The *Advertiser*'s Owners

1856–1870
Henry Martyn Whitney

1870–1875
James Auld and James Black

1875–1876
James Black

1876–1878
Henry L. Sheldon

1878–1880
James Black

1880–1887
Walter Murray Gibson
(acting as front for Claus Spreckels and
his Honolulu affiliate, W. G. Irwin & Company)

1887–1888
W. G. Irwin & Company

1888–1894
Hawaiian Gazette Company
(Henry Martyn Whitney major stockholder)

1894–1899
Hawaiian Gazette Company
(W. R. Castle family major stockholder)

1899–1931
Lorrin A. Thurston

1931–1961
Advertiser Publishing Company, Ltd.
(Lorrin P. Thurston, Robert Thurston, and
Margaret Thurston Twigg-Smith principal stockholders)

1961–1993
Thurston Twigg-Smith family

1993–
Gannett Company, Inc.

Presstime in Paradise

Presstime in Paradise

The Life and Times of *The Honolulu Advertiser*, 1856-1995

George Chaplin

A Latitude 20 Book
University of Hawai'i Press
Honolulu

Library of Congress Cataloging-in-Publication Data
Chaplin, George, 1914–
Presstime in paradise : the life and times of
The Honolulu advertiser, 1856–1995 / George Chaplin.
p. cm.
"A latitude 20 book."
Includes bibliographical references and index.
ISBN 0-8248-1963-2 (cloth : alk. paper)
ISBN 0-8248-2032-0 (pbk. : alk. paper)
1. Honolulu advertiser.   I. Title.
PN4899.H66C43   1998
079'.96931—dc21   97-35954
CIP

University of Hawai'i Press books are printed on
acid-free paper and meet the guidelines for permanence and
durability of the Council on Library Resources

Designed by Janette Thompson (Jansom)

Contents

Preface

AS WE near the twenty-first century fourteen decades have passed since the founding of the *Pacific Commercial Advertiser*, now *The Honolulu Advertiser*, one of the oldest newspapers still publishing west of the Rockies.

More often than not it has been a tumultuous time, as the paper bridged the events from monarchy into statehood. It has reported on whaling vessels and nuclear submarines, on horse-drawn carts and satellites flashing by, on wars near and far and peace in between, on Honolulu's growth from sleepy town to fast-paced metropolis.

History is an untidy business. Institutions, like individuals, can have periods both of notable service and of flawed performance. Newspapers are no exception. As it moves toward its sesquicentennial, the *Advertiser* has had several owners and editors who have stood out as near-giants, others who have been able journalists, and a few who were either incompetent or outright scoundrels concerned less with the public welfare than their own opportunism.

Walter Lippmann in the 1920s said "newspapers do not try to keep an eye on all mankind." Covering news of Hawaii was and is in itself a unique challenge. This island state is the only one with a majority of people having roots in Asia and the Pacific. It is the only state with its integral parts separated by stretches of ocean. It is the only state to have been bombed from the air by a foreign power.

Technology has greatly extended the paper's reach, but it remains essentially a local chronicle, as it has been from its inception. Like the Islands, it has had its good times and its bad. For most of its existence to date, with striking exceptions, it largely mirrored the views and policies of the establishment. In that sense, its behavior calls for evaluation in the context of the times. In the years when Oriental ascendancy was feared, it was racist. When workers strived for higher wages and better conditions, it was stridently anti-labor and, in one period, engaged in "Red Scare" hysteria. But as the community mellowed, so did the *Advertiser*.

Economically, it has had its ups and downs. In the 1950s, under an inept publisher and an aged editor, both frozen in the past, the paper was in rapid decline and would have died had not Thurston Twigg-Smith, a missionary descendant with fifteen years on the *Advertiser*, staged a palace revolution to gain control from his uncle, Lorrin P. Thurston, and then negotiated a joint operating agreement with the rival *Star-Bulletin*. A fresh management team of publisher and editors brought the *Advertiser* into modern-day Hawaii. Today it flourishes as the largest and leading daily in the Islands.

A veteran Connecticut editor, Herbert Brucker, said, "Like other business-es that get the world's work done, journalism must be a profitable enterprise. But unlike all the others, it performs a public service without which self-government ceases to exist." Put another way, a newspaper is both business and public trust, with an obligation to "serve the governed, not the governors."

If a paper is forthright, it will from time to time irritate public officials, who would prefer that it be their mouthpiece, and they will strike back with their own brand of vituperation. But this is an ongoing occupational hazard that has to be accepted in stride.

The only way for a newspaper to avoid criticism is to serve up pabulum and that is not what the founding fathers had in mind when they adopted the First Amendment to the Constitution, guaranteeing a free press. That assures not only the right to print but, perhaps more importantly, the right to read. Fortunately, a free press was affirmed for Hawaii as far back as the Constitution of 1852, a tribute to the monarchy of the time; two lapses occurred later, during the provisional government and during martial law in World War II. (While press freedom does not mandate responsibility, any decent newspaper accepts the need for it.)

THIS BOOK seeks to record both the internal operations of the *Advertiser*, at times arcane, and its relationship with the community on which it impacted and which, in turn, impacted on it.

On a personal note, I tried to seek whatever detachment I could. Since I spent twenty-eight years in the editor's chair, in a period of considerable ferment at the paper, I worried about "I" popping up all too often. One day, chatting with political scientist Dan Tuttle, a longtime friend and erstwhile contributing columnist, I expressed my concern. He volunteered to write an appendix "About the Author." The result is overly generous, but better, I believe, than subjecting the reader to a barrage of "Is."

I wanted to write about the life and times of the *Advertiser* simply because I felt that needed to be put down. It was not an easy task and there were moments when I doubted that it would ever be finished. But it is—and I hope that it adds a useful bit to the colorful cavalcade of Hawaii's history.

Acknowledgments

THIS BOOK is the result of much material and much help, with research and writing spread over the ten years since my retirement from *The Honolulu Advertiser.*

I owe a debt to numerous persons, but most importantly to Ingrid Peterson, without whose diligent and comprehensive research this history would not have come to fruition. She was the consummate literary detective, ferreting out the most elusive facts. My gratitude to her is unlimited.

Bea Kaya, who Gavan Daws has called the "custodian of the *Advertiser*'s memory," and her faithful and cheerful staff in the library of the Hawaii Newspaper Agency were always helpful as I searched through miles of microfilm for salient information.

Considerable assistance was provided by Rick Thompson, Mary Ann Akao, and Susan Shaner of the Hawaii State Archives; Barbara Dunn of the Hawaiian Historical Society Library; Mary Jane Knight, Lela Goodell, and Marilyn Reppun of the Hawaiian Mission Children's Society Library; Dr. Michaelyn Chou, Lynette Furuhashi, Dr. Nancy Morris, and Jean Kuble of the Hamilton Library of the University of Hawaii; Linda Laurence and Mary Judd, Punahou School archivists; Marguerite Ashford, Jane Short, Betty Kam, and Stuart Ching of the Bishop Museum; Laureen Blackum of the Brigham Young University (Hawaii) archives; Lila Sahney of the Watumull Foundation oral history project; historian Pauline King; and University of Hawaii student Larry Carter.

My former *Advertiser* secretary, Jessica Wise, was extremely helpful, as were secretaries Leslie Ann Kawamoto, Jane Arita, and Pat Fong and stamp collection researcher Mary Mitsuda.

Hearty thanks to Iris Wiley, former executive editor of the University of Hawai'i Press, for wise counsel; to William Hamilton, director of the press, for his kind assistance; to the readers he assigned to review the manuscript; to John Strobel, *Advertiser* news editor, for his eagle eye in copy-reading the manuscript; and to Freda Roth Hellinger for deciphering and converting my patched-up final draft into acceptable condition on her word processor.

I also owe great appreciation to writer Douglas Young, who provided me with a copy of his extensive interview with Thurston Twigg-Smith, filled with information and insights.

My longtime colleague, veteran author Bob Krauss, was enormously generous in sharing his own research notes and thoughts on the *Advertiser*'s background and always being available for counsel.

A number of former *Advertiser* staffers sent me recollections. Elaine Fogg Stroup's ran to eighteen typed pages, a veritable treasure trove. Also contributing were Scott Stone, Irva Edwards Coll, Hugh Lytle, William Hutchinson, Alex MacDonald, Betty Peet McIntosh, Harry Albright, Robert Monahan, Eric Cavaliero, and Robert Trumbull, some of them now gone. David Pflaum of KGU thoughtfully came forward with valuable material on the radio station's history. The late Professor Donald Johnson kindly let me read the galleys of his history of the City and County of Honolulu. And Dan Tuttle was overly generous in his "About the Author" at the end of the book.

Attorneys J. Russell Cades, Jeffrey Portnoy, and William Cardwell were most helpful on legal issues.

Capping all of the assistance from the above was the steady encouragement of former *Advertiser* publisher Thurston Twigg-Smith, who at times must have wondered, as on several occasions did I, whether the paper's fourteen decades could be pulled together in a single volume.

To all who assisted I express appreciation and aloha, for without their participation, whatever worth marks this undertaking would have been substantially less.

THIS HISTORY is dedicated to Esta, my wife and closest friend of sixty years, and to my son and daughter, Steve and Jerri, and their spouses, Carol and Peter, who have been unfailingly supportive during this project and in my earlier times of writing and editing history-on-the-run.

Part I

1856–1880

A "Reliable Domestic Newspaper" Is Born

TODAY'S HONOLULU with its frenzied freeways and crowded skies, its sky-scrapered Waikiki and downtown, its vast shopping malls, its satellite "dishes" and TV towers, seems unrelated—save for the glittering blue-green ocean and majestic cloud-crowned mountains—to the raffish little seaport of the 1850s.

It was then a frontier community of grass-thatched native huts, some with adobe walls, and of government and commercial buildings and foreigners' residences of clapboard, stone, or coral blocks cut from the reef. There were no sidewalks and "all were compelled to be middle-of-the-road men and women" as they walked in paths and streets that rotated between dust and mud.[1] Along with no electricity, there were no telephones and no streetcars, and interisland steam navigation was in its infancy.

But there were excitement and anticipation in the air. It was a decade that was to see the first biennial session of the legislature; establishment of a post office, the Honolulu waterworks, and a gas street-lighting system; opening of the first bank; the harbor's first dredging; opening of a flour mill; the wedding of King Kamehameha IV and Emma Rooke; completion of the Sailor's Home; the start of a foundry; a new fire engine and the arrival of the first shipment of Alaskan ice; increased sugar production stimulated by demands of the California Gold Rush; local talk of annexation by the United States and even a treaty draft with a statehood provision, intended solely to stave off threats from other nations. And it brought the publication of a new independent weekly newspaper to compete with the government journal, the *Polynesian*.

In 1853, Hawaii's first general census showed 73,137 persons on all islands; in Honolulu the population fluctuated up to some 12,000, depending on the whaling season influx. Of these, 1,687 were resident foreigners, led by Americans, followed by British and other nationalities. Even so, the town exuded something of the flavor of New England. The missionaries and many of the businessmen were from there and so were most of the whaling ships and their original crews, based in Honolulu and Lahaina for the exciting search for oil and bone.

It was in this upbeat environment in the rough and remote seaport that Henry Martyn Whitney, the Kauai-born son of missionaries, on July 2, 1856, brought forth his *Pacific Commercial Advertiser*, not Hawaii's first newspaper by any means, but now the oldest continuous one. (*The Pacific Commercial Advertiser* was variously called by that name, by the shorter title of the *Commercial*, and, in time, *The Honolulu Advertiser*. For brevity and clarity I call it the *Advertiser* throughout this book.)

There were two separate editions—one of four pages in English and one with three pages in English and the fourth in Hawaiian. The fourth English page, which was dropped in the Hawaiian edition, contained ads, port news, and reprints from other papers. The subscription price: $6 a year locally, payable in advance; $7.50 "to California or the U.S." Advertising, in English or Hawaiian, was to cost ten cents a line for the first insertion, five cents for each subsequent insertion. Neighbor Island agents would accept payment for either subscriptions or ads.

In commenting, the *Polynesian* ignored Whitney's statement that "the necessity for a reliable domestic newspaper devoted to inter-island commerce, agriculture and the whaling interests of the Pacific, and independent of government control and patronage has long existed." But it did acknowledge that the new paper would "very considerably interfere with a sort of monopoly enjoyed" by itself. Then, after warning Whitney to represent none other than the Hawaiian nation, it proffered its good wishes.[2]

Henry Martyn Whitney, founder of the *Pacific Commercial Advertiser*

But this gesture was soon replaced by hostility, which led to an acrimonious feud between the self-directing *Advertiser* and the royal regime's obedient editorial voice. There were frequent, abrasive exchanges in the florid language of the day.

Whitney was an affable man, but his editorials showed firm notions of what a newspaper should be. He felt, as America's founding fathers had, that the press should be a watchdog on government, demanding reform of official abuse. He saw the newspaper as a teacher, his major reason for having a page in Hawaiian and for later founding a Hawaiian-language paper for native consumption. He was a good reporter, a clear writer, albeit in a lush Victorian style, a campaigner for what he felt was equitable and against what he perceived as evil. He was strong on human rights, but his editorial positions tended toward the moralistic, tinged on occasion with self-righteousness. These qualities, displayed in bridging a half-century of active involvement in the public affairs of the Islands—including serving in the legislature in 1855 and on the Privy Council of State, 1873–1893—stemmed from his roots and his rearing.

He was born June 5, 1824, at Waimea, Kauai, where Captain Cook had first stepped ashore forty-six years before. His parents, Samuel and Mercy Partridge Whitney, had come from New Haven, Connecticut, to the Islands

July 2, 1856. The front page of the *Advertiser*'s first issue.

with the first company of missionaries on the brig *Thaddeus* in 1820 and had been speedily assigned to set up a mission on Kauai.

In due course the Whitneys—he had been a mechanic and a teacher— had to decide on the education of their children. Maria, the first white girl born in the Islands, was sent to America in November 1826, followed five years later by Henry and his older brother, Samuel, Jr., and later by a younger sister, Emily. Henry and Samuel went around Cape Horn with a whaling skipper, who gave them quite a thrill: he took them out in a whaleboat that killed a whale. Once ashore, Henry stayed with Hervey Ely, a flour manufacturer, and his wife, a cousin of his mother, in Rochester, New York.

He was a frail child who had not begun walking until he was a year and a half old, and his father back in Hawaii fretted both about his health and his seeming indifference toward religion. But when eighteen Henry joined the church and that came as welcome news to his parents.

He did well in high school—the Rochester Collegiate Institute—and had planned to enter college in 1841, but he suffered a deafness that was to be permanent—due, his father thought, to early illness—and so he chose to go into the printing trade.

In 1841 he began work first in Rochester, then in Hartford, but by May 1845 was in the New York pressroom of Harper and Brothers, a highly esteemed publisher; in his two years there he worked his way up to foreman. In keeping with tradition, however, he moved around and spent two years in the printing room of the American Bible Society Printing House in New York.

He also was familiar with the leading newsmen of the day. As a later *Advertiser* editor, Walter G. Smith, wrote retrospectively, "Horace Greeley, James Gordon Bennett, James Watson Webb and Henry J. Raymond [were] among those with whom he came into more or less frequent contact. His favorite paper, however . . . was Colonel [William L.] Stone's [New York] Commercial Advertiser—the sober and useful organ of the men who were building up the commerce and trade of the metropolis and of the Union."[3]

Late in life, when his recollection could have been dimmed by time, Whitney spoke of a connection with Colonel Stone's paper—and that was often repeated in subsequent articles—but no such record has come to light. Even so, Whitney "must have respected it to have named his own newspaper as he did."[4]

In his mid-twenties, Whitney seemed ambivalent on whether to return to the Islands. In August 1848 he wrote his sister Maria that because of his "plans and prospects" and the "wide ocean" lying between them it might be months and even years before they'd meet again. He said that his poor vision required a business that would not demand much of his eyes. He liked horticulture and gardening and was thinking of farming. But in earlier letters to his mother, which included news of his engagement to Catharine March, a native of New Hampshire who had moved to Brooklyn, he raised the possibility of returning home.

On November 8 his mother wrote that she had mentioned his interest to Dr. Gerrit Judd, a medical missionary who was the kingdom's minister of finance and a leading adviser to Kamehameha III. A week later Judd wrote Henry that the Privy Council had adopted a resolution offering employment in the government printing office and authorizing up to $600 for passage.

Judd wrote that if Whitney's talents justified it, he could wind up as editor of the *Polynesian*. And he conveyed Mrs. Whitney's hope, which he endorsed, that Whitney marry before coming.

In those days, mail service between Hawaii and the United States was unbelievably slow. Routing mail or passengers through Panama, as was sometimes done, was faster but riskier. Judd's letter to Whitney did not reach him in New York until some five months later, in April 1849.

Whitney now had the opportunity to stay in printing without endangering his eyes by personally setting type. He quickly wrote a letter of acceptance to Judd, along with a strong recommendation from his cousin-by-marriage, Hervey Ely.

On May 25, two days before his marriage to Catharine, Whitney got off a second letter to Judd. He said he had no doubt that the editor of the official paper "receives much the same treatment from opponents of the government that a fort does in a siege." But he pledged "to discharge faithfully and manfully whatever duties may be imposed on me," so far as they didn't impinge on principle.

Then he told Judd "it may perhaps be found better for me to undertake merely the post of Director of Government Printing at first, assuming the editorship necessarily involves a responsibility for the tenor of the editorial articles—but we can judge more definitely after my arrival in Honolulu." This reservation showed a discerning judgment. Otherwise, Whitney would have found himself in untenable circumstances, serving as a government voice in full and unquestioning support of all official policies, clearly at odds with his staunch belief in an unfettered press. (His late father had once subscribed to the *Polynesian* for him, so he was not unaware of its editorial thrust.)

In his older days—it was in 1903, a year before his death—Whitney recalled that getting from New York to California "was no light job." He said, "I came by way of the Isthmus, and had to wait a long time to get a passage to Panama. It cost me $200 in gold that far, when I did get it." Since "that was in the days of the gold excitement in California they did not have steamers enough to take people away from the Isthmus, and so I had to wait three or four weeks to get a passage to San Francisco. And that cost me $300 more."[5]

In San Francisco Whitney met Dr. Judd and Princes Liholiho and Lot, who became Kamehameha IV and V. He recalled, perhaps jokingly, "I came from New York to meet them. They came from the Islands to meet me."[6] But their meeting was happenstance. Judd and the princes were headed for France to try to resolve a misunderstanding between Hawaii and that country, and Whitney fortuitously arrived while they were en route.

About October 23 Whitney left the West Coast for Honolulu on the brig *Robert Bruce,* "making the run in fourteen days." In reminiscing a half-century later, he said that when he and other passengers departed San Francisco that port was a forest of shipping, and "all were surprised to find another similar forest here [in Honolulu], comprising the large fleet of whale ships, which at that time found the Arctic and Okhotsk seas nearly as profitable as were the gold places of California."

Whitney had to wait about three months for his bride to arrive on January 29, 1850, but it was satisfying to be home. Looking back a half-century later, he said, "Everybody was good to me in Honolulu. I was put in charge of the government printing office at once, the royal family was kind to me, and for two or three years I was editor of the Polynesian paper. I had everything my own way."[7] Whitney's obituary in the *Advertiser,* August 18, 1904, said that "Dr. Judd wanted a practical man to take charge of the Polynesian. . . . He told Whitney that they had had several editors who had thrown up their jobs and cleared out to California, joining the rush to the newly found goldfields."

There had indeed been a vacancy in the *Polynesian* editorship when Judd offered employment to Whitney, but by the time he arrived from New York Edwin O. Hall—a printer and a secular agent for the Sandwich Islands Mission—had been editor for six months and the post was never again available to Whitney during his tenure at the government printing office.

His misrecollection was simply a lapse of an aging memory. He was in charge of the official printing operation and business manager of the *Polynesian,* but apparently had no say in the editorial room.

Whitney and his wife quickly became a part of the community. Their first house in Honolulu was made of adobe, "thatched with pili grass, which had been built in the front yard of what is known as the Chamberlain house," on King Street, across and down the street from Iolani Palace.[8] Their first child, Hervey, was born there March 26, 1850. Of Whitney's initial earnings of $23 a month, $10 went for board. Later, the family acquired property on Piikoi Street, below King, and built a comfortable one-story home called Kewalo. When Piikoi Street was extended toward the ocean in 1900, this dwelling had to be removed and another built some feet back.

During the forty-seven years of their marriage, Catharine Whitney made her own mark as a suffragist and dedicated community worker. She was a leading member of Bethel Church, the recording secretary of the Woman's Board of Missions and the treasurer of Stranger's Friend Society—Whitney's staunch helpmate from the beginning.

A year after Whitney's return to Hawaii, and while still with the government printing office, as an additional duty he was named the Islands' first postmaster on December 22, 1850. A bit later he wrote to a cousin that his postal salary was not yet fixed but was to be about $1,000 a year or the profits from the operation. "I'm getting to be one of the head men, you see."[9]

As it turned out, it was not until the following September that the Privy Council set the salary—not at $1,000 but at $250 a year, retroactive to December 1, 1850. Whitney held the postmastership for five and a half years, during which he set up an efficient postal system, issued stamps, and inaugurated branch post offices.

He also started free interisland mail service. His successor changed this to paid delivery and was supported by the *Polynesian*, but opposed by the *Advertiser*. Whitney later acknowledged that requiring postage had not reduced the volume of mail, as he had feared, and that the stamps were actually popular.

His appointment by the minister of the interior had followed a proclamation by King Kamehameha IV that "there shall be established a post office in Honolulu and for the time being the Polynesian office is declared to be the post office." That office was a two-story building on what is now the corner of Merchant and Bethel Streets. Until that time people had to make their own arrangements for outgoing mail with captains, crewmen, or friendly passengers of departing ships. Handling of incoming mail was worse, ranging from the casual to the chaotic. Letters, periodicals, and packages were simply dumped "on the floor of the counting room of the consignee of the vessel, or of the harbormaster's office, and those expecting letters gathered around the pile to assist in overhauling or 'sorting,' picking out their own and passing over their shoulders, the letters, etc., of those standing in the outer circle."[10]

On Merchant Street between an earlier structure at the corner of Bethel Street, far left, and a frame building was one (largely obscured but with its lookout tower visible) in which the *Advertiser* had its first editorial rooms, from 1856. Printing was done in a small frame building in the rear. (Photo: R. J. Baker Collection. Bishop Museum.)

Empowered by the Privy Council, Whitney on October 1, 1851, brought out the first Hawaiian stamps, dubbed "the Missionaries" because that group was the prime user, in mail bound for the United States. Two-cent, five-cent, and thirteen-cent denominations designed by Whitney were hand-set and printed on the government presses.

Because all were on extremely thin, porous paper, of the two-cent stamps used as postage on newspaper and other periodical wrappers, only fifteen have survived. The five-cent issue, needed to pay the Hawaiian rate to have a letter accepted aboard a U.S.-bound ship, and the thirteen-cent one, which covered both the ocean voyage and delivery within the United States, also became rare and thus extremely valuable. So coveted are these stamps that in the 1890s a Parisian who sought to buy a two-cent Hawaiian stamp from a friend and was refused, murdered him and stole the stamp. Some real-life Hercule Poirot tracked him down and he confessed.

The supply of these stamps ran out, and the government turned to engraved issues printed on the East Coast by American Bank Note Company, which also ran out from time to time. To fill in, the government produced what are known as "the Numerals" from 1859 to 1865. These were first printed at the government printshop and, after its founding in 1856, at the *Advertiser*. Thus, the *Advertiser*'s linkage to Hawaiian stamps runs back to their inception.

Stimulated by this relationship, the *Advertiser*—headed until recently by a missionary descendant, Thurston Twigg-Smith—gathered the world's most complete and most valuable collection of the stamps and postal history of Hawaii, regularly honored at international philatelic expositions. Interestingly, the collection included the "Parisian murder" stamp, which had gone through several sales and which *Life Magazine* once called "the most valuable substance on Earth."

Whitney rendered solid service as postmaster, but his heart was in printing. On February 24, 1851, he and Hall, the *Polynesian* editor, proposed to buy the government printing establishment. They got nowhere. On December 1, 1853, wanting to concentrate on printing for the government, Whitney submitted his resignation as postmaster to Interior Minister John Young. An attempt was made to dissuade him and the next month he consented to stay on "until some change could be made," although his desire to be relieved remained "as strong as when I tendered my resignation."[11]

On December 8, 1854, he again sought to buy the government printing operation, for $5,000. He proposed to make the *Polynesian* "more independent" and issue it semiweekly—and to put out a weekly native newspaper, with material translated from the *Polynesian*. He sought free use of the building, after which he would rent or move. And the government printing would be done "quite as cheaply as . . . now."[12] The government rejected his offer.

Earlier that year, the post office moved next door from its corner location to Honolulu Hale (Honolulu House) when Whitney—turned down in his effort to acquire it—was granted a lease on March 1. This was a two-story coral structure with a lookout tower built about 1835, and for years it served as Hawaii's seat of government.

At Honolulu Hale, which was entered through an archway surmounted by a golden crown, the first floor then was divided between the post office and a Whitney-owned stationery and book store, which also sold weeks-old newspapers and magazines from the United States and other foreign lands. Whitney was also into another enterprise; between 1853 and 1856 he, along with George Gower and Asa G. Thurston, operated a struggling flour mill, Hawaii's first, utilizing wheat grown on Maui. But most of the work fell on Whitney and he finally extricated himself, moving on to an interest much closer to his heart, the establishment of an independent newspaper.

2

"New Type, a New Press, a New Building"

IT DOES not appear to be recorded when Henry Whitney determined to start his own newspaper and commercial printing operation, but the idea must have been germinating all during the time he sought in vain to buy the government printery and to be released from his postal duties.

While postmaster, Whitney observed that the public was eager to get the latest news, but the local press seemed "to have very little public spirit in getting out 'extras.'" So as important news arrived from San Francisco, elsewhere in the United States, and Europe, he posted bulletins on his office door.

Aside from the printer's ink that ran in his blood, there undoubtedly were other considerations propelling him toward an independent newspaper. Philosophically, he did not take kindly to government policies being supported without question by an official press. He clearly identified with the American business community, which felt unfairly treated by the *Polynesian*.

Missionary influence in the government, once so strong, had steadily waned. Kamehameha IV and his bride, Emma Rooke, the adopted daughter of an English physician and her Hawaiian aunt, were perceived as strongly pro-British. (The king's visit, as Prince Liholiho, to England in 1849–1850, heightened his appreciation of their royal system and the Anglican Church and made him increasingly wary of proannexationist Americans in the Islands.)

Another "reason," clearly subject to debate, was advanced for Whitney's founding of his paper. It involved *Polynesian* Editor Charles G. Hopkins, a naturalized Hawaii citizen of British origin, urbane, Bohemian and antimissionary, and his friend Abraham Fornander, a rather intellectual and caustic Swedish university student who turned whaler, settled in Hawaii, married a Molokai chiefess, and in January 1856 brought out the first issue of his *Sandwich Islands' Monthly Magazine*.

The *Polynesian* for a long time, as was the tradition, had given members of the Sandwich Islands Mission a 50 percent discount on their subscriptions to the newspaper. When Hopkins suddenly began charging full price, some forty mission members reportedly dropped the paper. Fornander, who enjoyed acerbity, wrote, "They could stand much; they could bear to have their measures condemned, their opinions ridiculed, their candor called in question, but could not stand this. Political influence and personal consistency may be sacrificed in these hard and degenerate times, but the dollar—never. . . ."[1]

Eleanor Harmon Davis, a retired Hawaii public librarian and biographer of Fornander, writes, "The resulting quarrel between [mission] members and [the government] newspaper appears to have been the immediate cause for the founding of a new journal, the *Pacific Commercial Advertiser*, at this particular time."[2]

Thrum's 1877 almanac pungently assessed the government weekly: It "had degenerated from quite a readable journal into anything but a *news* paper." It gave as an example of the *Polynesian's* ineptitude its devoting of six lines to a whaling ship that limped into port after being dismasted far at sea "when any other paper would have gloried in the opportunity of furnishing a column description of it."[3]

There had been talented writers on some of the earlier Hawaii publications, but few, if any, had Whitney's professional background. Perhaps because of this, Whitney liked to think of the *Advertiser* as Hawaii's first independent newspaper. In fact, there had been numerous ones before, although they had died by the time he returned home from the United States.

Like many another place, Honolulu actually was a sizable graveyard of newspapers, starting with the first secular English-language sheet, the weekly *Sandwich Island Gazette and Journal of Commerce*, founded July 30, 1836. Edited by Stephen D. Mackintosh, a fiery, young, free-wheeling Bostonian, and then by a committee of Honolulu residents, it was—according to Henry L. Sheldon—"coarsely and violently offensive to the government of the day," although Kamehameha III had granted permission to print, and "abused the American missionaries without stint."

With few exceptions, Mackintosh backhanded the missionaries as "conceited and ignorant blockheads by whom the honored epithet dunce has been deserved."[4] The paper's circulation was tiny, about one hundred, and it died after three years, on July 27, 1839.

Came next, August 15, 1839, the *Sandwich Islands Mirror and Commercial Gazette*, a monthly with the policies of its predecessor. It lasted eleven months. It was followed on June 6, 1840, by a much better paper, the weekly four-page *Polynesian*, established by a recently arrived Bostonian, James Jackson Jarves, whose "notable place in Hawaiian history and letters rests on his books rather than on his newspaper editorship."[5] It was independent in policy, but there were not enough foreign residents to sustain it and it expired in eighteen months. But in May 1844 the *Polynesian*, at least in name, was revived as the official organ of the government, and Jarves, who had been away, returned and became its editor until 1848, when he left for good. He was succeeded by C. E. Hitchcock (January 29–December 16, 1848), followed by Charles Gordon Hopkins (December 23, 1848–May 12, 1849), then by

Edwin O. Hall (May 19, 1849–June 30, 1855), then by Hopkins again, until succeeded by Abraham Fornander on October 6, 1860.

New papers continued to sprout quickly and just as quickly wither. Of the *Cascade* (1844–1845), the *Monitor* (1845), and the *Oahu Fountain* (1848) there is little mention. The weekly *Sandwich Island News* made more of a ripple. It was begun September 2, 1846, by "A Committee of Foreign Residents," with Peter A. Brinsmade, a commercial representative of Ladd & Company, in charge. It was against the government, with which Ladd & Company was in litigation, and also antimissionary. Overtaken by economics, it faded out on August 25, 1847, was resuscitated by a different management November 4, 1847, but lived only until April 14, 1849, its readership having suffered when many foreigners left Hawaii to join the California gold rush.

Henry Sheldon, who had returned to Honolulu after panning for gold in California, established the *Honolulu Times*, a weekly, on November 8, 1849, and was its editor until May 1, 1850. The paper, moderately critical of the government, survived only until February 19, 1851. January 14, 1852, saw the advent of the *Weekly Argus*, with Matthew K. Smith as editor, a position assumed in March by Fornander. It was the "outstanding opposition paper at mid-century. . . . Liberal from its inception on Printer's Row . . . it was a one-man operation and the foremost opposition voice to the government," especially critical of Dr. Gerrit Judd, still a leading minister of the crown. It was suspended in the summer of 1853 because of the smallpox epidemic, resumed in January 1854 as *The New Era and Argus*, and closed its doors the following year. Although the official *Polynesian* called the *Argus* "a sewer for discharging filth," it later hired Fornander as its editor.[6]

While by conventional definition it was not a newspaper, notice needs to be taken of *The Friend*, established in 1843 with the title of *The Temperance Advocate and Seamen's Friend* and edited for more than forty years by the Rev. Samuel C. Damon. It focused on morality and sailors' welfare and continued publication until June 1954.

At thirty-two, with high enthusiasm, Whitney was undeterred by the long roster of vanished newspapers. He felt the time was ripe, and he was ready to set Island journalism on its proper path. He established an editorial office on the second floor of Honolulu Hale, which continued to house his stationery and book store and the post office, until the new Kamehameha IV post office was built in 1870 on Merchant Street at Bethel, where it still stands, occupied by a state agency.

For printing, Whitney erected a two-story frame building in a lot just waikiki of Honolulu Hale. This was directly across Merchant Street from the old Bishop Bank and the adjoining Kaahumanu Street, which then ran to the waterfront but later was but a fifteen-to-twenty-foot remnant serving as the entry from Merchant Street to a municipal parking lot. (Where the Honolulu Hale and the *Advertiser*'s printing facility stood is now a small park, between the 1870 post office and the building housing the Cunha Alley Arcade. Honolulu Hale remained for many years as a historic structure but grew dilapidated and unsafe, and finally, in 1917, the government auctioned it off for $10 for razing.)

Foreign Minister Robert C. Wyllie had some qualms about the *Advertiser* being the Islands' only independent newspaper. Accordingly, on June 30, 1856, two days before Whitney went to press, the government amended the law relating to the government paper. The amendment read: "The editor of the *Polynesian* shall conduct his paper free and independent of all government influences and responsibility, excepting only in regards to the publication of notices and communications by authority of the government or any of the departments thereof."

This was purely cosmetic and so recognized. Even the *Polynesian's* editor couldn't restrain his facetiousness:

> The Polynesian is, as it were, thrown out of gear, and left in a disconnected state to perform its own small gyrations, neither receiving its impetus nor taking its time for the governmental machine. . . . It is a satisfaction to know that hereafter Law and Fact will walk hand in hand. . . . Whatever naughtiness the editor of this paper may commit he only will be liable to a turn over the knee; upon his small clothes only will the ferule rattle. . . .

Whitney had ordered an Isaac Adams New Patent Press from Boston, but its delivery was delayed about eight months, and so he began with a Washington hand-powered press, capable of printing several hundred copies an hour. In reminiscing much later Whitney proudly said that his first issue came from "new type, a new press, a new building and, in short, everything new from the ground floor to the ridge beam."[7] In actuality, the press was probably a used one, but it served its purpose.

A great deal has been written about the lure of printer's ink, but less about the painstaking work required to provide a product for the reader. In some aspects, the printing process of Whitney's day was not that far advanced from Gutenberg. It was basically a hand craft, simple, but slow and tedious. With one hand a printer plucked individual letters of type from a case and placed them in a composing "stick" held in the other hand. As words that were formed with the individual letters began to fill a line, he "justified" it by spacing the words so that the line came out flush left and flush right. The lines then were put in a "galley," a long, shallow metal tray from which proofs could be pulled and the content checked for accuracy.

The type from a number of galleys was then assembled inside a metal form or "chase" that stood on a mobile table, usually of steel, called a "stone" or "turtle." The chase was "locked up" with large "keys" and then slid from the table onto the flat bed of the press, which printed two pages at a time on one side of the paper. Usually one pressman kept the type inked and another fed in the blank sheets. A hand-operated press sometimes required a third man.

After the press run was completed, the type and rollers had to be cleaned of ink and the type restored to the case, a letter at a time. The capital letters (or upper case) were distributed to one set of compartments, the smaller letters (lower case) to another.

Whitney was a jack of all trades—publisher, editor, ad salesman, printing foreman. Joseph O. Carter, who doubled as ship and customs house reporter and *Advertiser* accountant, recalled that the paper started with two journeymen setting type, "Stephen Wescott and, I think, Alex Bolster," and three apprentices, James Auld, Peter Porter Kauhema, and William G. Brash, the first two part-Hawaiian.[8] The printers worked ten hours a day, six days a week. Auld later became head pressman for fifteen years, and Whitney described him as a faithful and competent mechanic. No one would have suspected that he would later play a larger role in the *Advertiser* story.

Since the town's English-speaking residents were eager to see what Whitney and colleagues would produce, publication morning—July 2, 1856—brimmed with anticipation, and a small crowd poured into the printshop. It included Charles R. Bishop, A. S. Cleghorn, Dr. Gerrit P. Judd, Dr. Hugo Stangenwald, Dr. John Mott-Smith, S. N. Castle, Amos S. Cooke, John T. Waterhouse, and Captain "Preserved Fish" Wilcox, among others.

Whitney was to expansively recall that the spectators were "all anxious to see the long-expected people's organ, which was to open a new era and bring prosperity to the whole kingdom. At last the signal was given, the wheels began to revolve and the papers to reel off."[9] The first copy, with three pages in English and the fourth in Hawaiian, was handed to reporter Carter, who gave it to Arnum W. Field, "who declared that he would not part with it for $20."[10] Carter contented himself with the second copy; others were passed out to the charter subscribers as quickly as their names could be taken down. The first edition of two thousand was extended to three thousand, many of them sent to residents' relatives and friends in the United States.

The *Advertiser* began as a five-column four-pager, fourteen by twenty inches, with the columns lengthened by an inch two months later. The format was dull and gray, enlivened only by an engraved illustration which adorned the page-one masthead, sketched by Whitney while perched atop an American guano clipper ship, looking inland from Honolulu harbor, and engraved and electrotyped in Boston.

Whitney remarked in 1899, "It is safe to say that no daily paper now printed in the United States carries a vignette more widely known, or that has not been changed during a longer period than that" of the *Advertiser*.[11] Actually, when the *Advertiser* went daily in 1884, it had a new front-page vignette designed by John Andrews of Boston, while using the old cut on the continuing weekly edition.

The custom of the day in American newspapers, one that Whitney followed, was to run a great many ads on page one. In his first issue fifty-two ads took up three of the five columns. In the first column, Whitney ran a publisher's notice of circulation and advertising rates, then his prospectus (largely a repeat of earlier announcements elsewhere) and at the bottom of the space a rather weak joke about a prospective juror asking to be excused because he had a breaking out between his fingers and the judge solemnly instructing the clerk to "scratch that name out."

Column two was titled "Varieties" and down the length of the page carried several score short items proffering homely hints, puns, witticisms, and anecdotes, apparently lifted from American newspapers, magazines, and books.

Examples: "If you wish to cure a scolding wife, never fail to laugh at her until she ceases, then kiss her. Sure cure and no quack medicine." "Happiness is very easily procured. All that's required is to spend one hour a day helping somebody." "It is good to know much, but better to make good use of what we know." "Beware said the potter to the clay, and it became ware." "I shall be indebted to you for life, as the man said to his creditors as he ran away to Australia."

The ads ranged from three-liners to two ads that occupied the entire fifth column. One promoted S. C. Hillman's news agency, a Whitney competitor, offering publications from the *London Illustrated News* to *Leslie's Gazette of Fashion* to the *Nantucket Mirror* to newspapers from Boston, New York, Philadelphia, Cleveland, and other cities.

The second and even larger ad was by Thomas Spencer, ship chandler and importer, who appeared to list every single item in stock, running the gamut from oars to butcher knives to camel's hair "pencils."

Only a few advertisers listed prices, such as H. Dimond, selling "clocks, brass, hour-striking, for $6.00." Some advertisers' names are familiar today: Charles Brewer, commission merchant; Samuel N. Castle and Amos S. Cooke, doing business as Castle & Cooke, importers, wholesalers, and retailers in general merchandise "at the old stand, corner of the King and School Streets, near the large Stone Church"; H. Hackfeld & Company (now Amfac), general commission agents. Others included importers John Thos. Waterhouse and E. O. Hall; C. H. Lewers, carpenter and lumber merchant; and M. C. Monsarrat. Above the *Advertiser* office was photographer W. Benson's "Polynesian Daguerrean Rooms." He would take pictures "at all hours of the day and in any weather."

Finally, a touch of mystery in the ad of Albert G. Jones of Jones Hotel: "The undersigned hereby gives notice that he intends leaving the Kingdom." He chose not to give a reason. Through its advertising, the American business community, which appreciated the *Advertiser*, was clearly out to support Whitney, and the *Polynesian* was soon to acknowledge the loss of much of this patronage.

Page two provided local news and commentary; as was the style of the day, facts and opinion were inseparable. The first column covered markets, from sugar and molasses to building materials to potatoes. The next column contained shipping information, including arriving ship passengers, and exports and imports; marriages; deaths; an *Advertiser* notice that copies of the first issue would be given to all foreign residents, including nonsubscribers, so that all choosing to take the paper could do so. Then came the start of Whitney's first editorial, pledging to encourage "every branch of lawful industry" and "to second the government in all its honest efforts to improve physically and mentally the condition of the body politic." But Whitney also pledged "to frown with imperious scorn on every attempt to infringe popular rights and on every act that tends to violate the confidence reposed by the nation in those elevated to authority—in a word the public welfare—these we conceive to be the end and aim of a public press. . . ."

The editorial continued the length of the third column and spilled over into the fourth. Below the editorial was the big news story of the first issue, the two-week-old wedding of twenty-two-year-old King Kamehameha IV and his twenty-year-old bride, Emma Rooke, in the "Stone Church" (Kawaiahao). It was a well-written, detailed, and thoroughly respectful article, which must have pleased the king and queen. It continued over into column five; just below it were "Notes of the Week," nine short items, such as: Mangoes were in the market, but high-priced. In a trial, the new fire engine, named Kamehameha, "threw a stream from the inch nozzle about 95 feet in height. The hose, however, did not stand the test . . . two lengths of 50 feet each having burst."

Notes in the next issue reported a Hawaiian murdered by "one or two Chinaman [*sic*]" who had been stealing his taro; the election of officers of Fire Engine No. 1; a broken leg suffered by John Dominis when a horse kicked him below the knee; the robbery of $800 belonging to the Hawaiian Agriculture Society from the home of its treasurer, George Williams, while he was at the July 4th ball at the courthouse; and the presence of the steamer *America* taking on coal, brought earlier for her from Boston, for her passage to China.

Volcanoes were hot news then as now, and Captain Law of Kawaihae, an *Advertiser* agent for circulation and advertising, reported that the volcano goddess Pele was once more becoming restless. An earthquake had cracked his stone house and a lava stream from Mauna Loa "which was formerly tending towards Hilo"—to within eight miles of the town—"has now branched off and is running to the southward where less injury will be done."

The first issue also carried some foreign news, but it was old—from San Francisco a month behind, from London ten weeks, from Sydney twelve weeks.

The main interest, of course, was in the United States. At the *Advertiser*'s birth that country consisted of thirty-six states and territories, with lands west of the Mississippi, except for California, largely unexplored. Franklin Pierce was president, with country lawyer Abraham Lincoln little known outside Illinois. Slavery was an accepted institution in the southern states. Morse telegraph and the railroad were experimental. Most cloth still came from hand looms. River paddleboats and ocean sailing ships were the dominant

water transport. The blacksmith, shoemaker, and tinker were essential pur-
veyors of service. Women had few legal and no political rights.

But it was evident that the world, like Hawaii, was in ferment, and
Whitney wanted native Hawaiians as well as haoles (Caucasians) exposed to
the news. Hence his printing of one page of the *Advertiser* in Hawaiian—in the
separate edition titled *Ka Hoku Loa O Hawaii*, the Morning Star of Hawaii.

Fluently bilingual, Whitney used the Hawaiian version of his name, Heneri
M. Wini, and wrote in Hawaiian with an appropriate flourish: "Aloha, o you
close friends living in the towns, the country, the valleys and beaches from
Hawaii to Kauai. Great aloha to you. Behold today there is opening the dawn
of the Morning Star of Hawaii, to be a torch illuminating your home. . . ."

Whitney promised that "articles intended to encourage industry and an
improvement in the domestic and social habits of the native race will be prepared by persons well fitted for the task." In pursuance of this, he would soon
be inveighing against the hula, which he saw as licentious, a disgrace to the
Islands, promoting immorality and indolence and impeding progress.

Whitney also aimed "to create a literary taste" among readers. Qualified
contributors were to be invited to present material on the history, geography,
and nature of Hawaii and neighboring island groups, as well as "such discov-
eries and travels as may be of general interest."

He acknowledged that the experiment might not work, and as time
passed he felt this to be the case. On September 25, 1856, after thirteen issues,
Whitney announced he was dropping the Hawaiian-language page, the space
being needed "for the foreigners during the time the whaling ships anchor in
the harbor." But he hoped to resume it in probably three months, when he
expected a new and faster press to arrive.

To those readers who had prepaid the $6 yearly subscription, Whitney
owed $4; he said he'd credit that against a resumption of publication. But it
was five years, in 1861, not three months, before Whitney published again in
Hawaiian. This time it was not a page but a complete newspaper, the *Nupepa
Kuokoa*, and, remarkably, it continued until December 1927.

On the *Kuokoa*'s publication day, the *Advertiser* printing office by 10 A.M.
"was almost taken possession of by the excited natives." News of the paper
"spread like wildfire," and by the end of the day six hundred to eight hundred
Hawaiians had shown up to buy copies. Demand continued during the next
several days, and the press run was expanded to four thousand with the need
for a third edition of five hundred or one thousand anticipated. While subscribers would be first-day buyers—"the natives are generally poor"—the
healthy demand showed "the avidity of the native population for more information and shows their mental starvation."[12]

Another Hawaiian-language paper, *Ka Hoku Loa o Ka Pakipika* (The
Morning Call of the Pacific), one of whose editors was David Kalakaua, called
Whitney's *Kuokoa* a missionary paper. Rubellite Kinney Johnson, a student of

the era, says: "Despite [publisher] Whitney's diligent efforts to keep the Kuokoa strictly secular, the accusation was not without justification. Whitney was the son of the Rev. Samuel Whitney. The editor, L. H. Gulick, was the son of a missionary. The board was heavily missionary. The rivalry between the two papers allowed a form of mild, witty banter to take place between the debating readerships. . . ."[13] Sometime between 1866 and 1870 yet another missionary son, Curtis J. Lyons, edited the *Kuokoa*. A Big Islander, an alumnus of Williams College, a surveyor and meteorologist, he also served as assistant editor of the *Advertiser* early in Whitney's ownership.

Hawaiian-language newspapers attracted a wide following. Gavan Daws writes that during the 1860s and 1870s "the declared circulations were three or four times greater than those of English-language papers. [The larger] Hawaiian-language papers, however, were edited, published and otherwise directed by white men as often as not. The degree to which they led or reflected native opinion cannot be ascertained very clearly."[14]

Whitney at times wrote harshly about the Hawaiians, at other times generously. In one instance he could say,

> Though inferior in every respect to their European or American brethren, they are not to be wholly despised. . . . They are destined to be laborers in developing the capital of the country. . . . In proportion as they come into contact with foreigners and acquire correct habits . . . in that proportion do they rise in our estimation.[15]

And yet in his first editorial in the Hawaiian-language page, he wrote:

> The intellectual eyes of the native race have been opened for years, but beyond a few elementary volumes and some charitable attempts to provide newspapers for them, they have been and are still left to grope about, seeking light, but finding little or none. There are intelligent natives here and throughout this group, who are desirous of knowing what is transpiring throughout the world and who, finding their own dialect too limited, are striving to learn the English language.

And later, discussing the jury system, Whitney wrote:

> There have been . . . some who [have] questioned the wisdom of the practice, especially in the country, where it has frequently been remarked that a trial by a native jury was little less than a farce. But the late case involving a fish pond dispute of the Sylvas vs. Nahaolelua [a former Maui governor] . . . goes to show that a Hawaiian jury is sufficiently educated to be entrusted with the adjudication of questions of right between man and man without respect of persons. This appears more emphatically, when it is remembered that wealth, influence and power, including the Prime Minister among counsel, were arrayed on the side of the party defendant [who was found by the jury to be at fault and fined $500].[16]

Whitney's interest in the welfare of the Hawaiians was appreciated by many of them, but not all. At one point he wrote critically of native boatmen who he felt were overcharging for their services—and threatened to put a boat in competition unless they lowered their fees. Outraged, the boatmen organized and determined that Whitney must be eliminated. But to avoid violating the law against murder, they resorted to an ancient rite, *anaana*, the process of praying one to death with the help of a kahuna, a traditional priest. They needed and presumably obtained, although how is a mystery, something from Whitney's person, a strand of hair or fingernail or the like, for use in the solemn ceremony. At night the kahuna, carrying a white pig, approached the Merchant Street offices of the *Advertiser*. Finding the fence gate locked, he lifted the pig, its feet tied, and deposited it on the other side of the fence. At midnight he began quiet incantations in the interest of spiritual murder. His voice grew louder during the night and at daylight the kahuna retired, leaving the hapless pig behind.

On reaching his office that morning, Whitney inquired about the pig and learned from a native about the boatmen's intent. Whitney's reaction was to order the pig tossed into the harbor and then to invite another *anaana* ceremony, directed at *Advertiser* representatives. He offered to provide seats in front of his building for any kahunas and a cage for the white pig. Then the kahunas could repeat "the weird incantations composed of our contemporaries' editorials upon the wickedness of the Advertiser." Later, if they wished, his detractors could adjourn to a nearby saloon to celebrate.[17]

Another assault on Whitney, this one potentially far more dangerous, came from a highly unusual source, the official U.S. representative to Hawaii. It was triggered by the Civil War, on which Islanders were divided, but with most, including Whitney, vigorously supporting the Union. (The kingdom was deliberately neutral to try to avoid trouble with either side.)

The *Advertiser* had printed one or more letters by Dr. Charles Guillou critical of U.S. Commissioner J. W. Borden, who favored the Confederacy. Borden heard that yet another letter was to be published and sent the legation secretary, a Mr. Hanks, to the paper to see if this was so. Whitney said it was.

That afternoon, Borden came calling and when he got no satisfaction, he said—according to Whitney—"I have, then, only one mode of redress left to me," pulled out a Bowie knife, and led Whitney to conclude he intended to use it on him.[18] Whitney retreated to the door of his office, opened and closed it, and yelled to J. W. Austin, a nearby attorney. Responding, Austin questioned Borden, who calmly said he carried a knife to protect himself against insult. Whitney had gone downstairs, and Borden, who had diplomatic immunity, left.

Although Austin said he saw no apparent intention by Borden to pursue Whitney or use the knife, Whitney complained to Foreign Minister Wyllie. This triggered an exchange of seven letters, all printed in the *Advertiser*. The incident was ended with the government's decision that Borden's explanation left Whitney without any reasonable ground of complaint.

Years later, Whitney recollected that Borden was "recalled by President Lincoln, as soon as this affair was known in Washington, and nothing further ever transpired regarding it."[19] At some point, it's said, Whitney was again assaulted, caned "by an irate shipmaster who apparently mistook him for the editor of a rival newspaper that had been criticizing the conduct of mariners," but no record of that is at hand.[20]

The year before the Borden incident Whitney, in an editorial, had written: "Those who dream that an editor's life is one of unalloyed bliss are very much mistaken."[21] The time ahead did little to alter that view—even though, like most editors, Whitney enjoyed his work.

3

"Going to Sea without a Passport"

FOR MUCH of the *Advertiser*'s history, the Pacific Ocean was Hawaii's life-line—commercially and informationally. Once the Islands' closed and delicate ecosystem was ruptured by Western arrivals, the foreign residents and increasingly the native Hawaiians became dependent on the outside world. Much of the food and most of the other necessities of life came in by water and local products went out. Incoming news was provided by foreign publications and mail, all conveyed by ship, and by personal accounts of those aboard. Not until the Pacific cable made connection early in this century did the Islands receive same-day news.

Henry Whitney quickly focused on the waterfront and whaling, the leading industry, for which the Islands were a natural magnet. He assigned Joseph O. Carter to ship-news reporting, in addition to his other duties as the newspaper's accountant. Carter worked on the *Advertiser* until 1872, during part of that time doubling as a waterfront correspondent for the *New York Herald*. Subsequently, he served in the legislature, became a trustee of the Bishop and Campbell Estates and Kamehameha Schools and president of C. Brewer & Company. Outspoken in public affairs, he at times clashed with his brother, H.A.P. Carter; his nephew, George B. Carter, became the second territorial governor.

After Carter, who died in 1909, at seventy-three, the *Advertiser* down the years continued to have able waterfront reporters. Albert P. Taylor, a lively journalist and a specialist in Hawaiiana who became an official archivist, covered many of the big port stories.

Much later, Ray Coll, Jr., son of the longtime *Advertiser* editor, Raymond S. Coll, reported shipping news for fifteen years before returning to the newsroom as news editor and financial editor. Many others earned names for themselves recording the happenings of the harbor. Elaine Fogg Stroup, who subsequently operated a news clipping bureau in Honolulu, was one of the finest.

Going back in time, Whitney also did his share of marine reporting. He believed in enterprise in chasing the news, seeking to get it before his competitor, the government's *Polynesian*—but within two weeks of the start of the *Advertiser* this zeal almost cost him his life.

He attempted to board the ship *Fanny Major* offshore while she was making eight or nine knots. The *Polynesian* of July 19, 1856, reported, "As he was just preparing to get on deck his boat went from under him and was capsized. He had a rope in his hand, to which he held fast, and being drawn under the barque's counter his life was for some time in imminent danger. When rescued he was quite insensible." Whitney, either modest or embarrassed, carried only a sentence or two on his narrow call.

The marine beat could be hazardous even closer to shore. An *Advertiser* reporter getting news as the bark *Yankee* was leaving the wharf "found himself going to sea without a passport." He jumped for the wharf but landed under it, not far from the vessel's keel. On climbing onto the dock, he looked at his watch, to time the incident, but found it waterlogged.

News was obtained not only from ships coming to Honolulu but often from U.S. West Coast vessels bound for China without an Island stop. Whitney hired boats so reporters could intercept the ships between Diamond Head and the mouth of Pearl Harbor to get firsthand information and copies of available U.S. newspapers. Starting in 1857 the *Advertiser* was helped in this by a marine telegraph erected by Postmaster Jackson on a knoll just back of Diamond Head. Its operator on a clear day could sight ships from twenty to twenty-five miles in either direction and, using large arms on a sixty-foot pole, signal their approach. This was valuable not only to the press but to harbor attendants and postal authorities, who could go out, collect mail, and sort it for faster delivery.

In 1866 a new and improved marine lookout and a higher semaphore were put on the roof of Honolulu Hale on Merchant Street, making it easier for suburban residents to see the signals. As a further aid, at the *Advertiser*'s suggestion, many ships from San Francisco hoisted the American flag on the mainmast on sighting Diamond Head, thus enabling the mail boat to be sent from shore.

Whitney maintained close ties with the mariners who brought him news, as evidenced by the typical item that "we are as usual under obligation to our San Francisco friends, Captains Lovett and Smith, and Purser Horton of the Comet, for favors in the news line."[1] Or this: "Captain Gove kindly hove-to his ship"— the *Torrent*, seventeen days from San Francisco, bound for China—"and supplied us with a file of papers to June 6, for which he will accept our thanks."[2]

But not every skipper was that cooperative. One clipper captain was given copies of the *Advertiser* on his arrival and was solicited for U.S. newspapers in return. He rebuffed the reporter, declaring he had more important business than hauling newspapers around the world. An annoyed *Advertiser* writer sharply responded: "That master ought to be promoted to the command of a canal boat or sent into the forecastle. Such cases are not common. Sailors visiting this port are generally thorough gentlemen or at least treat the press gentlemanly."[3]

But even when captains were willing, they didn't always have newsworthy material. In 1861, Whitney, still personally ship-chasing, was at the signal station when a clipper ship was sighted. He rode out to Waialae just in time to get into a rowboat with a Captain Babcock and six oarsmen. Halfway across the channel to Molokai they found the ship *Iconium* becalmed and boarded her. Disappointingly, she was from Australia, not San Francisco as anticipated, and they got hospitality but no significant news.

Whitney once before had chased the same ship for fifteen miles. This kind of earnestness sometimes produced an *Advertiser* scoop. A passing skipper left for King Kamehameha IV a West Coast newspaper reporting on developments following the Crimean War, a Russo-Turkish conflict in which Britain and France joined against Russia, Florence Nightingale introduced women to army nursing, and Tennyson wrote "The Charge of the Light Brigade."

Reporter Carter, knowing that, as a matter of course, the paper would quickly be forwarded to the *Polynesian*, prevailed upon the messenger to let him see the story and quickly jotted down a summary. It was a Sunday, which Whitney strictly observed. He was persuaded, however, to let his staff come in at midnight and prepare an extra. Meantime, Andrew Potter of the *Polynesian* was given the king's newspaper and planned, on reaching his office Monday morning, to immediately get out a paper with this latest and exclusive news. One can imagine his dismay on being greeted by a newsboy shouting, "Advertiser Extra."

All news from abroad was avidly read in Honolulu, but it was always long after the events. For example, in 1858 the clipper ship *Polynesia* arrived January 13, twelve days from San Francisco, carrying U.S. mail of December 5 and European material up to November 22. The time from New York to Honolulu was thirty-eight days—equaled only once before.

At times there were great gaps in the news, and journalists desperately reached for the scissors and glue pot for other than local material.

Time, of course, brought speedier movement of news. Word from San Francisco in June 1860 was that the Pony Express had shortened the transit time to San Francisco from New York or Boston to twelve or thirteen days for letters and that telegraphic dispatches could be sent through in nine or ten days.

By 1862, thanks to the telegraph, California newspapers had begun receiving U.S. East Coast and European news simultaneously with those in New York, so the Islands would be depending more on San Francisco papers and far less on those from New York and Europe.

In 1867 Whitney predicted that within ten years declining costs would make feasible the laying of a submarine cable between the United States and the Islands. In November 1858 a U.S. surveying schooner, the *Fenimore Cooper*, had taken the necessary soundings on a forty-three-day passage from San Francisco. With the forework done, said Whitney, "we bide our time."[4] He would live to see the cable completed, but it would be in 1902, twenty-five years later than he forecast.

In 1869, the *Advertiser* and other publications as well as letters from Honolulu were taking twelve days for delivery in San Francisco, twenty days in New York, and a shade under thirty days in London. Whatever the elapsed time, the harbor was central to the receipt and dispatch of all cargo, however small or large—and Whitney, in editorials, constantly called for improving it and the waterfront.

Another concern of the *Advertiser* was the safety of the interisland vessels, the "poi coasters." Whitney wrote that many were in poor condition and too often captained by inexperienced men who frequently were drunk. This discouraged "pleasure voyaging of foreigners among the islands."[5]

Safety aside, the coasters could never be cited for speeding. Anyone wanting to see a Big Island volcano was ten days getting to Hilo and after a crater visit and a week's wait was seven days from Hilo to Honolulu—thirty days in all.

On a visit to California in 1870 Whitney was greatly impressed with the importance there of steam navigation. He urged the legislature to find the best vessel possible or provide incentives for private action. But it was another two years before a viable service was established. The use of steam in coastal vessels sometimes enabled the *Advertiser* to be delivered to all islands on the day of publication. But that didn't end Neighbor Island circulation problems. Letters from Hilo and Kau, among other communities, said their papers were as much as two weeks late. The *Advertiser* printed a notice that it mailed papers at the post office on publication day but "over the mails we have no control."

The *Advertiser*'s interest in poi coasters was vastly overshadowed by its enthusiasm for whaling ships, the more the merrier. The paper saw the Islands providentially located as the center of whaling activity, as a "recruiting depot for the 10,000 seamen engaged in the whale fishing," and destined to play an enormously expanded role in Pacific commerce.[6]

Whaling had followed the fur and sandalwood trades and for almost half a century dominated the economy of Hawaii, which serviced and provisioned its ships, provided skilled boatmen, and purveyed rowdy recreation for the visiting seamen.

In August, September, and October, whalers drew supplies and recruited crewmen in Hawaii and took their harpoons south to equatorial waters for the winter. Then about March or April they returned to the Islands and prepared for summer hunting off Alaska and Japan, well up into the Arctic. The *Advertiser*, at its outset, was euphoric about whaling.

From his first issues, Whitney was determined to comprehensively cover shipping in general and whaling in particular. By September 1856 the *Advertiser* started regular fall and spring publication of the "North Pacific Whalemen's Shipping List." This extensive feature included names of ships and captains, year of sailing, the owners, the last whaling area, the season's catch in oil and bone, plus remarks. At times, statistics were compiled to show the total value of the catch. The information was collected by an *Advertiser* staffer who boarded every ship from the north and interviewed her officers. Newspapers in New Bedford, Boston, and New York regularly quoted the *Advertiser*, which gained the reputation of printing the most accurate accounts of northern whaling. In April 1857 it was stated that keeping the list up-to-date "requires more labor . . . than all the rest of the paper."

Native Hawaiians—the whalemen called them Kanakas—were much in demand as crewmen because of their boating skills and the need to replace dead sailors, deserters, or those kicked off by skippers on reaching shore.

When the government newspaper complained that the almost five hundred native seamen constituted labor needed for sugar plantations, Whitney dipped into his ever-ready well of sarcasm: "To think that these men should be ambitious and enterprising enough to embark in a venture which nets them $150 a year when they might, by settling down as agriculturalists, have meaner food, poorer lodgings and perhaps one-fifth the amount as a result of the same term at home. Surely their wings must be clipped. Gentlemen of the government will at once prepare a penal enactment for insertion in the Civil Code. . . ." [7]

The reality was that boatmen, native or otherwise, fully earned their pay, for whaling was a dangerous occupation. Obituaries of lost ships—from treacherous ice, collisions in fog, running aground in poorly charted waters, or plain lack of seaworthiness—were not infrequent in the *Advertiser*.

The waterfront was in everyone's consciousness, but for varied reasons. Hordes of sailors were in town every day, from merchantmen and coasters, and twice a year the whalers barreled in, their pockets loaded with accumulated wages, their minds intent on whiskey and women. These were readily provided by a rapacious mix of saloons, dance halls, gambling dens, bawdy houses, and other dives, a pleasurable haven for men long at sea, starved for sex, thirsting for drink. To many residents, the carousers were an affront, but to merchants they were riches from the sea. It is estimated that in a busy year the "sporting ladies" would take in $120,000, and of this, $100,000 reached the merchants. When added to income from provisioning and shipyard work, the combined sum, figured at $1 million or more, was vastly beyond the annual government revenue.[8]

The bright lights and pleasures of Honolulu drew hundreds of rural women. Prostitution was against the law, but the forces of supply and demand overwhelmed its enforcement. Hawaiians generally were highly vulnerable to venereal disease, against which they lacked immunity. Women selling sexual favors to sailors, and often receiving a VD infection along with payment, returned home to spread the contagion. It was, as Gavan Daws put it, "the great waster" of the nation.

In 1860 the legislature sought to cope with venereal disease by passing the "Act to Mitigate Evils and Disease Arising from Prostitution." It required ladies of the evening (and usually of the daytime, too) to register with the sheriff or face jail and to undergo medical inspection at the newly built Queen's Hospital. The *Advertiser* inveighed against the statute, saying "it will neither lessen the amount of prostitution; nor is it calculated to abate the evils which flow from it."[9]

In contrast to numerous such editorials, Whitney wrote little on the evil of prostitution itself. He adopted a laissez-faire position that those engaging in commercial sex did so voluntarily and the government couldn't compel people to walk in the paths of rectitude. So, while highly moralistic on many subjects, on prostitution the *Advertiser* twinkle-toed its way down the sidelines.

One might speculate, fairly or unfairly, that Whitney editorialized so sparingly on the subject because he was a businessman as well as an editor. Whaling was Hawaii's economic pillar, and the merchants who depended on the sailors and prostitutes for much of their trade were also his key advertisers, and with them his solvency and survival rested.

The swings in whaling activity continued to largely determine the economic rhythm of the Islands. By 1859 Whitney, once so high on the industry, was predicting whaling would rapidly diminish "in the next two or three years." But he was encouraged that other exports were gaining ground: "Our sugars receive the highest awards in Paris and California; our hides and wool begin to be quoted in the Eastern market reports; our coffee tickles the palates of connoisseurs at the East, and even in Europe; California stuffs her beds with our pulu"—a fiber from tree leaf ferns—"and luxuriates on our sweet potatoes. . . ."[10] Many felt, he wrote, that Hawaii's economy would benefit as other enterprises supplanted whaling.

By 1861 Whitney was railing at the government for taking no remedial action in developing Island resources to cushion the blow. He wrote that despite his cries of urgency, the king's ministers were concerned only with their own aggrandizement and "persisted in bringing poverty on the people, ruin on the country and lasting disgrace on their own names."[11]

One looking for even a small bright speck in the dark could find Honolulu a quieter place, so much so that the *Advertiser* could call for a trimming of the thirty-five-man police force, since, with whalers gone, the town was "inhabited by orderly foreigners and the most peaceful native population in the world."

With whaling's death, a fledgling sugar industry began to come into its own, with enormous impact on Hawaii's destiny—and even on Whitney's control of the *Advertiser*.

"We Shall Not Flinch from the Issue"

AUTHORITY IS never completely comfortable with a free press. The job of the journalist is disclosure, while the instinctive reaction of government, when there are mistakes or active chicanery, is secrecy. So the very nature of the two institutions tends to fuel an adversarial relationship.

Even in a democratic republic the tug-of-war between government and press creates inevitable tension. In the Hawaiian kingdom, given the differences in culture and the conflicting agendas of local and foreign elements of the community, it was surprising that a free press could even exist. And yet the government, although it had its own official voice for many years, permitted it.

This was primarily due to the liberal Constitution of 1852, which clearly reflected American political thought. "Granted by His Majesty Kamehameha III . . . by and with the advice and consent of the Nobles and Representatives of the People in Legislative Council Assembled," it provided in Article 3 that "all men may freely speak, write and publish their sentiments on all subjects, being responsible for the abuse of that right; and no law shall be passed to restrain or abridge the liberty of speech, or of the press."

So Henry Whitney and other Hawaii journalists, like their counterparts in America, were given constitutional protection. A new constitution, proclaimed in 1864, as Kamehameha V sought to increase the powers of the crown, retained the prohibition of laws restraining the liberty of speech or of the press, but added: "except such laws as may be necessary for the protection of His Majesty the King and the Royal Family." In the Constitution of 1887, promulgated by Kalakaua under pressure, that exception was stricken.

Whitney in his first editorial in 1856 emphasized that the *Advertiser* would be "untrammeled by government patronage or party pledges, unbiased by ministerial frowns or favors." He told his readers: "We must be left to our judgment to act with entire independence. To commence on any other basis would be to render our sheet what every former attempt has been, the tool of a party or the mouthpiece of a [cabinet] minister." Later in July, he promised to base the *Advertiser*'s stories on facts and then make appropriate comment,

no matter what party, clique, or individual interest may be damaged or promoted by our fearless discharge of our duty. Private reputation we consider
sacred and with it we shall never meddle, unless an individual seeks to make
himself an object of public notice, by his acts or publication. But public men
we view only as servants of the people, and all their official acts open to public comment, approval or condemnation.[1]

Whitney lost no time in translating these words into action. From the outset his editorials fairly bristled over perceived official derelictions. In the first
six months he inveighed against these, among others:

- A lengthy delay in dredging Honolulu harbor, "nearly two years from the
  time authority was given. . . ." That editorial hit a nerve, for the next
  issue reported that the dredge "has stretched out its dormant limbs
  preparatory to making submarine explorations in the harbor."
- The government's failure to provide Honolulu with a large enough supply
  of water from adequate springs and through adequate piping, and at less
  than existing rates.
- The government's lack of an official whose duties are "to examine into
  the expenditures of each department, to see whether public monies are
  properly collected, properly kept and accounted for, or used for private
  advantage."
- The lack of a proper system for managing the roads of the kingdom. A
  general superintendent was needed to give personal attention to the laying out and construction of new roads and bridges. "The drive toward
  Ewa could, at no great expense, be made pleasant; and that out toward
  Waialae returning by the beach around Diamond Head, and through the
  coconut grove of Waikiki, is a very pleasant one, if only a good road was
  completed. The drive to the Pali is the finest around Honolulu, but the
  road is very stony and generally very muddy." The person who gets there
  in a carriage "generally boasts of it as an uncommon feat."[2]

The fact that this fusillade brought no rebuke or retaliation from the king
attests to the worldliness of Kamehameha IV and his willingness to tolerate
diverse viewpoints, no matter how annoying.

Ironically, the strongest potential restriction against the press surfaced in
the American-influenced Provisional Government's Constitution of 1894, which
after granting freedom of speech and press provided that "the Legislature may
enact such laws as necessary to restrain and prevent the publication of public
utterance of indecent or seditious language."

This was at a time of public unrest after the 1893 toppling of the monarchy, but although "several Hawaiian newspapers were established for organized opposition against the Provisional Government," no reprisals were
taken against them.[3]

Even when the press is deemed free, libel laws are essential to protect innocent persons against published defamation. But they can be, and sometimes are, utilized in attempts to stifle legitimate expression, and some public officials will not hesitate to label as criminal, even treasonable, any press criticism that gets under their skin.

It is hardly surprising that given his zeal Whitney was to be exposed to both types of assault. When he likened the *Advertiser* to "a little bark launched on the uncertain tide of life," he foresaw that it would not always sail smoothly. "There are often squalls and gales slumbering unnoticed on the horizon of the most tranquil sky, while reefs and shoals are to be met in every voyage."[4]

He proved more clairvoyant than he might have wished. As early as his seventh issue of the *Advertiser*, August 14, 1856, he found himself involved in a charge of libel. The offending editorial charged the government with bad faith in renewing the license of the Royal Hotel and saloon on the Bethel square, since it had promised the Sailor's Home Society it would not do so. The antiliquor society, which on the basis of that pledge had built its home nearby for $14,000, was a haven for sea captains and crews and had most merchants and foreign residents as members.

The society's trustees vigorously protested the hotel relicensing, and Whitney editorialized, criticizing the Privy Council but concentrating his heaviest fire on Foreign Minister Robert C. Wyllie, whom he accused of dominating Prince Lot, the acting minister of the interior, on this matter.

Whitney seemed unconcerned that he was taking on one of the ablest and most powerful cabinet officers in the history of the Hawaiian monarchy. Wyllie, a dapper, mustachioed Scotsman who accumulated considerable money as a merchant in Latin America and London, came to the Islands in 1844 on the invitation of a friend who was British consul general. The next year he became minister of foreign affairs and served until his death two decades later. On the side, he owned and operated Princeville Plantation on Kauai, which long afterward would become a deluxe resort.

Whitney declared that the people "demand of Mr. Wyllie some explanation . . . or in default thereof they have the right to inquire why the affairs of the Kingdom are placed in irresponsible hands."

Then followed a rapid-fire exchange of seven letters, thinly coated with politeness, all reproduced in the *Advertiser* of August 21. Wyllie wanted to know if Whitney's editorial had the sanction of the trustees of the Sailor's Home Society. When Whitney replied he had written on his own authority, Wyllie said he had insulted Prince Lot, while directing "malicious falsehoods" against himself. He threatened to sue for libel unless Whitney immediately retracted.

Both Wyllie and Whitney hired lawyers, and Whitney editorialized, "If the government is anxious to make the attempt to muzzle this sheet and gag the expression of public opinion regarding public servants then let the contest come now. . . . We shall not flinch from the issue (even if it costs) our last drop of blood."[5]

After some further maneuvering, the word scuffle ended without court action. But given his strong will and crusading spirit, it was inevitable that Whitney would build a reservoir of resentment among officials and that a goodly number, eager to strike back, would seize on an early opportunity. Some felt that had arrived when a sixteen-line item appeared in the *Advertiser* of May 23, 1868.

The item concerned Rear Admiral H. K. Thatcher, commanding the U.S. North Pacific Squadron. A year and a half earlier, when Queen Emma cut short her state visit to the United States on the death of her adoptive mother, Thatcher had brought her home aboard his flagship. For his kindness, the king decorated the admiral. When, considerably later, Thatcher was transferred to the Charlestown Navy Yard, Whitney linked his recall to the decoration, which he intimated could have been designed to influence the admiral's official conduct.

Two days later, the legislature began debating a resolution declaring that Whitney for a long time had sought to bring the king, government, judiciary, and people into disrepute and contempt before the world and that in the current session he had maliciously attacked its honor and dignity. The aim: to have the attorney general criminally prosecute Whitney.

One House member after another sounded off, mostly against Whitney, then David Kalakaua spoke: "I have no personal motives in the matter, but I think that calling an editor to an account is below the dignity of this House. It is trifling with a common editor of an insignificant paper. . . . I care nothing for the personal attacks this paper has made on me, but I deny that the liberty of the press should be suppressed."

The bottom line was that Attorney General Stephen Phillips took no action on the resolution and the entire furor evaporated.

Whitney doggedly continued to target his editorial fire on official shortcomings, one of the more glaring being favoritism in the award of government contracts. He declared: "Let not officers of the government be pecuniarily interested in the public works."

He berated the government for having earlier named Theodore C. Heuck as director of the Bureau of Public Works while he continued to maintain his own architectural and contracting firm and personally awarded it no-bid jobs.[6] This was the same Heuck who three years later was shielded by Police Magistrate John Montgomery from having to stand trial for allegedly buying stolen whalebone. The *Advertiser* felt there was abundant evidence that Heuck had acted knowingly and that there was probable cause to take the case before a jury.

The government's newspaper, the *Gazette*, successor in 1865 to the *Polynesian*, defended the official no-bid policy as providing the best workmen and brushed aside any question of conflicts of interest. Gavan Daws has observed that "Heuck's Honolulu was far from being Tweed's New York," but allowing for respective differences "there was a similarity in tone."[7]

Despite Whitney's constant criticism of the Hawaiian government, its ministers, and policies, in the *Advertiser*'s early years he was exceedingly respectful of the king. This was dramatically borne out by his paper's treatment of outrageous conduct by Kamehameha IV on September 11, 1859. The king four years earlier had appointed as his personal secretary Henry A. Neilson, a handsome young man of a distinguished East Coast family, which included Neilson's nephew, E. H. Harriman, later of railroad fame.

Neilson had few duties, other than serving as a drinking and traveling companion to the king. He enjoyed a bohemian life, which included a mistress whom he squired at royal functions. Someone poisoned the king's mind with the suspicion that Neilson was having a liaison with Queen Emma. During a visit to Lahaina, and after considerable brooding, his majesty went aboard his schooner and spent the night, all of the next day, and well into that night drinking heavily. On coming ashore, he took a pistol, went to Neilson's quarters, and at close range shot him in the lower chest. On sobering, the king made belated inquiries that convinced him his jealousy was entirely without basis. Filled with remorse, he sank into a deep depression and talked of abdicating.

Three days after the Lahaina tragedy, the *Advertiser*, under "Notes of the Week," said, "Our readers may expect that we should say something in regard to the melancholy affair which occurred at Lahaina on Sunday last. But there are so many vague rumors afloat that we forbear for the present giving any version of it."[8]

The following week the paper, under a small heading, "The Shooting Affair at Lahaina," noted dissatisfaction by readers over its silence, then added:

> We were assured by the government editor that a statement would be made in his paper, on Saturday last . . . and in deference to His Majesty we preferred waiting for such official account.
>
> The reason why no statement was made in the Polynesian last Saturday was that the account as drawn up had not been returned from the King, but is expected today or tomorrow, when it will be immediately published.
>
> We are not blind to the gravity of the case, if current rumors are correct, but reasonable deference to His Majesty, who is the principal actor in it, should allow him first to make such public statements as justice to His people demands.

A week later, seventeen days following the shooting, the *Advertiser* ran a long lead article starting with the report that the king wished to abdicate his throne and return to private life. It said that while in a sense the tragedy—of which it gave no details—was a private affair and the king was immune to prosecution, it was also a public affair that merited journalistic comment. That comment was restrained and equivocal. The king's deed violated the laws of man and God and could not be justified. But, if the king's suspicion of Neilson had been well founded, the public would have "imperiously demanded" his meting out of justice and "public sentiment would have fully justified and acquitted him of evil intent." As it was, the king's remorse showed him "to be a man in every sense of the word, a man of refined and tender feelings, and worthy of the position he holds."

The *Advertiser* appealed to the king to retain his throne: "The interest of the kingdom, the interests of every subject, or resident, demand that the king banish forever the idea [of abdication] from his mind and maintain the position which the God of nations has decreed to him and in which every subject will loyally support and defend him."

On October 1, the government paper carried a brief statement that "the rumors in regard to His Majesty's abdication are, we are happy to say, without foundation." The king apologized to Neilson by letter and provided him with the best of medical care. But the victim remained bedridden until his death thirty months later.

In its "Notes of the Week" the *Advertiser* of September 12, 1862, carried a brief item: "Yesterday morning Mr. Henry A. Neilson died in this city. In former years he was well known but for two years and a half has been confined to his room by the unfortunate occurrence which is familiar to all. His funeral will be held at 4 P.M. today." Neilson was buried in Nuuanu Cemetery in a grave left without a marker.

Amid the Press Battles, a Shocker

WHEN THERE are two or more newspapers in a democratic society, competition is their lifeblood. But the rivalry between the *Advertiser* and the *Polynesian* went far beyond the norm. It was bitter, persistent, and often personal.

One major reason was that at the *Advertiser* Henry Whitney was running an independent private-enterprise newspaper, while the government-subsidized paper was a spokesman for and defender of official policy and performance. This assured an inevitable, continuing clash in editorial philosophies. Another reason was that both newspapers operated commercial printshops, and the government competed with Whitney for private accounts.

Whitney paid taxes—$1,000 or more a year—on his revenue of some $22,000 from printing, periodicals, and books, while the *Polynesian* and its printshop paid nothing. Thus, argued Whitney, in seeking private business the government printshop undercut him and other printers in town. So for years a considerable amount of his time, energy, and editorial space went toward contending for "just rights" against a "government monopoly." He asked what the public would say if their government went into importing and retailing and sold goods below cost "at the public expense" to government employees.

The first and only kind word from the *Polynesian* came July 5, 1856, just after the *Advertiser*'s first issue. Editor Charles G. Hopkins complimented the newcomer on its overall "neatness," which "altogether distances the Polynesian, for the office was ordered out entire and not like ours got together by parcels as opportunity or necessity drove."

The very next month the *Polynesian* took after Whitney for his commentary on the government's financial distress and a few weeks later for the *Advertiser*'s call for a government auditor to keep an eye on officials' traditionally unaudited accounts, used "to suit their whims."

At one point Editor Hopkins of the *Polynesian* complained there was little news in Honolulu and what there was became as stale as "sliced cucumbers" before seeing print. You're lazy, Whitney lectured him; there's enough news "in our little world to fill a dozen papers of heavier caliber than yours, if you will only hunt it up. There's the rub."[1]

Beyond indolence, the *Advertiser* accused the *Polynesian* of plagiarism, declaring it should not "borrow our editorial columns without at least giving a fair credit." It cited two examples: a ship's manifest "condensed only with hours of labor was copied from the Commercial [Advertiser] as original." And a report on the cargo of the schooner *Kamoi* "filled out by the captain and addressed to the publisher of the Commercial [Advertiser] was actually copied and printed first in the Polynesian. We like to see a little enterprise, but don't take others' copy and set it up as original news."[2]

So it went. When the *Polynesian* printed an extra with some important ship news eight hours after the *Advertiser,* Whitney labeled it the "fastest terrapin" in the country and suggested it should stick to publishing laws of the kingdom.[3]

At times the language was rough. Once, Whitney had published, in advance of the *Polynesian,* a statement of government finances and expressed thanks to the registrar of public accounts for making it available. The *Polynesian* did not feel Whitney had been grateful enough. Thus lectured on manners, Whitney showed his disgust: "The public look upon that journal as they do on an insane person, with pity—almost contempt—and treat it as unworthy either of their patronage or support. . . . Like an unwhipt truant schoolboy, it needs an occasional use of the birch to bring it to a sense of responsibility. . . ."[4]

Despite the journalistic animosity, toward the end of 1858 Whitney had submitted to the Privy Council an offer to do the government's printing. For ordinary printing he would charge $3,800 a year, with lowest-rate additional charges for "extraordinary" jobs. Included was the printing of any departmental gazette in English or Hawaiian, not more than once a month. For printing a Hawaiian-language weekly with the same size and circulation of the government's existing *Hae Hawaii,* he would charge $1,500 a year.

The next month Prince Lot read Whitney's proposal to the Privy Council, which voted to leave it to the "wisdom of the Minister of the Interior."[5] Nothing came of this. But Whitney had the satisfaction of seeing his drumfire against the government printing bureau gradually have its effect. The budget for 1860 was cut sharply, eliminating, among other posts, the deputy directorship held since the spring of 1857 by Fornander. In October, after five years as director and editor of the government press, Hopkins resigned, citing financial considerations.

On October 6 Fornander succeeded Hopkins, taking on a mountainous challenge. In his farewell commentary Hopkins wrote, "If it be any satisfaction to those who put their heads together to undo the Polynesian, I am willing to confess before the first blow is struck that I think it very likely their machinations will succeed."[6]

Hopkins was prophetic. The *Polynesian* of November 2, 1860, brought the news that the government was getting out of the printing business. The *Polynesian* and the official printshop would be operated under lease by Fornander, who, at least, would have the contract for government printing.

The next two years were marked by combat between the two papers over the Civil War. Whitney was vigorously pro-Union. Fornander took a neutralist position, for which Whitney labeled him "our secessionist neighbor."[7]

Fornander, like Whitney, was a strong-willed man and he worked hard to make a go of the *Polynesian*. But the odds were against him, and in late January 1864, at his request, the government released him from his contract. Some days earlier, Whitney apparently had gotten wind of Fornander's intentions and so on January 18 met with Minister of the Interior George M. Robertson and on the next day submitted to him in writing an almost unbelievable proposal. Under it, the *Advertiser* and the *Polynesian* would be discontinued, merging into a new weekly, the *Royal Hawaiian Gazette*.

The *Gazette*, wrote Whitney, would be "published at my risk and expense and all receipts accruing from it [would] be mine." The papers would go "to all paid subscribers of the above two papers during the term they have paid for," and, excepting the king and cabinet members, no government officers would receive the *Gazette* free of charge. He would take over the printing covered in Fornander's contract and would bind himself for five years in return for $3,800 a year, payable quarterly by the government. The *Polynesian*'s office would be closed, and its presses and type would be stored for the duration of the lease, unless needed to execute the government printing, in which case he had the option of leasing them on "equitable terms."

Then came the shocker:

> The editorial columns of this (proposed) paper shall be under the control of His Majesty's Ministers, to express the views of the government, and all such articles are to be handed in at least 24 hours before the time of publication. The editorship of the Gazette [is] to be placed in the hands of a competent person, to be employed by me, and paid at my expense. . . . The Kuokoa newspaper, now published by me, will become the exponent of government policy, so far as the King's Ministers may wish to use it as such. Both papers are to be open and free to discussions on current events or topics, written in a temperate tone.

As icing on the suggested cake, he added: "As I retire from the editorial charge of the Commercial Advertiser, I am to resume the office of Postmaster General with the approval of the King."

Whitney's proposition was so diametrically opposite of everything he had written and practiced on independence that it defies understanding. If his motivation was recorded, it has not come to light. One is reduced to simply asking questions: Was the *Advertiser*, despite its claims of success, actually in desperate financial circumstances? Did Whitney fear the government would retrieve the *Polynesian* and, in a new approach, fund it so substantially that it might push the *Advertiser* to the wall? Or did the businessman in Whitney rationalize that being manager rather than editor would relieve him of any responsibility for what the paper printed, or didn't? Was the postal job suggested to assure a steady income, in contrast to the ups and downs of publishing? Was he unconcerned about what his peers would think, if they became aware of the proposal—which apparently did not become public?

All that is certain is that Henry Whitney, who exuded rectitude and adherence to principle, was proposing to manage a propaganda sheet for the government, in the process eliminating the *Advertiser* and leaving the community without a separate and independent editorial voice.

Were the letter to the government not in his own hand, one would be tempted to dismiss the communication as someone's notion of an intemperate joke. While the government pondered Whitney's suggested deal, Fornander in his valedictory in the *Polynesian* of January 30 said that in journalism "we have encountered obloquy, traduction, malevolence, but we lived down all that, and the path we tread, though not smoothed, is illuminated by the knowledge that our moral integrity has been vindicated and recognized even by our assailants."

The government, tired of the financial drain, discontinued the *Polynesian* on February 6. Then, four days later, Interior Minister Robertson gave Whitney his answer, but not the one that was wanted: "Your proposal . . . having been considered by His Majesty's Government I have the honor to inform you that I am not at present authorized to accept that proposal, either in its original shape or as subsequently verbally modified." (No record of the modification is at hand.)

"The publication of the Polynesian newspaper having ceased, the Government will issue its proclamations and executive or other notices in the Commercial Advertiser, for the present."[8]

So Whitney, with the field to himself, could afford to be gracious about the now-dead opposition: "For all [the Polynesian's] faults, it had some good qualities. . . . We shall regret standing alone. . . . There has no doubt been much unnecessary bitterness at times expressed. 'Let bygones be bygones.'"[9]

In 1899, only a few years before his death, Whitney wrote that with the demise of the *Polynesian* in 1864

> the ministers sought to make an arrangement with the publisher of the
> Commercial Advertiser by which it would become the semi-official organ of
> the Hawaiian Government, and receive all its patronage of advertising and
> printing. This was firmly declined by the editor and publisher who would not
> relinquish the independent platform on which it was established and had
> been conducted for ten years.[10]

Whitney was seventy-five at the time and his memory may have gone awry; in any event, it was a clear case of history being rewritten.

Back to 1864: the *Polynesian* was discarded by the government only a month before King Kamehameha V began a campaign seeking changes in the

Constitution of 1852 to centralize more power in the throne. Apparently the king and his cabinet failed to anticipate the sharp controversy—and the value of having an official newspaper to showcase their position and influence the election of friendly delegates to a July constitutional convention.

The *Advertiser*, which on the *Polynesian*'s departure had shifted its publication day to Saturday and was now getting all government notices requiring English, did not exploit the situation. It evenhandedly printed letters of widely varying opinions and a series of articles by Attorney General Charles C. Harris explaining proposed constitutional changes.

The convention deadlocked over the king's demand for a property qualification for voting, which would negate the universal suffrage assured in the Constitution of 1852. The king dissolved the convention, and for some days Hawaii operated as an autocracy without a written constitution. The *Advertiser* on August 20 labeled it "an oligarchy ruled by a ministerial cabinet of four." That same day, the king's signature ramrodded through a new constitution prepared by his inner circle.

The *Advertiser* had long been a thistle in the government's anatomy, but on limiting suffrage it shared the royal view, especially with regard to the legislature. The constitution was redrawn, proclaimed by fiat, and prevailed for twenty-three years.

As it developed, the *Advertiser* had the English-language field to itself for just eleven months. Its January 14, 1865, issue carried a paid notice that the *Hawaiian Gazette*, a weekly, would be published starting on Saturday, the 21st, at the government printing office and that subscribers, at $3 a year, should send their names to J. H. Black, the publisher. He doubled as foreman with Henry L. Sheldon joining as editor.

On the day the *Gazette* was to come out the *Advertiser* said that if it was confined to the promulgation of official orders, notices, and laws, "as we understand it to be," monthly or semiweekly issuance should suffice. But the *Gazette* took on a full newspaper format, so sniping between the two publications was predictable.

The *Advertiser* of March 11 looked down its nose at the "puerile compositions" appearing weekly in the *Gazette* and said that if some of the writers were examined by a competent board they "would hardly be acquitted of the charge of lunacy."

In April 1865, after more than eight years of carefully nurturing the *Advertiser*, Whitney felt the need for a sabbatical. He ran a notice in large type, informing all that he would be leaving on the bark *Comet* to visit San Francisco, New York, and Washington for about six months. In his absence, Joseph O. Carter, Jr., was empowered to act for him, in full charge of the paper.

Two weeks after assuming the editor's chair, Carter unloosed a volley at the *Gazette*. That paper had reproduced from "an English periodical" an article that was actually a thinly veiled attack on the missionary element. It impugned the motives of the early advisers of the Hawaiians, accusing them of "officious intermeddling" and ambitions to usurp royal power. Carter was sure that it was the work of a local resident "celebrated for his fatal facility in defacing foolscap."[11]

Carter further excoriated the *Gazette* for defending increased power for the king and "the illegality of trampling on the Constitution of 1852." In so doing, Carter appears to have taken a stance quite the opposite of Whitney's. Whereas Whitney favored property qualifications for voting, Carter said that any notion that universal suffrage was incompatible with a monarchial government was "absurd," unless by monarchy one meant autocracy. Carter wrote:

> partial suffrage in some of the States of the American Union, is found to be a retrogression, and steps are being taken to remove the restriction. Here, universal suffrage under a monarchial government [was] tested for 12 years [1852–1864] and the fruit of it culminated in the convention to resist ministerial aggression upon its rights.
>
> We will only add, the elements of that convention exhibited a proof of national advance in a knowledge of civil rights and duties perfectly astounding to fogy monarchists, who desire to keep the common people in respectful tutelage to a privileged class for indefinite centuries.[12]

After a twenty-eight-week absence and more than eighteen thousand miles of travel, Whitney was back in harness, eager to share his experiences with readers "scattered from the western shore of Niihau to the green fields of Kau." The sight of Diamond Head evoked from him paeans of praise for the Islands, "an Eden-like home of perpetual spring and balmy winds, 'where the bee banquets on through a whole year of flowers.'"

In his journeys, he had run into erroneous opinions—one that Hawaii was under British rule, this stemming from an English Episcopal bishop's presence; the other that the Hawaiians were "relapsing into their former state of barbarism."

Some American and British newspapers, in covering Queen Emma's successful visit to Europe, had referred to the natives as "eating Captain Cook." Whitney's response: "The [earlier] Hawaiians, whatever else they may have been, were never cannibals." Of Queen Emma he wrote, "She is indeed a truly noble woman, fit to grace the royal circle of any European sovereign, and far superior to many European noble women in moral culture, simplicity of heart, and all that goes to make an exalted female character."

During Whitney's U.S. visit, the Civil War ended; he opined that "every American may justly be proud [of the country] as the only power on earth that could have subdued such a rebellion or survived such a war."[13] His later advocacy of annexation should have surprised no one.

Whitney praised Carter, his surrogate editor, noted an "increasing subscription list and a generous advertising patronage," and pledged to maintain the *Advertiser* as a "welcome guest" in readers' homes and "a valuable assistant" in the "counting room."[14]

Yet less than three months later, on January 10, 1866, there was startling news. A notice appeared over Whitney's name offering the *Advertiser* for sale—and the printing establishment connected with it. "Possession will be given at the close of the current volume, June 30, 1866."

In his next issue he intimated that he had been approached by prospective buyers. When none appeared even after a second "for sale" notice, he sought to recover any lost ground by announcing that as of July 1 the paper would be nearly doubled in size, with new type, new paper, and a larger office to enable him to print both the news and all the ads submitted.

In his traditional anniversary editorial, Whitney on July 7, 1866, wrote: "At one time, lately, the publisher thought of disposing of the paper, but the probability is that he will continue to publish it ten years longer, if life and health are spared."

He said that as the *Advertiser* entered its eleventh year, while it was not easy to have "every type, every sheet of paper, every (overseas) article brought in over thousands of miles," the paper had been able to make it financially. But he and the *Advertiser*, in addition to battling the government paper, were soon to face competition from another source. J. J. Ayers of the *San Francisco Morning Call*, who had been visiting, decided to move to Hawaii—and word in the California papers was that he had bought a press and a stock of type and intended to establish a newspaper.

The *Advertiser* observed in June 1866 that if the government wanted to sell or close its printing monopoly it would open the field for a second printing office and paper and that would be welcome, since Ayers was understood to be a good printer and a good editor.

In August Ayers let it be known that he planned to issue a paper starting September 4, independent and, here was the big news, daily from Tuesday through Saturday. Its name: *The Daily Hawaiian Herald.* After its first issue, the *Advertiser* acknowledged that Hawaii had "actually entered upon a new era in [its] newspaper history." And it congratulated proprietor Ayers for having "the nerve to break through the thick crust of popular skepticism."

The *Herald*'s pages were small, twelve inches by fifteen, but it was "large enough to keep our island metropolis posted in all current events." Whitney said he hoped it would succeed as a second independent paper, and if it didn't it would be the fault of the government's subsidized *Gazette* and printshop.

As the days passed, the *Herald* continued to "grow in favor." But while praising its new competitor, the *Advertiser* deplored the *Herald*'s intention to print police reports, fearing no good would come from it. "In a small, one-horse town like ours, everybody is known to his neighbor and is supposed to possess a character; and everybody is liable to err and fall into the hands of the police, often too eager for their prey. Now we object to the publication of the alleged or actual offenses which are continually brought before this inquisition."[15]

In late August, Sheldon resigned from the *Gazette*, having found Black difficult to work with, and joined the *Herald* as a reporter. The *Advertiser* in November noted an improvement in that paper and said that if it gained financially, as well as in the news department, it would be a success.

But newspapers can't live on praise alone. A month later, in mid-December, the *Herald* had to close. Its circulation had not risen beyond two hundred to three hundred copies a day, and publisher Ayers had found out the hard way that Honolulu was not yet ready for a daily.

In the next couple of years, two other publications were started, *The Punch Bowl*, a monthly established by J. H. Black, and a weekly called *Bennett's Own*. Whitney expressed the hope that both would succeed, but then got in his usual dig at the government paper: "So long as the sleepy, super-annuated hebdomadal [weekly] which issues from the government press monopolizes the place of a second lively and a spirited weekly paper, it is of little use to try to attempt anything new in this line, except for amusement."[16] Neither of the new publications was long-lived.

As with the *Polynesian*, much of Whitney's energy was devoted to fulminating against the *Gazette*, its "moral turpitude . . . want of decency . . . and demoralizing influence."[17] In October 1866 the *Gazette* named as its editor Dr. John Mott-Smith, who had been a legislator from Kohala—and Whitney scoffed at his suggestion that the post sought him out. The fact is, he said, Mott-Smith had lobbied for the job for the past six months.

Whitney's ire was specifically directed at what he called dishonorable behavior by Mott-Smith. The *Advertiser* in its last issue had intended a sentence to read that "no man can take [the *Gazette* editorship] and retain the respect of the community." It came out that no man could take that position "and retain his position as a member of the community." Whitney that very morning visited Mott-Smith and called his attention to the error. But, said Whitney, Mott-Smith deliberately concealed that the error had been personally corrected by Whitney and, instead, quoted the erring sentence. Whitney exclaimed this act "is unworthy of a member of the fraternity."[18]

The battle between the papers had all the earmarks of a weekly boxing match, both weaving, ducking, trading punches—not infrequently below the belt—and crying "foul." In sniping at an *Advertiser* story, the *Gazette* was not reluctant to charge that Whitney would go to any length "to gratify the personal animosity he feels" toward those with whom he differs.[19]

Along with the name-calling went rivalry for getting the news first. Take the case of Captain Hamilton and his whaling bark *Sea Breeze* arriving with a long, newsy report prepared by the skipper for the *Advertiser*, with whom he enjoyed cordial relations. He had on board the captain of the bark *Cayalti*, which had suffered piracy and murder, the details of which would make lively reading. The *Gazette*'s marine reporter, saying the two papers were on good terms, conned Hamilton into giving him the material, which he quickly printed. The *Advertiser*'s name had been erased and that of the *Gazette* substituted in the reporter's handwriting.

Declared the *Advertiser:* "We have always desired to be on good terms with the Gazette, but if to retain their good will we are to submit to such discourteous treatment, we shall be compelled to decline the honor. A fair, honest competition in securing news could but be advantageous to the newspapers and the public and such competition we invite."[20]

The editor of the *Gazette*, Dr. Mott-Smith, was often absent, and G. Von Gosnitz, who had been conducting the government press in the interim, resigned in March 1869, and the *Advertiser* rejoiced "at his independence." It declared that "no man who has any self-respect can remain in a position where he is compelled to sink his individuality so utterly and disgracefully." The *Advertiser* was puzzled that Mott-Smith's name was still appearing as director of the *Gazette* since he "distinctly gave us to understand that he had severed his connection with the paper and confessed that it had been distasteful to him."[21]

Not long after, the *Gazette* announced it was cutting its rates on ads and job printing by 25 percent, and Whitney charged this was designed not for public benefit but to injure "and perhaps suppress" the *Advertiser* and the *Kuokoa*.

In that same issue Whitney said "in an argument with a Government official, we were plainly asked if we did not like the condition of affairs here—why did we not leave the Kingdom? Our answer to him and his colleagues was and is that having been born here and established a home and a business, we do not intend to be driven from them."[22]

6

Praise and Presses, Letters and Lava

THE *ADVERTISER* was warmly regarded by Honolulu's American community, both by merchants and the missionary element, as a fair-minded spokesman. They felt that Henry Whitney could be counted on to present their viewpoints, while serving as a buffer between them and a government about which they frequently had doubts. They also were comfortable with his entrepreneurial instincts, including his promotional bent.

From the very outset, he was never one for modesty where the paper was concerned. On New Year's Day, 1857, the *Advertiser* was just a six-month-old "infant," but its "lungs" were lusty. Whitney proclaimed that from a list of two hundred names circulation had grown to one thousand copies each week. He reiterated that he was publishing an independent, not an opposition paper, and not "the first line of disloyalty" to the sovereign had appeared. But the paper had "been opposed to the blind, one-sided policy of ministers [which] was fraught with evil to the public weal" and would continue to resist it.

In that same January 1 issue Whitney further showed his promotional flair by quoting other publications' testimonials to his efforts. The *New York News* saw the *Advertiser* as "one of the handsomest papers in point of typography and general appearance that comes to this office."

In the *San Francisco Town Talk*, "Friend Bowlin" said, "We are pleased to see [that the *Advertiser*] gives every evidence of prosperity. In comparison to the Polynesian, it is a steam engine to a dog cart."

The *Boston Advertiser* called the *Advertiser* "a very neatly printed paper, and intelligently conducted, with an adaptation to the business purposes of the inhabitants of the islands. . . ."

Whitney's readers, given a friendly outlet, were not slow in utilizing it for candid, often pent-up expression of their feelings. The first letter to the editor appeared in the second issue, its author complaining of the shortage of wharf space and asking why the government didn't "sell out water privileges" to people who wanted to build docks "to aid the commerce of the country."

Other early letters dealt with inland transportation: "Anyone riding from Honolulu to Wailua can testify to the wretchedness of the roads and bridges, except where the road is naturally good. At the present time one of the bridges is absolutely impossible for either teams or saddle horses, and this is one of those most needed."

Then there was a spate of letters about the quality and performance of the Honolulu police. Complaining of "the utter insecurity of our town at night," a writer said: "Judging by the number of robberies which we hear of almost daily, it is not unreasonable to suppose that many of our native policemen are either in league with some band of housebreakers or are, in many cases, themselves the thieves."

Excessive language was encouraged by the use in signatures of initials or pseudonyms, which seemed the vogue of the day in letters to the editor, in the Islands and in the United States. Readers thus had no way of knowing whether the letters were bona fide or of being able to judge any vested interest by the writers.

In late March 1857 the *Advertiser*'s long-awaited Adams New Patent Power Press, which cost $2,000, arrived from Boston on the bark *Raduga*. Its composition rollers "were cast in Boston and must be 10 or 12 months old, yet they were nearly as good as new." No machinist at hand knew how to assemble the machine, but William Hughes, who operated the harbor dredge, took on the task and had the press in operating condition in two days.

The *Advertiser*'s next important acquisition of equipment was a Ruggles Combination Job Press, capable of printing up to one thousand impressions an hour. The newspaper carried a pen-and-ink sketch of it and announced it now had a variety of "new and fancy types and materials," with more to come, and hoped "soon to be able to print all kinds of bill-heads and small jobs, at as low prices and as neatly as can be done either in San Francisco or Honolulu."[1] It subsequently conveyed that with its assorted "new and elegant type" it "was now prepared to execute book, job and fancy printing in every variety with neatness and dispatch."[2]

With the close of the *Advertiser*'s first year, it announced it was expanding its size to enable more news and ads. It was getting new readers on the other islands, and since production was costing between $500 and $600 a month, it encouraged subscribers to be prompt in renewing their subscriptions.

The paper had not "been expected to repay the cost [of the new equipment] the first year, but it had done more towards it than the publisher had any right to look for."[3] Because of the expense, Whitney had not yet employed an editor, performing those duties in part himself, but in the year ahead he hoped to hire one. And when subscribers demanded it and were willing to bear the expense, he was ready to move from weekly to semiweekly.

Whitney felt that during its first year the *Advertiser* had maintained "a conservative bearing" while being "unequivocal on all matters of general interest." Its independence in taking to task erring government officials had "in some cases given personal offense." But that was an acceptable part of getting out a paper "for the public good."[4]

The leading articles during that first year were generally prepared by persons "classed among the most intelligent and reliable men in the kingdom."[5] Whitney had said, "This journal will be conducted on the European plan without any announcement to the public of the names of its editorial contributors. This will enable us to introduce into the editorial columns a greater variety of style on all topics to which the paper is devoted."

With contributed articles and its regular features, Whitney felt the paper was making steady progress. In July 1858, as the *Advertiser* entered its third year, he said it was finally breaking even, but without allowing any pay for him.

By the following March the paper was boasting that it was selling up to fifteen hundred copies an issue, taking its advertisements to almost every farmhouse and foreign resident in the kingdom, as well as throughout the Pacific.

To add editorial strength Whitney had taken on Henry Sheldon as associate editor and head printer. Sheldon held that post until September 1859, when J. H. Sleeper succeeded him and the paper went semiweekly. Sleeper was twenty-six, a New Hampshire man whose father, the mayor of Roxbury, Massachusetts, had been for many years editor/publisher of the *Boston Journal*. He had come to Hawaii primarily for his health and learned to read and speak Hawaiian.

Only a month after the semiweekly was inaugurated Sleeper died, after a five-day illness, and since no experienced successor was available, Whitney announced that the paper would have to revert to a weekly.

That same year Whitney bought the presses, type, and furniture of the Mission Press, founded in 1822 and for many years thereafter the only printing operation in the Islands. The *Advertiser* printshop had been doing the mission work for the previous year or two after the Hawaiian Evangelical Association found it could get better work at less cost than doing it itself. The agreed sale price was $1,300, which Whitney was to pay in printing. This was a plus for the *Advertiser*, but it could never take good fortune for granted.

With the outbreak of the Civil War came a sharp rise in the price of newsprint, due in part to a scarcity of cotton and cotton rags used in its manufacture, and in part to price-fixing by a cartel of papermakers who controlled the industry. The *Advertiser*, which had been buying some of its paper from Germany for four or five years, would have to rely more on that source, although there was an extra cost of some 20 percent. The paper hoped it could avoid a jump in subscription rates, especially of the *Kuokoa* "which, at the present price of stock, barely pays for the white paper alone."

Thus it came as a surprise when the *Advertiser* announced that it was reducing advertising rates for regular customers by about one-third, "lower than those of weekly New York papers." The reason surfaced in its next issue: the *Polynesian*, the government paper, had lowered its charges by that amount.

Beyond that, the *Advertiser* claimed proof that the *Polynesian* had printed some notices for half-price, thus "studiously and stealthily" seeking to injure its rival. But determined to remain the Islands' "leading advertising medium," the *Advertiser* was "countering this move."

On the news side, in some weeks, because of exciting Civil War reports, the *Advertiser* was issuing one or two extras. Some readers asked why these weren't free. The *Advertiser* explained that the government-subsidized *Polynesian* had confused matters locally by giving away extras.

If any Neighbor Islanders wanted *Advertiser* extras they would be provided, with additional billing. But getting papers to the other islands on time was not easy. The postal service left much to be desired, and to former postmaster Whitney delays in delivery of the *Advertiser* were especially galling.

Under the heading "Is there no relief?" the *Advertiser* cited complaints from Kauai. A Hanalei reader got three issues of the *Advertiser* at one time, one of them a month old. A Waimea subscriber cited irregular delivery, not only of the paper but of all mail. This despite the fact that hardly a week passed without a vessel leaving Honolulu for some Kauai port.[6] A number of copies of the *Advertiser* clearly addressed in large type to Kauai wound up instead on the island of Hawaii and were returned to Honolulu.

These "eccentricities of the mails" spurred a complaint to the minister of the interior by Whitney, who had lost two subscribers and had many others wondering "why their papers are from two to four weeks getting from Honolulu to them." Whitney wrote that it might be best to abolish the postal service "and return to the old mode of letting papers and letters reach their destination as best they can." He didn't mean it, of course, but the post office's "grossest and most inexcusable negligence" frustrated and angered him.[7]

Then, as now, few days in newspapering were without their aggravations. Except when the government press and cabinet antics were involved, Whitney was usually a man of peace, but he had his limits. Came a day when plantation owner John Montgomery found his horse's tail clean-shaved and on the mane a note saying the hair could be retrieved at the *Advertiser*, where it was to be used "to brush off type." The paper "had never heard of . . . a more mean, cruel and contemptible act . . . a disgrace to a Botany Bay convict." Given the villain's additional offense of trying "to disguise himself by imitating a lady's handwriting, few will hesitate to say that he merited a coat of tar and feathers."[8]

On other occasions, Whitney was more restrained but still annoyed when he felt the paper was being treated improperly, as when it was denied various court decisions for publication. He blamed it on "the dog-in-the-manger policy" of the interior ministry.

He could put his vexations aside by turning reporter in a different setting—thus satisfying his zeal to inform his readers—and this he did from time to time. For example, a great eruption of Mauna Loa on the Big Island on April 7, 1868, prompted a hasty trip there by Whitney and the production of an extra featuring his dispatches from Kealakekua.

He had witnessed "the most grand, brilliant and awe-inspiring scene probably ever afforded to the people of these islands." From Kealakekua he and a
party of ten, plus guides, followed the old road through the Kona district on
the island's western side. On ascending a ridge near Kahuku he viewed a valley "floored over with a pavement of . . . lava from 10 to 29 feet deep . . . from
a crater about 10 miles up the mountain."

That afternoon he saw a fresh flow from a new crater "at least one and a
half miles in extent" destroy farmhouses with the lava "varying from five to
fifty feet in depth." He described the "river of fire" running to the sea, "surging
and roaring like a cataract, with a fury perfectly indescribable." At night "the
scene was a hundred-fold more grand and vivid—the crimson red of the lava
doubly bright, and the lurid glare of the red smoke clouds that overhung the
whole, the roaring of the rushing stream, the noise of the tumbling rocks
thrown out of the crater, and the flashes of electric lightning—altogether
made it surpassingly grand." From Kau, on the south side of the island, "the
scene is even more beautiful."

From residents of Waiohinu he learned there had been an estimated two
thousand shocks prior to the eruption. On April 2 a giant earthquake, felt on all
the islands, generated a damaging tidal wave that hit Kau. So with the volcanic
beauty came the cost. The whole Kau district, where the earthquake had been
centered, was "a field of desolation and probably $500,000 would not restore it
to what it was a month ago. It is no wonder that the foreigners are leaving the
place, with the intention of never returning to it again. The number of deaths
will be between 80 and 100."[9] By coincidence, Kilauea had erupted in concert
with Mauna Loa, but its lava "had poured out harmlessly far back in the hills
on worthless barren lands. The villain of 1868 was Mauna Loa."[10]

7

"No Opening Offered" for Mark Twain

WHENEVER HE traveled in the United States, Henry Whitney sent back letters to the *Advertiser* for publication. In January 1869, he wrote that San Francisco is no doubt a great place for money: "Fortunes are made and lost more rapidly and easily than anywhere else in the world—but for quiet and safe business and real home comforts and happiness, there is nothing here that will compare with our own lovely islands."

That warm word picture of Hawaii could have been equally written—in fact, exuberantly expanded upon—by a stranger who earlier visited the *Advertiser* and identified himself as a correspondent of the *Sacramento Union*. He asked for a job, but as Whitney was to recall thirty years later:

> Having a good assistant—Nat Ingalls—who was a very clever writer, no opening offered for him. Still, an occasional joke played on an unsuspecting victim, and racy items of news, made the stranger's visits very welcome, and showed that he had a fund of humor ready for any occasion. He was not only an inveterate joker but also smoker, at least one box of cigars disappearing every week on an average. He made himself perfectly at home in my office, but would seldom leave without a parting joke. I became quite attached to the stranger, who proved to be Mark Twain—a nom de plume [for Samuel Langhorne Clemens] then hardly known beyond the border of California, as he was just beginning his literary career.[1]

In point of fact, Twain had been dropped by the *San Francisco Morning Call* for unacceptable work. His enjoyment of life, it seemed, turned considerably on his disinclination to let facts impede a sentence that fiction could enhance. William G. Brash, an early *Advertiser* printer, alludes to this in his clear recollection of Twain: "He virtually made the Advertiser his headquarters and Mr. Whitney liked to have him around, as did the printers. . . . Of course Mark Twain's first writings about life in Hawaii were full of exaggerations, but no one minded in the least. Everything he wrote was eagerly read and produced great merriment."[2]

Whitney also enjoyed Twain's humorous reporting but, ever the editor, felt he would be more reliable if he stuck to the facts.

The richness that marked Twain's vocabulary did not extend in his early days to his wallet. He was usually out of money, but partly offset this deficiency by being an adept borrower, "not [of] cigars only but books as well. . . . to supply the historical part of the information needed to enable him adequately to fulfill his mission to write up the Islands." This from the late territorial Governor Walter Francis Frear, who in his enjoyable book, *Mark Twain and Hawaii*, tells of the so-called "Jarves history episode."

James Jackson Jarves, who had founded the *Polynesian* as an independent newspaper in 1840, wrote an excellent history of the Islands. In borrowing—it would be more accurate to say purloining—the Jarves history before sailing back to California, Twain felt the book belonged to the Rev. Samuel C. Damon, editor of *The Friend*, and the day he boarded the ship, he wrote Damon that he was taking the Jarves book with him: "I 'cabbage' it by the strong arm, for fear you might refuse to part with it if I asked you. This is a case of military necessity . . . so just hold on a bit. I will send the book back within a month, or soon after I arrive."³

In *The Friend* of August 1, 1866—Twain was in the Islands for four months and a day from his arrival March 18, going home in July—Damon wrote that he wished all who borrowed books were "equally conscientious" and he called on those having his books "to return them instanter."

In a follow-up *Advertiser* article, after quoting *The Friend*'s story, Whitney wrote:

> If there is anything worthy of commendation it is the trait of conscientious honesty. 'An honest man,' says the proverb, 'is the noblest work of God.' But that isn't what we were going to say. It is simply this—that the book which Mark borrowed is ours, not the Friend editor's. At least we loaned Mark a copy and shall claim the volume when it arrives. We admire Twain's ready pen, and if the History referred to helps him in getting his letters about the islands all correct, we shall not begrudge the voyage it has taken, albeit the work is now so very scarce, that it is worth its weight in gold.⁴

A decade later, a story in the *San Francisco Morning Call* carried an implication by Whitney that Twain still had not returned the book. As far as Twain was concerned, his "crime" was against Damon, not Whitney. In a letter March 2, 1867, to the *Alta California*, he wrote "I have mailed to Father Damon, in the Sandwich Islands, the Hawaiian History I stole from him a year ago."

Frear wrote that just when the book reached Hawaii was uncertain, but, minus its cover, it was in Damon's library at his death. Whitney was either mistaken about the ownership or just out of luck. What is obvious is that Twain, by circulating the news of his misdeed, converted a liability into an asset in his writing and lecturing.

Twain read Whitney's comments on the Jarves book and—playing on his oft fantasy of cannibalism in the Sandwich Islands—lobbed this back after learning that a China-bound steamer was expected to stop in Honolulu in January:

> I expect to go out in her. . . . I am going chiefly to eat the editor of the Commercial Advertiser for saying I do not write the truth about the Hawaiian Islands, and for exposing my highway robbery in carrying off Father Damon's book—History of the Islands. I shall go there mighty hungry.
>
> Mr. Whitney is jealous of me because I speak the truth so naturally, and he can't do it without taking the lock-jaw. But he ought not be jealous; he ought not to try to ruin me because I am more virtuous than he is; I cannot help it—it is my nature to be reliable, just as it is his to be shaky on matters of fact—we cannot alter these natures—us leopards cannot change our spots. Therefore, why growl?—Why go and try to make trouble? If he cannot tell when I am writing seriously and when I am burlesquing—if he sits down solemnly and takes one of my palpable burlesques and reads it with a funeral aspect, and swallows it as petrified truth—how am I going to help it? I cannot give him the keen perception that nature denied him—now, can I?
>
> Whitney knows that. Whitney knows he has done me many a kindness, and that I do not forget it, and am still grateful—and he knows that if I could scour him up so that he could tell broad burlesque from a plain statement of fact, I would get up in the night and walk any distance to do it. You know that, Whitney. But I am coming down there mighty hungry—most uncommonly hungry, Whitney.[5]

Many years later, in 1895–1896, Twain embarked on a world lecture and reading tour and expected to make his first foreign stop in Honolulu, but delay in sailing precluded it, disappointing both him and those planning to attend his reading at Independence Park, at King and Sheridan Streets. The *Advertiser*, after voicing regrets, went on to say: "He told the truth about us, in the early days, and he made fun of our weak points. As a missionary of humor he has rendered good and great service. [His writings] have driven away care and anxiety from many moody minds, and have served a better purpose than drugs and faith cures. . . ."

When Twain died in 1910, the *Advertiser* hailed his thirty-eight years of literary activity:

> It has been irresistibly laughter provoking, but its sole end has never been to make people laugh. Its more important purpose has been to make them think and feel. And with the progress of the years, Mark Twain's thoughts have been finer, his feelings deeper and more responsive. Sympathy with the suffering, hatred of injustice and oppression and enthusiasm for all tends to make the world a more tolerable place for mankind to live in, have grown with his accumulating knowledge of life as it is. That is why Mark Twain has become a classic. . . .

Twain and Hawaii gained from each other. And although Whitney needled Twain for his exaggerations, it was always in a fashion that reflected underlying friendship. And Twain, who for a time stayed at Whitney's home, appeared closer to Whitney and the *Advertiser* than to any other individual and institution in Hawaii.

"Scheme to Crush the *Advertiser*"

HENRY WHITNEY dreamed of the time when he could enlarge the *Advertiser* to have "an agricultural department" and carry articles "to promote the introduction and cultivation of new staple products."[1] He staunchly favored all crops that he regarded as beneficial to the Islands—sugar, rice, coffee, cotton among them—but he had a special fondness for cotton and was responsible "for the initial efforts toward its cultivation."[2]

Whitney "wanted not only to stir up the Hawaiians living on their own land to help themselves and increase the prosperity of the islands, but he also wanted to reduce the cost of printing by the use of locally grown cotton for the production of printing and writing papers."[3] During the Civil War, when growing cotton in the South was disrupted and prices went sky-high, Whitney obtained and distributed Sea Island cotton seed and bought whatever cotton was produced and brought to the *Advertiser*'s office on Merchant Street.[4] At the paper, Whitney had fifteen men and women operating gins, powered by foot, which extracted the seed so he could ship the lint to Boston. It was of high quality and brought up to a dollar a pound.

Even after the Civil War the *Advertiser* continued its campaign. In 1868 it offered $1,000 in prizes to local growers. In four years Whitney paid growers between $25,000 and $30,000 in gold for the cotton, which New Orleans experts considered equal to that of Georgia's sea islands.

Since cotton-growing techniques were not fully understood in the Islands, Whitney and others were involved in research and tests. These were "still under way and were quite promising when the sugar era dawned in Hawaii, and cotton, potatoes, wheat and other experimental crops retired before the triumphant march of the gilded newcomer."[5]

While Whitney championed diversified agriculture, he never lacked in enthusiasm for sugar. In 1858 the *Advertiser* expressed its belief that "our sugar plantations for the past two years have been the most profitable branch of business in the Kingdom and that it will continue so for years to come."[6]

Sugar was highly labor-intensive and as production expanded at an explosive rate, the need for plantation workers grew and there were not nearly enough locally. To provide official approval of contracting for foreign labor, the government in 1850 adopted the Masters and Servants Act. Chinese workers were recruited, 195 from Amoy, augmented shortly by another 100, and then a steady flow. They came on five-year contracts, at $3 a month, plus transportation, food, housing, clothing, and medical care. They were mostly picked on the basis of availability—off the streets—rather than farming capabilities, and this ensured considerable friction.

On completion of their plantation contracts, jobless Chinese created a crime problem, and the *Advertiser* in 1859 foresaw major trouble from former "pirates and criminals, cut-throats and murderers," who were "unruly and desperate."[7]

The fear actually stemmed from the behavior of a recalcitrant minority. Most Chinese were law-abiding, and the reputation of those in business remained untarnished. Whitney hammered away at immigrants, but stressed that his remarks applied "only to the class of low Chinese known as coolies. We have among us numbers of Chinese merchants, men of probity, respectability and standing, fathers of Hawaiian-born families and the best of citizens."[8] There was even a millionaire businessman, Chun Afong, who came in 1849.

To face labor problems, the sugar growers in 1864 organized the Planters' Society, and an official Bureau of Immigration was established to supervise labor importation. Private enterprise was barred from bringing in workers without express sanction of the bureau. In urging the agency's creation, Kamehameha V saw the government as "the proper agent to carry out such a measure. . . ."

The bureau tried to mandate civilized treatment of plantation workers, but without much success. There were penal provisions for violations of civil contracts, to dissuade laborers from running away. There were jailings and there were floggings by insensitive supervisors. While this latter mistreatment was prohibited, it was in private and who was to bring charges? Contracts could be transferred from one plantation operator to another. The workers were indentured rather than free and were regarded by many of their masters as peons.

Early in the expansion of sugar, Whitney had argued that there were enough Hawaiians to work the plantations, if only comfortable housing were provided, but by mid-1867 he was acknowledging that with the native population rapidly decreasing, it was essential to import workers—but not from Asia. To him its people were "barbarous and pagan idolaters . . . who are incapable of Christian civilization and never will assimilate or amalgamate with either the Hawaiian or Caucasian races."[9] But the volume of Chinese immigrants steadily grew—by 1884 they would constitute 22.7 percent of the Islands' 80,578 residents—and Whitney hung on to the subject with a stream of editorials.

In time he coupled his dislike of coolies with militant opposition to the government's control of contract immigration. His argument with official labor policy began when contracts of workers at the late Foreign Minister Wyllie's plantation on Kauai were assigned to the buyers of the property at an executors' sale. To him this was illegal and would not stand up before "a disinterested bench of judges."[10]

Over time, he altered his stance on who should be admitted: "No reasonable man objects to the introduction of emigrants from China, Japan or elsewhere, if procured under a fair system of contract [in] a purely commercial transaction, entrusted to reasonable and faithful persons. . . . Government should be only a guardian or protector of the rights of servant and master—to see that each performs his engagements to the other."[11]

Whitney was pursuing an odd mixture of positions, one reflecting the racism prevalent then and for many decades thereafter among whites worldwide, the other a strong civil libertarian espousal of human rights.

The *Advertiser* took comfort from a U.S. Senate resolution of January 16, 1867, declaring: "The traffic in laborers transported from China and other Eastern countries, known as the Coolie Trade, is odious to the people of the United States, as inhuman and immoral."

"The Senate," said the paper, "likened it to the slave trade, but using fraud instead of force to make its victims captive."[12] It subsequently pointed out that the Chinese Immigration Society of San Francisco imported coolies, who refunded the advance for passage and were free to pick their own employer— and that the same system prevailed in New York.[13] By contrast, the Hawaii policy was to make the laborer "a servile tool, a chattel, liable to be transferred, assigned, sold at auction or imprisoned as a felon for no crime but the non-fulfillment of his contract."[14]

In the fall of 1869 the issue of the coolie system grew white-hot, first with the Planters' Society calling a meeting in the courthouse, followed some days later by the first of several citizens' assemblies at Kaumakapili Church.

The planters' meeting, and a follow-up session, adopted a series of resolutions embracing these points: A foreign labor supply is essential to Hawaii's agricultural prosperity; the Chinese in general have been "faithful, industrious and reliable" and while the Bureau of Immigration should seek Polynesians it should continue to bring in Chinese; laborers' contracts should continue to be made with the bureau, but with bureau approval individuals may recruit their own workers; assignment of contracts should continue to be permitted; and, if possible, a reasonable number of married women should come with the immigrants.

An *Advertiser* editorial declared that those at the planters' meeting consisted chiefly of government officials with a few sugar planters and their factors and accused the *Gazette* of seeking to make it appear that resolutions adopted there reflected public opinion.[15]

At the initial church session, heavily attended by Hawaiians but with some foreigners also present, there was overwhelming opposition to continued government-directed contracting for coolies.[16]

There were three more gatherings at the church, drawing audiences of up to five hundred. Whitney spoke at the final citizens' meeting and was on a five-member committee that produced resolutions which the assembly adopted. These stated that the law of supply and demand should govern immigration, without government interference; that further introduction of coolies was undesirable; that the penal statute for enforcement of contracts be repealed; that government funds be used to help attract Pacific islanders; that some protective measure be devised against high U.S. tariffs.

Whitney also read a letter from more than a score of Chinese merchants opposing the contract system for coolies: "We believe that a much better class of men for plantation and other kinds of work can be procured from China by some arrangement for the encouragement of free immigration."[17]

In at least one instance local Chinese went to the docks to warn arriving coolies not to sign contracts, and they didn't. Soldiers had to be called to quiet the situation.

Whitney continued his crusade, month after month. On September 3, 1870, he restated his stand on the labor question "which has agitated the community for the past two or three years":

(1) The coolie trade, "as now carried on," is "inhuman and revolting" and should be abandoned in favor of free immigration of "white or colored laborers from any foreign country."

(2) The government should act not as a principal "in immigration enterprises," but as a protector of immigrants, making all necessary regulations and impartially enforcing them."

(3) The Masters and Servants Act "being unconstitutional, ought to be amended; and the penal clause, in particular, should be abolished." Labor contracts, "mutually and knowingly entered into" are a necessity, "but all attempts to enforce them by penal enactments are despotic." The penal clause, "like the law of imprisonment for debt . . . can only be viewed as a relic of barbarism." He was not indicting the plantations as such, but stressed "the system in vogue tends to foster abuse and injustice."

By this time, many sugar planters felt Whitney had gone too far and must be stopped. For them, it was a crucial time. Replacements would have to be found for many coolies whose five-year contracts were ending. And even more laborers would be needed if the U.S. Senate approved a pending reciprocity treaty that would permit Hawaii sugar to enter duty-free and thus assure a marked expansion in sugar acreage.

In August 1870 plantation operators on Maui gathered to seek ways to squelch the *Advertiser* crusade. Whitney, in an editorial titled "Lawless Proceedings," reported on the meeting held "for the purpose of taking concerted action against the paper and its publisher. After discussing their grievances in an excited manner, resolutions were passed, expressing a determination to stop the circulation of the 'Advertiser' and 'Kuokoa' as far as in their power, and not to deal with any person or persons who patronize these papers. They even went so far as to threaten merchants in Honolulu that, if they continued to support the paper, they would withdraw from them their trade and patronage."[18]

Whitney had the names of those "concerned in the plot" but had no desire "to retaliate on men who have been our personal friends for nearly a quarter of a century." He charged that the Maui action "was done chiefly under promptings from parties in Honolulu," but did not elaborate.

Finally, he declared that the planters who were involved had laid themselves open to prosecution for violating a Hawaii law making it a criminal offense to conspire "to injure any man in his trade or occupation." The *Gazette* scoffed at this, contending Whitney in his paper had slandered the planters as "slave-holders and slave-drivers whose business he had sought to injure" and that if anyone should be indicted it was he.[19]

Hard on the heels of the Maui planters' attack came another ominous development for Whitney. Black & Auld, whose establishment the year before of a Merchant Street printshop the *Advertiser* had greeted with enthusiasm, announced they would begin publishing a new weekly newspaper, *The Commercial Herald.* Their prospectus in the September 7, 1870, *Gazette* said,

> The time has evidently arrived when a new exponent of public opinion in the islands is imperatively demanded. . . . We believe that the Master and Servant Act [*sic*] is, in the main, just, right and fit for the state of society which exists, or is likely to exist, in the Hawaiian Islands. The same remark applies to contracts for labor for a term of years, intelligently entered into and justly enforced. . . .

Three days later, Whitney, referring to the prospectus, declared:

> The Ministry and three or four capitalists not satisfied with having defeated [in the legislature] all attempts to repeal or amend the odious Master and Servant Act [*sic*], nor with supporting the bonded labor system in a subsidized Gazette, are now concentrating their thunders for a terrible onslaught upon the Commercial Advertiser, which has had the temerity to speak its mind on subjects of public interest.

By going squarely on the side of forced labor, Whitney wrote, the new paper "intends to advocate the entire system of double time, fines, imprisonment, transfer and sale of contracts and indefinite term of servitude, which now obtains under the present law." Public sentiment was being defied, he said, and the "prime movers in the scheme to crush the Commercial Advertiser out of existence" were all hiding themselves behind the thin screen of So & So, Publishers and Proprietors."

But it was to no avail. Whether by orchestration or happenstance, the announcement of a new weekly coinciding with the planters' pressure for an advertising boycott of the *Advertiser* produced a formidable squeeze play. On page one of the September 24 issue, in a signed statement "To the Patrons of This Paper," Whitney announced that it was his final edition as publisher and editor, he had sold the type, presses, and supplies to Black & Auld, which would publish the *Advertiser* while also operating a book and job printing business. He said that for the past two years he had wanted to sell the paper and its printshop, had advertised it for sale, but several negotiations were unproductive. The Black & Auld offer "was so liberal and accompanied with such guarantees, regarding its future course, that all objections on my part have been overcome, while the interests of its patrons appear to be well secured."

The Maui planters' resolution and the loss of a few subscribers had no influence on the sale, he said, except possibly to improve the amount offered him. Since starting the paper in 1856 his sympathies had been "warmly enlisted in behalf of the laboring classes both native and foreign," and he urged his "young and enterprising" successors to follow suit. He hoped in their hands it would continue to supply "the wants of the foreign community" in the Islands.

Although the sale of the *Advertiser* was announced on September 24, it was not finalized until at least two days later when Black & Auld signed a "memorandum of guaranty" in the presence of Sanford B. Dole. The new owners pledged to retain the paper's title and "to advocate liberal principles; to conduct the paper independent of the control of Government or any political party or clique; to open their columns for the free discussion of any Commercial or Political Question of interest to the community or nation so long as communications are couched in moderate and proper language."

On labor, Black & Auld believed "some laws regulating . . . the system are necessary, but while they will support the present laws until some amendment or substitute is proposed, they will encourage the discussion of any amendment likely to benefit all parties concerned."

Personal matters would be avoided, and in free discussion of questions appropriate to a general newspaper "a tune of calm reason" would be insisted upon. The owners "intend to sustain the present form of Government—the Constitution and Laws of the Kingdom, with loyalty to the King and justice to all classes."[20]

Attached to the guaranty was a memorandum in Whitney's handwriting: It was mutually understood that all printers would keep their jobs; that Black & Auld, if they wished, could pay off their notes before they became due.[21]

Two years later, on October 12, 1872, Whitney wrote to the *Advertiser*, responding to a letter to the editor which said that while he had stood by his beliefs he so harangued his readers on labor policy that he "shivered his lance" and had to sell. Not so, declared Whitney. He had over a two-year period negotiated "with parties residing abroad at from $10,000 to $12,000 but neither of these parties came to satisfactory terms. When, therefore, an offer of $15,000 was made it was the opportunity long desired and the bargain was closed at once." The labor issue played no part, he said, and the planters' campaign cost him only one "business card" ad and subscriptions "of ten or 12 planters" on Maui, whom he named.

In his recollections many years later Whitney wrote that he sold the *Advertiser* because he wanted to take his family to the United States for a visit—and they did go on May 1, 1871, for six months. A biographer of Sanford Dole repeats this explanation, then adds that Dole, Henry Carter, Edward P. Adams, and William L. Green "discussed the advisability of joining the venture, but apparently did not do so. Dole, asked to edit the paper, felt obliged to decline. . . ."[22] Green was then approached and accepted.

So it was that almost a decade and a half after he had started his feisty, crusading newspaper and done battle with the government, its *Polynesian* and *Gazette,* and the early sugar barons, Henry M. Whitney was out of the *Advertiser.*

But he still had the *Kuokoa*—which he had reacquired by January 29, 1870, after its transfer to L. H. Gulick on January 1, 1865—and in it he continued to campaign against the official labor policy. Except for a gap from 1878 to 1886, printer's ink would keep him active in Island journalism for the remainder of the kingdom and beyond.

9

"Press Has All the Freedom It Could Desire"

WITH HENRY Whitney offstage, James Auld, James H. Black, William L. Green briefly, and Henry L. Sheldon moved to the forefront of Island journalism. It would be a time of shifting philosophies and, in the case of one editor, humiliation and heartbreak.

In true Horatio Alger style, Auld, an *Advertiser* printing apprentice at its start in 1856, wound up as junior owner of the paper, with Black, only fourteen years later.

James' father, Andrew Auld, a Scot, had come to the Islands in 1816 as a teenager and found work as a carpenter. His third wife, Kamoku Kauole, apparently was James' mother. From printing apprentice, James worked his way to head pressman of the *Advertiser*, then in October 1869 he and Black opened a printshop and also operated a news, book, and stationery business. When they bought the newspaper they sold the shop to Thomas G. Thrum, who had been Auld's classmate and regarded him as an extremely bright student.

Black, the senior proprietor, had a colorful career. Born near Philadelphia in 1830, he went as a forty-niner to California, where he and three others struck gold and equally divided $74,000. During much of the 1850s he worked as a printer at the *Detroit Free Press*. When the Civil War erupted, he joined the 24th Michigan Volunteers and served as an orderly sergeant. He was wounded twice in the right leg, first in the bloody battle of Antietam, and limped thereafter. He later felt he had joined the wrong service: "I should have shipped in the navy and today I might have been a big man."[1]

Advised to go west for his health, he worked in Sacramento, then in San Francisco, where he claimed he made $80 a week. A doctor suggested he move to Hawaii, and he arrived on the *Eldridge* September 1, 1864. Years later he said that Charles Gordon Hopkins, who was briefly minister of the interior,

> wanted me to go into the printing business. I did so in the old Polynesian office where the postoffice [at the corner of Bethel and Merchant Streets] now stands and was called the Government Printer. Later I went into the shipping business and was master of a vessel between here and San Francisco. Then I

returned to the printing business again. . . . I worked for a time until I had trouble with C. C. Harris, minister of foreign affairs, when I resigned. I went to San Francisco and bought a printing outfit and came back here with it.[2]

He and Auld went into business and, in addition to commercial work, printed a short-lived monthly journal of commentary, the *Punch Bowl*.

After they acquired the *Advertiser*, they approached Whitney and asked if he wanted to take a one-third interest, since it seemed uncertain that Auld could meet his payments on notes held by Whitney, but he declined.

Auld may have been short on cash at the time, but in 1862 he had married Uwini Tyhune, a well-known Chinese merchant's daughter, who bore him five sons. The family accumulated valuable property, including the Tyhune store site on the corner of Nuuanu and Hotel Streets.

At the *Advertiser*, Auld began as publisher and Black as editor, although nothing in Black's past suggested any writing experience. Black took on William L. Green as co-editor on October 1, but he stayed only until mid-December. Why Green even accepted that post is a puzzler, since he was already a prominent business leader with more than enough to occupy him. An educated Londoner, capable and versatile, Green in 1844 had built and operated the first screw-steamer on the Atlantic coast of South America, mined for gold in California but lost all his money, and in 1850 worked his passage to Honolulu as a sailor, joining and then becoming a partner in Janion, Green & Company, which preceded Theo H. Davies & Company. He established the Honolulu Iron Works, was a founder and first president of the British (later Pacific) Club, held the presidency of the Honolulu Chamber of Commerce for fifteen years, served in the Privy Council and the legislature, headed the ministries of interior and foreign affairs, and finally was prime minister during the Kalakaua regime.

Green was also a respected student of geology, and his book, *Vestiges of the Molten Globe*, was published and hailed in London. At one point he was acting British commissioner and consul general, although as a businessman and sugar planter he personally favored Hawaii's efforts to negotiate a reciprocity treaty with the United States, which would strengthen economic and, undoubtedly, political links between Honolulu and Washington.

It became clear, however, that the United States at the time was "not much interested in either reciprocity or annexation,"[3] and given this reality Green expressed himself in a lengthy article in the *Advertiser* of November 19. He titled it "Reciprocity Treaties, Annexation and Federation" and declared that

> this hankering after something we have not been able to get has had a most injurious effect on this country. . . . It is time the idea of either reciprocity or annexation be dropped once for all. Let us depend upon our own resources, and upon the markets of the world, and make the most of opportunities which we have, and of which no one can deprive us.

It may be that Green's particular interest in being at least a short-term editor was his desire to counteract any damage done by Whitney's powerful campaign against the government's being in the contract labor importation business.

The new owners, on buying the *Advertiser* and scrapping plans to produce the *Commercial Herald*, declared they were standing by the prospectus for the *Herald*, which had endorsed the Masters and Servants Act as essentially "just, right and fit for the state of society which exists, or is likely to exist, in the Hawaiian Islands."

Some criticism of this, in which the "new" *Advertiser* was called a "pro-slavery paper" and part of the "coolie ring," put them on the defensive, and they said in an opening editorial that their language was intended to save them "from being committed to any of the objectionable details of the law, if objectionable they may be."[4]

An accompanying editorial, dealing with a controversy over a "coolie ship" that touched at Honolulu en route to South America, said "a senseless clamor has been got up connected with the Chinese labor questions, with what object is not so clear."[5]

In the same issue the *Advertiser* commented on Island journalism:

[T]he intelligence disseminated by the public journalist, both native and foreign, has been and is a marked type of our civilization and progress, albeit, that journalism may have descended at times into the province of too caustic censure and personal invective. . . . Under our constitutional Government, the press has all the freedom it could desire, and by the character it possesses, is one of the most powerful exhibits that we can present of our advancement as a people to foreign nations.

Black & Auld's second issue recommended government involvement in several endeavors. It hailed the government's running of the interisland steamer *Kilauea*, but felt its "first care and duty" was to make it pay its own way. It urged the government to order, on trial, a new steamroller for road-building; to import a number of good "well-bred saddle horses, draught horses, bulls, rams, jacks, etc.," from the nearest and cheapest market and to sell them at public auction, pocketing the profit or loss.[6]

The following week, in reporting on the funeral of the dowager Queen Kalama, consort of Kamehameha III, the *Advertiser* praised the late king's establishment of constitutional government, voiced sadness that "the people of pure native origin are also passing away," but foresaw a "mixed race" over which it desired "the Hawaiian Dynasty to be perpetuated." This may have been a way of distancing itself from proannexation elements in the community.

Bland or not, the paper was getting solid patronage from advertisers, and more ads than usual were being placed on page one. Those in business undoubtedly were pleased when the importance of the harbor was extolled editorially and the government was called upon to provide more wharf space;

to build a narrow-gauge railroad track 'round the wharves so cargo could be conveyed from coasters to foreign-bound vessels and for transshipment from one foreign vessel to another; to erect a large fireproof waterfront building for sugar storage; and to lower Customs House storage rates, especially on ship's stores and liquors.[7]

In November there appeared a long editorial on the problems and potentials of the sugar industry. It almost certainly was written by Green because it reflected an intimate knowledge of the history and operation of the plantations.

Some matters were less weighty. At a concert, many women's gloves were ruined by the printer's ink coming from the programs. One woman's light silk dress showed an impression of the program. The *Advertiser* noted that "several ladies and gentlemen transferred as much lamp-black from their hands to their countenances as would have made them available for negro minstrels. . . . These bills were not printed at this office—and we will further state that we never print programs with this description of ink."[8]

When Green left the editorship, he was succeeded by Henry L. Sheldon, who was a reporter on the *Advertiser* at the time Whitney sold it. A Rhode Islander with a good basic education, Sheldon had worked as a young East Coast printer before sailing on a trading ship from Salem to Fiji, then to California and on to Hawaii in 1846, when he was twenty-two. Subsequently, he returned for some months to California, divided his time between operating a San Francisco paper, the *Californian*, and digging for gold, then came back to the Islands, where he spent the rest of his life.

A talented writer as well as a skilled printer, he worked on probably more local papers than any other journalist in Hawaii's history—the *Honolulu Times*, which he founded in November 1849 and edited for most of its one-year existence; the *New Era and Weekly Argus*, the *Polynesian*, the *Daily Hawaiian Herald*, the *Hawaiian Gazette*, the *Advertiser*, and later the *Saturday Press* and the *Daily Bulletin*. He produced "more editorials and contributed more copiously to current topics making up our Island newspapers than any other writer."[9]

The late Riley Allen, highly respected editor of the *Star-Bulletin*, called Sheldon one of Hawaii's "most competent editors and skillful writers of the early days—one of the outstanding figures" of Island journalism.[10] Among his contributions was a series of "Reminiscences of Honolulu," covering the period from his arrival in March 1846 to January 1863. These were published in the *Saturday Press* beginning September 3, 1881.

In 1849 Sheldon married Hannah W. Munn of Honolulu, who was part-Hawaiian, and of their four sons, one who went into printing became well known. John Kahikina Sheldon was an *Advertiser* and *Gazette* printer and editor of several Hawaiian-language papers and served as Hawaiian interpreter in court and in the legislature. He was also an authority on native folklore. In 1891 he was fined $100 for typesetting libelous articles as a printer for *Ka Leo O Ka Lahui* in a suit brought by Lorrin A. Thurston.

Henry Sheldon served several terms in the legislature, representing the Big Island, but later in life twice failed to be elected. In a further detour from journalism, he was named in 1859 as judge of the Third Circuit in Kona, a post in which his fluency in Hawaiian was helpful. The next year he was commissioned as a government land agent in the Kona district and in that capacity was instructed to sell certain government lands for cash, collect lease rents on fishponds, and remit to the ministry of the interior. Surprisingly, in February and March 1864, Interior Minister Charles G. Hopkins requested Sheldon's Kona land accounts for examination. This was followed by his arrest on a charge of embezzling $735 in government funds.

It was the start of a tragic chapter in an otherwise constructive career. Some insights may be gleaned from a series of highly personal letters from Sheldon to the Rev. Samuel C. Damon.[11] On June 24, 1864—his fifty-fourth day of confinement after his arrest, but before his trial—Sheldon wrote: "I have been led by God's spirit to reflect upon my wilful [sic] and reckless course of sin during the past seven years—if I have truly repented . . . I count 'these bonds' a blessing."

His trial of July 6–8 brought a conviction and a fine of $1,200 or three years in prison. The Privy Council was petitioned to reduce the fine to the $735.36 embezzled, to be paid by friends. The plea was rejected by a sixteen-to-ten vote, and ever the journalist, Sheldon acknowledged that relaxing his sentence "might become a bad precedent." Why his friends did not pay the additional $464.64 is unclear, although Sheldon felt it was "almost too much to expect."

What is recorded is that on July 4 he began serving his Oahu Prison sentence, and from September 8 until January 6, 1865, he worked on the "gang," presumably at hard labor. He wrote that while he had been fearing this, he deserved it, but "it will be terrible" for his wife and children: "The family broken, soon to be houseless and homeless objects of charity—'tis very hard. But they are in God's hands."[12] In his desperation he sought financial help from Damon, $10 to pay a family medical bill and $8 for house rent.

Damon, visiting him in the prison, said Whitney had heard that letters posted on a bulletin board attacking the *Advertiser* were written by Sheldon from his cell and that Whitney was "personally aggrieved." Sheldon confessed to Damon that he had written them "carelessly and no doubt with more ascerbity [sic] than the matters demanded." He said he did it to earn money for his family, that his wife "received a certain sum for each of those letters."[13]

Sheldon heard in January 1865 that the government was starting a new paper, the *Hawaiian Gazette*, but he wrote to Damon that "the idea of employing a certain individual"—meaning himself—"in the editorial department does not apparently weigh sufficiently to induce an effort towards his freedom."[14] Did this prompt Damon to approach the minister of the interior, who would be responsible for the *Gazette*, the successor to the *Polynesian*, with James H. Black as foreman printer?

That's unknown, but whether prompted or not, Minister Hopkins, himself a former *Polynesian* editor, soon decided Sheldon would be useful. So Sheldon the prisoner became Sheldon the editor, both of the *Gazette* and of the official Hawaiian-language paper, the *Au Okoa*. He petitioned for restitution of his civil rights, but for that he had to wait six years.

In April 1866 the Privy Council credited Sheldon with most of his fine for services rendered but ruled he still had to pay $300. On August 26, with his debt virtually cleared, Sheldon resigned as editor because of conflict with Black. He complained to F. W. Hutchinson, the new minister of the interior, that Black's

> extreme vulgarity and profanity of language and unbounded self conceit have been sufficiently distasteful to me in the past. But latterly, since the Friday on which he got drunk and had or tried to have a fight with me in the office, he has adopted a systematic course of encroachment upon my province as editor. My selections from foreign files he inserts or not, according to his whim or fancy, but selects largely himself and very foolishly heads these clippings— 'Editorial Items'—thus subjecting the paper to the charge of literary theft.

Black opened his editorial mail and made it a point in the office—even before Sheldon's printer-son—"to speak in the most contemptuous manner of me." Further, Black, instead of submitting proofs to him, read them himself, even though it was "well known that he is not a good proof reader." Sheldon said he was not a fighter: "It is utter misery to me to live in a constant quarrel, and this man is quite destitute of reason and fairness."

And yet, four years later, here was Sheldon again associated with Black, this time at the *Advertiser*. Did this mean that Black was now yielding his title of editor to Sheldon? Did he assure him of a free hand? If not, how could Sheldon— except possibly for dire need of employment—stomach a man he despised?

The questions go unanswered, including why Sheldon's name did not appear on the masthead. At some point he—or perhaps the "responsible publishers" listed on the masthead—felt it desirable to explain why the *Advertiser* had "no ostensible declared editor."[15] Two reasons were given. If an expressed viewpoint was "unpalatable," the tendency would be to focus on the writer, if identified, and question his motives. Secondly, the paper was speaking not as an individual but as an organ of the "collective public." How convincing this was is anyone's guess, since on the editorial page an editor is really presenting management's viewpoint, which may or may not coincide with that of the "collective public."

During Sheldon's first holiday season at the *Advertiser* he began publishing semiweekly. But within a month, once advertising became normal again, it reverted to a weekly.

Under Sheldon's editorship the *Advertiser* moved from passivism to the old Whitney style of pounding away at official shortcomings. The paper was especially agitated by the way the government sought to meet the need for a hotel in Honolulu. In an early issue under Black & Auld it had advocated fill-ing in two or three acres of reef land, putting in grass and trees, then erecting "a nice, moderate-sized, two-story, suitable brick or stone" hotel and outhous-es, to be advertised not only in Honolulu but in San Francisco and Australia and leased out for five-year terms." If necessary a loan should be obtained to carry out the project.[16]

As steamship service to Hawaii from the United States, Australia, and New Zealand brought more travelers, the government decided to act, although not on the scale or with the financing the *Advertiser* had in mind. A corner site was bought at Hotel and Richards Streets, and the Hawaiian Hotel (later named the Royal Hawaiian Hotel) was erected in 1871 and leased for five years to Allen Herbert. Of the $116,528 cost, $42,500 was raised by sale of hotel bonds to individuals, with a return pledged from rent rather than interest.

Just after ground had been broken, the *Advertiser* called the planned hotel "a large blunder," with its four hundred rooms unlikely to be filled.[17] The pro-ject was "either the product of an impracticable visionary or a cunningly con-trived scheme for the personal aggrandizement of somebody, and the erection of a fine roomy government house."[18] A few weeks later the paper criticized the government for issuing the original bonds without legislative sanction and called the project "a good-sized elephant."[19] Money was being "squandered by ministers upon an insane project. Ministerial patronage is a powerful engine; alternate wheedling and threatening may go a long way with a Hawaiian legis-lature . . . but it will require . . . cunning forced by bald necessity . . . to induce the next Assembly to swallow the bitter pill of the new Hotel."[20]

The *Advertiser* correctly predicted the legislature's annoyance, although the government got the needed votes, but was far off the mark in condemning the hotel. As historian R. S. Kuykendall wrote, it "was an ornament to the city and filled a real need in the community, for which it became an important social center," winning "praise from travelers and from local residents who patronized it."[21]

The *Gazette* used the hotel question to jab at the *Advertiser*'s new owners—"young men not aspiring to any literary reputation, but to be skillful and laborious practical printers." The *Gazette* said the community had hoped for independent journalism and noted that Black & Auld had initially "employed as editor a gentleman of great literary taste and acquirements; of great experi-ence, undoubted discretion and gentlemanly associations; and the first numbers of the new issue seemed to justify our hopes . . . but soon the connection was dissolved between the editor and the proprietors," presumably because "they could not agree." Since then, continued the *Gazette*, the *Advertiser* reads as it did "under the old management resorting to opposition, pure and simple."[22]

But the fact is that officialdom invited it. In April 1871, for example, after public advertising the Interior Ministry sold at auction a tiny storage room for $13.50. Why, the *Advertiser* wondered, was there no such public competition for "supplying the leper establishment on Molokai, the army and the prison with necessary provisions and other supplies."[23]

The paper also was concerned about the spoils system, about government officials who were also engaged in private business and manipulated any bidding process to their own advantage. And it criticized the government for its willingness to let C. C. Harris, minister of foreign relations, pick ten boys at the reformatory school to work as indentured apprentices on his Kaneohe sugar plantation. Fortunately, this attempt to get inordinately cheap labor was thwarted by the Board of Public Instruction, which had a guardianship role.

The *Advertiser* stressed that if there was open bidding for contracts to supply public institutions "all suspicion of unfairness and favoritism would be disarmed and we should no more hear disreputable stories of the doings of 'rings,' which on a small scale savor of New York corruption."[24]

And there was the recurring theme of government waste. The *Gazette* had done the printing for the legislature during the 1872 session. The bill was $1,742. "The same work could have been done elsewhere in town for about half the money."[25]

As with Whitney, the government's carrying on a printing business competing with private shops nettled Black & Auld. When Matthew Raplee, director of the government press, died on February 15, 1873, the *Advertiser* coupled praise of him with a recommendation that the administration rid itself of needless, heavy printing expense, which it put at $117,864 over nine years.

It's just possible this citation of a public burden played a part in the government's decision only a month later to get out of the business. The *Gazette* of March 26, 1873, announced that as of April 1 that newspaper and the Hawaiian-language *Au Okoa*, together with presses, office, and material, were leased to—here he was again—Henry M. Whitney. Interior Minister Edwin O. Hall, in an official advertisement, said the government would be "in no wise responsible for any views expressed in such newspapers, except for what may appear under the head of 'By Authority.'"

Three days later the *Advertiser* seemed to substantially shift gears. It had "always opposed the policy of government" conducting a printing business "in competition with or opposition to private enterprise." But "we hold that Ministers will always require a recognized organ and at the present time more than ever."

Then it sought to preposition its new competition: "The Gazette, though nominally divorced from Government bed and board, will, under certain understood conditions, become a quasi-Government organ. We shall watch its course with curious interest, as an independent journal coming into existence under peculiar circumstances born of a mixed parentage."[26]

Whitney, already publishing the *Kuokoa*, quickly folded the *Au Okoa*, which had published since April 1865, and the *Advertiser* moved to fill the vacancy with a short-lived new native newspaper, *Ko Hawaii Ponoi*.

In July the *Advertiser* began its eighteenth year with a declaration that "its circulation, its popularity and its influence" had not diminished. And it proudly reported that for the first time in the Islands three power presses were at work at one time, a Hoe, an Adams, and a Gordon. The first had recently come from New York and was "the farthest west that a Hoe cylinder press had yet traveled."[27]

It then opened fire on Whitney's *Gazette*, pointing out that it was getting the government's printing and, together with the *Kuokoa*, all the legal ads. "Indirectly the Treasury of the country is supporting a government press. . . . We can but smile to see the champion of free competition today is the Director, in all but name, of the same government press, which he strove so earnestly to overthrow. Truly, time works wonders."[28]

Clearly irate, the *Advertiser* kept the darts flying. It stated that the *Gazette*,

> not being satisfied with being the reputed Organ of the Ministers, has the temerity . . . to speak for His Majesty personally. And it does this in a most presumptuously silly style and babbles about His Majesty's 'solemn and long considered resolve to effect a [reciprocity] treaty, if one can be made.' . . . Has the doctrine become obsolete that Ministers are alone responsible for the Government policy? How much longer will the Gazette be permitted to drag the Royal name into the pool of politics?[29]

The *Advertiser* kept trying to hang the government mantle on Whitney. But then it obtained two jobs outside of ministerial control—printing of a schoolbook and, for the legislature, publishing ads about proposed constitutional amendments.

So Whitney, tongue in cheek, congratulated the *Advertiser* on its "having been selected as the official organ of the Hawaiian government.[30] The *Advertiser* failed to find any humor in this and called the article libelous. A week later it explained its elevated blood pressure: "Once and for all—and we shall decline to allude to the subject again—no printing for Ministerial Departments is offered for competition; the Gazette gets the whole of it, by a foregone conclusion."[31]

The situation continued to rankle the *Advertiser* as it sniped away at the *Gazette*—whether for inaccurate reporting; or falsely accusing *Harper's Weekly* of lifting a photograph of Kalakaua from it when it was from a Hawaiian-language paper printed by the *Advertiser*; or for using obscene language in its native paper, the *Kuokoa*; or for a statement on Whitney's bookstore bulletin board that the *Gazette* had the largest circulation of any Island paper.

That was "a downright falsehood. Our books will show that the circulation of the Commercial Advertiser is by far the largest of any newspaper in the city (excepting The Friend)."[32]

The *Advertiser*, though largely shut out from government print jobs, was abundantly busy. It boasted that in seven days its printers, "all Hawaii-born boys," had set up and printed the *Nuhou*, the *Hawaii Ponoi*, *The Friend*, the *Advertiser*, and a nineteen-page "Second Interregnum," some sixteen thousand impressions of press work, "besides a goodly amount of casual job work. This will do very well for these Islands or for any other country for that matter."[33]

In January 1872 the *Advertiser* felt so confident about business that it announced the Saturday weekly would be augmented by a semiweekly appearing Tuesday and Thursday mornings—containing foreign, commercial, and shipping news, local items, editorials, and local and transient advertising. The semiweekly, which lasted for a year, would be for sale at the office, at the bookstores or from the carrier, W. J. Maxwell, at ten cents a copy. Meanwhile, any shortfall of foreign news in the Honolulu press could be offset by sub-scription to U.S., British, and Australian papers, available through Thomas G. Thrum, 19 Merchant Street.

When Sheldon became editor, the focus shifted almost entirely to local content. He seemingly lacked Whitney's enthusiasm for reporting the latest U.S. and other news from abroad. Some things, however, remained the same. The old complaint of plagiarism of Honolulu articles by the San Francisco newspapers was raised anew.

Advertiser and *Gazette* stories about the loss, by shipwreck, of the USS *Saginaw* at Midway were appropriated without credit, with the Californians' efforts confined to using scissors. The *Advertiser* said, "We admire cheek and impudence to a degree. . . . In the case of a newspaper it adds to its circula-tion and influence . . . but these things may be carried too far."[34] The *Gazette* a few days later reprinted the *Advertiser*'s gripe with full approval. But such agreement was rare. The norm was for each paper to look for any opportunity to disparage the other, as if revealing the competition's alleged sins was proof of one's own virtue.

The newspapers feuded against a larger backdrop of considerable politi-cal stress—and some violence. When Kamehameha V, the former Prince Lot, died December 11, 1872, on his forty-second birthday, the *Advertiser* wrote that he "was distinguished for keen judgment, firmness of purpose and stabili-ty of character."[35] That was at odds with former owner Whitney's earlier denunciation of the monarch's autocratically imposed Constitution of 1864, which greatly strengthened royal powers at the expense of the electorate and to the distress of the foreign community.

The king, a bachelor, was succeeded by his cousin, William Charles Lunalilo, thirty-seven, a confirmed alcoholic, as well as tubercular, but he was also intelligent and a charmer, witty, and clever. His reign, however, was brief and turbulent, marked by the disbanding of the army following a mutiny and conflict over whether Pearl Harbor should be leased to the United States for fifty years in return for a treaty admitting Hawaiian sugar duty free.

The reciprocity plan was developed by Whitney, who presented it to King Lunalilo on January 27, 1873, but it did not become public until February 8, first in the *Advertiser*—which did not mention Whitney, but said the time was opportune to offer a harbor and coaling station in the Pearl River to the United States—and then in the *Gazette* on February 26. The king, while cool to cession, consented to having a treaty negotiated, with him then deciding whether to sign or not. Meanwhile the *Advertiser* and the *Gazette* both favored reciprocity and Whitney's plan, but not annexation. On June 14 the *Advertiser* revealed the government's decision to submit the Pearl Harbor ploy to Washington.

This triggered a passionate outburst of organized opposition by Hawaiians and Britishers, and by November the king withdrew the Pearl River offer before the United States could respond.

There was a further emotional complaint from the native Hawaiians over government policy toward those afflicted with the ancient scourge of leprosy. Early in the decade the *Advertiser* criticized "half measures" that were permitting some lepers to remain in Honolulu and even allowed one from the Molokai colony to come back to town to take care of personal business.

> If the law for the isolation and removal of the lepers is not at once and fully
> carried out, the whole people are doomed to become a nation of lepers in a
> very short time. . . . It is a grave and sad thing to sunder families and doom
> men to perpetual banishment from home and friends, but the greatest good
> of the greatest number compels us to it.[36]

Soon after that appeared, the paper said "a few good men—Christian men—have mildly questioned the 'policy' of this journal in keeping before its reader so persistently the subject of Leprosy in these islands." Critics said this hurt Hawaii's image abroad and recommended that the *Advertiser* follow the "masterly inactivity" of the government newspaper, "which scarcely ever refers to the dismal topic." But, said Editor Sheldon, the sense of duty as public journalists would not allow the *Advertiser* to "conceal the truth or to fail in giving an alarm when danger threatens the public weal." Hence, its insistence on vigorous measures "to protect and preserve the remnants of the Hawaiian race from the ravages of this scourge."[37]

Ignorance, fear, and bureaucracy were all part of the picture. And scandalous conditions at the settlement reflected an out-of-sight-out-of-mind mentality, evidenced in a letter the *Advertiser* quoted from the *Kuokoa*, signed "From the Lepers."[38] The conditions described were pitiable. There was not enough to eat. Utensils were in short supply. The sufferers needed warm wear. They wanted basic mail service, "a postmaster appointed for this place, and a separate mail bag to be forwarded to and from Honolulu." The reason for this is that letters sent "never reach their destination. What becomes of them? We are of the opinion that they are willfully thrown away." And, finally, they wanted decent burials. The dedicated work of Father Damien Joseph de Veuster in his sixteen years on Molokai, before he himself died in 1889 of the disease, helped bring improved conditions. But the government policy of isolation remained deeply resented by the Hawaiians and this "added to the turbulence of the times."

On February 3, 1874, Lunalilo's poor health and compulsive drinking led to his death. Both David Kalakaua and dowager Queen Emma, the widow of Kamehameha V, sought the throne. The *Advertiser* editorially declared Kalakaua's claims to the throne "are in every respect paramount to those of any other personage that can be named. Any attempt to thwart the well-known will of the people is to be profoundly deprecated, for the sake of the peace and future prosperity of the country."[39]

Kalakaua won the election, and one of his first acts was to name William L. Green, the former short-term editor of the *Advertiser*, as his foreign minister. Then, riding the momentum of his victory, he with his queen, Kapiolani, toured the Islands, pledging to restore Hawaiian pride and power. At each stop he was joyously welcomed, and the *Advertiser* noted that in short order he had restored the people's confidence.

A personal visit to Washington led to a treaty providing two-way duty-free admission of agricultural and other products.

Sugar and rice boomed, plantations expanded, and the cry for more foreign labor sounded anew. At the *Advertiser*, business also seemed to be going well, but, for reasons unexplained, Auld broke with his co-owner in early June 1875, and from June 12 only Black's name appeared on the masthead. In 1880 Auld became foreman of the *Advertiser*'s job printing and in 1883 was foreman at the *Hawaiian Gazette*. He died while abroad in 1903.

On Saturday, July 14, 1875, the one thousandth issue of the *Advertiser* was marked by a dinner hosted by Publisher Black for some twenty-five members of the press, including the founder, Whitney. The *Advertiser* made no mention of the function, but in his July 28 *Gazette* Whitney carried a laudatory story that included the names of some of those present when his first issue went to press nineteen years before. He concluded by expressing "the same aloha we have always had for the Advertiser" and warm wishes for "its continued success."

While appreciating his kind words, the *Advertiser* didn't let them dull its competitive spirit. Exactly a month later, while Editor Sheldon was on his first vacation in four years, the *Advertiser* shared this appraisal of Whitney's *Gazette* with its readers: "Erratic, sensational, superficial, dogmatic; when beaten in argument or . . . finding itself on the losing side of a public question, it straightway loses its own temper" and descends to "coarse and slanderous attacks. Its editor is seemingly unaware that these invariably fail in their effect—excepting in animals too low for gentlemen's game. . . ."[40]

Did this incur Whitney's unrelenting enmity? Not at all. Three years later, listed as "an occasional contributor whose favors are always acceptable," he was writing articles for the *Advertiser* from his farm at Keaiwa, Kau, on the Big Island. They were in the form of letters, each addressed to "My Dear Sheldon."

On January 1, 1876, Black announced the sale of the *Advertiser* to Sheldon. The reasons, undetailed, were "purely of a private and personal nature." Black said with "pride and satisfaction" that in the almost five years since he and his former partner, Auld, acquired the paper "its career as a business concern has been a success, its circulation and patronage have largely increased, and its influence, it is believed, has been beneficial to the best interests of the country at large."[41]

In the next issue, Sheldon's first editorial as proprietor, publisher, and editor expressed his philosophy: "The newspaper should be a conservator of public morals, an upholder of law and justice, and an educator of public opinion in all that is for the real welfare and progress of a community. . . ." He pledged support for the planters and graziers, for the merchants and traders. "We belong to no party but the party of Hawaiian independence and progress." He foresaw "a noble future for Hawaii Nei," with the press having a special mission to "accelerate the coming of the era of national prosperity." Finally, he promised "free and outspoken" discussion, criticizing "when occasion may require, without fear or favor; but always with due courtesy to persons, if severe upon measures."

A few months later, Sheldon outbid Whitney's *Gazette* for a government contract to print one thousand copies of a thirty-five-page book. The bid: $74. Later that year Sheldon won another government printing job against the *Gazette* for five hundred copies of the legislative session laws of 1876 in both Hawaiian and English at $2.50 a page.

The *Advertiser* from time to time sent "messages" to its advertisers and readers regarding their relationship with the paper. It reprinted a piece from the *Cincinnati Gazette* saying editors are busy people, that three-fourths of those who call to see the editor "have no business properly with [that] individual" and if there's something to convey, put it in a letter.[42]

Sheldon complained of people who, in his absence, made themselves at home in his office, left things in disorder, and even mutilated his file by clipping articles. Henceforth, "these treasures will be guarded by a particularly savage dog."[43] And he printed a diatribe against "puffing"—people requesting "puffs," which are really advertisements which should be bought and paid for "in a special column appropriately labeled."[44] Sheldon also sought to dispel another misimpression, that ads are sometimes left in the paper to fill space. "We can't afford the room," but any ad placed without an expiration date does continue "until ordered out and will be charged accordingly."[45]

Finally, correspondents were put on notice that letters written on both sides of the paper could not receive attention. Such communications had to be rewritten, and the staff already had "other employment."[46]

Meanwhile, over at the *Gazette*, after three years at the helm, Whitney had had enough, and the government offered to further lease or sell the paper. Surprisingly, Sheldon entered the picture. He wrote Dr. John Mott-Smith, minister of the interior, that he had heard Whitney was terminating his *Gazette* lease and he would like to acquire it. But his bid failed, and at year-end, after three months of interim editing of the *Gazette* by Dr. C. T. Rodgers, T. Crawford MacDowell, a lawyer and former editor from Harrisburg, Pennsylvania, formally took over. The new lease ran from January 1, 1878, to December 31, 1879.

Was Sheldon unhappy at the *Advertiser*? If he had obtained the *Gazette* lease, what would he have done with the paper he already owned? Did he entertain a dream of buying the *Gazette*—possibly through a front—at the end of his lease and then merging the two papers, which, certainly for a time, would have given him a monopoly?

Perhaps it was to assure two voices, and to hope for at least one friendly one, that led the government to turn down Sheldon's offer. Obviously, the king and ministers were sensitive to the *Advertiser*'s constant criticism. Even so, they must have been pleased by the paper's editorials in 1877 and 1878 on the wider role perceived for Hawaii in the Pacific. Sheldon linked this to his concern over the growing loss of independence by Pacific islands. The British control over New Zealand's Maoris, the French involvement in Tahiti and the Marquesas, the apparent American and German threat to Samoa—these all seemed a sign of more to come. The *Advertiser* urged a Pacific confederation and a common Polynesian flag, which would tend to discourage outside interference without diminution of independence. In brief, "Polynesia for the Polynesians."[47]

A subsequent editorial recalled the late Foreign Minister Wyllie's hope of

an Empire of the Pacific, with a Kamehameha at the head and Honolulu the capital—a confederation of Chiefs which should be recognized by the great Powers. In the event of such an empire, the religion, civilization and laws of Hawaii would necessarily be extended south and west throughout the ocean. Events passing at the present time seem to indicate that Mr. Wyllie's dream may yet be not all a dream.[48]

This was tied to the paper's urging that more Polynesians be attracted to Hawaii, with as many women as possible accompanying men, not only to work on the sugar plantations, but to amalgamate with the Hawaiians and stem the tragic population decline.

Clearly a staunch supporter of the Hawaiians in general, Sheldon still felt that more haoles should be playing an active role in government. He sought to persuade foreigners to forgo their usual apathy and vote "to secure the return of a sufficient number of able, intelligent and independent men of their own class as shall operate as a check upon the crude legislation and erratic pro-clivities of many of the native members, as witnessed in the two last preceding assemblies."[49]

In 1874 there was one foreign-born representative in the House; in 1876, three, whereas, Sheldon said, they used to average never fewer than twelve.

"A fair proportion . . . in view of the material interests involved would be ten." He described the Hawaiian members, with some honorable exceptions, as "blatant demagogues, pliant office-seekers, ignorant impracticables, or simply hungry seekers after the loaves and fishes of the position. . . ." He stressed he was not condemning the whole race as unfit to be legislators, but unlike twenty years before, the best did not put themselves forward.[50]

His entreaties failed. A later editorial said that with an election coming in February 1880, foreign-born voters were still unresponsive, with the result that Honolulu, capital and seat of wealth, was "the worst represented [legislative] district in the country." The representatives were "anything but creditable to the intelligence or civilization of the country." With Honolulu sending four members to the House, "we can and should elect two foreigners—unless we choose to continue in our present anomalous condition of taxation without representation." The paper felt that some two hundred registered voters of foreign birth in the district could easily elect two of the four members. Sheldon, who had announced for the legislature, hoped to be one of those two elected from Honolulu, but kingdom-wide only three haoles made it. Those who failed to vote were quickly scorned as "laggards and traitors."[51]

Somewhat earlier, after two years and eight months as owner of the *Advertiser*, Sheldon had resold it to Black, but remained as editor—with no apparent change in policy. There was no public explanation of Sheldon's action, but a possible clue may be found in a letter he wrote to the Rev. Samuel Damon. Referring to "peculiar circumstances of trial and difficulty" not of his making, he said he sinfully "sought the wrong source for strength & consolation" and had suffered mentally as well as physically.

His membership in Bethel Church was in jeopardy at the time, and it may be that his problem, brought on by economic pressures at the paper, was drinking. If so, he was not the first, nor would he be the last, editor to discover that running a news and editorial operation and running the business side, including advertising, circulation, and production, require quite different skills. Some journalists combine both, but they are a decided minority. Sheldon, although relieved of the publisher's responsibilities, still had plenty to occupy him.

There was some positive news: The first artesian well in the Ewa section of Oahu was dug by James Campbell for "irrigating the several hundreds of acres" in the neighborhood,[52] and the telephone had come to the Islands, first to Maui, then to Honolulu. "The sanctum sanctorum of the editorial room may converse freely with the publication office without the labor of going down and upstairs. Very shortly we expect to see numbers of these useful instruments employed by businessmen in our city."[53]

With the acknowledged good came the controversial issues—and, of these, few were more recurrent or contentious than the importation and sale of opium. As the *Advertiser* noted, from 1860 to 1874, vending of the drug was authorized by the government, with two license-holders paying up to $26,000 each, against an upset price of only $2,000. But after 1874 opium could only be imported by the Board of Health for medicinal purposes, with a heavy penalty for illegal possession.

In mid-July 1878 the legislature passed a bill again legalizing public sale. The king vetoed it, but not before a sharp division was evident in community thinking. The *Advertiser* noted that "intelligent Chinese merchants" were against licensing, feeling that under the ban opium use had declined.[54]

A year later the *Advertiser* declared that frequent seizures of smuggled opium proved that barring importation had failed. The increased arrival of Chinese had brought a larger demand for the drug. Some supplies, said the paper, had come in disguised as bean sauce, and there was the San Francisco case of opium ingeniously shipped in the hollowed-out heels of twenty dozen pairs of brogans. Licensing the sale, said the *Advertiser*, would stop the smuggling; the quantity sold to an individual should be regulated and a record of sales required for police inspection at any time.[55]

During the debate, the *Advertiser* printed, undoubtedly with great relish, that *Gazette* Editor MacDowell had been arrested on a charge of smuggling opium. He had returned from a visit to San Francisco, bringing back material invoiced for printing. In two of the packages, beneath a small compartment of legitimate oil, a customs guard found 149 tins of opium.

At a preliminary hearing, following his release on $1,000 bail, MacDowell pleaded ignorance of the contraband, saying he had acted on behalf of a good friend, Henry Bradley, who through his attorney took full responsibility.

MacDowell was cleared, but his problems were not over. A bit later he was called before the Supreme Court to explain why he had written an editorial charging the court with being vindictive in imposing hard-labor sentences for opium smuggling. He apologized, saying he meant no disrespect, and was let off with a reprimand and a bill for court costs.

In the same issue reporting the outcome, the *Advertiser* editorialized that liberty of the press was an important principle, but its abuse becomes license, "and the very worst of tyranny is the result, dangerous to the rights of life and liberty themselves."[56] The editorial did not explain how criticism of a court constituted tyranny; nor did it comment on the attempted intimidation implicit in a court's hauling an editor before it for expressing an opinion.

In any event, MacDowell later that year, 1879, returned to Pennsylvania, accompanied by a farewell punch from the *Advertiser*. It seems that MacDowell had endorsed the arrival of 560 Chinese as "good news," which led his competition to observe that "the result of flooding these Islands with a race of pagan cockroaches" did not bother MacDowell, because he was leaving Hawaii.[57]

And when the government announced that the *Gazette* would be sold to the highest bidder in front of Aliiolani House, to take effect January 1, 1880, the *Advertiser* possibly hoped to scare off a purchaser. It is said the newspaper business was the poorest paid and anyone's best luck would be to not have the *Gazette* "knocked down to them today."[58] If that was a ploy, it failed, and Black's brother-in-law, Robert Grieve, for some years previous the paper's foreman, bought it for $1,875 cash.

Then, perhaps to mollify Grieve, the *Advertiser* said that the first *Gazette* editorial since MacDowell's departure, probably written by "one of the new combination" who would be operating the paper, was "a decided improvement on the slipshod style which has characterized that journal during several past years. We recognize the change . . . as a relief from the usual weekly dose of crudities and absurdities."[59]

While frequently insightful as to both men and measures, the *Advertiser* was not immune to grievous miscalculation. The case of one Celso Caesar Moreno is instructive. A soldier of fortune, a naturalized Italo-American, he landed in Honolulu in 1879 on a steamer from China with several schemes in mind. The *Advertiser* on November 14 described him as an "energetic and persevering promoter of a trans-Pacific telegraph cable. . . . He is a polished gentleman, a thorough man of the world."

Moreno had several goals in mind: a possible cable deal, a Hawaiian government subsidy for a Chinese steamer service to and from the Islands in connection with laborer importation, and a chance for him to benefit from his suggested opium-licensing measure to make Honolulu the processing and distribution center for the entire Pacific area.

Kalakaua endorsed the steamship subsidy in a message to the legislature. At first, the lawmakers rejected the plan but did a snappy about-face after Moreno greased enough palms. The *Advertiser*, reversing its earlier assessment of Moreno, charged "open and wholesale bribery" by an "impecunious adventurer." But Kalakaua had his back up. By royal prerogative he terminated the legislative session, demanded his cabinet resign, and among his replacements was Celso Moreno, as minister of foreign affairs, after instant naturalization as a citizen of the kingdom.

The uproar among foreign diplomats and the business and professional community led Kalakaua to grudgingly obtain Moreno's resignation, but before the charlatan's departure from the Islands a few weeks later, the king gave him a secret commission as minister plenipotentiary, empowered to negotiate neutrality treaties with foreign powers. Moreno took with him three young Hawaiians for education in Italy; one was Robert W. Wilcox, who would later leave his own mark on Hawaiian history.

The *Advertiser*, with the public, was "heartily glad" to bid Moreno "an everlasting farewell."[60] And its distaste for him was equally intended for Kalakaua and his ministers, reflecting how the paper had moved within a decade from a conciliatory stance toward the government to one of disapproval and, at times, hostility. Was any of that attributable to Black or was it almost entirely Sheldon's doing?

Whatever the answer, it would appear that by the spring of 1880, Sheldon was no longer in charge editorially. For it was then that Black approached Sanford Dole, who had been writing for the *Gazette*, about taking the editorship of the *Advertiser*. Dole wrote that he would accept the post at a salary of $25 a week,

> it being understood that I shall be allowed full freedom of expression in the management of the paper, and shall be consulted in regard to all literary material which may be provided from other sources and that I shall not be responsible for commercial articles or shipping data. If I assume this work I shall be available for work and consultation before 9 a.m., from 12 to 1 p.m. and after 4 p.m. and shall expect to do the greatest part of my work in preparation at home evenings.[61]

Black agreed, but Dole edited only two *Advertiser* issues, May 22 and May 29. On the latter date he wrote Black that

> you do not pretend even to carry out your part of the terms of the agreement nor have I any reason to suppose that you intend to do so in the future; my own articles are revised and sometimes suppressed without consultation with me, to make room for adverse articles upon similar subjects from other pens; literary material from other sources is published without my advice and editorial articles written by others are inserted without my knowledge or advice. I have therefore to say that it is useless for me to go on in this way, and to notify you that our agreement is at an end from this date.

He asked for and received a $50 check on Bishop & Company, with a note in which Black wrote: "I regret you should come to such a hasty conclusion and hope what has occurred will not break your friendship towards the Advertiser."[62]

Dole wrote his brother George on Kauai that as near as he could judge Walter Murray Gibson was the real editor and that he was now "fancy free and attached to no paper," but would soon resume writing for the *Gazette*. Alfred S. Hartwell "is getting tired of the Gazette and is very anxious to transfer it to me or some one else, but I don't bite worth a cent."[63]

Later that year, however, Dole agreed to edit the *Gazette* starting the following January (1881), but not handle the news department, which W. R. Castle was to head. As it turned out, Alatau T. Atkinson became editor at the start of 1881 and held that post until 1887.

This strange business with Dole and the machinations of Moreno were but a modest prelude to the bizarre period immediately following in *Advertiser*— and Hawaiian—history.

Part II

1880–1898

10

"To Be Invariably Loyal to His Majesty"

THE 1880s were a time of growth in Honolulu: horse-drawn streetcars in service on King Street; a rapidly expanding telephone system; the start of construction of the Oahu Railway and Land Company; better steamship service, both interisland and trans-Pacific, coupled with harbor improvements; the first commercial canning of pineapple; and recognition of the potential of tourism.

It was also a time of great political turbulence, much of which emanated from a multifaceted dreamer and schemer, Walter Murray Gibson. On August 30, 1880, he bought the *Advertiser* from James H. Black, who claimed an average profit of $3,000 a year in his ten-year ownership.

The paper's editorial policy was quickly intertwined with the aims and actions not only of Gibson, but of King Kalakaua and sugar king Claus Spreckels. They made a fascinating and fearsome triumvirate, powered by a wide range of motives in an environment of greed and glitter.

Gibson was charismatic and single-purposed, with larger-than-life visions of unchallengeable power. Tall and erect, white-haired, bearded, with piercing blue eyes, he outwardly brought to mind an Old Testament prophet, walking the land, spreading a fervent message. But one who met him described him as "wise as a serpent, but hardly as harmless as a dove."[1] He was brilliant in his maneuvering, an articulate Hawaiian-speaking seller of ideas, with a highly flexible conscience. However much he attained, he hungered for more; his appetite for status and acclaim was insatiable.

When in 1878 Spreckels asked the government for certain water rights for $500 a year to irrigate Maui land, Gibson, then in the legislature, ran interference for him. When Spreckels bought a questionable claim to crown lands and then sought to swap that for twenty-four thousand Maui acres in fee simple, Gibson successfully led the fight in his behalf. When Spreckels made between $100,000 and $200,000 as the agent on the $1 million in Hawaiian coins bearing Kalakaua's profile, Gibson was working hand-in-glove with him.

Gibson was a son of poor English parents, whose lineage he fancifully embroidered. After living in Canada and on the U.S. East Coast, he became a gun-runner to Latin America and a revolutionary in Indonesia, where the

Dutch slammed him into prison, then let him escape. On June 30, 1861, he and his daughter, Talula, arrived in Honolulu from San Francisco.

Gibson reportedly sent a fellow passenger to the *Advertiser* with clippings about him and word that he was available for lectures. In its next issue the *Advertiser* called Gibson a "well-known traveler" who it hoped would lecture on the "social conditions and commercial importance of the Malaysian group," a subject he had addressed in California.[2]

It soon came out that Gibson, a convert, was establishing a Mormon settlement on Lanai. His religious persuasion, combined with his pro-South leanings in the Civil War, just under way, put him under suspicion among Hawaii's Yankees.

By November 1861 the Lanai Mormon community, financed by native contributions, was under way. The following March the *Advertiser* printed a report of a system "worse than slavery," with "eight or ten kanakas . . . harnessed to a plower and driven like mules."[3] Gibson denied the forced labor and said it was a voluntary effort before they had horses. Some months later, the *Polynesian* praised Gibson for his "philanthropy and social reform,"[4] and the *Advertiser* quickly responded: "When an effort is made through the court journal to foist [Gibson] upon the world as preeminently a philanthropist, a model citizen, a saint, and the first practical exponent of the editor's favorite theory of Roman 'communes' we think it due the public that the sham should be unmasked."[5]

Gibson came into control of about thirty thousand acres on Lanai, the title to which wound up in his name. Complaints to the mother church in Salt Lake City brought investigators and, in the spring of 1864, Gibson's excommu-

Walter Murray Gibson controlled the *Advertiser* **from 1880 to 1887 for the benefit of King Kalakaua, sugar magnate Claus Spreckels, and himself.**

nication by Brigham Young. But he retained the land and operated a planta-tion and ranch with his two newly arrived sons as overseers.

In September and October 1872, the *Advertiser* (after Whitney had sold it) printed a series of five articles by Gibson on immigration. From Asia he favored bringing in a moderate number of Japanese laborers, but for repopu-lating the country he advocated looking to the "brown races" of Malaysia, with its population of thirty million.[6]

In 1873 he moved to Honolulu and on February 23 began publishing his own newspaper, the Hawaiian-and-English-language *Nuhou*, with the racially volatile theme of "Hawaii for the Hawaiians." In thus establishing himself as the haole champion of the natives, Gibson clearly was laying the groundwork for his own advancement. As early as its April 9, 1873, issue the *Gazette*, of which Whitney had become editor, said the *Nuhou* "blows its own horn and is evidently aiming to elevate the Shepherd [of Lanai] into public notice if not public office."

When the *Nuhou* ceased publication in April 1874, Gibson began writing controversial columns for the post-Whitney *Advertiser*.

In 1878 Gibson ran for the legislature from Lahaina, campaigning in his fluent Hawaiian, and was easily elected. That was the beginning of his nine stormy years in Island politics. He was disliked and distrusted by the planters and merchants, and his status and influence depended entirely on Hawaiian grass roots and kingly support.

Acquiring the *Advertiser* would give him a potent platform for achieving recognition and, in the process, move him closer to the dominant role he craved in Island affairs. So it was that on August 28, 1880, Gibson entered into an agreement with Interior Minister John E. Bush. The government advanced him $5,000 toward buying the *Advertiser* for $15,000—this $5,000 to be repaid by doing official printing and binding to that amount. Gibson was "to conduct, manage and edit" the newspaper and "to support the Hawaiian Government and its policy, and pursue a line of discussion . . . best calculated to carry out the measures of His Hawaiian Majesty's Government," and "to be invariably loyal to His Majesty."

The paper's rates were to be "fair and reasonable"; in return he was assured of the public printing and binding of all the cabinet-controlled depart-ments for at least two years. If Gibson failed to comply with the agreement, he was to refund the money advanced minus that canceled by completed printing and binding. The government funds were forthcoming on August 30 and on that date Gibson purchased the paper.

Gibson named Auld as printing foreman; his son-in-law, Fred Hayselden, as company agent, later titled manager, to handle communications and account payments; and Frank Godfrey as assistant editor "to attend to adver-tisements and business of a local nature."[7]

In later life Godfrey suffered an ignominious ordeal when he circulated false reports about his hospital experiences during a cholera epidemic, and a group of masked vigilantes treated him to a coat of tar and feathers. He unsuccessfully sued the kingdom for $50,000.

Within days of Gibson's first issue of the *Advertiser* on September 4, 1880—using a steam-powered engine to run the presses for the first time in Island journalism—he had started two other papers, the *Wednesday Express* and the companion *Elele Poakolu*, which was bilingual but soon dropped its use of English.

So Gibson was covering both English- and Hawaiian-language readers. To counter his policies, a group of merchants established yet another paper, the weekly *Saturday Press*, but it lasted only until mid-1886. Dole, among others, hoped it would starve out Gibson, but it didn't, despite the fact that the town's leading firms—such as Dillingham, Hackfeld, McInerny, and Brewer—had pulled their advertising from the *Advertiser*.

In his initial issue Gibson pledged to advance the quality of journalism in the kingdom; to promote "the welfare of the Hawaiian people of all races"; to seek "to avoid all strife and personalities"; and to defend against "any disloyalty to the Hawaiian throne."[8] But four days later the *Gazette* opined that Gibson, "if we mistake not . . . will now do strifes and personalities enough for the whole town."[9]

So Gibson was off and running with his new papers. But a few storm clouds were forming. When Interior Minister Bush left his post on September 27, his successor, H. A. P. Carter, took a dim view of the government's agreement with Gibson. He wrote Gibson on October 5 that Edward Preston, who had been attorney general until about two weeks before the Bush-Gibson deal, advised him that the contract was illegal.

In the next day's *Wednesday Express* Gibson said that because of the $5,000 advance for public printing he had agreed to conduct the *Advertiser* as a semiofficial organ. He added that Bush and his fellow ministers "felt greatly the need of an organ—not so much to defend their views as to present them fairly."

By the following May, Carter actively sought to recover the $3,000 that had not yet been spent on official printing. He also had his chief clerk withdraw five government ads from the paper. Gibson promised to repay but didn't, and Carter on June 6 sued in the Supreme Court. Gibson finally handed over the $3,000, plus $11.25 in court costs, but called it an injustice. Rumor had it that Spreckels had lent him the money.

But Gibson was not long rid of legal proceedings. The next involved Attorney General William N. Armstrong, who went with Kalakaua on his 1881 round-the-world trip, doubling as acting commissioner of immigration. Before the royal party's return, the *Advertiser* charged Armstrong with "treason." His "crime": He had focused, charged Gibson, on attracting only foreign plantation labor, not farmers and artisans who could make it on their own. Armstrong, on his return, arrested Gibson on a charge of criminal libel, and he was indicted on January 2, 1882. The case came up the next month, and the *Advertiser* gave it voluminous coverage, as if Gibson was thoroughly enjoying the commotion he had caused and the attention he was getting.

His defense was that no malice had been alleged and without it there would be no libel under the law. On January 27 the prosecution announced it was dropping the case. Gibson had apologized and that was acceptable to Armstrong, although there was no mention of this in the *Advertiser.*

Gibson was not slow in propounding his theme of Hawaii for the Hawaiians. In his fourth issue he bitingly declared that the opposition press— the *Gazette* and *Saturday Press*—believed "the management of the country belongs to certain well-recognized business rings and their friends; His Majesty should recognize these rings, or cliques, as the 'community': the opinions or desires of the Hawaiian native people are hardly worth taking into consideration; what we [of the opposition press] say, is what everybody says or thinks."[10]

Thus, in the first month of his editorship, Gibson bluntly served notice that the business community, for which Whitney had been a spokesman, was now the *Advertiser*'s implacable enemy.

In April 1881, in an effort to boost circulation and retrieve advertising, Gibson started new columns in both the *Advertiser* and the *Elele Poakolu.*

In "Lies of the Week," which dealt with gossip and innuendo, he dismissed rumors that Spreckels helped him acquire his newspapers. The other column, "Street Talk," was a ghoulish contrivance in which a "doctor" did unflattering "post-mortems" on well-known residents, some living, some dead. This "body-snatching" led Dole to snort that "no paper in Honolulu has ever been guilty of such a contemptible outrage."[11]

Gibson took it all in stride, but interestingly the bizarre columns ceased with the return of the king October 29 from his global travels, and the editor-publisher resumed his dignified stance, while reveling in his influence. He had encouraged the king's global tour and planned the itinerary, and with the monarch back home, Gibson encouraged a lavish coronation for him and Queen Kapiolani, held nine years after Kalakaua had ascended the throne.

Gibson's power initially came not only from his newspapers but also from his continued presence in the legislature as chairman of the finance committee and the acknowledged leader of the native Hawaiian group, which held the majority. In 1882 he ran for his third term, this time from Honolulu, and was overwhelmingly reelected. Of his critics the *Advertiser* said: "The stupid and cowardly spirit of slander was handed a signal rebuke from a free, generous and independent people."[12]

His steady rise to power in public office was climaxed when Kalakaua on May 20, 1882, finally rewarded him with the post Gibson had long yearned for and felt he deserved—the prime ministership. As an additional plum, he was named minister of foreign affairs. The following year, when vacancies occurred in the offices of attorney general and interior minister, Gibson temporarily acquired those as well. His Machiavellian maneuvers, persistently pursued, had brought him to the pinnacle. Small wonder that, at sixty-one, he became known as the "Minister of Everything."

The *Advertiser* was more powerful than ever, having a few weeks earlier, on May 1, 1882, begun publishing daily, Monday through Saturday, while retaining the weekly edition.

On May 22 a notice proclaimed that Gibson "has withdrawn from the editorial management of this journal. Mr. Joseph Webb is now chief editor of the. . . . Daily and Weekly." It was soon clear, however, that the *Advertiser* was continuing to reflect Gibson's views. The *Saturday Press* saw "the Minister of Foreign Affairs and the editor of [the *Advertiser* as] two souls with but a single thought, two hearts that beat as one."[13]

The *Advertiser* regarded fault-finding with Gibson as "paltry, personal antagonism . . . ever since he showed his hand in public affairs." The critics were barking like "a bad pestilent cur at the heels of a great, calm, indifferent mastiff."[14]

The paper could also be counted on to come to the ready defense of Kalakaua. The opposition sheets were hammering away at the power of the king, contending that he was going far beyond the bounds of constitutional government by controlling patronage and using muscle to influence legislation and elections.

The *Advertiser*'s answer was a series of editorials, almost certainly crafted by Gibson, upholding the king as "the first man who has been on the Hawaiian Throne with the brains and ideas of a statesman."

Editor Webb served until August 13, 1883. This period saw a rapid and confusing turnover of *Advertiser* editors and business-side managers. After Webb left, the *Advertiser* was edited briefly by Charles R. Buckland, a friend of Spreckels who had worked as a journalist in his native Tasmania before moving to San Francisco. On August 20, Buckland printed a well-written account of two raids on local opium dens, augmented by a commentary that much of the drug importation was by foreigners who made a huge profit selling to Chinese.

The only thing wrong with the *Advertiser* story, as the *Gazette* gleefully revealed two days later, was that, except for a few local touches, it was plagiarized, a nailed-down case of "literary thieving." The *Gazette* ran side by side a May 12 story from Frank Leslie's *Weekly*, describing an opium den in New York City, and the *Advertiser*'s sprightly account of three months later. The two were identical. The *Gazette* stuck its dirk in a bit deeper by wondering if the *Advertiser* story had been "suggested," a dig at Gibson, the alleged suggester of *Advertiser* content.

The *Saturday Press*, tongue deep in cheek, said the *Advertiser*'s appropriation of the "sensational article" from the Leslie publication showed that Gibson was "merely anxious to give the obscure writer in the obscure sheet from obscure New York the benefit of the wide circulation and enviable reputation of the Pacific Uncommercial Maladministrator."[15] It called Buckland a "talented" young amateur, but said he didn't even know the history of his own paper, having misidentified the *Advertiser*'s first press.

By September 3 Buckland had left the *Advertiser*—voluntarily or otherwise—and become editor of the *Bulletin*. The *Saturday Press* soon charged that, under him, the *Bulletin* had become "either the paid or the unpaid second fiddle to Mr. Gibson's official mandolin."[16] The *Advertiser* acquired another short-term editor of doubtful competence, one Charles Carson, whom the *Saturday Press* branded as a "liar-in-chief" for Gibson.

But Carson clearly was not destined for journalistic glory, at least not in the Islands. The *Bulletin* on October 12 carried a rumor that the *Advertiser* was about to change hands, and on October 15 it did. Gibson, suffering from weakness brought on by a persistent cough, sold the paper to former *Advertiser* editor Webb and Edward C. Macfarlane, owner of the *San Francisco Wasp*. Three days later, Carson left for Puget Sound. That same week the *Advertiser* reported the death at fifty-nine of former editor Henry Sheldon, who was praised as both a good journalist and the "best translator of English into Hawaiian."[17]

The *Advertiser*'s new owners candidly stated their object was to make money and they would achieve that by putting out "a good and useful journal." They were satisfied to support the "existing order of things," but as reforms seemed needed they would be advocated "with vigor and without fear or favor."[18]

The *Gazette* suggested that Webb, while editor, would retain his post as acting secretary to Foreign Minister Gibson. The *Saturday Press* praised Macfarlane as a supporter of good government but dubbed Webb "a thick and thin defender of the Gibson policy" and said the *Advertiser* would continue to be edited by Gibson from the Foreign Office.

Webb's staunch support was appreciated by Gibson, but his standing with some others in the community was less than satisfactory. There was the case, for example, of attorney Clarence W. Ashford, during one of the leprosy scares that from time to time swept the Islands, fueled by the antigovernment papers and dismissed by the *Advertiser* as absurd.

Ashford had written the *Bulletin*, urging that every schoolchild be required to have a medical examination and a Board of Health certificate showing no contagious disease. A follow-up letter to the *Advertiser*, signed "Paterfamilias," said that since Mrs. Ashford had been a recent teacher at the Fort Street school, she and all other teachers of the past five years—as well as everyone else in the community—should also have to get a health exam and certificate.

Ashford demanded the real name of the letter-writer. When Webb replied that he would have to get the writer's permission, Ashford threatened to horsewhip Webb if the letter in the daily was reprinted in the weekly *Advertiser*.

When the paper came off the press with the letter, Webb personally carried a copy to Ashford, prepared for either a peaceful or combative resolution. Ashford asked Webb to take a seat, then suddenly swung a chair and brought it down on Webb's head. The *Advertiser* account said that Webb partly warded off the blow, with Ashford then trying to strangle him. The editor yelled for help, and Dole ran in and prevented further violence. It was all reminiscent of the assault-by-bowie-knife on *Advertiser* editor Whitney by the pro-Confederate U.S. minister two decades before.

In June 1884, Webb, having sold his *Advertiser* interest to Macfarlane, again stepped down as editor. Daniel O'Connell, a Spreckels recruit, described as a "fire-eating Bohemian," came from San Francisco with his wife, five children, and a nurse to accept the post.[19] The paper "change[d] from 'its gentlemanly tone with complete command of temper' to one brashly raucous, bristling with barbs of satire. . . . Brilliant, witty, bold." O'Connell was strongly antimissionary and pro-Gibson.[20]

He soon aroused the ire of Whitney, who called him "one of the worst specimens of that class of editors which are becoming so numerous in San Francisco and California. He was imported by Ed Macfarlane, and in my opinion is a disgrace to the profession, ridiculing Christianity and everything that is good. I was never so ashamed of my old paper as now."[21]

But even more serious criticism of the *Advertiser* was just ahead. The paper suffered one of its most telling setbacks of the Gibson era when the legislature's finance committee, controlled by independents after the 1884 election, issued a blistering report of financial favoritism and worse.

For the first eighteen of the twenty-four months covered by the report Gibson still headed the *Advertiser* while prime minister and minister of foreign affairs. The committee found that *Advertiser* rates for printing and advertising were higher than elsewhere; that some *Advertiser* bills had been paid twice; that the paper had delivered in unfinished condition a book of rules for king's guard volunteers at a price of $630, against estimated proper charges of not more than $280 for a completed job. Committee chairman Godfrey Brown called the $630 bill "a highway robbery . . . probably pushed through the Minister of Foreign Affairs at a time when business was dull in the newspaper office."[22] The committee also reported that $500 had been paid to the *Advertiser* in 1882 as an advance on printing, but with no work done.

Gibson's son-in-law, Hayselden, former *Advertiser* manager who had wound up as secretary of the Board of Health, did not go unscathed. The board's ledger showed numerous erasures and some doctoring of entries. And eyebrows were lifted over bills submitted by Hayselden and paid for $3.50 each for seven turkeys plus two corsets and a bustle.

Gibson responded that the committee was "unmistakably prejudiced," with much of its evidence "inferential"[23] and that Hayselden's turkeys, corsets, and bustle were gifts to ladies who made decorations for King Kalakaua's coronation. This last led Dole to suggest the ministers be called the "turkey cabinet" because of their "disposition to gobble up public funds."[24]

The *Advertiser*, pointing out that the cited problems preceded Macfarlane's ownership, said that overall the legislative report showed "an astonishing negligence and lack of system in the conduct of Government affairs" and attested to the value of investigation and of a "good, healthy opposition."[25] At the same time, it decried the "shallow sneaking warfare" and "the mendacious assaults" on the *Advertiser* by its sloppy enemies.[26] And it absolved Gibson, whom it declared to be "an honest, energetic and capital official," against whom there was no proven evidence of having used public money for his own benefit.[27]

A subsequent exchange outside the legislature between Gibson and Henry Waterhouse led J. T. Waterhouse, Sr., to shake his stick at Gibson and declare, "You're a rogue, sir. You've been carrying on this Government in a rascally manner." Gibson told him, "Keep that stick down and I'll talk to you." At this point Henry Waterhouse came up and gave Gibson a push that brought him to his knees. Bystanders broke it up, and the *Advertiser* condemned Waterhouse for being violent "toward a man so much his senior." Apparently that ended the incident.[28]

All in all, it was not a glorious time for Hawaii journalism. And a Washington lawyer-writer, David Graham Adee, brother of a U.S. State Department under secretary, said so. After a stay in the Islands representing a steamship company, he wrote an article in an American journal on the Island press. Quoting "a gentleman . . . who knows," he wrote that

> Honolulu is cursed with mongrel editors and newspapers and now there is another paper [the *Hawaiian*, being started] which may prove a curse or a blessing. Several of these so-called newspapers are given to most contemptible criticisms of the government. They are mismanaged by scrubs, unhappy beings, disappointed adventurers and chronic growlers and detractors, but so far as their influence goes away from their own office, it is a mere blank or void.[29]

Whatever the reason, on September 15 *Advertiser* editor O'Connell left Hawaii and was succeeded by David W. C. Nesfield, who only two weeks before had come over from the *Hawaiian* to serve as local news editor. "An exceptionally brilliant man from the Coast," he had been a music critic for the *San Francisco Post* before arriving in the Islands in April 1884.[30] He had a fine baritone voice and sang at benefit concerts. Mysteriously, he lasted as editor for only a week and then sailed back to the coast "to recruit his health."[31]

The ubiquitous Webb again returned. But he was not part of the ownership, which the following January changed again, with articles of incorporation filed for the paper by Edward C. and Clarence W. Macfarlane. And a month later they had a new editor, with Webb being succeeded by Robert C. Creighton, who came as Spreckels' man from San Francisco.

The fact that neither Macfarlane held an office, although listed as the sole stockholders, raised the question of who really owned the *Advertiser*. Spreckels' influence there was evidenced by his sponsoring of O'Connell and Creighton and also of auditor W. M. Gifford, who was chief clerk of W. G. Irwin & Company, in which Spreckels was a partner.

Any doubts about Spreckels' monetary involvement in the *Advertiser* were erased when in March 1885 he began erecting on the ocean side of Merchant Street, near Fort Street, a new building for the paper. Said to be the first such structure in Honolulu constructed purely for newspaper use, it was a two-story wooden plant. The manager's and business offices, the composing room, and the presses were on the first floor, the editorial rooms and job printing compositors on the second. Also on the second story were carrier pigeon lofts, occupied by birds able to fly in news. The new building was occupied Monday, April 25. The press printed on Saturday in the old building and on Monday in the new.

Further light on Spreckels, Creighton, and the *Advertiser* was cast by a letter in which Creighton cited his and the *Advertiser*'s function: "I have been in charge of the Govt paper on these Islands for the past twelve months having come here specially for that purpose."[32]

When a new cabinet was named on June 30, 1886, under Prime Minister Gibson, Creighton was appointed minister of foreign affairs, after becoming a "denizen"—an alien admitted to citizenship—the day before. Toward the end of his June 30–October 13 service, he was additionally named secretary of war and navy. This all affirmed the convenient relationship between Spreckels and Gibson.

Succeeding Creighton as *Advertiser* editor during his three and a half months in government was Arthur Johnstone, serving until late September. He was followed briefly by Mason W. W. Gilbert, a recent arrival from either New Zealand or Australia, who later became auditor of the *Advertiser.*

When in October Spreckels split with Kalakaua over finances and angrily sailed for California, Creighton was out of the cabinet and back as *Advertiser* editor. He demonstrated Spreckels' control by doing an about-face and becoming critical of the very government for which he had been an enthusiastic mouthpiece.

Soon smarting under the *Advertiser*'s negative drumfire, the government moved to acquire the paper, agreeing to pay W. G. Irwin & Company, representing Spreckels, $7,500 down and $13,000 within a year. The *Advertiser* of June 2, 1887, reported:

> At a meeting of the stockholders held Tuesday afternoon [May 31] a portion of the stock changed hands, thus involving the necessity for a change in its management and a modification in the expression of its views on public matters. . . .
>
> With this issue the Advertiser takes a new departure, and its best efforts . . . will be directed towards expressing faithfully and fairly the opinions of His Majesty's Government.

That same day the *Daily Bulletin* declared: "The Government resumes control of the paper [the *Advertiser*] and it henceforth will be published as a Government organ."

Four days later Gibson wrote H. A. P. Carter, Hawaii's minister in Washington, that the paper "is now held in the interest of His Majesty's Ministers and will be a semiofficial organ of the Government."[33]

Creighton gave up the editorship, and while the paper did not publicly name a successor, Gibson engaged Horace Wright, a well-educated Foreign Office clerk, to assist in the preparation of editorials. It would be like old times. There was nothing in Gibson's diaries to indicate that he did not feel everything was under control and would continue to be.

But big trouble was brewing. The longtime antagonism of the business community was being brought to a boil by an opium bribery scandal. The king appeared to pocket $71,000 for an opium-selling license paid by a Chinese rice farmer who, when outbid by another, was unable to get his money back. The businessmen were vigorously reacting to what historian Jacob Adler termed "a regime of political corruption unlike anything known in the previous 40 years of constitutional government in Hawaii."[34]

At long last, Gibson put aside his myopia. On June 26, he acknowledged in his diary: "Increasing rumors about public discontent, and there is an armed league in opposition to the Government."

On June 27 the *Advertiser* reported that the streets were rife with politically motivated rumors and lies about Gibson, including a report that he "was preparing to leave the country on the next steamer." That same day the *Bulletin* declared that in time the *Advertiser* would be forced to admit that more than a "few malcontents" wanted government change for the public good.

Resolutions adopted at a June 30 mass meeting at the Honolulu Rifles' armory and addressed to the king requested, among other actions, that a new cabinet be created; that Gibson be "dismissed from each and every [government] office held by him"; and that the king make "immediate restitution" of the $71,000 "obtained by him [for the unissued opium license] in violation of law and of his oath of office. . . ."

Anticipating at least the demand for a new cabinet, the king had already obtained Gibson's resignation and those of his colleagues and asked W. L. Green to put together a cabinet. When the king realized that this would not lessen the clamor for across-the-board reform, he caved in to the other demands, including acceptance of the so-called bayonet constitution, which took away much of his power.

Meanwhile, Gibson, suffering with tuberculosis and realizing his Hawaiian adventure, with his dream of everlasting glory, was at a humiliating end, sailed July 12 for San Francisco, where he died January 21, 1888. A month later his body was returned to Honolulu for viewing by thousands, predominantly native Hawaiians, at his former residence and a funeral service at the Cathedral of Our Lady of Peace.

Born into the Anglican Church, Gibson had become a Mormon and died a Catholic. He was buried in Honolulu, then in Lahaina, in a special vault from which his casket at some point disappeared.

The *Advertiser*, because of the political turbulence surrounding Gibson's ouster and Kalakaua's reduced powers, carried no full-scale editorials between June 29 and August 3, 1887, substituting cautious comments and foreign news. It did print an item on the king's receiving and signing the new constitution and published the text without comment, for "lack of space."

But suddenly, on August 4, Creighton resurfaced as editor and the paper was replete with local editorials. After four days he announced he was buying the paper and promised an independent course, but that fell apart and editorial duties went to Wray Taylor, a descendant through his mother's family of King Lunalilo and a sometime organist at St. Andrews Episcopal Cathedral. He continued until the following May and in later life was official custodian of the Royal Mausoleum in Nuuanu Valley.

11

"Laws of U.S. Are Good Enough for Hawaii"

THE GOVERNMENT failed to make the remaining $13,000 payment for the *Advertiser*, and the paper was once again in the hands of W. G. Irwin & Company. But with Spreckels at bitter odds with the government, the firm lost interest in newspapering.

Thus it came to pass that Henry Whitney, the founder of the *Advertiser* in 1856, was again to be a major player in the paper's life. This was by way of the Hawaiian Gazette Company, in which he and his wife held majority stock. At a *Gazette* stockholders' meeting on May 22, 1888, of Whitney, Henry N. Castle, and his uncle W. R. Castle, it was resolved to buy the *Advertiser* if it could be had for $6,000. W. R. Castle was delegated to approach Irwin & Company.

The purchase was completed May 26 for that amount, the *Gazette* taking immediate possession, with payment of principal and interest to be completed within a year. The new owners quickly discontinued the weekly *Advertiser* and the daily *Gazette*, leaving the daily *Advertiser* and weekly *Gazette* with Henry Castle as editor of both papers and Daniel Logan as *Advertiser* night editor and later as managing editor. Whitney served as company manager and, on the side, as editor of the *Planters' Monthly*. The *Gazette* in 1889 moved its office and equipment into the *Advertiser* building on Merchant Street, which would be used until January 1896.

Castle, who was born in Honolulu of missionary parents and educated at Punahou and Oberlin College, was admired by Whitney for writing "vigorous, scholarly English that betrayed a familiarity with the best that men and books can give."[1] He was also noted for his keen and sometimes caustic wit.

Logan, who came to Hawaii in 1884 at age thirty-two, had worked for almost a decade on newspapers in Montreal, Nova Scotia, and elsewhere in Canada. He spent three years at the *Advertiser*, leaving in mid-1891.

Castle had been in newspapering for five years, having accepted an offer in September 1883, when he was twenty-one, to be virtually a one-man reporting staff for the *Gazette*, writing everything except editorials. But he was lacking in confidence. "I was strongly impressed with my unfitness for the position." He had planned to study law, but doubted that he would if he went into journalism. "It is a pity I do not know my own mind."[2]

Newspapering seemed to bore him; it wasn't profound enough. When the 1894 legislative session ended, he noted that, as a result, "the newspapers . . . have lost every vestige of what little interest they once possessed."[3] At heart he was an intellectual, a literary man far more comfortable on a campus, with books and academic discussion. So he took frequent leave to study in the United States and Europe, especially Germany.

With an election coming up in February 1890, Castle found politics confusing: "The white vote will probably be more or less divided, and, in general,

The *Hawaiian Gazette* in 1888 bought the *Advertiser* and moved it into its building on Merchant Street. The paper remained there until 1895, when it leased a structure on the ocean side of King Street, between Fort and Bethel, where it operated until 1913.

things are very much mixed up. There is a general spirit of dissatisfaction and restlessness abroad. . . ."[4]

His assessment of politicians was highly critical: "People's motives are so hopelessly petty and small, and their actions quite correspond. I am intensely sick of the whole thing, and only wish, with the psalmist, for a pair of wings, so that I may fly away anywhere and be at rest."[5]

On January 20, 1891, while Castle was away on an extended European visit, Kalakaua died in San Francisco of uremic poisoning. Nine days later, the *Advertiser* distributed a fifteen-hundred-copy extra, covering the arrival of his remains on the *Charleston* and their transfer to the palace, to lie in state for public viewing. The following morning it carried the proclamation of Princess Liliuokalani as the queen.

On February 5, the paper said Liliuokalani "ascends the throne of Hawaii with every presumption of a peaceable and happy reign." She has "the sanction of the constitution" and "the approval of her people and with a plainly marked path of duty stretched before her. To reign and not to govern has been accepted as the definition of the duty of a modern Constitutional Sovereign."

Thus, the *Advertiser*'s endorsement of the queen was conditioned on her abiding by the "bayonet constitution" and confining herself to a role similar to that of British royalty.

But Liliuokalani, a well-educated woman of strong will, had her own ideas about personal government. In time, rumors spread that she intended to scrap the "bayonet constitution," which she had sworn to uphold, and proclaim a new one, restoring and expanding on previous royal rights.

The *Advertiser*'s support rapidly dwindled. By February 18 it was criticizing the queen for demanding, as her first official act, the resignation of the cabinet, which refused to comply. The paper regretted her "open opposition to the constitutional representatives of the people," and feared she intended "to renew the conflict between Prerogative and the people, a conflict which for the last six years has kept the country in a turmoil." It cautioned that, if continued, this attitude could eventually have a "disastrous [result] to the privileges and powers of the Sovereign."

In August the *Advertiser* was critical of efforts by "one or two native papers" to "array the natives against foreigners" and likened it to instigators of atrocities in China against "missionaries and foreigners generally."[6]

Castle returned September 1 and was pleased that the *Advertiser* was being delivered to Waikiki subscribers, almost as far out as Diamond Head, by a special messenger on horseback and was also promoting its new illustrated Hawaiian Islands tourist guide.

But Castle's comfort was undercut a bit just before Christmas, when an *Advertiser* reporter "enjoying the weather and not looking for trouble" was assaulted on Fort Street by a Mr. Whaley, an "alleged tourist," who disliked "something which appeared in the columns of this paper." The assailant weighed twice as much as "the green reporter"—likely newcomer Frank L. Hoogs, who had a crippled right hand.

The paper stressed that the editor and publisher, not a reporter, were responsible for its contents. But it noted that "the Bulletin, Marshal [C. B.] Wilson and a whole lot of other queer people are congratulating 'the alleged tourist,' on his brutal and absurd exploit."[7]

No opportunity was missed to rail against Wilson (whose son Johnny years later would be a popular Honolulu mayor). The paper charged that the marshal "has allowed gambling, opium dealing and other forms of law-breaking to flourish unchecked and . . . is commonly reported to exercise a pernicious, illegitimate and occult influence" on the queen, which tends to bring her government "into contempt and disrepute."[8]

The 1892 session of the legislature ran from May into January 1893. It was of record length and highly inflammatory. The paper hoped the cabinet would resolve political differences, but that was not to be. Lottery and opium bills, which the queen would sign, were passed, and on January 12, 1893, a respected cabinet, headed by George N. Wilcox, resigned. The *Advertiser* blamed "a combination of opium smugglers, disappointed office holders and haole haters, aided by the powerful influence of the Court and the Police Department and the free use of bribery."[9]

A new cabinet was named, drawing a blistering editorial from the paper. The following morning, Saturday, January 14, the queen arrived in the legislative chamber and at noon officially terminated the session.

That afternoon the queen tried to promulgate a new constitution, giving her even more power than her late brother Kalakaua had had before "the bayonet constitution" was forced on him. The cabinet balked and the queen agreed to yield, but only temporarily, and the proannexationists saw the situation as dangerous and calling for swift, decisive action.

They had formed an Annexation Club, which quickly became a Committee of Safety, which intended to depose the queen, abrogate the monarchy, and form a provisional government, which would then appeal to Washington for annexation. The U.S. commissioner, John L. Stevens, and the captain of the USS *Boston*, then in the harbor, appeared to approve, and documents were drafted to establish the provisional government. On January 16 a mass meeting of some fifteen hundred was followed by the landing of 162 marines from the *Boston*.

The next morning, which was to see the overthrow of the queen, the *Advertiser* hailed the mass meeting as demonstrating "that the foreign community is weary of aboriginal dynasty. . . . The landing of troops from the *Boston* furnishes a guarantee that the persons and property of American citizens will be safe from violence."

Liliuokalani wanted to avoid bloodshed. Once Minister Stevens recognized the provisional government as the de facto regime of Hawaii, she had no choice but to step down, making clear that she was yielding, under duress, "to the superior force of the United States."

The next morning an *Advertiser* extra headlined "The New Era" and declared

> the people, weary of the conspiracies, usurpations, scandals and encroachments upon their rights which have marked the last years of the Hawaiian monarchy, have asserted the prerogatives inherent in every people to determine the form of their own government. . . . The change which has taken place, though carried out by the foreign population, is not in the interest of any class, section, creed or nationality, but will inure to the benefit of all. . . .[10]

Under the headline "Everything Moving Smoothly," the *Advertiser* reported on January 19 that the government, with Sanford Dole as president, had moved into Aliiolani Hale, assumed formal control of Iolani Palace and the barracks, and paid off and disbanded the household guards of the queen, who "had withdrawn to her private residence at Washington Place."

A five-man commission left for Washington to negotiate an annexation treaty with the United States. If they succeeded, the *Advertiser* said, "the day which made that mission possible should be marked in letters of gold, for it will have been a day of blessing to all classes in Hawaii."[11]

On February 1 an *Advertiser* extra front-paged, in larger than usual type, Minister Stevens' pronouncement that, in the name of the United States, he was assuming protection of the Hawaiian Islands, "but not interfering with the administration of public affairs by the Provisional Government." His action was "taken pending, and subject to, negotiations at Washington." An adjoining story gave this reason:

> The increased agitation on the part of certain whites of the class who have always been the curse of this country, coupled with the efforts of one English and one or two native newspapers to discredit the Government; to block its efforts toward the establishment of order, and in general to bring it into disrespect and contempt, have been the chief agency in spreading through the town a feeling of uneasiness and disquietude.

While Hawaii's government had changed, some other things hadn't. In a column adjoining editorials the ad of E. O. Hall & Son, L'd, asked, "Do you want the wheels of your buggy, brake or dray to run smoothly this year? Of course, you do, you ain't in love with a hot box and a wheel that won't go round. Just try a bottle of Climax Axle Oil and see how it works. It is far better than castor oil. . . ."[12]

Some Neighbor Islanders also were taking developments in stride. The *Advertiser*'s correspondent in Kohala, on the Big Island, reported, "The first excitement of the news from Honolulu is over and all is quiet there. The sugar mills of North Kohala are all in full blast. . . . While some have been making history, we have been making sugar."[13]

The *Advertiser* meanwhile was making cheer, or trying to: "If this country becomes part of the United States a boom in values may be expected without a precedent in its history."[14]

But when there was a move to fire the monarchy's employees the *Advertiser* objected, saying that anyone doing his job should be retained. To the radical element among the annexationists this was heresy, and they started their own mouthpiece, the afternoon *Hawaiian Star*—with a future *Advertiser* editor, Walter G. Smith, as managing editor. The Hawaiian-language paper *Holomua* labeled the rather sober *Advertiser* the voice of the missionary-sugar constituency and the turbulent *Star* a dispenser of "a mass of . . . pultaceous pabulum" to the laboring class.

To counter the assertion that the revolution was the work of the missionaries' descendants, the *Advertiser* reported that fewer than thirty-five of the two thousand members of the Annexation Club were of missionary stock and the same was true of only eight of 101 cabinet members since the early 1840s.

In Washington, a treaty of annexation was worked out by the Hawaii commission and the outgoing administration of President Benjamin Harrison and was sent to the Senate. But when Grover Cleveland succeeded Harrison in the White House, he and Secretary of State Walter Q. Gresham recalled the treaty and sent former Democratic Congressman James H. Blount to the Islands for a four-month fact-finding study.

When he completed his mission and prepared to leave, the *Advertiser* on August 8 carried a glowing editorial, praising him as a statesman, "the right man in the right place," retaining "the respect and friendship of both sides." Assured by Dole that order was firmly established, Blount removed the marines. He submitted his findings to Secretary Gresham, who let time pass until mid-October before making his report to President Cleveland. The upshot was that a new minister to Hawaii, Albert S. Willis, was sent to express Washington's "sincere regret" to the queen for Stevens' "reprehensible conduct" and to favor her reinstatement to the throne, with a grant of amnesty to all who had opposed her.

Six days after Willis arrived in the Islands on November 4, Gresham's letter to Cleveland was printed in East Coast newspapers and in due course made its way to Hawaii. Gresham said: "Should not the great wrong done to a feeble but independent state, by an abuse of the authority of the United States, be undone by restoring the legitimate government?"

The *Advertiser* was livid: "A democratic government restoring a dethroned monarch bearing such a history. The whole world would cry out—'shame.'"[15]

With no chance of Liliuokalani's retrieving power, the Cleveland administration tossed the hot potato to Congress, which after two months of hearings generated the Morgan Report, described by historian Ralph S. Kuykendall as managing "to exonerate from blame everyone save the queen."

On December 23 Dole personally handed Willis a letter formally rejecting Cleveland's proposal to hand back the government to the former queen. The

Advertiser reported that the jubilant expectation of royalists that the monarchy would be restored was succeeded by depression and gloom.

As 1894 arrived, the *Advertiser* foresaw a bright future, "chiefly because the time has come when the white population of Hawaii, and the saving remnant of the aboriginal population, will no longer submit to the rule of a monarchy which is corrupt, reactionary and heathenish, and which is out of touch with the tendencies of the age."[16]

But on February 12, the *Advertiser* acknowledged that annexation "seems to be impractical at present" and reported the leaders of the "emancipation movement" have "wisely chosen the next best thing and seek an independent republic for themselves."

A constitutional convention was convened May 30, and with the constitution's adoption on July 4 the Republic of Hawaii was proclaimed, with Dole as president.

The political scene over months had grown relatively quiet, but journalistic life had its turbulent moments. Editor Castle had written critically of Paul Neumann, who had been Liliuokalani's attorney. When Neumann demanded an apology, Castle asked for specifics. Neumann provided none, but again insisted upon a retraction. When it was not forthcoming, Neumann stopped Castle, walking with his bicycle on Merchant Street, and struck him in the mouth with his walking stick.

When Castle sought to respond, he was grabbed from behind by W. H. Cornwell, and Neumann struck him three more times, on the head, opening a gash and drawing blood. Castle regarded it as royalist revenge—a "wild and erratic cyclone of cane and whiskey"—and took no criminal action. But he did run a news story titled "A Most Cowardly Attack" and an editorial stating that the paper's freedom of the press would not "be abridged by the threats or violence of any number of cowardly ruffians."[17]

Castle had a strong city editor in Ed Towse, a Maine native who had moved to the Wyoming frontier with his Indian-fighting father and, being an adventurous type, had been attracted to Hawaii at age twenty-six by the 1893 revolution.

Towse and others on the *Advertiser* staff had high respect for Castle and his adherence to principle. When a draft of the constitution for the pending republic guaranteed free speech and a free press, but prohibited "writing, speaking or printing anything favoring the restoration of the monarchy," Castle was outraged. He called this an abridgment of the liberty of the press and asked: "Is there any wisdom or expediency in depriving the royalists of the right to express in a peaceable manner their views? It pleases them and it does not hurt anybody."[18] He lost, but the paper's faith in itself and the future remained undimmed.

It established a book bindery in the commercial printing department and bought two Linotypes, Hawaii's first typesetting machines and, readers were told, a year ahead of the *Times* of London. It installed a Babcock Dispatch roller press, then rated as the fastest flat-bed newspaper press built. The paper jumped from six pages to eight, moved editorials from page two to page four, and started carrying news stories on page one, moving ads inside.

Promotionally minded, it called itself "the leading paper in the Hawaiian Islands. It has a larger circulation and prints more live news than any other Island paper. Price 50 cents a month, in advance," soon raised to 75 cents. "Ring up Telephone 88 for home delivery."[19]

In August 1894 Whitney offered to sell his majority stock in the *Advertiser*'s parent, the Hawaiian Gazette Company, for $17,500. The Castle family emerged as owner, and Whitney yielded his general oversight of the *Advertiser*, the *Gazette*, and the Hawaiian-language *Kuakoa* on September 10. W. R. Castle was elected president, and the company expressed appreciation for Whitney's long years of service.

In November Editor Castle took his fourth trip to Europe, to further his studies in German, but he found his stay unsettling. He wrote his wife: "There is no scholarship in me."[20] Then, in a reversal of earlier pessimism, he foresaw a bright future for himself in Island journalism. But it was not to be. Tragically, en route home in January 1895 he and his daughter Dorothy were drowned when their North German Lloyd steamer *Elbe* was rammed and sunk by another ship in the North Sea. He was thirty-three, Dorothy, five.

In a eulogy before the Hawaiian Bar Association, J. A. Magoon said: "The appearance of the daily morning Advertiser, edited by this young man, was looked for with no little dread by the wicked and corrupt government that existed prior to 1892, and with no little eagerness by those who were battling for the right, and for intelligent and just government in this land."

When Castle had been away studying, it appears that Dr. C. T. Rodgers, author Arthur Johnstone, and former Attorney General W. N. Armstrong served at different times as temporary editors.

Johnstone, who would later become city editor, was an Iowan who came to the Islands in the early 1880s, taught at an Episcopal institute, and married Julia Afong, an attractive, well-educated daughter of wealthy Chinese merchant C. Afong.

Johnstone became friendly with Robert Louis Stevenson, who first visited Hawaii in 1889, staying at the San Souci resort for his health. When Stevenson heard that San Souci was criticized for selling liquor illicitly he fired off a letter of protest to the editor of the *Advertiser* which also conveyed his thorough distaste for the existence of telephones.

Johnstone wrote glowingly of Stevenson, but a *Star-Bulletin* columnist a half-century later called Johnstone a failure as an editor, who fought the planters, the government, and business interests, and attacked annexationists for sending what it called stories of restlessness in Hawaii to mainland newspapers. Interestingly, this stance did not deter the Gazette Company from hiring him as interim editor when Castle was away, nor Lorrin Thurston from accepting him on the staff later on.

Whatever Castle thought of Johnstone, in a New York stopover on his way to Europe in the fall of 1894, he had been impressed by a twenty-three-year-old reporter for the *New York Commercial News* and offered him the managing editorship of the *Advertiser*. To relatives, Castle wrote, "He was the only reasonably low-priced man who had any of the experience I particularly wanted." The young man thus selected is little remembered for his three years at the *Advertiser*, but is prominently identified with its opposition, the *Star-Bulletin*, and with his service as governor of the territory of Hawaii.

Wallace Rider Farrington, a native of Maine, was a journalist from boyhood. At fifteen he was editor of his military academy journal and, four years later, business manager of his college paper. On graduating in 1891 from the State College of Maine, he worked on papers in Maine and Massachusetts. After accepting Castle's offer, Farrington landed in Honolulu on November 22, four and a half months after the republic was established, and the Personals column noted that "W. R. Farrington, an experienced young newspaperman, arrived on the Alameda and will be on the Advertiser staff."[21]

Two examples of *Advertiser* ads in bygone days. On the right, after a cholera outbreak in August 1895, a drugstore plugged patent medicine for the disease, 25 cents per bottle. In November 1903 McInerny was offering "Stein-Block smart suits and spring overcoats" for $15 to $35.

Six weeks later, on January 4, 1895, Farrington was elevated to the editorship, replacing interim editor W. N. Armstrong, whom he greatly respected. Two days after that, the republic was exposed to a small, abortive revolution led by Robert W. Wilcox, but quickly put down. Wilcox was sentenced to death, others to lesser terms, but all but one were freed on January 1, 1896. The *Advertiser* observed that it was "the last act in what was nearly a bloody tragedy . . . [but] let bygones be bygones."[22]

The *Advertiser* declared that the republic had "shown itself amply able to maintain itself against all comers." And Farrington declared, "The spirit of '76 is in the air . . . we are making history."[23] A staunch Republican and instant annexationist, he charged that Cleveland had "done all in his power to overthrow the Republic of Hawaii and has been balked at every step." But annexation would have to wait until another and much larger conflict had its impact.

Although a newcomer, Farrington quickly gained the respect of his readers, who already had a high regard for the paper. Farrington's biographer, Thornton Sherburne Hardy, said that of the Honolulu newspapers, "In volume of advertising, intelligence and tone of its editorials, presentation, variety and choice of its news, the *Advertiser* stood head and shoulders above its competitors," which included the *Evening Bulletin*, the *Hawaiian Star*, the semi-weekly *Hawaiian Gazette*, and "several come-and-go papers published in the Hawaiian language and a swarm of fly-by-night gossip and rumor sheets."[24]

Although public interest was dominated by the uncertain political scene, the *Advertiser* attracted attention with a crusade against downtown prostitution. It deplored the heavy concentration of brothels on Nuuanu Avenue and Maunakea, Hotel, and Pauahi Streets, where schoolchildren had to pass "the dens of women . . . with their hideous, powdered faces peering at passersby with a brazen effrontery." And it said its reporters investigating the situation had been threatened by hoodlums, "a crowd of gamblers and blackmailers." It wanted "every licentious Asiatic" driven from the business area or, "better still, sent out of the country."[25]

At the time, Farrington was only twenty-five, but he wrote editorials worthy of a far more experienced editor. And he was not reluctant to take controversial positions at odds with strong economic and political forces. For example, he strongly favored attracting Americans to work on the plantations. It was "a vital question" to him "whether the Anglo-Saxon and the Hawaiian [are] to be protected against the inroads of the Asiatic"—specifically, at that time, the Chinese.

If, by today's standards, Farrington appeared narrow on this subject, he was liberal on others. He believed that the native Hawaiian population, which far outnumbered the haoles, should exercise full rights of citizenship at the polls. He advocated higher education for women and said they "should know politics and have the right of voting."[26] He urged the building of schools that were "well lighted, well ventilated and arranged generally upon modern ideas."[27]

He opposed executive sessions in the legislature "when matters pertaining to local men and affairs are under consideration."[28] He tended to agree with "a general impression" that corporations "are reaping all the gold from the soil and are not bearing their proportional share of the financial burdens of the Government."[29] He favored temperance, but felt that the public had to be educated since "as long as there is a taste for liquor, liquor will be sold."[30] And, in drunk cases, he favored penalizing the seller.

Of course annexation was the hot issue of the time, and Farrington fervently pushed the cause.

Hawaii interest ran high as Americans went to the polls on November 3, 1896, to decide between William McKinley and William Jennings Bryan for president. The day before, Farrington wrote that, regardless of who won, the campaign in Congress for admission should begin at once. "We must not lose time in announcing that Hawaii is still at the door of the U.S." On November 17, the *Advertiser* printed a story headlined: IT IS McKINLEY.

The *Advertiser* was exultant because of McKinley's support of annexation: The people of Hawaii "believe that with a strong, thoroughly American administration, the stars and stripes, the American flag, will wave over Hawaii, never to be hauled down."[31]

Farrington flayed the sugar people who opposed annexation because it would end the use of contract labor. "They are willing and anxious to hold the labor system down to the level of degenerate serfdom provided sugar pans out its usual quarterly profit. . . . They want nothing but the dollars and a fat thing from the reciprocity treaty."

And to those who were upset that Liliuokalani had quietly left for the United States, presumably to lobby against annexation, he reminded that having been given a full pardon by the government "she has a right to do whatever she wants."[32]

The Annexation Club adopted a resolution favoring the earliest practicable annexation, and Farrington editorialized that "Hawaii asks for admission to the American union without quibbling over labor laws, immigration laws, sugar laws, or any other law. The laws of the United States are good enough for Hawaii."[33]

On July 1, 1897, McKinley urged the U.S. Senate to ratify a U.S.-Hawaii annexation treaty, but the session ended without action.

Farrington was disappointed but confident that Hawaii's day would come. Meanwhile, he was making his mark not only in the editorial rooms but on the corporate side of the paper as well. At the annual meeting of the Gazette Company in March 1895 he had been elected secretary. The following month the by-laws were amended to say there would be an editor-in-chief, appointed by and responsible to the board of directors, but who would have charge of the company papers' direction and contents and authority to appoint and remove members of the editorial staffs.

Meanwhile, the paper had moved from 318 Merchant Street to 68 South King Street, in the Von Holt block, and began using for the daily *Advertiser* and semiweekly *Gazette* a "perfecting press," which "printed, cut, pasted and folded papers ready for delivery," permitting a later news deadline and presstime.[34]

In June, Farrington's contract was renewed for the year beginning November 25 at $2,100 a year, and in August he was elected president of the company. The next May he was reelected, and the company's balance sheet reported "a prosperous condition."[35] But a shocker lay ahead.

In June 1897 Farrington, for reasons unclear, suddenly resigned as *Advertiser* editor "to take effect on arrival of Mr. W. N. Armstrong," who was abroad. In a resolution the board declared that during Farrington's tenure the columns of the *Advertiser* "have been characterized by a cleanliness in journalism and honesty of purpose which have been appreciated by the board and the readers of newspapers in Hawaii."[36]

Despite this glowing appraisal, the company publicly made no mention of Farrington's action, confining itself to a bare-bones notice atop the editorial page: "Today W. N. Armstrong takes charge of the editorial department of the Advertiser."[37]

Farrington had arranged for Henry Whitney to fill in for him until about mid-July or the earlier arrival of Armstrong, "it being understood that in case Mr. Armstrong should not return by the middle of July or thereabouts, Mr. Farrington will return to reassume the editorial management."[38]

Armstrong did return, and Farrington and his wife, whom he had married in San Francisco the previous October, settled in Fitchburg, Massachusetts. He apparently was unhappy there, for a year after leaving the Islands he was back, having accepted an offer to become editor of the *Evening Bulletin.*

Armstrong brought to the *Advertiser* editorship an impressive background. The son of an early missionary, Dr. Richard Armstrong, and a Yale graduate, he had practiced law for many years in New York City. At the end of his interim editorship two years before, he had reminded readers that newspapers are "mercantile ventures . . . not prone to greatly vary from the average demands of the readers." He presciently added that "in the racial contest, which the Caucasian here has on his hands and which will grow sharply as time goes on, and the issues become clearer, there will be a supreme need of unity of thought and action. In this, good journalism should become a powerful agency, and should demand the constant cordial and, indeed, unusual support of its readers."[39]

Armstrong had a habit of writing a variety of editorials in advance and putting them in a desk drawer. Whenever he was absent, the composing room foreman selected what he felt would be suitable for the next issue and had it put into type. On such occasions, one reporter recalled, the foreman was "the real editor."[40]

The paper expected the prevalent antiannexation sentiment from the Hawaiians but was mystified by the lack of enthusiasm by the Portuguese—some sixteen thousand—who would get the right to vote.

When some antigovernment members of the legislature needled the administration, the *Advertiser* pleaded: "Stand by the Government you have put in office. There are hardly 2,000 of us 'able-bodied' men who are trying to hold the fort of white civilization against 80,000 or more who oppose us. We need to make our frontage solid as granite."[41]

The paper no longer feared a restoration of the monarchy and even suggested, when Liliuokalani's niece Kaiulani landed in Honolulu after a stay in England, that she officially be called "Princess."

But there remained a general nervousness over what might be ahead, and Armstrong editorialized that Hawaii could well use a study by social scientists:

> Here is a singular mixture of races, a little Babel in its way, a rag-bag full of curiosities, odds and ends, a museum full of the queerest humanity, above all is a government founded on a political theory of the Anglo-Saxon type, of which 90 percent of the people who live under it know nothing, either by racial instincts or education, and scattered all about the premises is an uncomfortable amount of social dynamite.

But the subject, he said, was being ignored.[42]

Of one thing the paper felt certain, however: that with or without annexation, the "planting interest" would become "the political master of the situation here." In an unusually candid editorial, tinged with cynicism, Armstrong wrote:

> It will dictate the measures it requires and make them into laws. If the islands remain independent, it will be the government in reality. If there is annexation, it will have the ears of the leading men in Washington.
>
> The sugar interest will do here just what the large railroads and insurance corporations of America do. These become dominant forces in politics, because they are forced to it.
>
> They buy justice and legal privileges, because they are for sale in the Legislatures. So long as the people elect corrupt men to office, the business interests of a semi-public character must pay for protection. These predictions are made upon the usual course of events in other countries and the same course may be anticipated here."[43]

While Armstrong was clearly proannexation, he was regarded by some as wishy-washy because he wanted advance assurance from Washington on matters of local concern. The *Star* dubbed him an "aged lady who is shaking her curls in the editorial chair of the Advertiser."

But such a judgment proved hasty. When the Hawaii Senate ratified the annexation treaty in September 1897, Armstrong declared, "The bolt has been driven through on this side. It remains for the Americans to put a lock nut on the other side. If the American Senate will take as cheerful and hopeful view of the act as we do, it will not delay responding to our quick ratification. . . ."

Annexation remained on hold in Washington until the Spanish-American War, which erupted on April 25, 1898, with the sinking of the USS *Maine* in Havana harbor. The war quickly took on a Pacific dimension because of the Philippines, and Honolulu's immediate strategic value as a midway coaling station between San Francisco and Manila virtually guaranteed annexation.

Still, some in Hawaii, including the *Advertiser*, waffled over abandoning neutrality, for fear of retaliation by the Spanish fleet. But President Dole quickly assured the United States of the Islands' wholehearted support.

On June 1 three Philippines-bound American troopships, preceded by the USS *Charleston*, arrived in Island waters. The next day twenty-five hundred troops established Camp McKinley in Kapiolani Park. Crowds welcomed "the boys in blue," and the *Advertiser* reported that "from end to end of the city 'Old Glory' floated from every housetop" in a bright glow of patriotism.[44]

The paper, which soon began sporting red and blue ink, joyously reported Hawaii was "in the hands of Americans," adding that "Hawaii covers the Boys in Blue with her leis of flowers and to them all gives her greeting ALOHA."[45]

When the first troops sailed westward, the June 4 *Advertiser* said, "So good-bye, Boys in Blue. Plant Old Glory in the Far East, not in hatred . . . but in the name of the enlightened people of the world."

July 14, 1898. Annexation and the Spanish-American War victory topped page one.

As the second troopship convoy dropped anchor in Honolulu, the paper not only welcomed it, but, regarding the Islands' status, asked, "Where are we?" The same issue reprinted a Denver *Rocky Mountain News* cartoon showing Uncle Sam pinning flags onto a world map while acknowledging, "By gum, I ruther like your looks."[46]

On July 7, Hawaii finally rated such a flag! Annexation was a reality. Breathing relief at the word from Washington, the *Advertiser* shouted, "IT CAME AT LAST."[47] The next day it produced a poem on page one that in part said:

And the Star-Spangled Banner
In Triumph Shall Wave
O'er the Islands of Hawaii
And the home of the brave

On Friday, August 12, a brief and simple ceremony transferred Hawaiian sovereignty to the United States. The American community watched and listened with quiet satisfaction and then cheered as the Stars and Stripes rose to the top of the pole at Iolani Palace to the strains of the national anthem.

For the few native Hawaiians present and the thousands who did not attend, as their flag was lowered earlier to the haunting notes of "Hawaii Ponoi," it was the tragic climax to decades of declining population, power, and pride. They felt dispossessed of their traditions and their values, uncertain of their identity, fearful of the future. As the *Advertiser*, which carried Old Glory in color on page one, reported: "To the Hawaiian it was pathetic. As the last strain of 'Hawaii Ponoi' trembled out of hearing, the wind suddenly held itself back" and the flag "descended lifeless. . . . No man who is a man escaped a pang of sentiment or sorrow when there descended from the State building for the last time the flag of a nation that has so long held an honorable and noteworthy place in the great family of the greater commonwealths."[48]

The banner over the *Advertiser* masthead that day proclaimed that "Hawaii Becomes the First Outpost of Greater America." But it would take two years—until June 14, 1900—before Congress established the territory of Hawaii, U.S. citizenship was conferred, and Dole was appointed governor.

On the eve of the transition, the *Advertiser* editorially assessed the outlook:

Our sugar can never be removed from the American free list. We are assured of the cable and of a naval station at Pearl Harbor. Capital, unless driven away by some unfortunate renaissance of fanatical politics, will flow hither in a steady and flooding stream. . . . We look to see Honolulu and Hilo in a few years' time as populous, respectively, as Los Angeles and San Diego. . . . Old Hawaii will vanish with much of its picturesqueness and charm of primitive racial customs; new Hawaii will come with the intense activities that mark the American commercial spirit.

On the first day of the territory, the paper declared:

We are now in the visible presence of American Hawaii. Back of it is aboriginal Hawaii filled with picturesque and poetic memories, but soon to be a
thing of tradition and romance. Behind is the garland and the song; before is
the whirr and rush of commercial life, a realization of Seward's dream of
Pacific Empire, a sound of hoarse whistles and rushing wheels at the crossroads of the ocean. . . .

It expressed the hope that "all true Hawaiians will put behind them the
old times of strife and dissension . . . and pulling together will look forward
with light hearts . . . to the Hawaii of the twentieth century."

At the same time, Editor Armstrong ran a balance sheet on the missionaries' performance in the Islands. Their major contribution was to establish permanently "a system of education, which has no peer in the tropics."

Armstrong separated those missionaries who had come seventy-eight
years before from the "trader and merchant of those days [who] robbed the
kings and debauched the women and demoralized the men with rum" and the
legions of whalers who "in search of oil, which was gold . . . threw away their
principles before they crossed the equator and believed the Devil reigned
under the Southern Cross," with only "churches, schools and good government" standing in their way.

It was education, he wrote, that "dispelled the fear of American statesmen that the native population would be a menace to good government,
though it might not be in itself sufficient for self-government." He credited the
missionaries with

planting of the institutions of civilization here although [they] could not
maintain them in their integrity. . . . The result of their works, valuable as it
was and is, is still disappointing, when measured by the standards erected by
their own hope and enthusiasm.

It was not strange that they failed to comprehend the conservative power
of the racial habits in mind and morals. What the value of the assets which are
turned over to the American people today, will be in a century, no one can esti-
mate. Another balance, struck off a hundred years from now, will show.[49]

Part III

1898–1931

12

An "Itching for Printer's Ink"

AFTER ANNEXATION, with Henry Castle dead, his relatives viewed the *Advertiser* as a burden and offered it to Lorrin A. Thurston for long-deferred payments without interest. Thurston, just back from Washington, where he had been the Island government's envoy, "had dabbled enough in 'Printer's Ink' to have an itching therefor, and eventually succumbed to the arguments presented thus having 'wished upon me' the ownership" of the *Advertiser* for a reported $5,000.[1]

Three and a half months later, on January 28, 1899, Thurston became president of the Gazette Company, the *Advertiser*'s parent. He brought, at age forty, a colorful and controversial career, with a pivotal impact on Island history. His character and his dynamism reflected his lineage. He was the grandson of Asa and Lucy T. Thurston, who had come from Massachusetts with the first company of missionaries in 1820. His maternal grandfather, Lorrin Andrews, had taught Hawaiian boys at the school at Lahainaluna, Maui, to set type, engrave, and print; he also translated part of the Bible into Hawaiian, produced a Hawaiian-language grammar and dictionary, and issued the first Island newspaper, *Ka Lama.*

Lorrin's father, Asa G. Thurston, who died at age thirty-two when Lorrin was a year old, had been an interisland skipper, operator of a small Kona coffee plantation on the island of Hawaii, and a government clerk in Honolulu. His mother, Sarah, at one time taught at the Royal School in Honolulu.

As a boy, Lorrin swam almost daily in the Kapena pool in Nuuanu Stream. The family moved to Maui after his father's death, and his first job for pay, at twenty-five cents a day, was during vacation on the I. D. Hall ranch; providing his own horse, he carried water to workmen on a fence-building job. In 1872 he came to Honolulu as a boarder at Punahou School, where he earned his spending money, including fifty cents a week for caring for the president's horse.

Once, with other boys, he hid and fed for several days two Portuguese, who said they had been at sea without pay for two years, until their ship sailed and they turned themselves in to police and got laborers' jobs.

He had a brother, Robert, four years his senior, who had been in charge of the Punahou carpentry shop. Robert cut his foot while reef fishing, it became infected, and he died at nineteen from blood poisoning.

Near graduation at Punahou, Lorrin was expelled by Principal Amasa Pratt, who gave three reasons. Lorrin on Sunday evenings had taken liberties in quoting a Scriptural verse reflecting on women teachers; on a stairway, he had kicked a bucket of water from another boy's hands and the racket it made in tumbling down the stairs disturbed the entire school; when he was instructed to rewrite a composition because he had used the ampersand (&) instead of "and" throughout, he wrote microscopically except for extra-large "ands."

He acknowledged the first incident, which was his response to a dare. As to the next, he explained the bucket had been accidentally kicked into the boy, who had taken a poke at him. He admitted the tiny writing on his revised composition but said he resorted to that, against which there was no rule, because the only criticism of his work was use of the ampersand. "Thus," he later wrote, "I 'graduated' from Punahou."[2]

Then, although he had hoped to be an engineer, he accepted an offer from attorney Alfred S. Hartwell to be his office boy, utilizing his knowledge of Hawaiian as an interpreter, while having the chance to study law. He received $4 a week, but got a dollar increase when he took on additional duties as jani-

Lorrin A. Thurston, a powerful and controversial figure in Island life from his earlier years, served as publisher of the *Advertiser* from 1900 to 1931.

tor. He also earned $5 a month "for pumping the organ at the Fort Street Church for rehearsals on Friday evenings and at two services on Sunday."[3]

In Lorrin's second year with Hartwell he was paid $600 and in his third year $1,000. When the attorney felt, after a stint as attorney general, he could no longer afford a clerk at that pay, Lorrin applied to and received from the court his own license to practice law and set up in Wailuku, Maui—where he earned $75 in his first month and $85 in the next.

He then accepted a job as head luna (supervisor) and bookkeeper at Wailuku Sugar Company at $125 a month, stayed for eighteen months, then took the $1,800 he had saved over four years and entered Columbia University law school in New York City. His classmate Theodore Roosevelt was to later prove helpful when Thurston had official missions to Washington.

After two years at Columbia, Thurston returned to Honolulu in late 1881, became an assistant to Hartwell and then a partner with W. O. Smith and W. A. Kinney, and spent the next several years building a law practice.

But his taste for politics remained strong, abetted by his training in the law. He served in the kingdom's House of Representatives, as interior minister in Kalakaua's reform cabinet, and as a member of the House of Nobles.

On February 21, 1884, he married Clara Shipman of the island of Hawaii, whom he had known at Punahou, and on February 1, 1888, she gave him his first son, Robert Shipman Thurston. On May 5, 1891, at the age of thirty-one, she died in childbirth, as did her infant.

In the 1893 showdown with Liliuokalani, Thurston "probably more than any other man" overthrew the throne and led the campaign for annexation.[4] But his opposition to the monarchy was not new. Gavan Daws writes that "as a fledgling lawyer with a strong sense of right and wrong, he saw delinquency, political and moral, all around him during Kalakaua's reign—the stuffing of ballot boxes and the selling of offices, the drinking of too much gin, the dancing of the hula, the smuggling and smoking of opium."[5]

Thurston wrote political columns for the *Gazette* and, during the 1884 legislative session, vitriolic editorials for the *Bulletin*. In 1887 he became the prime mover in establishing the reformist Hawaiian League, later the Committee of Safety, with muscle provided by the voluntary Honolulu Rifles.

He drafted the "bayonet constitution" stripping Kalakaua of excess powers, and once Liliuokalani was on a collision course with business leaders, he dictated the proclamation unseating the queen, ending the monarchy, and establishing the provisional government, pending annexation.

Once that was achieved, he shifted his energies to the *Advertiser*, becoming publisher in 1900, a year after having assumed the presidency of the company.

The editor, W. N. Armstrong, had stepped down on November 15, 1899, to be succeeded by Thurston's choice, forty-nine-year-old Walter Gifford Smith. In his farewell editorial, Armstrong said, "The average intelligence of this little community is higher than that of any community with the same number of

white citizens to be found on the Mainland." He added that Hawaii's location
and history had

> served to force the life of the community into conservative channels and
> have partially severed its intelligence from progressive action, excepting in
> the matter of public education. . . .
>
> The incoming editor assumes the serious task of commenting upon
> affairs at the time of a radical and final absorption of an independent sover-
> eignty, with an extraordinary mixture of races, by the Greater America.

He expected many major problems to be resolved in Washington, but
with plenty of local questions on which the *Advertiser* would need to "inform
and aid" its readers.

Smith, quite in contrast to Armstrong's "cultivated style," was a "swash-
buckling, soldier-of-fortune news writer."[6] But in his opening editorial he
pledged that "the conservative traditions of the paper will be respected."
While promising an effort to "add to the interest, variety and scope of the
news columns," he said it was not yet "practicable to make a metropolitan
paper in Honolulu. . . ."[7]

A New York state boy, a military academy classmate of artist/author
Frederick Remington, Smith was a National Guard captain at sixteen, a
Republican stump speaker at nineteen, a Cornell freshman at twenty-two.
Early in his career he bought an interest in the *San Diego Sun*, campaigned to
revive the declining lemon industry there, and was responsible for the 350th
anniversary celebration of Cabrillo's discovery of California. He came to
Hawaii during the provisional government to edit the *Star*, became active in
the Annexation Club, and was on the commission named by President Dole to
draft a constitution for the republic.

He returned to San Diego in 1894, but later that year, as a war correspondent, covered the Japanese invasion of China for the *San Francisco Chronicle*.
After peace, he declined a Chinese colonelcy and spent the next several years
as the *Chronicle*'s assistant city editor, then chief editorial writer, sandwich-
ing in lectures on his war experiences.

In 1899, he returned to the Islands and edited the *Advertiser* for ten years.
The time, the paper would later write, "was one of transition from the old Hawaii
to the new, and, journalistically speaking, it was exciting to a degree. . . . In
candor, in honesty, in devotion to high ideals and in utter fearlessness of expression, The Advertiser which Walter G. Smith edited was a paper in a thousand."[8]

In that yeasty period, the *Advertiser*'s top reporter was Albert P. Taylor, a
utility player who could cover anything but specialized in marine news. He
would go out to an incoming ship with the pilot boat, usually rowed by a half-
dozen husky Hawaiians, rummage around for mainland or foreign newspapers, and possibly grab a quick celebrity interview. Returning, he would dash
up Fort Street, turn into King, and once in the *Advertiser*'s office, between

Fort and Bethel, hand the papers to Editor Smith, who would parcel them out so staffers could capsule worthwhile stories.

Born in St. Louis, Taylor had become enamored of William Jennings Bryan's free-silver philosophy and worked in Washington for the Democratic Party during the McKinley-Bryan race. After Bryan lost, he went to Cuba, became an officer in revolutionary forces resisting Spanish rule, and was involved in an attack on sugar plantations near Havana. Arrested by the Spanish, he was threatened with summary trial and execution, but U.S. representatives in Havana intervened, and Taylor was freed on condition he not return.

Back in Washington, he was introduced in 1897 to Lorrin Thurston, who hired him as secretary in the annexation campaign. Once that was attained, he shipped to Honolulu and became secretary to Judge (later governor) Walter F. Frear, chairman of the commission to draft the Organic Act. Joining the *Advertiser* in 1899, he served intermittently for a quarter century.

Covering local news in those days depended on leg power. Although transportation was available by mule-drawn streetcars and horse-drawn hacks, the *Advertiser* had no expense fund for reporters. Taylor, in a 1930 reminiscence, wondered what "Walter G. [Smith]" would say

> if he saw the Advertiser's reporters today, hurtling off on a new story to the other side of the island in a high-powered auto, and returning in a few hours. The trip around Oahu, even 23 years ago by auto, was an all-day affair. What would he say if he saw a woman, an Advertiser reporter, stepping into an air-plane at Rodgers Airport [forerunner to Honolulu's present one] to be sent to Kauai or Maui or Hawaii to cover a story? Or what would he think of the morning edition of The Advertiser being loaded into an airplane and the bundles dropped on Maui and Hawaii one and two and a half hours later?[9]

But Smith didn't lack imagination. On July 2, 1906, he devoted a section of the paper's fiftieth anniversary edition to a vision of Honolulu on the same day in 1956. The "Balboa Hotel," fifty stories high, had three thousand rooms, "rates $5 a day." If you pushed a button, it would draw your bath. Electric waiters delivered meals to your room. "You press a button in any room and the News of the Day will be Told You from the Phonographic Tube." Page one featured an illustration of a dirigible with the caption, "Reginald Dillingham and bride in their new aeromotor," which he was driving. Mars would be flashing ideographs to Earth. And the *Advertiser* would bring out "hourly editions."

To Taylor, serving under Smith was "inspirational. . . . He waged war against whatever he believed to be detrimental to public interest, sparing no one when he believed he was right. . . . He had a code of ethics and he believed his reporters should live up to them. Of course, we were many types and temperaments, but we worked well."[10]

Once under the American flag, the Islands held a special lure for journalists, many of them with substantial talents. In the early years of the new century those who worked for a time on the *Advertiser* included: Herbert P. Williams, former literary editor of the *Boston Herald;* Frederick O'Brien, a city editor who later would gain fame for his novel *White Shadows in the South Seas;* the paper's first paid columnist, Will Sabin, who became noted for his poetry; John Fleming Wilson, who developed into a successful short-story writer; Henry Wadsworth Kinney, who wrote several novels; Allan Dunn, a scenario writer and magazine contributor; Herbert M. Ayres, author, poet, and athlete, who started the paper's sports page; cartoonist Ralph O. Yardley, who also did pen-and-ink illustrations; Wade Warren Thayer, who came from the *San Francisco Chronicle* on a promise of $25 a week, covered police and courts, then, having a law degree, passed the bar and in time served as territorial attorney general and secretary of Hawaii, had a successful business career, and became a national leader in the Boy Scout movement. Another *Chronicle* man, Fred Holsheiser, came in 1900 to organize and direct the *Advertiser*'s reference library.

One highly touted addition to the staff proved more of an embarrassment than an asset. Mortimer L. Stevens, who came from San Francisco in January 1900, had reportedly founded Alaska's first daily, in Skagway in 1898. The *Advertiser* welcomed him as "a notable athlete, a versatile musician and a traveler" in addition to his ten years of newspapering.

But less than a month later Stevens was making personal headlines. After reading an article in the *Republican* that he felt impugned the reputation of a young mainland woman, a childhood friend visiting the Islands, he went to the office of *Republican* Editor Edwin S. Gill. He asked if any follow-up story was planned. When he failed to get a response from Gill, who treated the matter as a joke, Stevens struck him in the face. Gill brought out a .38-caliber revolver, shot Stevens in the right leg, near the hip, then turned himself in to police. He was charged with assault and battery with a deadly weapon and released on $1,000 bail. Stevens was treated at Queen's Hospital.

The *Advertiser*, while not defending Stevens' behavior, editorially called the incident deplorable and said "an editor who would insult a defenseless woman . . . might be expected to shoot an unarmed man."[11] The *Star* called for law and order, but the *Bulletin* sided with Gill. The *Los Angeles Times* called Gill "a rash individual of the smart-aleck type" who "has succeeded in making himself ridiculous in more communities than one."[12] Several months later, Gill quietly left the Islands, his bail was forfeited, and the *Republican*, a money-loser, died. Stevens recovered, but it is not apparent whether he continued at the *Advertiser*.

When Thurston bought the paper it had neither a photography nor a photoengraving department. Business manager A. W. Pearson ordered engraving equipment from the mainland, and Carl S. Andrews, a Thurston relative, operated it. The first halftone engravings in local newspapers appeared in the *Advertiser* in January 1900.

The paper's first photographer was James A. (Jimmy) Williams who, at nineteen, began in 1902 and remained until 1931, when he resigned to take over the longtime photographic business of his father. Jimmy's younger brother, Alfred, joined him in 1903 and served until his death in 1934.

The more prominent of the two, Al snapped the Prince of Wales, Mrs. Teddy Roosevelt, confidence men, murderers, football stars, surfers, and statesmen, claiming they all looked alike to him since his aim was simply to bring back a good picture. He was a quiet, modest fellow but had no hesitation in clambering up a wildly swinging Jacob's ladder to photograph notables on an incoming ship. One experience he later laughed about was hardly funny at the time. To get a shot on the opening night of the Princess Theater, he and an assistant set up his camera on the roof of the fire station at the corner of Fort and Beretania Streets. As the theater doors opened, he fired his flashlight gun; something went awry, there was an explosion, and he and his helper were badly burned. But his primary concern was that the picture was blurred.

A future commercial photographer of some standing, On Char was an *Advertiser* newsboy at the time. Recalling those days when he earned $9 a week, and he and his three younger brothers helped support a family of ten, he said, "I used to sleep in a box [outside the press building] so I'd be first to get the papers when they came out. We used to buy 20 papers for 50 cents. We sold them for five cents, so for every two papers we sold we made a nickel. As soon as you'd finish selling them, you'd run back to the office and buy more papers."[13]

The *Advertiser* tried to give the newsboys stories they could shout about. One that ran for days was the infamous Chinatown fire. In December 1899, after plague had been detected and the Board of Health isolated the area and militia surrounded it, the *Advertiser* said that only burning would prevent a fresh outbreak of the disease. The Board of Health resisted until cases were discovered some distance from Chinatown. President Dole and his cabinet then urged drastic action.

On New Year's Day 1900 the *Advertiser* editorialized that its suggestions "that fire should take the place of rose water as a disinfectant were carried out yesterday in one part of Chinatown and we hope to see it speedily followed up in other parts. . . ."[14] But wind carried the blaze out of control. Flames obliterated thirty-eight acres, from the waterfront to Kukui Street and from Nuuanu Avenue to the stream at River Street, and some seven thousand Chinese, Japanese, and Hawaiians had to be housed for weeks in quarantine camps.

The paper wanted one part of old Chinatown converted into a park and another part "as a white man's business quarter," with "a new and sanitary Chinatown to be constructed somewhere in the suburbs. When this city reaches 100,000 population it must either have use of the old Chinatown for business" or encroach on residential neighborhoods. "We would rather see the Asiatics pressed back than the owners of Honolulu's most beautiful and stately homes."[15]

Another series that grabbed public attention was a spirited crusade against gambling and a suspiciously tolerant police force. One top-banner story related how the paper exposed and shut down "the Punahou [neighborhood] nest of gamblers."[16] Information sent to San Francisco police brought the response that the operator of the high-stakes game, one Billy Hurt, alias T. W. Allen, was a notorious swindler and cardsharp. He threatened to sue the *Advertiser* for libel, but then fled to San Francisco.

The paper followed up by publicizing "Commodore" Nicholas Weaver, who came to the Islands after being booted out of German Samoa for a land-fraud scheme. He, too, left for the coast. In exposing Hurt and Weaver, the paper indulged in a bit of back-patting, observing that it was the duty of the territory's leading newspaper to protect the people of Hawaii against such "vermin."

Most attention was focused on wide-open gambling in a soon-restored Chinatown, often with police passing in front of the known "dens" but saying they had no power to interfere. The most popular game was *che fa*, in which players picked one of thirty-six words on a sheet (e.g., dog, man, arm) and winners were drawn at random. An *Advertiser* reporter witnessed the way in which four out of five *che fa* "banks" announced the outcome, with dozens of bicyclists racing down principal streets shouting or holding aloft placards with winners' names, while police, said the paper, conveniently vanished.

While small games were raided, large ones were not, despite the *Advertiser*'s printing of pictures or descriptions of their locations. Several persons suspected of giving the *Advertiser* information were harassed by police. Deputy Sheriff Henry Vida acknowledged punching a former detective whom he regarded as an *Advertiser* "spy." A former police officer was berated by Sheriff Arthur Brown for presumably giving the paper information and was told he could expect no job in town.

Asked the *Advertiser*: "Has it come to pass in Honolulu that a man who is even suspected of helping the crusade against gambling must take risks of personal violence or persecution from the police?"[17]

Advertiser staffers themselves were not immune to retribution. Reporter Herbert M. Ayres was outside the fishmarket waiting for a car when a gambler exposed in a story that morning reviled him for "taking bread and butter out of his mouth." He aimed a heavy cane at Ayres' head, but the reporter caught it on his forearm, which spurted blood. Ayres knocked the man down while two policemen simply watched. The crowd separated the two, and one of the officers told Ayres he was looking for trouble and to make himself scarce.[18]

Several evenings later, six police officers in plain clothes stationed themselves opposite the *Advertiser* and appeared to be noting who entered or left the building. When a reporter drifted nearby they gradually peeled off.

Editor Smith, in a speech at the Methodist Church, charged police connivance with gamblers, intimating bribery, and urged widespread citizen action. "If our reform public bodies, our Civic Federations and antisaloon leagues and churches would meet the expense of a crusade on a large scale, as the Advertiser is meeting them on a small scale, every single public gambling game in Honolulu could be ferreted out and its owners and patrons punished by the courts."[19]

Acting on the *Advertiser*'s revelations, the Board of Supervisors passed a tougher antigambling ordinance, and the paper's campaign gradually wound down.

The *Advertiser*'s hard-hitting brand of journalism was not confined to the criminal element. In mid-1902 it zeroed in on the rival *Bulletin*, disclosing that when that paper earlier boasted that "every department was making a dividend," it had, in fact, mortgaged its press to a foundry for $1,357.50, with documents signed by W. R. Farrington and A. V. Gear. And it revealed that even the Linotype machine that set up the story of prosperity was heavily "plastered" (mortgaged) to the Mergenthaler Linotype Company. The *Bulletin* sued for $15,000, but the *Advertiser* ferreted out and quoted from the mortgage papers and the case collapsed.

Meanwhile, the *Advertiser* seemed to be doing well. Its New Year's Day paper that year had been an eighty-pager, put together in ten days without interfering with the usual fourteen- and sixteen-page daily issues.

On December 20, 1902, the *Advertiser* announced that as soon as the cable news service began from San Francisco it would publish the "important

December 29, 1902. The cable brings same-day news to the Islands.

telegraphic news of the world," including a special service from Washington. It observed that the full Associated Press service would cost $1,500 a day, exclusive of the AP franchise, and no paper in a community smaller than 250,000 could afford that. So it would try a column a day, costing $73,000 a year, and give that a fair trial. To help defray the new cost, it was raising the daily subscription price about a cent a day, from seventy-five cents a month to $1.

It also revealed that it would bring out a Sunday edition, to cost twenty-five cents a month, with the daily reader having the option of taking or not taking it.

When the cable began functioning on January 3, 1903, with a message from President Theodore Roosevelt, the *Advertiser* called it a great achievement, "the handmaid of commerce, the harbinger of peace [through better understanding among nations], the unifier of peoples."[20] Historian W. Alexander equated the importance of the cable with Captain Cook's arrival, Kamehameha I's union of all the islands, the arrival of the missionaries, the treaty of reciprocity with the United States, and annexation.

On January 4, the *Sunday Advertiser* was born, with eight pages filled with cable news, sports, society, waterfront and business news, and a new chatty but unsigned column, "The Bystander," which began taking cracks at the *Bulletin*'s "verbal poverty and infelicity."[21] There was a congratulatory message from Secretary of War Elihu Root on the cable completing Hawaii's "union with the people of the United States." On the local scene, a long story reported on a fire that did $160,000 damage to the L. B. Kerr dry goods store, the warerooms of auctioneer James F. Morgan, and the Coral Building owned by the James F. Robinson Estate.

An editorial said "the coming of the cable impressed most businessmen with the need for such a paper," and it gladly noted a "lack of dissent in religious quarters," attributed to "a broadening of the doctrine of Sunday observance." The edition sold more than six thousand copies, many being sent to the mainland.

A few days later, the *Bulletin*, always eager to target the *Advertiser*, said jurors in an assault case were upset and "indignantly objected" to a racial reference in the *Advertiser* that "only one white man" was on the jury after defense challenges were exhausted. This followed an earlier *Advertiser* comment that no Hawaiian jury ever convicted a fellow Hawaiian.

Prince David Kawananakoa and several other jurors refused to continue sitting, and the judge said he couldn't blame them. One juror, W. H. Wise, said, "We all know that the Advertiser has been running the country since 1893" and wanted to continue, but he wouldn't stand for it.[22]

The *Advertiser* said the intent of the news item was mistaken, and the *Star* added that some of the Home Rule Party leaders who were on the jury were making it a racial issue to inflame Hawaiians. Attorney General Lorrin Andrews ruled there was nothing in the *Advertiser* item on which a contempt charge could be based. He added that criticism of a jury could not prevent that jury from fairly weighing the evidence and deciding, so the jury remained and the case proceeded.

In March the *Advertiser*'s parent company began producing a semiweekly newspaper dealing especially with official, corporate, legal, and financial notices, called *The Official and Commercial Record*. Its rationale was that with seven daily and weekly English and foreign-language newspapers in town a businessman and lawyer had to read them all or miss information important to him. These notices were to be collated and printed in the new paper, Mondays and Fridays, for a $2 a month subscription.

Meanwhile, the *Advertiser* was promoting its growing library, with information on a projected thirty thousand prominent figures, worldwide and local, being filed for quick use when required.

On the first anniversary of the *Sunday Advertiser*, Editor Smith said that while there had been other Island Sunday papers, this was the first to get a firm foothold, building the largest circulation in the city's history, with the daily *Advertiser* second and the Hawaiian-language *Kuokoa* third. It had grown from eight pages to ten and would go to twelve if more advertisers realized the paper's value to them.

The paper's progress was gratifying news to its founder, Henry M. Whitney. But failing health was to fell him on August 17, 1904, a year after he relinquished the editorship of the *Planter's Monthly*, a Gazette Company publication, and retired from a press career bracketing a half-century. Editor Smith said Whitney "may be set down as the most influential citizen of Hawaii during his active journalistic life."[23]

Some months after Whitney's death, the *Advertiser* adopted a new and much more modern page-one masthead, the first since the paper's birth. Although the longtime engraving appeared "antique and rustic," it was to be preserved, since the drawing for it was done by Whitney from the sails of a ship that had brought him back to the Islands.

On July 2, 1906, the *Advertiser*'s fiftieth anniversary was celebrated with a heavily illustrated 120-page issue recalling the history of Island agriculture, politics, the military, whaling, religion, and other fields. An article on the Thurston-headed Gazette Company noted that the paper

employs a large staff of writers, maintains a library, takes the Associated Press night cable service and is illustrated. It is set by a battery of four linotype machines. The Sunday Advertiser, which is alone in its field, is regarded as the brightest, most original and enterprising paper in insular America, just as the [daily *Advertiser*] is the most progressive journal in that vast and populous region. The Gazette Company regularly employs about 100 men and women, has eight presses, the largest number of linotype machines known to any single publication office in Hawaii, the most complete job department and bindery and an efficient art department, with photographic adjuncts.

Ten years after Smith had covered the Sino-Japanese war, his sympathies with Japan were still remembered in that country. The *Osaka Mainichi Shimbun*, an important Japanese daily, wrote that Japanese residents in Hawaii "have come to consider the Advertiser as their own organ."[24]

But Smith's observations about the Islands during an extensive mainland trip presented a somewhat different picture. In an interview with the Macon, Georgia, *Telegraph* he said, "The Japanese [in Hawaii] are slowly acquiring commercial supremacy. . . . It is impossible for white labor to compete with the Japanese mode of living and workingmen and tradesmen are compelled to leave the islands." The only solution, he felt, was to attract white farmers, with the government augmenting private land with public. Should that fail, "we will be at a loss for an effectual way of fighting the Japanese commercially." He saw the "great population growing up of native-born Japanese" as threatening white domination of elections and voting "solidly for any policy favoring the interests of Japan."[25]

The same issue of the *Advertiser* that reprinted the Macon story also quoted a *Washington Post* editorial:

> It is a dangerous state of affairs when any integral part of the United States must call for American immigrants in order to save the Americans already there from being placed on a plane with coolie labor.
>
> The United States may be eventually compelled to govern a little Japan for the benefit of Japanese whose connections in peace and sympathy in war would be with Japan. . . . [But,] such a calamity will not be without its element of poetic justice. Americans wrested Hawaii from the people by force and fraud, and if only after a few years another darker race shall come into commercial possession of the stolen land, the Kanakas at least—the first to be despoiled—will unquestionably see in such a turn of events the avenging hand of fate.

In Binghamton, New York, Smith told the press there that out of a population of 151,000—65,000 of them Japanese—there were fewer than 8,000 whites and this number was declining while Orientals were increasing and those born locally would become voters. He added that they were entering all lines of industry and competing with the whites.

Smith's census figures of the Japanese posed the dilemma faced by other Islanders, especially the haole leadership. The very numbers of Japanese needed and sought for work on the labor-intensive plantations simultaneously generated frustration and fear that, in time, those locally born, plus those naturalized, would control the political scene and be partial to Japan.

On Smith's return to Honolulu, the rival *Star* interviewed him, and he reported that in Washington, accompanied by Ernest G. Walker, the *Advertiser*'s correspondent there, he found military men convinced that an American fleet would remain in the Pacific and that Honolulu and Pearl Harbor should be heavily fortified, thereby relieving the Pacific Coast of such a need.[26]

The Army also had its eye on the Islands. When construction started on what was to become Schofield Barracks, the *Advertiser* went way out on a limb: "Who knows?--it may be that there will be 20,000 soldiers stationed at the local forts at some future time."[27] What seemed a wild prediction came to pass not many years later.

In January 1907 Smith lost one of his most valuable staffers for two years when A. P. Taylor accepted the post of chief detective of the Honolulu Police Department.

A gutsy investigative reporter, he had been digging into Chinatown gambling and the subjects of his stories struck back. In November 1906 he had been arrested on a gambler's complaint that he had impersonated an officer and carried a deadly weapon. Since Taylor had been appointed a special policeman, the case got nowhere. The very next day, he and fellow reporter Roderick O. Matheson were arrested and charged with being found at night without lawful excuse inside the town's biggest gambling establishment. At trial, the prosecution folded, with the allegation against Taylor dismissed and against Matheson nol-prossed.

Some weeks thereafter, now detective chief Taylor made headlines when he captured a jewelry thief and recovered most of his booty, and again when he was put upon in "the Porto Rican part of the (Iwilei) tenderloin" by four Mexican seamen and rendered "partially unconscious by a blow to the base of the skull . . . and was kicked about the arms and shoulders" until uniformed police arrived and arrested two of the assailants, one of whom had Taylor's gun."[28]

When causing his arrest didn't work, the gamblers took a new tack. One Chinese "hui," or group, offered him $1,400 a week on an ongoing basis to protect its games and guarantee it a monopoly. It would give him a list of competitors and act as informers in securing the arrest of the players and operators. They told Taylor they had successfully bribed a previous police administration. Taylor clued in the attorney general, the sheriff, and *Advertiser* Editor Smith, who assigned Matheson to work with a detective. Taylor accepted a down payment from the gamblers; the police, who had him under close surveillance, closed in, and the bribers were arrested.

Taylor continued to be a popular target. A group of crap shooters injured his knee in a tussle, but he held on to the leader and the incriminating dice and got both back to the police station. Not long after, he was charged with assault and battery by a noisy police court spectator whom he had ejected and held at the station for twenty minutes. The man later unsuccessfully sued him and the sheriff for $5,000 for ill treatment and unlawful deprivation of his liberty.

Shortly before he returned to the *Advertiser* in 1908, Taylor's home was dynamited, but the nighttime blast, although close to the bedroom, left him and his wife unharmed. The *Advertiser* said Taylor was "feared and hated by every lawbreaker" on Oahu and the dynamiting was "the response of crime to his activity. . . ."[29] He returned to the *Advertiser* for five years, and even later in life his byline often appeared, mostly over historical pieces. He died suddenly in 1931, just after spending an hour and a half in the editorial rooms of the *Advertiser*, swapping recollections.

One of Taylor's legacies was his book, *Under Hawaiian Skies*, printed by the *Advertiser*, a colorful and comprehensive narrative of the Islands, which drew on his close relationship with members of former royal families and contained rare daguerreotypes of court beauties and prints of Captain Cook's visit.

When Editor Smith, because of ill health, left the paper and the Islands in September 1909 for San Francisco, Thurston wrote that he was "the best equipped and ablest all-round newspaper man who has ever wielded a pen in Honolulu.[30]

In early 1911 Smith returned to the Islands as editor of the *Star* and remained until the early summer of 1912, when after thirty years in journalism he assumed direction of Hawaii's tourism and other promotional activities on the West Coast and in Canada.

The *Advertiser* called it "a wise move and a good selection," and "The Bystander" column, bidding goodbye to Smith, took note of the merger of the *Star* and the *Bulletin* and welcomed its editor, Riley Allen. The same column sharply took to task local "patriots" who objected to an American of Japanese descent being chosen to read the Declaration of Independence at a July Fourth ceremony, reminding that the shapers of the Declaration and the Continental Congress "agreed unanimously that ALL men are created equal."[31]

Succeeding Smith was thirty-three-year-old Roderick O. Matheson, who had come from Ontario in 1904 and was night editor and editor of the Sunday *Advertiser*. At one point he left to be Governor Frear's chief clerk, but with the understanding that he would return on call.

In a farewell dinner honoring Smith, Thurston, and Matheson, hosted by the Japanese business community, Smith was thanked "for the fearless manner in which he had consistently upheld and defended the Japanese of Hawaii when he considered their cause a right one." In responding, Thurston said that Hawaii "now can no more get along without the Japanese than it can get along without the Americans, and I believe that we as Americans will profit as much by your presence here and by the presence of your children growing up as you will benefit by coming here to live amongst us and become Americans."[32]

Matheson quickly added a Sunday woman's page and expanded society coverage. On December 12, 1909, the *Sunday Advertiser* had thirty-six pages in five sections, hefty for those days. The following morning the paper carried a long story on its advertisers over the years, noting that "with the exception of [the ad] announcing the sale of the Isenberg property," the largest advertisement ever in the *Advertiser* was the day before, two pages for the Kaimuki Land Company.[33]

Matheson wielded a rather prickly pen and he was undeterred by the importance of a chosen target. In a 1913 editorial titled "Presidential Piffle," he needled President Woodrow Wilson, who, in addressing a joint session of Congress, referred to the Hawaiian Islands rather than the Territory of Hawaii and lumped them with Puerto Rico and the Philippines, adding that the Philippines merited more care than either of the other two. To which a disgusted Matheson wrote, "Oh, piffle."[34]

By 1913 the *Advertiser* had outgrown its plant in the Dimond Building on King Street between Fort and Bethel and planned to move to a new home nearing completion on King Street near Alakea. There, in a three-story reinforced concrete structure, it would have twice the old floor space. Designed expressly for the paper, the building was to occupy the entire lot between the offices of the Hawaiian Electric Company and the Occidental Hotel, and run clear through from King to Merchant Street.

An order had been placed for a new press with a four-thousand-copies-an-hour capacity that would print a larger, seven-column paper, as well as for additional Linotype machines, type cases, and a new style of type. The press would be on the first floor, along with job presses and paper storage, with editorial offices on the second floor, fronting King Street. The third floor would house the engraving and binding departments. Reserved for Editor Matheson was an enclosed room opening on an air shaft. The reporters had a better deal, with more light and ventilation. The city editor's desk in a full-view corner would enable him to keep an eye on his staff.

On Monday, April 14, 1913, the *Advertiser* made its bow "in its new make-up, issued from its new building, printed on its new press and with part of its

In 1913 the *Advertiser* moved again but remained on King Street through the 1920s, at first sandwiched between RCA and the corner building at Alakea Street. It subsequently acquired the rear part of the building, which fronted on Merchant Street. At the extreme left is the Hawaiian Electric Company. (Photo: R. J. Baker Collection. Bishop Museum.)

new dress. As soon after the Sunday edition had been printed in the old home, the composing room equipment was moved to the handsome new quarters. . . . Some equipment was still to come, delayed by a railroad interruption of three weeks on the mainland."[35] Somewhat later the paper acquired the adjacent stone building that still stands on the corner of Merchant and Alakea Streets.

In those days, recalled veteran staffer Jared G. Smith,

> we wrote our copy long-hand with pen and ink on daffodil-yellow work-sheets. The company supplied editor and city editor with Remingtons and A. P. Taylor, waterfront reporter, had his own. Lorrin A. Thurston, owner and editor-in-chief, used a pencil. His "copy" was interlined and corrected, blacked out with marginal inserts. Only one typesetter could get the hang of it and turn out legible galley proofs, which "L. A." again corrected.
>
> The *Advertiser* being a morning paper, we signed in at 1 P.M. and quit at midnight. The last [street] cars left King and Fort at set times, so from 11:30 on the office boy watched the clock and called the time. If you missed the last car, you walked home.[36]

As the paper was settling into its new home, Thurston felt it time to broaden its coverage, and he persuaded Smith, a Nebraska Ph.D., an expert on plant life in general and sugar in particular, to come aboard as agricultural editor. Smith had arrived in the Islands in 1901 to set up the federal experiment station, but after six years resigned to operate a tobacco firm at Kona on the Big Island. At forty-seven, he had no journalistic experience, but he was an author and poet as well as an authority on farming and soon was regarded as one of the *Advertiser*'s gems. He wrote lead editorials for six months, then branched out into every field except sports and society, and in time became financial editor for twenty-five years.

Retiring at seventy-four, and on pension, he continued to come in and write. He enjoyed cigars and always kept a metal spittoon by his desk. From an interview with Queen Liliuokalani he approvingly recalled that she was smoking a rich, black Havana cigar.

On one birthday late in his career when the staff presented him with a new typewriter, Smith rejected it; fortunately the trash collector hadn't yet picked up his ancient model. His younger colleagues revered him. A onetime news editor, William Hutchinson, called him the best writer in town, a crafts-man who could take the dullest subject and make it so interesting that fan letters poured in. Sanford Zalburg, a former city editor, wrote that Smith was "a warm-hearted man, happy with his work, happy with his fellow man," who used to tell others on the staff "it's been a wonderful life."[37] Elaine Stroup, a young reporter at the time, simply said he was one of the most remarkable men she'd ever known.

Smith's tenure at the *Advertiser* had stretched over forty-three years. Not far behind was Godfrey Alfonso, a contemporary with thirty-five years on the staff. Born in Portugal, he came to Hawaii with his parents when he was three, became a lawyer and legislator and editor of two Portuguese-language papers before joining the *Advertiser*. He covered police and courts and was sports editor when the great surfer and swimmer Duke Kahanamoku was in his prime and knocking off Olympic medals.

Many staffers, however, were short-timers who came, wrote, and moved on. Most left of their own volition, but not all. On December 16, 1911, the paper hired a new reporter, William G. Leonard, who it said had "worked on the New York World, the New York Herald, the Washington Star and Philadelphia papers. He was war correspondent for the Washington Star in Havana when the Spanish-American War broke out and represented that and other newspapers in Cuba during the struggle." He later served with the military in the Philippines and China and before coming to Hawaii had been "running a ranch near Portland, Oregon."[38]

In reality, Leonard was one William Francis Mannix, who had been fired from the *Philadelphia Press* for getting it into a million-dollar libel action. True, he had been a correspondent in Cuba, but most of his stories about atrocities there had been cooked up in a hotel restaurant. Spanish officials had arrested him and kicked him out of the country.

He became Leonard by faking letters of endorsement from West Coast clergymen. He was a smooth writer and something of a versifier, and the *Advertiser* much later was to observe that he "had a rather meteoric career in Honolulu and became known in a large variety of circles."[39] He also became known to the police when he forged a check and was fired. While jailed, he mixed fiction with fact in writing the memoirs of a Chinese statesman, Li Hung Chang. Houghton-Mifflin published it, and even though it was exposed and succeeded by an accurate version, the fake continued to be the better seller.

Pardoned by Governor Frear after some months, he continued hoodwinking the gullible, mostly through phony interviews with notables. Even his wife was conned by him. When in 1913 she quarreled with Mannix, sold the household goods, and sailed with her nine-month-old baby on the *Lurline* for her parents' home in Vancouver, he followed on the *Sonoma* and with a barrage of wireless messages effected a reconciliation and had her waiting for him on the dock at San Francisco.

The misdeeds of a Mannix were more than offset by the performance, at the paper and in the community, of such journalists as Walter Doyle, a colorful waterfront reporter, and Andrew Farrell, who worked on the *Advertiser* intermittently from 1915 until 1938 as a marine editor, sports editor, and territorial editor. He also compiled the three-volume *Memoirs of the Hawaiian Revolution* by Lorrin A. Thurston and Sanford B. Dole, published in 1936 by the *Advertiser*.

Tenure in the newsroom fluctuated, but the business side of the *Advertiser* was marked by stability. Charles S. Crane joined the paper in 1896, at age twenty-seven, as a clerk, rose to business manager succeeding the late A. W. Pearson, and remained for thirty-five years, retiring as executive vice-president. He turned to politics, was a Honolulu supervisor, then mayor and territorial senator. After ten years in California, he came back to live with his son Ezra, editor of the *Maui News* and an *Advertiser* alumnus, at Spreckelsville. He was a gentle and gracious man who complemented Lorrin Thurston's dynamic personality.

Another long-timer was George A. Seyde, who entered the paper's service as a bookkeeper in 1899 and, in time, became treasurer, a director, cashier, and chief accountant. A naturalized citizen from Germany, he came to Hawaii as a lieutenant in an Army engineering company that was bound for the Philippines but was reassigned to the Islands. In his forty years at the newspaper, he was at his desk each morning at six o'clock and for twenty-five years took no vacation.

Thurston and company aggressively pushed for circulation, and in 1914 the paper's daily figure was 4,610, up by 1,746 over five years. The Sunday issue stood at 5,985, going to "every responsible business house and English-speaking head of household in the territory."[40] Meanwhile, a special Newspaper Day Edition plugged Hawaii as "The Isles of Peace—No War; No Cold; No Storms; No Pestilence . . . Where Every Day Is June."[41]

The paper sought to bolster that image by campaigning for beautification. As early as 1905 it was fighting against billboards as an objectionable form of advertising. Seven years later it claimed "the day is almost at hand in this city when the billboard will no longer be respectable and when the only use for it will be to expound the merits of cigarettes and booze. When that time arrives the depressing effect of billboards upon real estate values will drive it wholly out of the residential sections of Honolulu."[42]

In 1913 it devoted an entire edition to supporting the determined efforts of the Outdoor Circle, an activist women's organization, against billboards. But it would take until 1927 to successfully pressure the legislature into outlawing them.

Another beneficiary of *Advertiser* backing was the annual floral parade in the early years of the century. An editorial declared that "no other city can present the same commingling of the races of the earth in (such) gorgeous national displays."[43]

13

From Streetcars to Volcanoes

LORRIN A. Thurston ran the *Advertiser* not only as chief executive but as a spirited writer, at the same time serving as a community promoter and builder. He helped organize the Honolulu Rapid Transit Company, which provided the city's first electric streetcars, and the building of the only standard-gauge railroad line on the Big Island. He had a hand in the establishment of the Pali Road, the shoreline drive between Koko Head and Makapuu Point, and the opening of Kapiolani Boulevard.

Because his missionary grandparents had settled on the Kona coast, Thurston had a special interest in the Big Island. He helped build the Hilo breakwater. As interior minister he had started the road from Hilo to the Kilauea volcano. He worked for creation of the Hawaii Volcanoes National Park, embracing the Kilauea and Mauna Loa areas and Maui's Haleakala crater, having enlisted the support of Theodore Roosevelt, his Columbia University classmate, and wilderness advocate John Muir. He felt the protected Kilauea area should not be just the crater and surrounding lava but fern and koa forests as well and carried the day despite the opposition of Bishop Estate and the Hawaiian Agricultural Company.

He was a prime mover in the establishment of a scientific observatory on the brink of Kilauea crater and was largely responsible for Thomas A. Jaggar, noted geologist from the Massachusetts Institute of Technology, becoming its first director. Thurston's personal exploration of the area led to the lava tube named for him. In the summer of 1911 he volunteered to help an understaffed team of two scientists register the temperature of Halemaumau, the key lava lake of Kilauea volcano.

As columnist Russell Apple tells it, "Thurston put his family to work. Thurston himself handled the reel that lowered the thermometer; his wife Harriet held the cable tight on its drum; son Lorrin [P.] shifted its coils; and daughter Margaret [with a flag] stood on the rim in heavy sulfur fumes to relay signals [from one of the scientists] down in the pit at the lake's edge." The temperature: 1,832 degrees Fahrenheit.[1]

Thurston had long been a staunch backer of tourism and in the late 1890s organized a company that built a hotel, forerunner of the Volcano House, on the edge of Kilauea crater. It failed to meet his expectations, and he sold his interest to George Lycurgus.

He favored entertainment for tourists, but not the kind of hula being performed. A signed editorial called the dancers "sweet-scented fakes" who "wheedle coins from sucker tourists" who think what they are seeing is authentic. His strong sense of missionary morality caused him to condemn the "salacious flavor" of "sinks of iniquity," language reminiscent of Whitney's decades earlier.[2] He was backed by the Hawaiian Civic Club, but Hawaiian activist Flora Hayes defended the hula as far more decent than the "cheek to cheek, bosom to bosom, thigh to thigh dances" of prominent Honoluluans on hotel roof gardens and aboard ships.[3]

In his editorial Thurston, who had headed the Hawaiian Promotion Committee, a predecessor of the Hawaii Visitors Bureau, asked whether the public wanted "the suggestive indecent hula to continue as one of our tourist assets?" *Advertiser* columnist Bob Krauss would later write: "Apparently the answer was 'yes' because the hula rapidly emerged from the underground and the tourist industry prospered."[4]

To help tourism, Thurston urged more advertising, more steamers, more hotels and plugged away for airport and harbor development. He and Benjamin F. Dillingham organized sugar plantations on Maui and the Big Island. He was responsible for setting up Hawaii's first combined charitable fund drive, the eighteen-agency United Welfare Campaign in 1919.

And with an eye to publicizing Hawaii, he helped bring the Press Congress of the World to Honolulu in 1921, drawing 108 publishers and editors from the United States and a dozen countries, from Greece to Guatemala. Duke Kahanamoku, showing his prowess as a diver, called for coins from the arriving ship, shortly coming up with a mouthful of nickels, dimes, and quarters.

Thurston enjoyed sports as a member of the Trail and Mountain Club and the Outrigger Canoe Club. A philatelist, he was also interested in conchology, and his Pacific Island excursions enabled him to build a one-hundred-thousand-shell collection, left to the Bishop Museum. On one of his trips, to Palmyra Island, he came across unclaimed Kingman's Reef thirty-five miles away, which the State Department erroneously said didn't exist, and announced he was annexing it and a tiny adjacent island for the United States. He was a fan of the Outdoor Circle and its work for beautification, and he also backed the group in its campaign to get women on juries.

As a goodwill ambassador for Hawaii, Thurston knew many celebrities, among them Jack London, who spent time in the Islands in 1907, 1915, and 1916, became enamored of the Hawaiians, about whom he wrote prolifically— and proudly regarded himself as a *kamaaina*, an old-timer, who enjoyed his Hawaiian name, Lakana.

As good friends, London and his second wife, Charmian, spent several weeks in 1907 at the Thurstons' home in town and at their Tantalus cottage, where Thurston marveled at London's work habits:

> After breakfast he would get a small wire basket in which he had numerous small writing pads covered with scribbled notes. These he would arrange in a circle before him on the dining room table and compile and write them up in shorthand. . . . He studiously and laboriously concentrated on his work until 11 or 12 o'clock when he suddenly would throw down his pencil and say with a sigh, "Well, my job's done for today."[5]

The Londons and Thurstons traveled together to Maui, where London was fascinated by the vast Haleakala crater. They relished each others' company, but Thurston subsequently took umbrage at London's short stories about lepers. The author was impressed by conditions at the Molokai colony, but his fiction derived from legends about exaggerated, often outrageous figures. His settings were the islands of Niihau and the Kona coast of Hawaii.

The *Advertiser*'s "Bystander" column, implying London had violated conditions on which he visited Molokai, labeled him a "sneak of the first water, a thoroughly untrustworthy man, and an untruthful bounder."

On January 7, 1910, from his California home, London fired back in a letter to the editor calling the columnist a mediocre reporter engaged in deliberate lying.

Thurston replied that while London's factual reporting on leprosy was truthful, his fiction exploited the agony and shame of a gentle and helpless people. This stimulated a lively exchange of correspondence which failed to resolve their differences.

Although London visited Hawaii four years later, at the peak of his world-famous career, and again the next year, there is no indication that the strained relationship between him and Thurston was mended.

But Thurston had far more to contend with than the unacceptable writings of a visiting author. Unsurprisingly, it was in the ever boisterous realm of politics. His first decade at the *Advertiser* paralleled the birth of the territorial government in 1900, of county rule in 1905, and four years later of the City and County of Honolulu.

Because the Organic Act, effective June 14, 1900, declared that all who had been citizens of Hawaii at annexation had become U.S. citizens, Hawaiians had a majority of the electorate. They formed a Home Rule Party, favoring "Hawaii for the Hawaiians," and took most seats in both houses of the first territorial legislature and elected perennial firebrand Robert W. Wilcox as the first delegate to Congress. Both the legislators and Wilcox proved irresponsible.

Early in the legislative session the *Advertiser* was critical of "laws loosely drawn, many of them in contravention of the Organic Act, all of them assisted in passage by men who cannot read or write the English language. . . ."[6]

After one term in Washington, Wilcox was defeated for reelection by Prince Jonah Kuhio Kalanianaole, who saw becoming a Republican as the best way to help his people and continued to serve until he died in 1922.

As to municipal government, the *Advertiser* as far back as 1878 saw it as needed to adequately provide local public services. As the 1900s got under way, Thurston tentatively leaned in that direction, premised on property and income restrictions on voting and his continued key role in the Republican Party. But once Congress insisted on unfettered suffrage, his newspapers took a fearful view of home rule and sought to dissuade those seeking to draw Hawaiians and some Portuguese into a "native party."

The *Gazette* bluntly declared that if color was to rule any part of the territory of Hawaii that color would be white. Both the *Gazette* and *Advertiser* urged the native Hawaiians to team up with the Republicans, who held power in Washington. At the same time, they sought to raise doubts as to whether Hawaii needed new layers of government, suggesting this would simply add new taxes.

The *Advertiser* continued to pound away at the home rulers as "malcontents and soreheads" and their party as a haven for the "weak or bad man,"[7] who takes to it "as naturally as a pig to the wallowing in the mire." And "in the science of government . . . they are children groping in the dark."[8] The Home Rule Party soon fizzled because of its own ineptness, and for decades the Republicans determined the territory's political fate.

November 5, 1902. Prince Jonah Kuhio Kalanianaole becomes Hawaii's nonvoting spokesman in Congress.

Legislation creating county government was adopted in 1903 but did not survive court challenges. And a new act, passed in 1905, with a gubernatorial veto overridden by the legislature, which then had to adopt remedial amendments, drew the wrath of the *Advertiser.* It said the lawmakers "passed a county act that no more constituted county government, as it is known on the mainland, than a king constitutes a kingdom."[9] But it was upheld in a court test.

After two Boards of Supervisors served Oahu, the new City and County of Honolulu government went into effect. The law enabling this, the *Advertiser* would much later contend, was passed by the Republican-controlled legislature because it anticipated the first Honolulu mayor would be Senator John C. Lane.[10] With splits in GOP ranks, however, a charismatic Hawaiian, Democrat Joseph J. Fern, a former Oahu supervisor, won the office by a slim margin.

The *Advertiser*, which went to press with eight precincts still out, precincts it was certain would go for Lane, carried as its page-one banner "Lane Mayor of Honolulu."[11] But the following day it had to eat crow with the headline, "Final Count Shows Majority for Fern."[12] The paper drew some satisfaction from a record crowd that watched election returns flashed from the *Advertiser* office on King Street, interspersed with lantern slides and movies. But its strong opposition to Fern and the concept of a democratic municipal government remained.

The headline the morning after Fern and the supervisors, mostly Republican, took office editorialized: "A Day of Official Burlesque Opens the new Municipal Government," with a sub-headline: "The mayor shows incompetence and the supervisors get things snarled." The accompanying story said, "If Noah Webster had listened to the mayor's inaugural address, he would immediately have issued an appendix to his dictionary." Supervisors, in working out rules and parliamentary procedures, "fussed themselves into wrong positions and made confusion worse confounded." The mayor's inaugural address would have been more effective, the paper said, "if he had been able to pronounce all the long words contained in it and had not substituted some of his own grammar for what had been supplied him." It noted that when the mayor finished, there was silence, no applause.[13] But Fern held the top spot from 1909 to 1915 and from 1917 to 1920, with John Lane finally winning it in 1915 for two years.

In Fern's final month in office, January 1920, he had several relatives on the city payroll, and the *Advertiser* took out after him and the supervisors, a majority of them Democrats, for "an orgy of salary boosting." The supervisors were held responsible for "a discouraging exhibition of incompetence, selfishness and political acrobatics." Qualified only "to manage a peanut stand," they were "squandering our money," paying salaries much higher than in private business to the mayor's chauffeur, three fish inspectors, and a milk inspector.[14]

But when Fern died unexpectedly in February, the paper used more gracious language. It noted his strong feeling for his people, as "a Hawaiian of the Hawaiians," so much so that "one of his false teeth was made from the bone taken from the skeleton of his grandmother and he wore cuff links that were made from bones of another ancestor." He was "a kindly, upright man, a credit to his race who did his best according to his lights." The *Advertiser* had "consistently opposed him because it did not consider him equipped for the position to which he aspired, but it always recognized his honesty of purpose, his respect and affection of so large a proportion of the voters that he was repeatedly elected chief executive of the city in the face of determined opposition." And his "political genius," the *Advertiser* acknowledged, "would have turned an old-time New York ward boss green with envy."[15]

When John H. Wilson, a Stanford-trained engineer and steadfast Democrat, entered the mayor's office, the *Advertiser* was soon on the attack. It charged him and his "Democratic political lieutenants" with treating city employees as their "personal chattel," pressuring them for campaign funds. It said the mayor might as well regard City Hall as his personal office building and rent out space for his own profit.[16] But at least the paper supported Wilson's effort to put phone and power lines underground.

In 1926, when for the first time in municipal history the Republicans captured full control of the government, headed by Charles N. Arnold as mayor, the *Advertiser* was ecstatic, with a headline proclaiming a GOP landslide. Editorially, it said "the citizens were interested in better government and continued prosperity." The Republicans had "put party principles as a whole above personal popularity and ambitions, preaching teamwork and harmony."[17] The morning after the election, scowling at an *Advertiser* reporter who asked for a reaction, a Democratic spokesman said, "We concede nothing. The Advertiser be damned."[18]

Even though the new administration, despite promises, raised taxes without cutting spending, the *Advertiser* before the 1928 election, calling Honolulu a "Republican city," praised Arnold's performance. But the electorate had other ideas and put Wilson back in as mayor.

Lorrin Thurston, despite his dyed-in-the-wool Republicanism, was annoyed when his party forced a well-regarded circuit court clerk, Democrat Harry Wilder, out of office to replace him with a GOP worker. He wrote: "This bald trafficking in public office for party advantage revolts the public conscience, . . . repels instead of attracting voters and weakens instead of strengthening the organization."[19] While "on political principles the Advertiser is Republican . . . it has not handed over its conscience or management to the local Republican machine."

But Thurston was considerably less than even-handed in his policy of covering the Democrats, who had no newspaper of general circulation in Hawaii. He didn't feel that fair play or community interests required the *Advertiser* to "furnish free space in which to advocate principles or measures with which it is not in accord," but did demand that those who differ in political opinion be able to buy space to present their views.[20]

He seemed uncaring that in foreclosing his news columns to political views and actions he disliked he was violating a basic tenet of journalism. The fact that he could have printed Democratic views and news and then ripped them apart on the editorial page obviously had no appeal. It was excessive partisanship that detracted from his role as a community leader.

Thurston essentially believed that municipal government, providing services such as fire-fighting, police protection, and garbage collection, should be nonpartisan. In 1925 he wrote that Mayor Wilson, a Democrat, "was unquestionably elected by Republican votes, because the voters thought he subordinated party to public interests. Ever since his election, however, he appears to have reversed that order and put party interest first."

He said, "Quit it, Mayor," act for the benefit of the whole of Honolulu "and not primarily as a wet nurse of the Democratic Party." He urged the Board of Supervisors to "forget, for a while, that you are Democrats and Republicans and give Honolulu the nonpartisan service which she sorely needs and is entitled to."[21]

During the 1926 political campaign, complete and unbiased news-column coverage was pledged, with opinion confined to the editorial page. But a month later the paper said that Democratic candidates had misconstrued that as urging an independent or split ticket. It declared that the paper was supporting the Republican ticket because its aspirants "were certain to be men worthy of the newspaper's wholehearted backing" and that its policy "met with the general indorsement of thinking people in Honolulu."[22]

In 1930, after a period of divided control at City Hall, George Fred Wright, a Republican, was elected mayor, and most of the supervisors were Republicans. Thurston used the occasion to admonish them to put public ahead of party: "One of the worst things which has accrued in Honolulu . . . with the establishment of American and city government here is the introduction and adoption of the spoils system."[23]

He was distressed that after every election the victorious party tended to sweep out all department heads of the opposite party so it could reward its faithful. Merit, not party membership, he lectured, should be the yardstick. Thurston's concern over what he viewed as the low state of Island politics was unrelentingly linked to his opposition to early statehood, an issue raised intermittently since annexation. In 1927 Thurston said, "I think Hawaii needs statehood as much as a cat needs two tails and no more."[24] He contended that presidential appointment of the governor and judiciary had worked well as Hawaii's "sheet anchor."

But in some other respects he was critical of Washington. In an article headed "Hawaii's Status in the United States. Are we in or out of the Union?" he objected to executive and congressional circles classing Hawaii with Puerto Rico, Guam, the Philippines, and "other possessions." Unlike the others, he argued, Hawaii was not a possession, neither conquered nor purchased, and had come into the Union by mutual agreement. But Thurston saw a growing crystallization of the view that Hawaii was "outside the Union," as witness its not getting money for roads and education on a par with the states.[25]

Fear of permanent discrimination led to a "Bill of Rights," drafted by Thurston, passed by the 1923 legislature, and signed by Governor Farrington, providing for a commission to secure more complete recognition of the territory's claims. Two years later this was buttressed by another act, the "Declaration of Rights," reminding that citizens of the territory were entitled to all the rights and privileges of American citizens, but some were being illegally and inequitably denied "free and unhampered passage" between mainland ports and Hawaii by the Bureau of Immigration.[26]

With Thurston as a consultant, a brochure was developed, citing chapter and verse on Hawaii's short count in federal funding. With a covering letter this went to the president, his cabinet, all members of Congress, governors, and private-sector leaders. The result was an increased flow of road, education, and other funds to Hawaii.

The *Advertiser*'s strong convictions on public issues, and Thurston's readiness to express them, could on occasion prove embarrassing. A case in point was a "Bystander" column that said native Hawaiians should realize that as a people they are dependent upon haoles for their education, food, and work, that they are regarded as children "who will never reach years of discretion."[27]

Thurston was out of town, but on his return he disavowed the column as uncalled for and distasteful. He observed that "in both legislative and county governments, the average Hawaiian has done quite as well and been quite as conservative as the average of his white colleagues." While some newcomers looked upon the Hawaiians "as an incubus, to be shouldered off the beach at the first opportunity," he said there was no such feeling among older residents.

Thurston called "The Bystander" column a "free-lance department, contributed to by various writers."[28] But it turned out that the column in question had been written by his own editor, Matheson. In an immediate open letter Matheson said he still believed he had written the truth and was not apologizing or retracting. It says something about Thurston's tolerance that Matheson stayed on for six years thereafter. The *Star*, declaring that the Islands "never had a better citizen or truer man" than Thurston, said he was speaking "from his neighborly heart and not from his discriminating mind."[29]

Thurston differentiated between the Hawaiians as a people and the monarchy he had helped to topple. In 1923 he took up the question of whether the Hawaiians are a dying race. He acknowledged the census figures showing that pure-blooded Hawaiians had plummeted from 142,000 in 1823 to 23,723 in 1920. He related this to the higher death rate, especially among children, because of bad living conditions.

Hawaiians, he wrote, had practically abandoned fishing and agriculture and country life to flock into Honolulu and the larger towns, "where most of them live in crowded, unventilated, insanitary tenements and shacks." Formerly plain and nourishing food had been replaced by an unwholesome diet in "cheap, dirty restaurants." To these negatives, he added "drink susceptibility, disease to which other nationalities have become partially immune; and immorality, incident to the crowded, promiscuous life in the tenements."

He suggested two main remedies: "Teach the Hawaiian women how to cook" and prepare proper food for their families and get the Hawaiians "back onto the land, where they will escape most of the moral as well as physical drawbacks of town life; produce simple, healthful food as the greater part of the diet; and raise their children in a healthful environment."[30]

On Christmas Day 1927 Thurston announced the demise of the weekly *Kuokoa*, the Hawaiian-language paper printed by the *Advertiser*, founded in 1861 and connected with the daily paper since 1898. For years it had the largest circulation in the Islands and for a long time was more profitable than the *Advertiser*. But its circulation had gradually dropped, and in 1926 it lost more than $4,000.

Thurston wrote that the "younger generation of Hawaiians, both of pure and mixed blood, get practically no information and little pleasure from reading Hawaiian. Many of them even speak it haltingly and uncertainly." But, with the older Hawaiians in mind, he offered free use of the *Kuokoa* subscription list to *The Hoku*, or *Star*, a small Hawaiian-language paper still published in Hilo.

While the condition of the Hawaiians was discussed from time to time, a much hotter subject, never latent for long, was "the Japanese problem." On this, as on so much else, Thurston had definite views, although they were not always in accord with what was being expressed in *Advertiser* editorials. As early as 1912 he labeled as a bugaboo any fear that the Japanese in Hawaii were a physical or political threat. Governor Frear, Benjamin F. Dillingham, Frank W. Damon, and a number of other leaders echoed his opinion, disclaiming any local peril, yellow or otherwise.

But the Japanese-language schools, with three hundred to four hundred teachers, mostly aliens, and twenty thousand or more students, constituted an issue that would not go away. Many Islanders favored closing them, and in 1919 the House passed such a bill, but the Senate killed it. When the next legislature was reconsidering restrictive legislation, Thurston warned that "the chief danger to the U.S. by citizens of Japanese descent will be by reason of unjust suspicion directed against their loyalty. . . . Engendering the belief among them that we do not trust them is . . . one of the most pernicious consequences of the present uncompromising demand for abolition of the language schools." He could think of nothing "more un-American . . . more inexcusably tyrannical than to make it a penal offense for a man to teach his own child his own language."

But he was on the Citizenship Education Committee, which insisted that the schools actively promote Americanism. The *Advertiser* said that while the direct object of the textbooks is to teach the children how to read and speak the Japanese language . . . the indirect object is to have the books consist of such material that the children will subconsciously absorb information therefrom concerning American life and institutions that will better fit them to become good American citizens. The two objects are not inconsistent.[31]

Thurston felt that the pending legislation might be softened by reducing the amount of time children spent in the language schools. His proposal for limiting such teaching to an hour a day or six hours a week, after public school, was incorporated in one of the two bills passed by the legislature in November 1920, regulating the schools so "Americanism of the pupil may be promoted."

In 1922 the Department of Public Instruction formulated rules for control of the schools, and Governor Farrington gave them the force of law. When a group of Japanese parents filed a court challenge, the *Advertiser* termed it a "seething agitation" and declared, "enough of the language schools."[32]

Thurston said "most emphatically . . . the fat will be in the fire! . . . This is American territory, dedicated to American principles, controlled by American citizens and it will be maintained as such, by the full powers of the American nation, against all comers and at all hazards!" He subsequently noted that "being in Hawaii not only with our acquiescence but on our invitation, the alien Japanese are our guests."[33]

But the U.S. Supreme Court ruled that the Hawaii regulations violated the federal Constitution: "The Japanese parent has the right to direct the education of his own child without unreasonable restrictions. The Constitution protects him as well as those who speak another tongue."

Editor Fred K. Makino of the *Hawaii Hochi* called it a victory not just for the Japanese but for Americanism and the U.S. Constitution, and he urged that cooperation replace hostility. The *Advertiser* responded positively, acknowledging that the high court had ruled "we had no right to do it, and that is that. We used a club—brute force. We said, 'You shall not.'"[34]

The *Star Bulletin,* however, said the issue was not finished, that restrictive language could be drafted within constitutional limits. Makino, while praising the *Advertiser* for sportsmanlike acceptance, accused the afternoon paper of jingoism and vindictiveness.

Thurston came to feel that time would solve the problem, and Governor Farrington thereafter shared that view "because the younger generation sees that the study of a foreign language must be secondary to a study of English, and that language must not be coupled with either religion or nationalism."[35] But that time was slow in coming.

14

Laborers "Cannot Run These Islands"

SUGAR WAS king in Hawaii, and in the early part of the twentieth century it was planted, harvested, and milled largely by Japanese labor. The Organic Act that broadened the electorate also ended the contract system on the plantations, dissolving the companies' legal authority over their laborers and removing a cap from worker dissatisfactions, which were quickly vented.

Annexation extended the U.S. ban on Chinese immigrants to Hawaii, placing a heavier dependence on Japanese, who in 1900 already totaled 61,111, or nearly 40 percent of the Island population. A planters' committee in the 1890s had described Japanese laborers as industrious, obedient, intelligent, and handy, but their main attraction was that they were cheaper and more docile than, say, white workers, had they been available.

The *Advertiser* shared the racist view of many planters that tough control was the best assurance of worker cooperation. Weeks after the Organic Act took effect, it said the way to treat discharged or runaway workers no longer obligated by contract to remain on the plantations was to "enforce the vagrancy law without giving the coolie much benefit of the doubt."[1]

During a 1905 strike of Japanese workers the paper said, "The plantation coolie is the lowest type of the Japanese race," quite different from those in business or the professions. "Offer him a compromise and he regards it as a sign of fear; yield to his demands . . . and he thinks he is the master and makes new demands; use the strong hand and he recognizes the power to which, from immemorial times, he has abjectly bowed. There is one word which holds the lower classes of every nation in check and that is Authority."[2]

During a Japanese strike of two thousand on Maui, police and workers collided in Lahaina. One striker was killed, three were wounded. *Advertiser* reporter A. P. Taylor said, "The Japs fired first."[3] An editorial charged that "the strike epidemic among the Japanese laborers is being nourished and spread by demagogues. A large number of Japanese, it is said, devote themselves to preaching discontent along the old familiar lines of the labor unions on the mainland. . . . It is a pity that there are not enough men of other nativity in the fields to replace them. . . ."[4]

The paper said that ever since they won the Russo-Japanese War of 1904–1905 the Japanese "feel on terms of equality with the whites."[5] Editor Smith, who had covered the Sino-Japanese War of 1894–1895, had the *Advertiser*, by arrangement with the *Hawaii Shinpo*, carry news of the later war in Japanese for the domestics in haole homes. The dispatches were of great interest to the Japanese aliens in the Islands since many of their sons under twenty-one were responding to draft notices from Tokyo.

The paper continued to hammer away that Japanese laborers were "making themselves conspicuous and dangerous by their insubordination, clamor, puerile demands and paroxysms of anger. . . . [They] must be taught that they cannot run these Islands, disturb agriculture and manufactures and initiate senseless raids, merely to suit themselves."[6] A day or so later a letter to the editor said that "because a thousand or more Japanese on one plantation show signs of violence during a strike, it is scarcely fair to say sixty to seventy thousand Japanese in Hawaii are doing so." It noted that the Japanese did not carry firearms and that only Japanese, not police, were hurt in Lahaina.

During a 1906 strike in central Oahu, the *Advertiser* asserted,

> A more obstreperous and unruly lot of Japanese than Waipahu is cursed with are not to be found in these Islands. . . . To discharge every Jap and put on newly-imported laborers of another race would be a most impressive object lesson to the little brown men on all the plantations. . . . So long as they think they have things in their own hands, they will be cocky and unreasonable. . . . Ten or fifteen thousand Portuguese and Molokans in the field would make a vast difference in the temper of the Japanese.[7]

The paper neglected to mention that efforts to attract workers of other races (except later, Filipinos) were unavailing.

In 1908, a group of Japanese who felt an industrial union, the Islands' first, was needed to coordinate strikes for better pay and benefits organized the Higher Wages Association. In May 1909 it triggered a major strike, primarily against a wage differential favoring haole overseers and mechanics against Japanese counterparts. Earlier, the *Advertiser* had denounced the *Nippu Jiji*, "the Japanese yellow journal of Honolulu," which supported the Higher Wages Association, vilified the sugar planters, and urged violence against the editors of the rival *Shinpo* and *Chronicle*, which it called "the planters' 'dog' and 'pig.'"[8] The *Nippu Jiji* accused the other papers of putting obstacles in the way of getting higher pay for workers. Its editor was indicted by the territorial grand jury as "a dangerous and disorderly person" who was encouraging injury to Editor S. Sheba of the *Shinpo* and his family.

Some months later a Japanese court interpreter badly wounded Sheba with a knife, calling him a traitor to his people. The *Advertiser* blamed the stabbing on Higher Wages Association "incendiarism" and said "the reckless teachings of the Jiji and the . . . association aroused within [the stabber] the fanaticism that lies latent in the breast of nearly every Japanese."[9]

Several Japanese journalists were fined and sentenced to ten months in prison. Years later Governor Charles J. McCarthy said, "The planters, through their attorney in Hawaii, steamrolled those Japanese—the leaders—put them out of business and they put some of the leaders of this strike in jail."[10] The strike was crushed, but wages and working conditions were improved.

In 1909 the *Advertiser* headlined "High Wage Conspirators Stir Up a Strike at Aiea Plantation" and said a walkout by fifteen hundred laborers for a pay increase was backed by "main agitators of the so-called Higher Wages Association." The governing body of that group was described as a "gang of malcontents and grafters," backed by an incendiary Japanese-language paper.[11]

But even as inflammatory editorials were appearing in his paper, Thurston personally was preaching a far different text. In an essay to the Social Science Association he was urging more humane treatment of sugar workers. He said many leave because there is "little home feeling." Workers were housed in barracks, in space so small "that there can be little privacy." They were used in "gangs," not viewed as individuals, and shifted from field to field. The remedy: give the worker "something to stay for." Mainland workers were being offered higher wages than Hawaii could afford, he said, so "we must offer counter-inducements, other than wages."

He favored giving or selling the laborers in fee a piece of land conditioned on working for three years. The laborer could create a home, raise food for his own use, a place where he could feel secure as an individual. He felt workers should get a larger percentage of profits and a longer-term contract.[12] The Japanese-language paper *Yamato Shimbun* praised Thurston's plan as a way to win laborers and their families to the soil.[13]

An executive of one of the Islands' largest corporations, C. J. Henderson, later wrote in some awe, "Here we have a community leader calling on industry to give away land, reduce profits, concern itself with the happiness of its labor force. Time has marched on."[14]

For a decade after 1909 there was little overt unrest on the plantations, but the turbulence was building below the surface and in 1920 it erupted. As a result, for much of the 1920s anti-Japanese hysteria wracked the Islands, triggered by plantation strikes and fueled by inflamed commentary by the *Advertiser* and the *Star-Bulletin*.

The *Advertiser*'s top headline on January 20, 1920, warned: "Japanese Cane Workers Threaten General Strike," with the story saying they would join Filipinos who had already walked out. While it quoted instructions to members of the Federation of Japanese Labor saying their position and intentions were legal and orderly, the paper said this was not a legitimate strike over pay and living and working conditions, but the result of an alien conspiracy to gain control of the sugar industry, Hawaii's lifeline.

The alleged plotters were the Japanese press, the language-school teachers, and the Buddhist priests from plantation temples. Labor organizers were really "agitators" and it was darkly intimated that wires were being pulled by those high in the Japanese government.

With all Oahu plantations shut down, the *Advertiser*—under the heading, "Shall Hawaii Be American or Alien?"—said the real question was whether Hawaii "is . . . to be an American territory or an Oriental province? . . . Is Hawaii to be dominated by American citizens or by aliens?"

The Filipino strikers were "mere cat's-paws, used by wily Japanese agitators to further the interests of the subjects of the Mikado and particularly the interests of the agitators. . . . The strike is merely being used by a dangerous set of aliens to hoist themselves into power. They must not be allowed to succeed."[15]

And a few days later: "Is Hawaii to be ruled from Tokio? . . . There is no question that a bold attempt is being made to Japanize these Islands. . . . This brazen attempt to defy American law, American customs and the American people must be smashed before it goes any further."[16]

This editorial was followed by one reiterating that the strikers must be crushed, since their goal was "in line with Japanese policy wherever they colonize," whether in Manchuria, Eastern Inner Mongolia, Shantung or Formosa. "They evidently fail to realize that it is one thing to bluff, bulldoze and bamboozle weak Oriental people and another thing to try to coerce Americans." The real issue, it cautioned, "is the future of Hawaii and it touches every person in Hawaii."[17]

February 23, 1920. Japanese workers' demands for better wages and working conditions were pictured as a conspiracy to dominate the economy.

The *Star-Bulletin* took the same racist line that agitators were seeking absolute control of the territory's twenty-five thousand Japanese plantation workers and if "they could gain the point they would be completely the masters of Hawaii's destiny as if they held title to the land and the growing cane. They would be the autocratic dictators of Hawaii's industrialism. . . . Is control . . . to remain in the hands of Anglo-Saxons or is it to pass into those of alien Japanese agitators."[18]

The *Advertiser* urged that with Oahu plantations tied up, financial support for the strikers from Neighbor Island laborers, still on the job, be cut off by a "lockout of all the Japanese and Filipinos."[19] A little later it sought to pressure acting Governor Curtis Iaukea to ask Washington to send armed forces against the strikers. But he took a neutral stance, convinced "that the racial issue has been deliberately emphasized to cloud the economic issues."[20]

Meanwhile, the *Advertiser* was campaigning for a return of Chinese laborers, who were barred by federal statute: "It's time to stop pussy-footing and say right out loud that what we want is a modification of the Chinese Exclusion Act to permit us to import Chinese for our agricultural industries."[21] Governor McCarthy went to Washington to push the idea, but without success.

The irony is that not many years earlier the *Advertiser*, along with other opinion-makers, was declaring a pox on the Chinese as unacceptable troublesome laborers and characterizing the Japanese as the perfect plantation worker, industrious but docile. The reality is that what the plantations wanted in their work force had not changed much over the decades: "People who were accustomed to subordination, to permanency of abode, and who have modest expectations in regard to a livelihood."[22]

The 1920 strike, in which attrition, police harassment, and criminal prosecution took its toll, ended after 165 days in defeat for the strikers. But not long afterward pay was increased and living conditions were improved. Unionism was slowly taking root, but when the Japanese labor group sought to affiliate with the American Federation of Labor, the *Advertiser* warned that this would enable plantation workers to penetrate other labor elements and asked: "Do you want a little brown man as conductor on your [street] car, to give you the signals and dictate to you?" Haole labor, it said, wouldn't stand for it.[23] The national AFL was wary enough to reject the Islanders' request.

In 1921 the *Advertiser* participated in a decision to send a high-level delegation, chaired by Walter F. Dillingham, to further push for a resumption of Chinese importation. He argued before a U.S. Senate committee that this was essential to blocking Japanese control. When asked why white labor wouldn't do, he replied: "When you are asked to go out in the sun and get into the cane brake, away from the tropical breeze, you are subjecting the white men to something that the good Lord did not create him to do. If he had, the people of the world, I think, would have a white pigment of the skin, and not variegated colors."[24]

That same year the legislature moved to "regulate" the Japanese newspapers. The bill was sponsored by the American Legion, which contended that the foreign-language press was so bellicose, so intent on fomenting opposition to authority, it had to be checked.

The *Star-Bulletin*, in agreeing, viewed the bill as a "protection of Americanism . . . against the insidious propaganda of hostile aliens."[25] But Lorrin Thurston opposed, saying that with U.S.-Japan relations "in a critical stage" this measure could be disastrous.

> The two countries are rapidly drawing near to a point where anybody with half an eye can see that they may soon be at war. And if war comes, it is Hawaii that will get scorched first, and badly scorched. A Japanese warship that could get within range of Honolulu would be justified in shelling this city. This is war.
>
> It would be almost a military necessity to take all the Japanese here and coop them up somewhere. . . . And what would happen to this town if all the Japanese were cooped up over in Molokai?
>
> But that's what's coming, what may come, if we put so much as one matchstick more on this pile of fuel waiting to burst into flames. I believe it is God's word I am speaking.[26]

Thurston agreed that some Japanese papers had "been publishing incendiary matter," but he felt the solution was not restrictive legislation but for the government to hire a qualified translator who would scan the papers and bring to the governor's attention those articles he should see. The governor, in turn, would place translations of such stories and editorials in a file that the public could read.

The Central Labor Council also weighed in against the bill as prohibiting free expression of honest opinion, but, with some last-minute amendments, it passed and Governor McCarthy signed it. It stated that publication in any language of articles tending to inflame racial prejudice or incite the commission of violence, sabotage, rioting, incendiarism, and sedition was a misdemeanor, punishable by fines and imprisonment. Publishers of foreign-language papers would have to file with the attorney general a copy of each issue and a translation of any article relating to the government of the United States or Hawaii or to any racial, industrial, or class conditions. In addition to newspapers, the law covered books, magazines, and pamphlets.

The legislature neglected to provide any funds for enforcement, however, and Attorney General Harry Irwin, who reportedly would have needed two translators full time to scan the foreign-language press, said this nullified the law's usefulness.

In 1924 a Kauai strike, mostly of Filipinos, turned violent, and at Hanapepe gunfire and knife assaults between police and workers left twenty killed—sixteen strikers and four policemen. The anti-Japanese feeling, which the dailies had kept burning, flared wildly. The *Advertiser* flatly declared, "This strike of Filipinos is backed by the Japanese, half openly here [in Honolulu], altogether secretly" on the plantations.[27] The Japanese, in fact, had stayed on the sidelines, albeit sympathetically. The *Star-Bulletin* swung even more recklessly, contending that Japanese support was augmented by "a heterogeneous group of 'reds,' 'pinks,' and 'yellows'—'wobblies' and communists and cracked-brain demagogues . . . doing their bolshevik best to turn Hawaii into anarchy."[28]

That same year Congress adopted the Japanese Exclusion Act, formalizing what had been a gentlemen's agreement between the United States and Japan, and Hawaii continued to search elsewhere for labor. The Philippines proved a fruitful source, supplying more than one hundred thousand workers by 1932.

Advertiser policy, whatever the nationality of the workers, remained on the side of the sugar interests.

"Blood Calls for Blood"

WORLD WAR I saw little military action in the Pacific, but it did have an impact on Hawaii. As early as 1914 the Islands began contributions to the Allied cause, with a food production and conservation program, a strong financial outpouring for Liberty Loan drives, and the sale of war savings and thrift stamps, involving not only adults but an "army" of schoolchildren as well. Some youngsters raised money to buy stamps by selling subscriptions to the *Advertiser.* And early on, the *Advertiser* and other newspapers solicited funds to assist Allied war widows and orphans, with printed acknowledgment of those contributing.

The newspapers also helped create and maintain an environment of fervent patriotism, sustained by the presence of a number of German ships, including the gunboat *Geier,* which sought a neutral haven in Honolulu's harbor. There was fear that their skippers would sink their own ships at the harbor entrance, thus blocking it, or blow them up at the piers, wrecking the facilities. But Washington declined action until Congress adopted a war resolution on April 5, 1917, then ordered the ships seized and, with any damage repaired, put into American service. The *Geier's* officers and crewmen were the first prisoners of war captured by the United States.

Despite the official U.S. neutrality between the summer of 1914 and the spring of 1917, there was no doubt where America's sympathy lay. Honolulu's German community—several hundred naturalized citizens and a roughly equal number of aliens—grew increasingly nervous.

Two years before the United States entered the war, the Honolulu branch of the National German American Alliance of the U.S.A. had complained to Lorrin Thurston that the *Advertiser* was "unfairly suppressing news to the disadvantage of the German interests." Thurston wrote a long, signed response that called the criticism untrue and stated the *Advertiser* had not yet taken "a positive editorial attitude" on the war. The reason:

> This is an isolated community, closely knitted together by ties of blood, marriage, business, political and social relations. It is an American community,

but the Germans and the British have both taken a most active part in building it up, socially, economically and politically. Side by side with the Americans, the Germans and the British . . . are an integral part of the bone and sinews and brains of this Territory. . . .

    In this small community . . . it is essential to the public welfare that every intelligent resident, irrespective of nationality, should cooperate for the common good. . . . [Despite] the fact that nearly every British and German resident of Hawaii has relatives "at the front," some of whom have already delivered the "full measure of their devotion" in support "of the right as they see it," . . . cooperation in local affairs on an at least outward friendly basis has been maintained during the past fourteen months of tension. . . . [a tribute] to the self-control and the level-headedness of the local representatives of the nationalities named, as well as of others who have strong convictions.

He then detailed some of the difficulties involved in giving an impartial and reasonably complete news report in a small paper eight to ten thousand miles from the scene. "The Advertiser is faced with a beer circulation and financial resources, and a reading constituency with a champagne appetite for war news. During the early months of the war the Star-Bulletin and the Advertiser were put to a joint expense of $2,800 to $3,000 a month for cablegrams alone—a prohibitive expense for 'country newspapers.'" Thus, only a skeletonized service was possible and that of only the major events. Beyond that was "the most rigorous censorship the world has ever known." News of most importance to sympathizers with Germany had not only "to run the gauntlet of the German censor, but is subject to deletion by the Allied censors as well."

The *Advertiser* had "republished innumerable articles by distinguished German scientists, public officials and sympathizers in support of the German contentions." There was a standing offer to the local German consulate that any news dispatches from it or the German embassy in Washington were welcome, limited only by space.

Thurston concluded by noting that officers of the German American Alliance were invaluable community members and a number were lifelong friends of his—and that the *Advertiser* had no reason to deal unfairly with them or their cause.[1] There is no record of whether this mollified the German residents.

But by early 1917 the *Advertiser* was openly eager to take on the "Teutons." On March 1, when a German plot to bring about an alliance with Mexico and Japan for an invasion of the United States was revealed, the paper declared that unless "there is nothing this side of hell that is too gross and insulting for our government to swallow in craven spirit, war will be declared upon Germany today."[2] Congress the next day granted the president extraordinary emergency power but stopped short of a war resolution.

On April 3, with the Associated Press reporting five Hawaiians among sixteen Americans believed drowned when the armed steamer *Aztec* was sunk without warning by a German U-boat off the coast of France, the *Advertiser* headed its editorial response "Blood Calls for Blood." It believed the news "will steel the arm of this nation and heighten resolve that there will be no laying aside of the sword until . . . the might of Prussia [is] humbled and rebuked in the one way Prussianism is capable of understanding. . . ." And it said "it should stir this community from its almost sluggish apathy," a misstatement given the community's active involvement in a wide spectrum of war-related programs.

When two days later the desired congressional action came, the paper, anticipating the action, had a single-page extra on the streets within minutes of the AP flash. More than two thousand copies were snapped up. The paper also quickly informed Governor Lucius Pinkham and military officials, and naval censorship was imposed on wireless and cable messages. On April 6 the *Advertiser* called it "a just war."

Some days later, when a party of German diplomats ousted from China was due to arrive on a Dutch ship, the *Advertiser* said they ought to be kept strictly to their ship and "then, after they have sailed, we should fumigate the waterfront."[3]

With U.S. entry into the war, there was an enthusiastic response from men of the Islands. Thousands registered for service on a designated day, and the *Advertiser* reported that they did so with a shout of joy at the opportunity to do something. Some ninety-five hundred Islanders saw active duty in the Army or Navy, with another two hundred in the British army, and more than one hundred died in service.

March 31, 1917. The United States moves inexorably toward a declaration of war against Germany.

When the first volunteers sailed, the *Advertiser* said that

Hawaii's roll of honor was lengthened by thirty-four names yesterday when
just that many red-blooded Americans, nearly all Hawaiian born, left
Honolulu to be placed in regiments believed to be ready for service in France,
followed by the strains of Aloha Oe and the cheers of hundreds of people
who packed the street in front of the wharf.

Every man in the company of volunteers was below draft age, some just
eighteen, none above twenty-one, and all volunteered in order to get to the
front as soon as possible. Every youth resembled a human flower garden, so
covered with leis as to be almost hidden. They responded to the cheers of
friends by singing battle songs and the melodies of Hawaii nei.[4]

Public attention was briefly diverted from the war by the death in
November of Queen Liliuokalani. On the day of her funeral the *Advertiser*
headed its editorial column with a poem, "Aloha Never Dies." Inscribed to her
late majesty by Philip Henry Dodge, the final verse said:

It is closed the royal chapter
Now in history it lies
Let it be Hawaii's legend
That aloha never dies.

An accompanying editorial noted that "some prominent in the funeral
cortege had been amongst those whose power wrested the scepter from her in
the days gone by, by their presence testifying to the universal respect the queen
had won in her latter years." And it said "her influence she exercised to induce
[the Hawaiians] to prove as steadfast and as loyal to the Flag—which fate had
forced upon them—as they had been previously to the flag which once waved
over Iolani and withstood the political storms of a hundred years."[5]

This spirit of aloha did not extend to the German presence in the community, which created high tension. In a public infused with patriotic zeal, many
regarded all residents of German blood as possibly disloyal and therefore to
be kept under close scrutiny.

The *Advertiser* had urged placing guards at the city water system, but it
took the discovery of typhoid germs in the Nuuanu water supply before this
was done, first with troops, then police. Suspicion of sabotage was intensi-
fied, despite a similar lack of evidence, in the finding of anthrax in several
Island cattle herds.

Anti-German sentiment was further fueled when George Rodiek, a key
executive in H. Hackfeld & Company, the Islands' largest enterprise, as well
as president of the Hawaiian Sugar Planters' Association and a former
German consul, was charged with involvement in a fanciful German plot to
overthrow British rule in India. He pleaded guilty to violating the neutrality
laws. He was fined and stripped of American citizenship, which was restored

some years later. Another Hackfeld man, a former consulate secretary, was accused in the same case and fined.

About this time, a series of *Advertiser* ads carried sermonettes under the pen name of "Dixie Doolittle." One questioned whether J.F.C. Hagens, a German-American, should continue as president of the Chamber of Commerce, although it acknowledged his loyalty to the United States. He refused to resign but did give up his vice-presidency of Hackfeld.

After President Wilson signed the Trading With the Enemy Act on October 17, the German-owned Hackfeld properties were seized, and the company's assets were sold to Island firms. Creating a patriotic image, the company became American Factors, Ltd., and the name of its department store was changed from B. F. Ehlers & Company to Liberty House.

Advertiser Editor Matheson did not confine his suspicion of disloyalty to those of German descent. He even targeted Governor Pinkham for what he felt was his lukewarmness toward America's entry into the war. Pinkham, in a June proclamation calling for a children's assembly, which he addressed, said "the United States of America through its representatives in Congress has decided it to be its duty and interest to take an active and leading part in this war. Its citizenship accepts the responsibility for all the cost in lives, tragedy and treasure."

In an editorial titled "Under What Flag?" Matheson called this a "gross misstatement" of the position of the United States and said the proclamation smacked

> almost of pro-Germanism. . . . Not a peep about suffering Belgium, ravished France, our own murdered citizens, our cause in the name of democracy against Hohenzollern tyranny, a Hindenberg butchery and a Zeppelin slaughter of the innocents. If "our Governor" cannot talk like a red-blooded American, why in Heaven's name does he insist upon talking at all?

He suggested that Pinkham let others talk who "have no mental reservations about the justice of our cause."[6]

Four days later Matheson was arrested in his quarters at the Seaside Hotel in Waikiki on a warrant charging him with criminal libel. The complaint, signed by City Attorney Arthur M. Brown, said Matheson was "a person of malicious evil and wicked mind" who brought Governor Pinkham "into disgrace, abhorrence, odium, hatred, contempt and ridicule."[7]

There was no affection lost between Brown and the *Advertiser*, which for years had attacked him for laxness, or worse, in ignoring big-scale gambling and having close ties to some of its key operators. Back in 1904 Governor George R. Carter had summarily ousted Brown, a fellow Republican, from his post as high sheriff for failure to enforce laws against gambling and illicit liquor sales, but for much of the time since, Brown had continued to hold public office by election or appointment.

In the current case, Defense Attorney Lorrin Andrews said Matheson had simply commented upon a public official in his official capacity. The city attorney's office, which had brought the action on its own initiative, argued that any published criticism of a public official was libelous under Hawaii's statutes. Two months later Circuit Judge William Heen threw out the case.

In June 1919 the *Advertiser* endorsed Democrat Heen in his race against Brown, seeking reelection, for the city attorney's post. An aide to Brown, Harry Terence Lake, brought a criminal libel case against Publisher Thurston and his new editor, Edward P. Irwin, because of Thurston's response to a published letter from a well-known Republican, W. O. Smith, supporting Brown. Thurston said Smith typified the "good citizen" who makes possible "the proverbial rottenness of American municipal politics by blindly voting the straight ticket" without regard to the record or qualifications of candidates."[8] Lake's complaint was that he feared Thurston's language might cause Brown to be "excluded from society."[9]

Editorially, the paper said if Brown "has any notion that he can bluff the Advertiser by filing actions for criminal libel against its editor and president of the company, he's barking up the wrong tree."[10]

Heen won and, in losing, Brown brought down with him most of the Republican ticket for mayor and supervisors. Lake's case got nowhere.

Matheson's anti-German emotions spilled over into his community activities. He served on a committee to carry out a mass meeting's resolution that persons sympathetic with Germany and who expressed disloyal or unpatriotic wishes should be taken into custody for the rest of the war, but the Justice Department in Washington declined to set up an internment camp.

Thurston stuck to higher ground, chairing a committee for establishment of an Army-Navy Y.M.C.A. This finally led to purchase of the Royal Hawaiian Hotel downtown for such a facility.

Meanwhile, Thurston was pushing anew for an old goal—a ban on liquor in the Islands. He supported Brigadier General F. S. Strong, who urged "bone-dry prohibition," declaring that 90 percent of the problems of enlisted men were traceable to saloons.[11] In the spring of 1917, eight thousand army personnel were stationed on Oahu, with the National Guard expected to be called up.

Hawaii had previously debated the pros and cons of prohibition. Thurston, in a 1910 paper to the Social Science Association and then in a series of *Advertiser* articles, favored prohibition as "the most efficient means of reducing drinking to a minimum."[12] Temperance proponents had sought a ban on liquor in Congress and the legislature but without success.

In 1914 *Advertiser* Sports Editor H. G. Lowry and Business Manager Charles S. Crane refused a demand by the U.S. attorney for certain typewritten pages that reportedly contained information on alleged liquor sales at Schofield Barracks, which was under grand jury investigation. After arguments by counsel, a federal judge ruled in favor of Lowry and Crane.[13]

When the Oahu liquor board closed saloons at an earlier hour, the *Advertiser* and *Star-Bulletin* called it a ploy to discourage a full ban. In May 1917 the just-adopted selective service law made it illegal to sell liquor to military personnel in uniform. The result was a proliferation of dives, many also offering prostitutes, to circumvent the law. Civilians meanwhile were free to drink.

In a lengthy editorial titled "Prohibition Should Be Fair," the *Advertiser* urged that "the restrictions now applied to the soldier apply to everyone and in that way remove the discrimination. If it be good for our boys in uniform to forego the use of intoxicants during the war period, it is equally good for the rest of us."[14]

One of the "Dixie Doolittle" ads in the *Advertiser* criticized the Elks Lodge, the Oahu Country Club, the University Club, and the Commercial Club for apparent resistance to prohibition. Elks' leaders brought the matter before the grand jury, in part to uncover the identity of "Doolittle." Testimony was given by a number of Elks, followed by three *Advertiser* representatives, Charles S. Crane, business manager; Edward P. Irwin, city editor; and George A. Seyde, bookkeeper. A resultant criminal libel indictment disclosed the authors of the "Doolittle" ads to be Managing Editor Matheson and Richard H. Trent, president of Trent Trust Company and a respected leader in civic and religious activities. Trent was tried and acquitted, and the charge against Matheson was dropped.

A new commanding general left liquor enforcement up to the police. The situation worsened, and the Women's War Work Council soon complained that vice conditions in the city were deplorable, with opium joints and houses of ill fame running wide open. In spite of efforts to prevent the sale of liquor to soldiers, bootlegging and "blind pigs" (or speakeasies) flourished.

By 1918, spurred by *Advertiser* and *Star-Bulletin* demands for a bone-dry Hawaii, public sentiment was beginning to have its effect in Washington. In March, President Wilson issued an order outlawing liquor on Oahu except in private homes for family members and bona fide guests other than members of the military. Maui and Kauai decided not to renew or issue liquor licenses after June, but the Big Island authorities declined to go along.

Congress finally acted, effective in August, to make the Hawaii ban territory-wide, while providing that within two years after peace the voters, at a general election, could decide on retention or repeal of the ban. But, in 1919, before that could take place, the Volstead Act for national prohibition went into effect.

The *Advertiser* came out of World War I in generally healthy condition, although its weekday circulation of 5,487 lagged nearly 2,000 behind the *Star-Bulletin*'s. The semiweekly *Hawaiian Gazette* fared less well, with a sharply declining demand, and at the end of November 1918 it was discontinued. As a result, on January 1, 1919, the name of the parent organization was changed from the Hawaiian Gazette Company, Ltd., to Advertiser Publishing Company, Ltd.

In December 1918, after nine years as *Advertiser* managing editor, Matheson left the paper to join the *Japan Advertiser* in Tokyo as news editor. In a farewell editorial he acknowledged he had "been given what amounted to practically a free hand, uncramped by tangling alliances, either politically or economically . . . a position enjoyed by too few American editorial writers." For this he credited Thurston "for the broad vision that is his and the untiring earnestness with which he devotes his talents and the agencies he controls toward the moral and material advancement of the Islands he loves."[15]

Jared Smith later wrote that Matheson's term of service covered the

> transitional decade between the old days of personal journalism . . . with all its fierce antagonisms, jealousies and friendships and the present wholly impersonal era that goes with the broadened field and multiplied staff of writers and news gatherers. It was inevitable that . . . Matheson, a graduate of the older order, should carry into his work the fighting spirit which aroused the enthusiastic approval of proponents of leaders, measures, movements and the policies, or the unqualified enmity of those on "the other side."[16]

Thurston was excessively kind to Matheson: "He has matured and is now at the zenith of his powers."[17]

After a year in Tokyo, Matheson gave up newspapering for a general advertising business in Yokohama. The *Advertiser* published a long letter from him taking issue with the paper's position that "Japan has not a shred of moral or legal right to an inch of China"—referring to Japanese acquisition by the World War I treaty of former German rights in Shantung. His successor, Edward P. Irwin, rejected Matheson's contention as fallacious reasoning and "an utterly unwarranted aspersion of the press of the United States and the motive of those who like myself look upon the Shantung award as iniquitous."[18]

Irwin, who, if anything, had a hotter temper than Matheson, was an Iowa native, a University of Kansas graduate, who, after newspaper work on the West Coast, came to Honolulu in 1906 to join the *Bulletin*. He married Bernice Piilani Cook, a public school teacher, who for years wrote the *Sunday Advertiser*'s "Kahuna Nui" articles under a pen name.

A ready scrapper, Irwin required six stitches to close a cheek wound inflicted by brass knuckles in a fight outside the baseball grounds. He went to work at the *Advertiser* but was fired in 1911 "for general unreliability and too frequent intoxication."[19] But rehabilitation was effective or memories were short, for on July 5, 1917, after editing a weekly, he was named city editor of the *Advertiser* when M. G. Maury, a veteran of military service in Cuba and the Philippines, was called to Army duty.

A year and a half later he moved to the top spot, which he held for two years, until December 1920. During that time he survived several criminal libel actions resulting from slambang editorials. For two years after leaving the *Advertiser* he edited the weekly *Crossroads of the Pacific*, then worked for a while on California newspapers, came back to Honolulu, and in 1925 began publishing the *Honolulu Times*.

In a blatantly racist article in the December 1924 issue of the magazine *Paradise of the Pacific*, he questioned whether Orientals were capable of becoming Americanized. He saw mixed marriages as creating "mental, physical and moral deficiencies." He saw the Japanese as "characterized by flat features, protruding teeth and short legs" and asked "if we want to incorporate such . . . in the American body?"

He contended that "the inner formation of the Oriental brain" created an outlook "hostile to our ideals." He argued that Orientals accepted the benefits of citizenship but shunned the responsibilities. Their children were entitled to "only such an amount [of education] as we think is best for them." And, finally, he said "what these Islands need is a little less sentimental nonsense and a little more sensible thinking."

He continued to carry his pugnacity beyond the typewriter. He had a fist fight in the territorial legislative chamber with Senator David K. Trask, who had demanded an apology for an article in Irwin's weekly. He mixed it up on the Alakea Street sidewalk with Loris Rosa, a city auditor's clerk, who was provoked by an article on the case of a suspended city treasurer charged with embezzlement. Rosa wielded a blacksnake whip and threw Irwin down, giving him a bloody chin. Rosa was fined $20, but on appeal the case was dropped.

"Talking through the Air"

IN THE early 1920s a man Lorrin Thurston had never heard of approached him and urged that together they get into radio broadcasting. When Thurston told him there was no money for such a venture, the man said he'd work for "practically nothing if he could use the station after broadcasting hours to find out some things he wanted to know about radio."[1]

The man was Marion A. Mulrony, a civilian radio engineer for the Navy at Pearl Harbor who earlier had built eleven stations in Australia at the request of the government there. He was a friend of Alexander Graham Bell, Guglielmo Marconi, and Lee De Forest and holder of several radio patents. With Thurston persuaded, Mulrony in 1922 sought and received, for prospective station KGU, the thirty-second broadcasting license in the United States, issued by Secretary of Commerce Herbert Hoover. Having resigned his Navy connection, he then worked out a deal with the *Advertiser* to share the license.

Ed Sheehan, writer and radio personality, later observed that Mulrony "put together a remarkably good broadcast unit out of a dream, determination, bailing wire and scraps of lumber. It was Hawaii's first station and Mulrony's whole life."[2] The station went on the air at 10:57 A.M. on May 11, 1922, with a few hellos by manager/engineer Mulrony.

The first official broadcast was at noon, from the third floor of the *Advertiser*'s quarters on King Street, near Alakea Street, with Governor Farrington, a former editor of the paper, heeding the admonition to speak gently. But following him, pianist Johnny Noble struck a strong bass note, blowing out a transmitter tube and taking the station off the air. It recovered by evening, when it featured "live" entertainment until the 9:00 P.M. cutoff required by its license.

The next morning's *Advertiser* described the first studio audience:

In a hastily assembled room . . . were gathered electrical experts [and] members of the Advertiser staff . . . who had come for a first glimpse and sound of this new marvel of science. On a long table was a profusion of wire and apparatus, and projecting from it—a long horn. Into this, the various performers sang and played and the sounds were mysteriously sent to those amateurs eagerly awaiting them. The onlookers in the operating room sat for an hour and a half, perspiration dripping, unwilling to seek a cooler location while yet the mysterious array of machinery was engaged in talking through the air.[3]

Seeking to build KGU's audience and its own circulation, the *Advertiser* offered a free $32.50 receiver for anyone getting eight one-year subscriptions or an $80 set for ten.

During its shakedown period, KGU broadcast two evening programs a week, each lasting just an hour or two, as determined by the musicians' interest. Power gradually was increased from fifty watts to one thousand by February 1930, when the Island radio audience was estimated at seventy-five thousand. On March 4, 1929, KGU had aired the inauguration of President Herbert Hoover, "the first important official trans-ocean short-wave broadcast in Hawaii."[4]

For several years KGU operated without advertising revenue. Even when it began to attract commercials, the income was exceedingly modest—$250 a month in April 1926. It took seven years to get the station in the black.

One of its early employees, bright and eager but with a tendency to overlook airing commercials, was finally fired. His name: Dave Garroway, who would become a national broadcast personality.

It took most of the 1920s for the potential of radio and the linkage between broadcast and print to be borne in on *Advertiser* management. The realization prompted strenuous efforts to have KGU become a member of the prestigious National Broadcasting Company network, and these finally paid off on November 14, 1931, with a salute from New York by such stars as Rudy Vallee and Russ Colombo. That same year KGU fed to NBC the eruption of Mauna Loa after hundreds of pounds of equipment were carried to the Big Island and miles of land lines laid. One of the microphones was dropped into the crater and explanations were provided by volcanologist Thomas A. Jaggar.

In 1934 when President Franklin D. Roosevelt visited Hawaii he ended with a speech over KGU: "I shall ever remember these days; days that are all too short; your flowers, your scenery, your hospitality—but, above all, the knowledge that America can well be proud of the Territory of Hawaii. And so I say aloha to you from the bottom of my heart."

During those early years many other colorful personalities spoke into the KGU mike, including Floyd Gibbons, Philippines President Manuel Quezon, Salvation Army General Evangeline Booth, Walter F. Chrysler, Gene Sarazen, H. V. Kaltenborn, Jimmy Stewart, and Shirley Temple.

In World War II KGU aired many entertainers who were in service— Marine Lieutenant Bob Crosby, Commander Eddie Duchin, Navy man Ray Anthony and his sailor orchestra, Orrin Tucker with his Navy choir, and Army Major Maurice Evans, the Shakespearean actor.

The station did many special broadcasts—flier Charles Edward Kingsford Smith's arrival in his *Lady Southern Cross*, Amelia Earhart's historic flight from Wheeler Field to the mainland, the start of interisland airmail in 1931, the first Pan Am Clipper's arrival in 1936, and, of course, the December 7, 1941, attack on Pearl Harbor.

The best-known names in Island broadcasting worked, at one time or another, at KGU—Webley Edwards, brash disc jockey J. Akuhead Pupule (Hal Lewis), Robert (Lucky) Luck, Joe Rose, Ezra Crane, Chuck Leahy, Jim Leahy, Ken Wilson, Les Keiter, Al Michaels, Gene Good, Stan Anderson, Earle Daniels, Owen Cunningham, Tom Moffatt, Ed Laurence, and Ron Jacobs, among others.

Presiding over the operation was Mulrony, a firm and reserved taskmaster, but, underneath, a warm and kindly man. He retained a strong Victorian streak and, as Ed Sheehan recalled, "If he went to the movies and saw Dinah Shore wearing a low-cut gown, her records were no longer played on KGU."[5] He even smashed records of performers he didn't like, including a young Bing Crosby. And he had little broadcast time for sopranos. But no one questioned his radio engineering genius.

In 1951 Mulrony gave up his rights as KGU's colicensee to the *Advertiser* for $25,000, plus a $500 monthly pension starting the next year, when he retired. He was succeeded by William O. Paine, his assistant manager, a bright, articulate man, a graduate of the Wharton School of Finance, who had come to KGU in 1938 and, with the exception of Navy service in World War II and three years following in California, had served continuously at the station.

In 1957, on its thirty-fifth anniversary, KGU got a 10,000-watt transmitter and erected a 300-foot tower at Kewalo Basin, superseding its two 150-foot landmark towers supporting the station's antenna atop the *Advertiser*'s home on Kapiolani Boulevard. It was now clearly not only Hawaii's first but its most powerful radio station.

17

"Where America and Asia Meet"

THE 1920s were to see a rapid turnover of *Advertiser* editors, followed by three decades of stability in that office.

On December 19, 1920, Sam B. Trissel, a native of Mark Twain's hometown of Hannibal, Missouri, who had come to the *Advertiser* only three months before, succeeded Irwin. The *Hilo Tribune* described him as "blond and fat and round-faced and jolly. His efficiency is of the quiet, genial sort, rather than tempestuous and aggressive. He writes lucidly, but there is a personal, homely touch to his style. . . . His punch doesn't knock you over, but it weaves itself around your heart. . . ."[1]

Twenty-two years before, as a mainland reporter with a yearning to travel, he enlisted as an infantry private and first saw Honolulu on his way to the Philippines. He liked Manila, stayed on as editor of several dailies there, then traveled to China, editing papers in Shanghai and Cheefoo and serving as Associated Press correspondent with Russian forces in the Russo-Japanese War. The West Indies called and in 1910 he became editor of the *Times*, in San Juan, Puerto Rico. During World War I, until the armistice, he served with the U.S. State Department in London, Petrograd, and the Hague. Then, before joining the *Advertiser*, he spent time in Europe, North Africa, and, once again, the Orient.

The day he became editor, the *Advertiser* published a fifty-page paper, at the time the largest ever in Hawaii without the inducement of a special edition. Three months later, on March 31, 1921, the paper's name was changed from the *Pacific Commercial Advertiser* to *The Honolulu Advertiser.*

The change reflected the view that Honolulu was not only the center of Hawaii but of "this great Pacific community," the place "where America and Asia meet." And the paper added, prophetically, that "Honolulu will be the spot where the first great shock will occur in case of conflict between the East and West" or "it will be the home of those who hold the peace and demonstrate that 'love' and not 'war' is the greatest thing in the world."

Trissel lasted until March 7, 1922, when he resigned, with a friendly comment from Lorrin Thurston. When he died in 1934, while at the *Los Angeles*

Times, Advertiser columnist Walter J. (Doc) Adams wrote fondly of him as a complex man, "almost Falstaffian in his boasting about past glories" and yet a "willing Samaritan . . . a one-man Community Chest . . . a sure-fire victim for the chiseler with a hard luck story . . . a man [Adams had] quarreled bitterly with, but could never dislike."[2]

Succeeding Trissel was Lawrence M. Monfort, named managing editor—the editor title having been shelved for some years. He stayed less than four months, leaving to direct publicity for Consolidated Amusement Company, a local movie theater chain.

Moving to the editorial helm from which he would steer the paper for thirty-six years, was Raymond S. Coll. The son of an Irish immigrant, he had begun his colorful sixty-seven-year career on the Connellsville, Pennsylvania, *Courier*, then in 1896 moved to Pittsburgh, where he worked for the *Daily News* and the *Times*. It was a turbulent era, and Coll covered strikes, riots, mine explosions, train wrecks. He loved politics and when Socialist Eugene Debs ran for Congress, Coll stumped with him through the Alleghenies, "sleeping nights with his head cradled on a saddle." He covered Samuel Gompers' fight for labor and reported on worker-management disputes in the late 1890s in Pennsylvania, Ohio, and West Virginia. He interviewed Andrew Carnegie and H. C. Frick of steel and coke fame. He covered federal moonshine raids in the mountains of Pennsylvania and West Virginia.

In those years he was an ardent liberal—some called him a radical—and he served as delegate to a Pennsylvania state Democratic convention. He was a fiery young man, quick to vent his temper, but also quick to cool it. "Although not a large man, he was physically rugged and gave the impression of size simply by the strength of his personality. The outstanding feature of his powerful face was the penetrating blue eyes which could be as cold as diamonds—and as cutting. Or they could twinkle with tolerance and amusement."[3]

In 1907 Coll went to Arizona to edit the *Bisbee Review* and two related papers, including the Douglas *Dispatch*, which a year later he leased and campaigned for statehood for the territory. A year short of that achievement, he returned to Pittsburgh as night editor of the *Dispatch*. In World War I he served as its correspondent first in the capital at Harrisburg and then in New York City. In 1917 he became managing editor and held that post until the paper was sold in 1921 and he and his wife Nan planned a world tour, with a stop to visit her sister and brother living in Honolulu.

After the smoke and dirt of Pittsburgh, they were captivated by clear skies and trade winds, and within two weeks Coll had bought a house. Nan asked how he could do that without a job, and he replied that he'd get a job, which he did, briefly as an *Advertiser* reporter, then in July 1922 as managing editor. His wife, whom he had wed in 1896 because, she said, he fell for her copper-red hair and deep dimples, loved Hawaii as much as he did. Years later she told an interviewer, "The Philadelphia Public Ledger was trying to find him. When they did, they offered him the editorship, but he wouldn't take it. He wanted to stay here."[4]

Coll was a great admirer of Lorrin A. Thurston and of Walter F. Dillingham, with whom he soon became chummy. In the conservative environment of the local establishment, he became a Republican but in the years ahead had great respect for Franklin D. Roosevelt and Harry S. Truman and maintained a correspondence with them, as well as with FBI Director J. Edgar Hoover.

Coll liked, and owned, a big car, but he never learned to drive. His wife, Nan, was his chauffeur and alongside of her on the front seat throughout the 1930s was their German shepherd, Bonnie. Once at the paper, Bonnie accompanied her master and spent the day in his office, as both companion and, if the need arose, as protector.

The staff additionally got a kick out of an old leather blackjack dangling from the coat tree behind his desk, a holdover from his Arizona frontier days. Unlike many mainland newspapers, the *Advertiser* in those years had no security guards screening visitors to the second-floor editorial quarters. Anyone had easy access, but there is no record that Coll was ever in danger.

Coll had a gifted and creative staff, highly motivated and achievement-oriented. Clifford Gessler, who came to the paper from Chicago in 1921, became a nationally recognized poet and author.

Arthur A. Greene, a Kansas lawyer who switched to journalism, joined the *Advertiser* in 1921, serving as city editor and editorial writer, while playing an active after-hours role in Democratic politics. In 1934 he was named by President Roosevelt to become secretary of the Territory of Hawaii. When Governor Joseph B. Poindexter was absent, Greene served as acting governor and, in that capacity, received child film star Shirley Temple. He had been described to her as an "old newspaperman," but she told him he was not at all old looking.

William Prohme, a Brooklynite, attended a Lutheran theological seminary but opted for journalism, working in Denver, Sacramento, and Los Angeles before becoming editorial page editor of the *San Francisco Chronicle*. He came to the *Advertiser* in 1924, first as waterfront reporter succeeding A. P. Taylor, then as editorial writer. He left with his wife Reyna to be associated with the revolutionary government of China under Sun Yat-sen. When that fizzled, he lived in Manila, Berlin, and Paris, then, in ill health, returned to Honolulu. As death approached, he wrote his own obituary and sent it to Editor Coll with the notation: "Dear Chief: Put this away in a drawer to use when necessary."

In 1927 E. G. (Ted) Burrows, a Cornell graduate, was recruited, and he, too, served as city editor. He went on to get master's and doctor's degrees from Yale and became a professor of anthropology at the University of Connecticut.

Reporter Donald Barr Chidsey went on to be a successful magazine writer and Thornton Hardy an associate editor of the *Saturday Evening Post*. Of Hardy, a colleague wrote that he "treated each reportorial assignment with scholarly dignity and the eager enthusiasm of a cub. He had a limitless capacity for condescension and an ability to keep it out of his writing that amounted to genius."[5]

Editor Coll's son, Ray, Jr., came to the *Advertiser* the same year as his father, 1922, and possibly suffered by being in the shadow of such a strong personality. In his time on the waterfront he wrote a lively column, "Shoreside Shorts." In World War II he turned combat correspondent, reported the first Superfort bombings of Japan from Saipan, was present at the Iwo Jima and Okinawa invasions, and covered the Japanese surrender on the battleship *Missouri* in Tokyo Bay. He then went to Washington to report on the hearings on Pearl Harbor. In 1947 he married Irva F. Edwards, who worked at the paper for many years. He retired in 1959 because of failing eyesight and died in 1970.

In May 1923 the long-practiced art of reporters going aboard incoming steamers offshore to search out and interview distinguished passengers before landing was summarily ended. The U.S. Public Health Service would no longer make prelanding inspections, thereby sparing ships a delayed arrival of up to two hours—but in the process precluding many a good story. Henceforth reporters would "wear their legs and patience out trying to grab an interview very hurriedly at the foot of the gangplank, or rushing around hotels to look up the newcomers."[6]

About the time Coll became managing editor, Charles E. Hogue, an Oregonian, signed on after working as a reporter and editor from Chicago to China. It was on one of his trips via Honolulu, on boat day, that he asked Coll for a job. Being told there was none, he left, but within hours was back with three news stories that cried out for page one. Suddenly, there was a job, and except for a few stints in government and with the Archives of Hawaii and the Hawaii Employers Council, he was at the paper until his death in the spring of 1959. He had served as city editor, news editor, editorial writer, and editorial page columnist.

An editorial called him "one of the brilliant, unconventional personages in whom the fast-disappearing tradition of nonconformist American journalism was sustained. . . . His friends all over the world would say his epitaph might be: 'Say it simply. Be dead sure you're right. Then let the chips fall.'"[7]

Offsetting the worldliness of Hogue was the effervescence of Ezra J. Crane, who made people think of Teddy Roosevelt because "he had some of TR's boyish enthusiasm and rambunctiousness." A political and sports writer, he "could be as blunt as a blow from a billy club. . . . When he had something to say— which was usually—he said it at the top of his voice."[8] He enjoyed a good scrap and never seemed to lack for one. He spent twelve years at the *Advertiser*, part of that time doubling as a Republican member of the territorial legislature, while his father, after many years at the paper, was mayor of Honolulu.

In 1936 Crane became editor of the *Maui News* and from time to time wrote heated critiques of Honolulu journalism. When he died in 1984 the

Advertiser said he had gone "clamorously along the way, shouting and laughing and fighting, having himself just one whale of a time—and making life interesting for everyone around him."[9]

The paper needed a first-rate artist and in Jerry Y. Chong it found him. An alumnus of Iolani and the University of California School of Fine Arts, he spent forty-eight years at the *Advertiser*, most of the time as head of his department.

In 1923 the paper acquired one of America's leading baseball writers, Bill Peet of the *Pittsburgh Dispatch*, as sports editor. He had begun his career in Boston, traveling with the Red Sox, then went to Washington and made road trips with the Senators. This led to sports editorships of two Cleveland papers and the *Washington Post*. He was a close friend of Grantland Rice, Ring Lardner, and other famed sports writers of "the golden age." His first love remained baseball, and as the *Advertiser* later put it, "Bill Peet knows baseball inside and out, and knew all about the scandals and idiosyncrasies of each player and could probably tell a lot about 'Babe' Ruth and his contracts, Ty Cobb, [Roger] Hornsby and the great [Grover] Alexander, and just how Judge [Kennesaw Mountain] Landis [the baseball commissioner], talked and handled baseball affairs."[10] He was an amiable, "square-dealing, hard-hitting newspaperman."[11]

In 1935 Peet was succeeded by Vernon (Red) McQueen, who held the position until 1965, despite a long bout with rheumatoid arthritis that made typing painful and forced him to walk with a cane. A star baseball and football player in high school and for a year at the University of Hawaii, he left the campus in 1928 to join the *Advertiser* sports staff. His "Hoomalimali" column became a sports bible for Islanders, probably because he favored unvarnished facts.

The late *Advertiser* cartoonist Harry Lyons said McQueen was a sports writer who told it like it was: "Red would sit down at his battered typewriter, light up a cigar and begin to pound away with those gnarled, arthritic, talented fingers of his and he wrote it straight. He never wrote, 'Willie Pastrami was the victim of an unpopular decision.' Red's typewriter spat, 'Willie Pastrami was robbed.' Period."[12] Some boxing promoters disliked him because he denounced dubious bouts, but that never deterred him.

He was liked and admired by readers and by the scores of visiting sports writers and athletes to whom he played host. He enjoyed being the center of attention, and as his colleague Monte Ito recalled, "He held court at Smile Cafe in Waikiki with its owner Sam Uyehara into the wee hours of the morning. Every night there were more than a dozen athletes or fans listening to his stories or recounting their own personal exploits."[13]

In 1955 he was the only newsman to accompany the New York Yankees in touring the Far East for six weeks. He covered Rose Bowl games, the World Series, mainland golf tournaments. In 1957 he was named the nation's outstanding sports writer by a *Los Angeles Times* board of judges that included Casey Stengel, manager of the Yankees; Dean Cromwell, former University of

Southern California track coach; and former tennis champion Ellsworth Vines. On his retirement in 1970, he became the first and only sports writer to make the Hawaii Press Club's Hall of Fame.

The *Advertiser*'s lively coverage in the 1920s was well received, but at least some readers questioned the use of "scandalous and sensational" news. The paper replied that it really hadn't played up crime and scandal, but perhaps the fear of publicity might be a deterrent. It cited reports

> that it is becoming almost a cult in certain circles in Honolulu for young men of prominence to tamper with other men's wives, and the ease and rapidity with which families are broken up, divorces granted, readjustment of couples made, wedding bells sounded once more and 'everything lovely again'— all conducted 'under the rose' without undue publicity.[14]

It quoted a recent letter about debutantes drinking and smoking and driving home drunk, smashing autos and occupants; cards for money; abnormal liquor consumption in high-toned clubs; violations of the Eighteenth Amendment by high officials as well as leading members of civilian society. The contention was that this misbehavior was generally known but the press was "mum" because it dared not publish the truth, which, far from being scandal-mongering, would put the fear of God in the hearts of those who needed that experience.

The *Advertiser* said that while reconciling opposing views on this subject was its dilemma, it was still more a community problem, and it invited discussion of it "in moderate language and in a spirit of sincerity."[15]

There was no such ambivalence in dealing with street crime. When a young white man was killed by the "Aala Park Gang" of Filipinos, the paper said "one's first hope is there is a scaffold at the prison large enough to accommodate some 20 Filipino murderers at one time. The simultaneous stretching of twenty necks would make this city safer for quite a while."[16]

At times, the paper was strongly at odds with police. A page-one story with a strong editorial flavor conveyed that traffic police, on issuing citations, were "childishly" blaming the *Advertiser* for a campaign forcing them to crack down. Meanwhile, "the other branches of the Police Department maintain their attitude of defiance in their determination not to enforce the law." That encouraged the "booze joints," the "high-priced houses of prostitution," and even the "little fly-by-night disorderly houses." The town's "vice dens" were more open than ever and quality liquor confiscated by police in raids on bootleg parlors was being distributed to friends, including certain clubs retailing it at twenty-five cents a drink.[17]

The paper wound up in court itself in 1924 in a freedom-of-the-press case after Editor Coll editorially took a judge to task for jailing a man who refused to pay his wife's $50 attorney's fee in a contested divorce. Coll was held in contempt by Circuit Judge John R. Desha.

On appeal, the Hawaii Supreme Court ruled that the judge was without jurisdiction to punish the editor for "an alleged contemptuous editorial" concerning a case already concluded. It left unsaid what rights a newspaper had to critically comment on a case still in progress. Helpfully, one justice reminded that the dignity of a court was in its own keeping.

Undeterred by the occasional legal challenge—a standard hazard for vigorous journalists—the *Advertiser* kept its eye on workaday needs. It began to match its talented editorial staff with improved production facilities.

In March 1922 the paper bought a new twenty-page duplex printing press with color equipment and a capacity of thirty thousand copies an hour and a four-color press for the Sunday comic supplement, highlighted by "Bringing Up Father," "Polly and Her Pals," "Down on the Farm," and the "Katzenjammer Kids." "Time only can prove," readers were told, "whether Hawaii is ready for this form of mental and artistic stimulation. If so, the Advertiser will continue to furnish the stimulant."

The start of the new press was proudly witnessed by R. H. Whiting, who worked one of the Islands' first two Linotypes, both at the *Advertiser*, in 1895. He was pleased to see that the *Advertiser* now had eight Linotype machines, thirteen job presses, and other state-of-the-art equipment.

On December 19, the Sunday *Advertiser* printed thirty-six pages, the largest regular paper produced in the Islands, with display advertising from 217 firms and classified ads from 254 persons and 10 mainland firms.

Several months later, an eight-page feature "magazine" was added to the Sunday issue. The contents ranged from a definition by film vamp Bebe Daniels of "my ideal man" to an illustrated story of crocodile worship in the Egypt of King Tutankhamen. A front-page statement by Thurston hailed the addition as "the beginning of the realization of a 'daylight dream' of what an ideal Sunday newspaper can be"—a news report, editorials, and entertainment.

Arthur Brisbane and other top syndicated writers and authors were added, including inimitable sports whiz Damon Runyon, Walter Lippmann on world affairs, and H. G. Wells on science. A weekly church page was added, edited by Lorin Tarr Gill, covering the Islands' religious life, with aid from the multiethnic department of the Hawaiian Board of Missions.

During this period, several individuals took jobs on the business side. Robert A. Thurston, a son of Lorrin A. Thurston, a graduate of Louisiana State University, worked in sugar before joining the *Advertiser* in 1923 as assistant to Walter Cameron, national advertising director. He succeeded Cameron on his retirement in 1926, held the post until 1952, then continued as a vice-president and director.

Another long-timer was Allan J. McGuire, onetime newspaper boy, who came aboard in 1921 as an office clerk and rose through the ranks to business manager in 1949. He retired in 1963, after forty-two years of service, many of them on the board of directors and as corporate secretary-treasurer. An alumnus of Punahou and the University of Wisconsin, he was regarded as one of Punahou's greatest athletes, a member of the class of '21, which swept all major interscholastic sports for that year. His community service included work on the Honolulu Charter Commission.

Strongly promotion-minded, the paper ran an editorial aimed at advertisers trumpeting the "best" circulation in Hawaii, reaching into homes of readers who "fundamentally comprise the purchasing public." It said that in local advertising it was leading "by many thousands [of] inches" and would soon be number one in national lineage.[18]

Between 1924 and 1928 the company's annual profits ranged from $28,549 to $70,020 and dividends from $13,471 to $22,500.

In September 1930 the paper sought new readers by starting a Sunday "bulldog" edition, which hit the streets about seven o'clock on Saturday nights, carrying the United Press world report, local news, and regular features of the daily editions and initially selling two thousand copies. A few months later it went daily, with Mayor Fred Wright pushing the press button.

To stimulate national advertising and provide "co-op" funds to help local firms promote their products, the paper entered into an agreement with the Katz special advertising agency, with offices in New York, Chicago, Kansas City, and Atlanta.

When a chiropractor withdrew his ads because the paper editorially supported vaccination, Thurston wrote that the paper depended on advertising and "could not exist a month without it," but would continue to express its opinions on public issues. That was better than allowing advertisers "to silence sincere editorial conviction by withdrawal of patronage and permit dictation of editorial policy of the paper by its advertisers."[19]

In seeking advertising, as well as prestige, some U.S. papers of the period tended to inflate their circulation figures. In Hawaii the *Advertiser* was the first newspaper to apply for and receive membership in the Audit Bureau of Circulation, which examines and verifies the number of papers sold, providing an accurate record of the distribution.

Getting papers to the Neighbor Islands in timely fashion was a longtime challenge, and to help meet it, symbolically at first, the *Advertiser* turned to the air. It had kept its eye on aviation since the day in 1910 when it headlined "Honolulu's First Bird Men Take To The Air." The accompanying story announced that "the Tuttle Brothers of Honolulu have become the contemporaries of the Wright Brothers of Dayton, Ohio and their names will be perpetuated in history as the first aviators of the Hawaiian Islands."[20] These pioneers, Malcolm and Elbert Tuttle, both Punahou students, had built a glider, which they successfully flew in the hills of Kaimuki.

Thirteen years later, when roads were blocked by a storm, *Advertiser*s were air-delivered to Windward communities by pilot Charles Stoffer; one of the towns, Kahuku, usually got its morning paper by afternoon train. Soon after, the same pilot dropped papers at Molokai, and the U.S. Army air service delivered a special *Advertiser* edition for the three days of the Maui county fair, the first time Maui readers ever got their papers on the morning of publication.

The cooperating military continued to periodically drop mail bags of papers on wharves, consigned to postmasters for delivery. On October 23, 1924, the *Advertiser* heralded the first complete airmail delivery to all major Neighbor Islands. But it would be ten years before dependable daily service was possible.

The paper's air-mindedness paid off in news coverage in September 1925 when Commander John Rodgers and his crew in a Navy PB9-1 on a San Francisco-to-Hawaii flight exhausted their gas and ditched. Reporters were quickly posted to all Neighbor Islands, with one put on a searching Navy destroyer. When the plane was found off Kauai a week later, the *Advertiser* was the first to print staff photos of the rescue, giving the AP a forty-minute world beat. Charles Fern, who headed the *Advertiser*'s Kauai bureau, was the first to reach Rodgers and his crew and get a firsthand story of their drifting for days. The paper had three different extras on the street, each with an update of the news, before rival papers went to press.

It was at about this time that the *Advertiser* moved along on plans to construct a new home that could accommodate it well into the future. For $90,000 it had bought land at the intersection of King and South Streets and Kapiolani Boulevard. With partial financing by a bond issue floated through Bishop Trust Company, it erected a three-story, half-million-dollar plant of Mediterranean renaissance design, providing two acres of floor space for the newspaper, its commercial printing and bindery, and radio station KGU and their three hundred employees.

It was occupied on January 27, 1930, and dedicated almost a month later, attracting twelve thousand people, including Walter Murray Vettlesen of Molokai, grandson of Walter Murray Gibson, the turbulent editor of the Spreckels/Kalakaua period, and former Governor Farrington, who looked in the library files for editorials he wrote when he was the *Advertiser*'s editor.

Thurston used the occasion to review some personal history. He said his memory went back thirty-seven years

> when I was engaged in helping the overthrow of the monarchy and helping to make Hawaii an integral part of the United States. . . .
>
> I want to say that I have no feeling against Liliuokalani, the last queen under the monarchy. For 10 years after the overthrow of the monarchy I did not see her, and when I did it was at a reception given by Prince Kuhio for a delegation of congressmen. When I walked in Liliuokalani was there and shook hands with me. . . . It was the last time that I saw her.
>
> During the last years of her life Liliuokalani was a changed woman. She had accepted American institutions in good faith. If she had had that same

January 27, 1930. The present *Advertiser* building on Kapiolani Boulevard was occupied. Visitors were greeted by a lovely patio with fountain and flora.

spirit during her early life she would have ended her life as a queen and this would still be a monarchy. But I do not believe there is a person living in Hawaii who is not better off and not happier with Hawaii an integral part of the United States than if it had remained a monarchy.[21]

Newspaper equipment had been smoothly moved from the old offices at King and Alakea Streets between 6 P.M. on a Saturday and 4 A.M. on Sunday without missing an edition. The news and editorial-page staff was quickly ensconced on the second floor, with most of the mechanical department and its ten Linotypes, a Ludlow typograph, and engraving and stereotyping equipment in an adjacent space toward the rear of the building. The business departments—national, display, and classified advertising, circulation, commercial printing, art, and promotion, as well as managers' offices—were on the first floor, facing Kapiolani Boulevard, and in the back was the twenty-four-page rotary duplex press with some color capacity. KGU was on the third floor, with its 1,000-watt transmitter tower atop the building. The new telephone number for all departments was easy to remember: 2311.

The open house on February 11 featured a tour of what an *Advertiser* story that day described as "the oldest continuously published newspaper west of the Rocky Mountains." *Thrum's Annual* hailed the stately new building "for its contribution to the progress and beautification of the city."[22] Even the *Star-Bulletin* fraternally printed a long editorial complimenting its arch rival.

Advertiser business office in the 1930s, on the first floor of the present building.

That September, Crane, manager for twenty-four years, was advanced to executive vice-president; Lorrin P. Thurston moved from assistant manager and secretary to manager and treasurer, and F. Dickson Nott became secretary. Lorrin A. Thurston, president and publisher, who had acquired the paper in 1898, was in declining health, and after some months abed he died May 11, 1931, at the age of seventy-two. He had played a major role in the movement of Hawaii from native kingdom to U.S. territory and in the subsequent development of plantations and railroads, tourism, and other elements of an expanding society. He was survived by his second wife, Harriet (Potter), two sons, Lorrin P. and Robert S., and his daughter Margaret (Mrs. William Twigg-Smith), then of New Zealand.

The *Advertiser* said that "in building the structure of modern Hawaii, he was perhaps the foremost artisan," with "an authentic genius for leadership."[23] His newspaper rival, the *Star-Bulletin*, praised him as "a man of ideals, courage and extraordinary energy" who had a "picturesque and highly dramatic career."[24]

Of Thurston's relationship with the staff, columnist "Doc" Adams would later write:

> his spirit still pervades the building. . . . He asked no man to do what he would not do himself. He required no man to 'yes' him as long as that man was honest in his disagreement and loyal to the paper. He never to our knowledge turned down an employee who was in trouble, but he did help with influence and cash to smooth those troubles out. And, best of all, he permitted no one, important or not, to impose upon the men who worked for him. . . .[25]

At the funeral service at Central Union Church, conducted by the Rev. Henry P. Judd of the Hawaiian Board of Missions, there was no music, a brief Biblical reading, and a briefer eulogy: "A mighty man in the community is lost. . . ."[26] Burial was in Nuuanu Cemetery.

Less than two months after Thurston's death, the *Advertiser* marked its seventy-fifth anniversary and called him the most vital figure in its history, crediting him with enlightened policies backed with the "rare intelligence, courage and aggressiveness that were his."[27]

Part IV

1931–1961

A Son Inherits the Publishership

IMMEDIATELY ON the death of Lorrin A. Thurston, his son by a second marriage, Lorrin P., took over the publisher's post. At a stockholders' meeting October 2, he was also elected president and director.

Named as vice-presidents and directors were Walter F. Dillingham, Mrs. Lorrin A. Thurston, and G. I. Samson. Charles Crane resigned his executive vice-presidency, finding no productive place in the new leadership, and went into politics.

The new publisher had begun his affiliation with the paper when, at fourteen, he was appointed as an *Advertiser* school correspondent at Punahou, the next summer becoming a "cub" accompanying regular reporters on the police and court beats.

When he finished Punahou, his father felt he was too young for college, so he spent a year at Lawrenceville, a preparatory school in New Jersey, before entering Yale in 1917. Soon thereafter he joined the Reserve Officers Training Corps and was an artillery instructor for a year, until the World War armistice.

He returned to Yale and graduated in 1921, celebrating the event by bringing the Yale swimming team, of which he was captain, to Honolulu. He then took special studies in newspaper promotion for some months at the University of Missouri Journalism School and on his way home in March 1922 observed editorial operations at the *St. Louis Post-Dispatch, Star,* and *Globe-Democrat,* the *Kansas City Star,* the *Chicago Tribune,* and the *Arizona Republic.*

At the *Advertiser* he worked for a year as a local advertising solicitor, then organized and headed the paper's first national ad department, while doubling as promotion manager. In late 1924 he was named assistant manager of the paper, and seven years later he was the top man.

In his first weeks at the helm the paper declared, in terms of policy, it would support the Republican Party, but in "territorial and civic affairs it will, as in the past, pursue a nonpartisan course."[1] That, of course, was a blatant stretching of the record and one that must have substantially elevated the eyebrows, if not the blood pressure, of Island Democrats.

Thurston was being asked to step into his father's giant footprints, but it was a demand beyond his capabilities. He fell short of his father's intellect, judgment, and dynamism.

He did faithfully pursue the family tradition of civic involvement, serving as president of the Honolulu Chamber of Commerce, a director of the Hawaii Employers Council, the Red Cross, and Children's Hospital, a member of the City Planning Commission, the Hawaii Volcano Research Association, the Social Science Association, the Hawaiian Historical Society, the advisory board of the Salvation Army, and chairman of the governor's advisory commission on state parks and historic sites. And, after an abrupt change of heart, he chaired the statehood commission that saw Hawaii finally take its rightful place in the Union.

Also like his father he envisioned an unlimited horizon for tourism in the Islands and the Pacific. He chaired the Hawaii Visitors Bureau before and after World War II and helped found and served as charter president of the Pacific Area Travel Association, the tourism promotion arm of Pacific Rim countries. Late in his career he showed vision in having the *Advertiser* acquire a half-interest in Honolulu's second TV station, KONA.

But his primary responsibility, the *Advertiser*, suffered from the fact that he was a publisher by inheritance rather than ability. He seemed to have little idea of what a hands-on publisher should be and do. He felt that making calls on major advertisers—a "must" for a paper steadily falling behind the *Star-Bulletin* in circulation and advertising—was beneath him and yet he neglected to get an advertising director capable of filling the void.

His lack of business acumen was matched by his indifference to the editorial staff. The reporters and columnists felt that Thurston regarded them as a cross he had to bear. He knew few by name. He rarely ventured into the department. And at annual employee parties, while he always congratulated the advertising and commercial printing departments, he failed to mention the writing end. The others directly generated revenues; the editorial department didn't, although without it there would have been no circulation, no advertising, no paper. The young turks in the newsroom irreverently dubbed him "Coconut Head," for reasons going beyond his sparse hair.

He was proud of his relationship with important mainlanders with whom the company had business relationships. KGU, as the NBC radio affiliate in the Islands, brought friendship with David Sarnoff, chairman of RCA, which controlled NBC, and the paper's exclusive reliance on United Press led to a cordial association with Roy Howard of Scripps-Howard, which operated the wire service.

But sadly, Thurston seemed remote from the realities of a rapidly changing Hawaii, and this was reflected in his assumption that since the *Advertiser* had long published, it was certain of survival. In a later family dispute in court, which Thurston initiated, Circuit Judge William Z. Fairbanks may have summed up the publisher's mindset when he described him as "living in the 19th Century in many ways."[2]

It was a mentality that would bode ill for the newspaper as time and events unfolded.

Race, Murder, and the Press

RACE RELATIONS in Hawaii were usually stable on the surface, as a way of getting along, but underneath there was always a swirl of tension over differences in color and culture, over submission and domination. Two capital cases within three years agonizingly brought this to the forefront.

In late September 1928 a kidnapping and cold-blooded murder rocked Honoluluans, but especially those of Japanese ancestry, to their very marrow and created a wave of hysteria throughout the community.

It began with a phone call to Miss Mary Winne, principal of Punahou junior academy, saying that Mrs. Frederick Jamieson, mother of ten-year-old Gill Jamieson, had been hurt in an automobile accident and that someone would be coming by to pick up the boy to take to her.

A taxi drove up and a youth in a hospital orderly's uniform, pictured as being of Oriental extraction, possibly Japanese, soon arrived, and Gill got in the car. What happened after that was told in detail by *Advertiser* writers Thornton Hardy, Ray Coll, Jr., and others in the days and months ahead.

Hours after the kidnapping, the missing boy's father, Frederick Jamieson, vice-president of Hawaiian Trust Company, received an envelope from a messenger boy. It contained a ransom note demanding $10,000 and was signed by "The Three Kings," conveying that a gang was responsible. The note said, "We want you to have utmost confidence in us. Have all fears swept aside. Do what we say and you will see your son again. Fight us and you will never see him again, nay, he will be but a shadow: lifeless."

That night Jamieson got a telephone call telling him to bring the money in cash to Thomas Square. Alongside the Academy of Arts, an individual with a handkerchief over his face and carrying a hammer in his hand got into Jamieson's car and told him to drive to a lane just past McKinley High School. There, Jamieson gave him $4,000—eight hundred $5 bills—but the receiver was too excited to count it. He took what was given him, said the Jamieson boy would be released, and ran off through nearby bushes. He later felt he had lost $6,000 while fleeing.

When nothing happened overnight, police searched for a criminal band: two hundred special deputies were sworn in, and twenty thousand schoolchildren were mobilized to help in an Island-wide search. The *Advertiser* reported police were "scouring the Island for trace of a band."[1]

A tip from the taxi driver who had been to Punahou led to Waikiki, and that afternoon, behind the Seaside Hotel on the Ala Wai Canal, in a grave-like hole in an area hidden by kiawe trees, the body of Gill Jamieson was found. He had been killed, it later developed, by steel chisel wounds to the head, then by strangulation with a napkin. His badly bruised body indicated he had desperately fought for his life. It was determined that he died shortly after leaving Punahou and well before the ransom note was sent.

The ransom bills' serial numbers had been listed, then publicized, and five days later—five days of community turmoil—a suspect who had passed several was arrested by detectives as he leaned against a store window on Fort Street near Beretania. Earlier his family noted he had been acting oddly, and his twelve-year-old sister aided police in locating and identifying him. From his room in a cheap hotel police recovered a pair of bloody pants and 782 of the 800 $5 bills he had been paid.

The suspect was Myles Fukunaga, and immediately upon arrest he confessed and also volunteered that he was sane and knew the difference between right and wrong. Fukunaga was a loner, a short, slightly built, rather bright, well-read but shy nineteen-year-old youth who could quote Shakespeare and Walt Whitman. He resented having to go to work rather than high school and lost his job at Queen's Hospital when he was abed with appendicitis. Earlier, feeling he was a failure, he had attempted suicide. His next job was as a pantry boy at the Seaside Hotel, and this familiarized him with its surroundings.

Hawaiian Trust Company, representing the Heen Estate, had pressed to collect rent from Fukunaga's parents for a cottage they occupied off South Beretania Street. This angered him, although there had been no mention of eviction. He planned revenge on the trust company, targeting Jamieson after learning he had a young son.

Fukunaga was an avid reader of crime stories, and his model was the Leopold-Loeb case in Chicago, where two young men from well-to-do families carried out the kidnapping and thrill-murder of a young boy. They, too, had sought $10,000 in ransom.

Word of Fukunaga's arrest spread like wildfire, and it took three companies of steel-helmeted National Guardsmen with fixed bayonets to control a crowd of twenty thousand massed in the streets around the police station.

Justice moved swiftly. By the first week in October jurors were being drawn in Judge A. E. Steadman's court. *Advertiser* writer Coll, reporting on the first day's proceedings, said that "references to death penalty, hanging, mob violence, premeditated murder and the like brought on a paleness of [Fukunaga's] cheeks, a nervous twitching of his hands and a futile licking of his slacked lips."[2] At each recess, he asked permission to leave the courtroom and stand in the judge's chambers in front of an electric fan.

Early in the trial his confession, remarkably detailed and seemingly forth-right, was introduced and then printed in the *Advertiser* and *Star-Bulletin*. In it, he said that "before I planned this, I was always a good boy. . . . I feel sorry that I have done this thing. . . . I know that crime never pays. I have studied enough about [it]. . . . I am a lonesome boy. . . . Books are my only friends."[3]

In court, he was asked by one of his court-appointed attorneys, Eugene Beebe, to read his confession for accuracy. He sat for more than an hour, reported the *Advertiser*,

> lost in the contents of the voluminous statement. He forgot for the time being that he was in court on trial for his life. To him it was a story. . . . From time to time he smiled and nodded his head as some passages would strike his particular fancy. . . . But for some reason or other it seemed different when [the prosecution] began reading it to the jury. . . . There was an entirely different expression.[4]

There was no defense testimony, and one hour and forty-five minutes after it began deliberating, the jury—multiracial, including a Japanese—brought a unanimous verdict of murder in the first degree. Forty-eight hours later, the interval required by state law between conviction and sentence, Judge Steadman, in a courtroom mostly filled with Japanese women, sen-tenced Myles Fukunaga to death by hanging. The youth held out his hand to attorney Beebe and thanked him for his efforts.

The *Advertiser* said that "never in the history of Hawaii has such a brutal, mercenary crime been committed. . . ." The fact "Fukunaga was not immedi-ately lynched, out of hand, indicates that the Honolulu community is deeply imbued with the principles of Anglo-Saxon justice and the predominance of law in this community. If ever a lynching were justified, it would have been the lynching of Fukunaga immediately after the facts of the case came to light."[5]

As defense appeals dragged through the courts, the *Hawaii Hochi*, a Japanese-language paper, raised the race issue in articles and later at a mass meeting attended by an estimated three thousand to five thousand people and addressed by the paper's owner. The thrust was that Fukunaga was insane and that in Hawaii there was one kind of justice for haoles, another for Orientals. In the process, a rival paper, the *Nippu Jiji*, which had had a staffer on the jury, was attacked.

On November 19, 1929, almost fourteen months after the crime and with appeals all the way to the U.S. Supreme Court exhausted, Myles Fukunaga went quietly to the gallows at Oahu Prison and twelve minutes and ten sec-onds later was proclaimed dead.

For the *Advertiser* there was a postscript. An editorial in the *Hawaii Hochi* titled "The Hymn of Hate" attacked the *Advertiser* for its editorial expressions that fairness had marked the trial and sentence and that it was unfortunate the *Hochi* had injected the race issue. In its editorial the *Hochi* said that a Professor Myrick, in writing to Governor Farrington, had stated that "a person who is in as good a position as anyone to know the inside of events" had told him that Fukunaga would have been found guilty of first degree murder "whatever the defense had been," adding that if the defendant had been a haole and the victim a Japanese, the verdict would have been entirely different. The *Hochi* said Myrick had informed it that the person who made the statements was Raymond Coll, managing editor of the *Advertiser,* and that the *Hochi* had "no reason to doubt the absolute truth of Professor Myrick's story."[6]

The *Advertiser* struck back hard, calling the statement attributed to Coll "an outrageous untruth uttered by a slinking weakling and given publicity by a charlatan and fanatic posing as champions of the Japanese in Hawaii." It said when it learned of Myrick's accusation it had requested he call at the *Advertiser* office and explain.

> Denounced in the most forcible terms one man could express to another as an unmitigated liar, he slumped down in his chair and admitted within hearing of witnesses that he had assumed to put in writing what he thought was in the editor's mind.
>
> Prior to that visit the editor of the Advertiser on his own initiative made the decision refusing to give publicity to a report Myrick offered to Governor Farrington, L. A. Thurston confirmed that decision when Myrick sought a hearing to have it reversed. The editor of the Advertiser never had any discussion of the Fukunaga case with Myrick. His only opinion from the hour Fukunaga was convicted to the day he was hanged was that he was sane, had a fair trial and deserved the death penalty.
>
> The Advertiser's only regret is that an element of the Japanese community may be influenced by a newspaper in their own language controlled by men who are as unprincipled as they are unethical.[7]

Traumatized as it was at the Fukunaga kidnap-murder, the community soon was to be shocked and stunned by an even more far-reaching tragedy.

Lorrin P. Thurston had been *Advertiser* publisher for only four months when, in mid-September 1931, the infamous Massie case erupted. Hawaii was faced with an explosive mixture of race and class distinction that thrust it onto the national stage, raising questions about the Islands' political relationship with the rest of the United States.

The central figure was Thalia Fortescue Massie, who, four years before, at age sixteen, had married Navy Lieutenant Thomas Massie on his graduation from Annapolis. She was the daughter of a disinterested father, a career soldier who had been military aide to the late President Theodore Roosevelt, and a dominating socialite mother, a niece of Alexander Graham Bell. A quiet, withdrawn young woman, she was unhappy with her husband, a southerner in the submarine service at Pearl Harbor, with whom she had frequent quarrels, and with his gregarious fellow junior officers.

On September 12, 1931, she reluctantly went with her husband to a dance at the Ala Wai Inn on Kalakaua Avenue. She had quite a bit to drink, which was unusual for her, and when a Navy lieutenant declined to draw up a seat for her at his table, she slapped his face and at about 11:30 marched out into the night. Her husband, meanwhile, was elsewhere in the two-story building. She wandered alone up Kalakaua, over the Ala Wai bridge, into John Ena Road to the point where it turns toward Fort DeRussy.

There, she said, a car stopped, two men got out, punched her in the face, dragged her inside, then drove to a brushy area on Ala Moana Road, where they and several others with them assaulted, then dumped her. She flagged an oncoming car and pleaded to be taken to her home in Manoa Valley. Her husband, failing to find her at the dance, went to a friend's house, phoned home, and was told by her that "something terrible has happened."

He rushed to her side, telephoned police, who sent two detectives. She told them that her attackers were Hawaiian, but, because it was dark, she could not identify them or get any numbers from the car's license plate. (She suffered from poor vision because of an ongoing systemic disorder.) She was taken to the emergency hospital on Lunalilo Street, where a doctor said she was under the influence of liquor and might or might not have been raped, but had douched before coming in. She was treated for a fractured jaw and facial wounds; no sex-organ bruises or abrasions or semen stains on her clothing were found.

As her husband and a detective were on the hospital porch discussing the case, a patrol car about fifty feet away was, within their earshot, repeatedly broadcasting the license number of a car involved in an incident at King and Liliha Streets. A passenger in a car driven by one Horace Ida had punched a Hawaiian woman after a near-collision and argument.

About 3:30 A.M. Thalia Massie went by request to the police station. She said she had, in retrospect, a fleeting glimpse of the attackers' license plate and gave a number one digit off the number police had broadcast. But the number she cited was identical with one on the detectives' desk within her vision. Asked whether the green dress she had been wearing was torn, she told police she didn't think it was.

Ida had been arrested, acknowledged the auto incident at King and Liliha, but denied knowledge of the Massie attack. The next morning police arrested David Takai, also of Japanese descent; Henry Chang, Hawaiian-Chinese; and Joseph Kahahawai, Hawaiian. That afternoon they picked up a second Hawaiian, Ben Ahakuelo, and charged all five with criminal assault. The first four had been taken to the Massie home and, after hearing them speak, Thalia Massie identified Chang and Kahahawai but said she wasn't sure about the other two. After Ahakuelo was arrested, he was taken to Queen's Hospital, where Mrs. Massie was undergoing further examination. She identified him by a gold tooth, although she had earlier said it was too dark to see any faces.

She identified Ida by feeling his jacket and saying it was like that worn by one of her assailants. There was no lineup. Only suspects were brought before her for identification, and the arrests preceded an investigation, the reverse of standard police procedure.

The case broke too late for coverage in the *Sunday Advertiser*. The next morning the paper headlined a "gang assault" by "fiends" on a young, kidnapped wife. The victim was described as a "woman of the highest character. . . . a white woman of refinement and culture," and the suspects as "gangsters."[8] A bulletin above the story linked the Massie case and the incident at King and Liliha Streets. Mrs. Massie was not named, in keeping with the general policy of the press then and for years later not to identify alleged rape victims.

That day's editorial, calling for swift, effective government action against "one of the most revolting crimes in Honolulu history," declared, "The safety of the women and children of Honolulu is a precarious thing as long as such degenerates are at liberty."[9]

From the outset, the contention of group rape was accepted as a fact by Navy officials and the "elite" of Honolulu and was reported that way. Editorials referred to the "rape gangsters," and news stories dealt with "the Ala Moana rape case" and later "the Massie rape case." When most of the public seemed to view the case as tragic but isolated, the *Advertiser* lashed out at the "alarming apathy" in sex cases and charged "the public frame of mind has emboldened sex offenders to the point where women are not safe outside their own backyards."[10]

Ironically, the *Advertiser* at the top of its sports page featured a game-winning sixty-yard touchdown run by one of the defendants, Ahakuelo, who happened to be a prize-winning athlete. The next day the paper apologized, declaring Ahakuelo was "not to be exploited in the sports columns until he completely clears himself of the ugly charges which he is facing." So much for the presumption of one's innocence until proven guilty.[11]

The five suspects were indicted; their trial started November 17 and ended December 6, when the jury—composed of six Caucasian-Hawaiians, two Japanese, two Chinese, one Caucasian, and one Portuguese (who in those days, because of their field-labor background, were regarded as a separate race)—was unable to reach a verdict.

The *Advertiser* editorialized that "Hawaii is on trial before the world" until the "rape gangsters" are duly convicted and sentenced. People were demanding that "womanhood be made safe in this city" and that police "laxity and inefficiency" was unacceptable as an excuse. "It is Honolulu's chief unfinished business to run down the Ala Moana gangsters and send them to the penitentiary for the rest of their days."[12]

At Pearl Harbor Admiral George Pettingill said "word has gone forth that [white] women cannot safely appear on the streets of Honolulu," and soon thereafter Admiral W. V. Pratt, chief of naval operations, in Washington, charged that in the previous eleven months in Honolulu there had been forty rape cases.[13] Official records showed only two.

Admiral Yates Stirling, commandant of the 14th Naval District, including Pearl Harbor, wanted the defendants jailed until their retrial but was told that under Hawaii law the men were entitled to bail. He felt Navy wives would be justified in carrying guns and "half suspected" that one or more defendants might soon be "swinging from the trees."[14]

Six days after the mistrial, Horace Ida was grabbed on Kukui Street by Navy men in several cars, taken to the Nuuanu Pali Road, beaten severely and left. But much greater trauma lay ahead. On the morning of January 6, 1932, Joseph Kahahawai, another defendant, had gone to the courthouse to report to a probation officer. Outside the building a fake summons was flashed at him, and he was put into a car and driven away. A cousin of his who witnessed this contacted police. The car, a Buick sedan, which turned out to have been rented for the occasion, carried Thalia Massie's husband at the wheel; her mother, Grace Fortescue; and, holding a gun on Kahahawai, a Navy enlisted man, Albert O. Jones. They drove to Mrs. Fortescue's cottage in Manoa.

She was so confident that a confession could be extracted from Kahahawai that, in arranging for his abduction, she had written to *Advertiser* Editor Coll, asking him to come to her house to serve as an out-of-sight witness. Coll refused, but he kept the letter secret, and in disposing of his files to a Hawaiiana collector three decades later he put an embargo on the letter while he was alive.[15]

Kahahawai, despite duress, apparently refused to confess and was shot to death. His body, swathed in a canvas sheet, was put in the car, which headed out Waialae Avenue toward Koko Head, where, police said, the plan was to weight the body and shove it over nearby cliffs into the ocean.

A police alarm had been sounded, and two squad cars chased after the now racing Buick. They overtook and stopped it near the entrance to Hanauma Bay, found Kahahawai's wrapped body, and arrested Massie, Mrs. Fortescue, the driver, and Navy fireman Edward J. Lord.

An *Advertiser* reporter, J. Stowell Wright, had followed the police cars and witnessed the arrests. He raced to the nearest phone and flashed word to the paper, which rushed out an extra, giving the town its first news of the startling development. Navy man Jones had been left at the Fortescue house to clean up the bloody mess but ignored abundant evidence of the murder. He had then gone to the Massie residence, where police found and arrested him.

As soon as word of the murder reached the mainland, flowers and supportive messages were wired to Mrs. Fortescue from such personages as Joseph Patterson, publisher of the *New York Daily News;* Mrs. Edward McLean, wife of the publisher of the *Washington Post;* and Gilbert Grosvenor, president of the National Geographic Society. The Hearst papers called the murder an "honor slaying" and declared: "Outside [Hawaii's] cities or small towns, the roads go through jungles and in these remote places bands of degenerate natives or half-whites lie in wait for white women driving by."[16]

Admiral Pratt wired Admiral Stirling that "under such circumstances, and for this crime, [American men] have taken the law into their own hands repeatedly, when they felt the law had failed to do justice."[17] This endorsement of lynch law upset the editors of both the *Advertiser* and the *Star-Bulletin*. The *Advertiser* said, "Vengeance which takes the form of execution cannot be condoned. No man or woman is justified in taking the law into his own hands and killing another." But it seemed to marvel at "the cool, daring and carefully executed plan" of the defendants.[18]

The *Star-Bulletin* called it an example of hysteria and reminded that Navy people are sworn to uphold the constitution and laws of the nation. And its publisher, one-time *Advertiser* editor and Island governor Farrington, wrote to the *New York Times* that Hawaii was neither riot-ridden nor race-mad and that mainland reports of race hatred and acute danger to women were viciously false and not at all reflective of the spirit of Honolulu.

On January 26 the grand jury indicted Mrs. Fortescue, Massie, Jones, and Lord. The next morning the *Advertiser* explained that "under its responsibilities to the law it could have done nothing less. Whatever one's feelings may be in the matter it must be agreed that the legal structure of government must be preserved and that an indictment was demanded under the conditions imposed by law."

On March 24 famed attorney Clarence Darrow arrived to represent the defendants. The trial began April 4 and ran through the month. In his summation, Prosecutor C. C. Kelley, taking note of the Navy's public pressure and advocacy of "the unwritten law," asked the jury:

> Are you going to give Lieutenant Massie [who was widely believed to have fired the murder weapon] leave to walk out? They'll make him an admiral. They'll make him chief of staff. He and Admiral Pratt are of the same mind. They believe in lynch law. . . . As long as the American flag flies on that staff, without an admiral's pennant over it, you must regard the Constitution and the law. Do your duty uninfluenced by influences of sympathy, by influences of admirals. As Smedley Butler, [a tough Marine general], said, "To hell with the admirals."

In return the *Advertiser* editorialized that the Navy was not on trial, but it and its personnel "have been particularly under fire without reason. . . . The motives of one of the Navy's most trusted officers . . . have been questioned." The paper suggested that the attitude of the territory's prosecutor was "not only consciously but deliberately one of disrespect and antagonism toward the Navy."[19]

On May 4 the jury—composed of six Caucasians, one Portuguese, two Chinese and three part-Hawaiians—declared the four defendants were guilty of manslaughter but recommended leniency. A week later Judge Charles S. Davis sentenced each to ten years in prison.

In the interim, great pressure was exerted on Governor Lawrence M. Judd to pardon the convicted. The secretary of the navy and 103 members of the U.S. House of Representatives wired Judd urging "prompt and unconditional pardon." The Hearst papers and some others boiled with inflammatory stories. Heavy local influence was brought to bear. Clearly, Judd faced a terrible dilemma. If he arbitrarily freed four murderers, law and order would have lost its meaning and Hawaii's credibility would be shredded. If, on the other hand, he let the long prison terms stand, bills in Congress, strongly pushed by the Navy, to change Hawaii's self-government to a military-controlled commission form might well pass.

Judd acted pragmatically. Immediately after the sentencing, he had Mrs. Fortescue, Massie, Jones, and Lord brought to Iolani Palace, and there he commuted their term to one hour in the custody of the Oahu Prison warden. In that way, he defused the tension but let their criminal records stand.

Although the Navy and, of course, the defendants were greatly relieved by Judd's action, the *Advertiser* was not. It said that in giving "a mere commutation of sentence" Judd had

> evaded the issue and again placed Hawaii in an unenviable light before the nation. The governor's action has the effect of a grudging acquiescence to a powerful public sentiment, whereas by granting a pardon he would have gracefully complied with that sentiment. . . . The impression will persist that Governor Judd has been evasive and ungenerous.

The paper again deplored Kelley's closing argument and called on the Chamber of Commerce to adopt a statement telling the world "there is no vendetta between the people of these Islands and our national sea force."[20]

The *Star-Bulletin,* which observed that the trial "was conducted according to the highest standards," was taken to task by the morning rival for "failing to recognize the importance of the Navy to the Islands and expressing the esteem in which its officers and enlisted personnel is held."[21]

Two days later the *Advertiser* said, "The governor should not have felt himself restricted by the legal factors of the case. Oftentimes the legal procedure has been flawless and yet, for reasons altogether outside the law, it is right and proper to pardon, to fully pardon."[22]

The inconclusiveness of the Massie case still hung over the Islands. But the Navy had reassigned Massie and the two enlisted men for duty elsewhere, and Mrs. Massie, taking the advice of lawyer Darrow, left with Mrs. Fortescue. As a result, without a complaining witness, the charges against the four remaining defendants were dropped.

But there were two official postludes. After the first trial, the Justice Department had sent Seth Richardson, assistant U.S. attorney general, and a team of ten to Honolulu to investigate judicial procedures. His thousand-page report said, "We found in Hawaii no organized crime, no important criminal class and no criminal rackets. We did not find substantial evidence that a crime wave, so called, was in existence in Honolulu . . . in comparison with crime records in cities of similar size on the mainland." He noted "no present serious racial prejudices. The races seem to be still carrying on together with exceedingly little friction." He found no facts substantiating reports of "alleged proclivity of members of the Hawaiian race in sexual crime."

But he was highly critical of "extreme laxity" and "inefficiency" in law enforcement agencies and said this had "given rise to a feeling of personal unsafety among a substantial portion of the citizenry."

And to Congress he sent a message: "The character of the territorial population, with its Oriental and Polynesian background, presents such an extraordinary experiment in the development of the American constitutional form of self-government among such people that no effort should be spared in providing proper conditions of law enforcement, and suitable administration of justice for the people of the Territory." He felt that the president, on recommendation of the territorial governor, should appoint the police chief and public prosecutor; this understandably frightened and drew no support from local leaders, who recognized the need for reform and were pursuing it.[23]

There was a second report of importance, following an investigation of the Massie Case by the Pinkerton National Detective Agency, commissioned by Governor Judd. A team of detectives had come from the mainland in June 1932 for a thorough study. The conclusion: "It is impossible to escape the conviction that the kidnaping and assault [of Thalia Massie] was not caused by the accused, with the attendant circumstances alleged by Mrs. Massie."[24]

Two years after returning to the mainland, Massie and his wife were divorced and both remarried. Massie at some point left the Navy for civilian life. Thalia Massie was successful in her third attempt at suicide, dying in 1963 from an overdose of barbiturates.

The Massie and Fortescue-Massie cases remain Hawaii's most sensational, and Theon Wright, who covered the trials for the *Advertiser* and remained until 1934, wrote one of several books on the subject. Newspaper behavior at the time, as a later observer noted, hardly constituted journalism's finest hour.

20

Editorial Policy Gets "Help" from the Big Five

LIFE INEXORABLY moves on, with reporters and editorialists never at a loss for material. Memories of the Massies faded and fresh headlines flared.

In 1932 the national depression and related issues led to a Democratic victory at the polls, mostly on the Honolulu city level but to a lesser degree in legislative seats as well. In analyzing the election results the *Advertiser* concluded that "the new voter, particularly those of Japanese or Chinese ancestry, and particularly the approximately 5,000 who registered between the primary and general elections, are congenitally Democratic in principle and vote Republican only through deep friendship for a candidate of that party, or in hopes of tangible reward in the shape of a job."

The paper quoted "a detached viewpoint" that "the Republican Party apparently has not yet realized that it must divorce the dominant business enterprises of Oahu from so direct control of the party, because the Democratic attacks on what they designated as 'the Invisible Government' of Hawaii prove to be one of the powerful arguments the Democrats had."[1]

Several days of national news was generated in July 1934 after President Roosevelt, on the cruiser USS *Houston*, landed at Kailua Bay, Kona. An unrewarding all-day fishing expedition, covered by press boaters including *Advertiser* reporters Ezra Crane and Henry E. Dougherty, preceded a visit to Honolulu, where FDR was honored with a multiethnic lantern parade.

His visit was more pleasant than the bank holiday he had declared a year earlier after runs on financial institutions across the nation. The *Advertiser* was chosen to print Depression currency, called "Honolulu Clearing House Certificates," scrip used for one day, March 11. When banks reopened two days later, the bills were redeemed and destroyed. The *Advertiser* was having its own financial headaches, with a loss of $26,829 for 1930, $4,789 for 1931, $45,080 in 1932, $41,682 in 1933, and $8,387 for the first five months of 1934, a net loss over the period of $126,767.

On a brighter note, on April 17, 1935, Hawaii entered the commercial air age with the arrival of Pan Am's Oriental Clipper, completing the first leg of a China flight via Pacific islands. The *Advertiser* hauled out its largest headline to greet the plane: "At last aviation is settling down to a solid basis in Pacific waters."[2]

By this time regular U.S. airmail service had been inaugurated in the islands, and, starting in 1934, the *Advertiser* was able to provide same-day news for many of its readers off Oahu.

Front-page coverage of big stories in both papers was often similar, but editorial pages were a different story. The *Advertiser* was the only paper to contend that children were being overeducated, and it wanted tuition charged in high schools, presumably to discourage attendance by all except the brightest:

> It is unadulterated cruelty to overfeed a child or a kitten, coddle and protect it and at maturity turn it loose to make its way in the world. . . . Cramming and stuffing book knowledge into the young . . . gives them no innate advantage or superiority over their unstuffed competition in later years. In practical affairs the latter often having the advantage. They become the employers of the over-schooled.[3]

When the legislature in 1933 mandated a $10 fee for high school students, the *Advertiser* alone gave its support. It called junior high schools "fads and frills" and said, "A boy or girl is entitled to just the amount of education the community can provide and no more."[4]

But four years later, when the legislature, under heavy thumping from the rest of the press, canceled the fee, the *Advertiser* accepted that even rural high schools might be useful.

In 1936 when the Hawaii Government Employees Association was formed, the *Advertiser* saw it as unwise, something that would work against the public and be subject to politics. The *Star-Bulletin* called it a constructive step, an improvement over the spoils system.

Private-sector unionization was having a rougher time. In 1935 businessmen organized the Industrial Association of Hawaii (ILA) "to combat radical unions and radical labor leadership."[5] George Pratt of the National Labor Relations Board, who held the first NLRB hearing in Honolulu in 1937, wrote of the close ties between the ILA, Army intelligence, and police in seeking to intimidate workers interested in union membership.

The waterfront was particularly volatile. On August 1, 1938, when some 250 striking longshoremen and seamen in Hilo marched to the docks and demonstrated against the unloading of a ship by strikebreakers, police fired into the crowd. Fifty-one workers were wounded, some severely, most of them in the back as they fled after initial shots.

The *Advertiser* briefly departed from its traditional antilabor stance, called the violence deplorable, and urged calm until the outcome of an inquiry by the territory's attorney general. In contrast, the *Star-Bulletin* was critical of the strikers, who in resumed negotiations acknowledged defeat after sixty-seven days off the job. Although no one was killed, the conflict became known as "the Hilo Massacre." A grand jury, after an eleven-day investigation, reported insufficient evidence to warrant any indictments.

Two reports in 1939 shed further light on the Islands' labor picture. After a number of hearings, E. J. Eagen of the NLRB reported that the "absolute control and domination" by the economic hierarchy over "the lives and welfare of virtually every individual is such that, had not their actions been somewhat tempered by some regard for the rights of human beings, the picture would be far different."[6]

Dr. James H. Shoemaker of the U.S. Bureau of Labor Statistics, who would later become chief economist of the Bank of Hawaii, reported that "the workers of Hawaii are economically isolated. [They] are completely dependent on a relatively restricted group of island enterprises throughout their whole lives." Of plantation workers he wrote that being associated with labor union activities invited blacklisting by plantation management "which in turn has its policies controlled from the offices of the factors in Honolulu."[7]

The *Advertiser*, defending business, said that Shoemaker "takes mild potshots at our interlocking directorates but acknowledges that they have been a natural development of an industry that built itself from nothing in a hundred years."[8] Labor historian Edward D. Beechert observes that the paper "omitted mention of Shoemaker's discussion of the role played by subsidies and tariffs in building the industry."[9]

Although the sugar industry in the 1930s was paying higher wages and providing better perquisites than competing mainland companies, the Big Five—the Islands' most powerful corporations—became concerned about a growing antibusiness feeling. They brought a hotshot advertising and public relations man, Sydney S. Bowman, from San Francisco to attract more tourists to the Islands and, at the same time, enhance the big corporations' image. He lured national magazine editors and writers with expense-paid vacations. And he enlisted the help of the Honolulu press.

In his book *Hawaii: Restless Rampart*, Joseph Barber, Jr., who contributed to such magazines as the *Atlantic* and *Esquire*, wrote that "Nominally independently owned, the two leading newspapers, morning and afternoon, had for years reflected more or less consistently the policies and viewpoints of local business leaders . . . [who] took it for granted that editorially the Honolulu *Advertiser* and the Honolulu *Star-Bulletin* should conform with their own interests."[10]

When Bowman felt labor was "getting too much notice" or speeches by "troublemakers" were being covered,

A series of friendly meetings with the publishers and editors was arranged, in which Bowman representatives emphasized the perils of building up "agitators" in the press. Specific news stories which had already appeared were alluded to, with suggestions as to how their treatment might have been improved. To the newspapermen involved, such meddling in editorial matters was little short of insulting. But they were hardly in a position to express their true feelings.[11]

Barber wrote that the Bowman organization sent suggested editorials to the newspapers. And he intimates that the tab was picked up for *Advertiser* Publisher Thurston's 10,000-mile swing of U.S. sugar operations.

> He visited mainland sugar-beet and cane areas and Puerto Rico in the course of his extended and expensive trip, and wrote a series of daily articles about his experiences for the *Advertiser*'s editorial page. Dwelling at length upon the miserable living and working conditions and poor pay of the sugar laborers elsewhere, compared with Hawaii, the articles were well edited by Bowman representatives in San Francisco and Honolulu and by executives of the HSPA [Hawaiian Sugar Planters' Association], before being sent finally with their collective blessing to the *Advertiser* editor.[12]

(Of Barber's specific allegations, no independent confirmation has surfaced, but there is no question about the papers' probusiness sentiments.)

Meanwhile, the *Advertiser* continued to be plagued by low circulation figures. In 1937, for example, the morning paper averaged 15,737 copies a weekday—12,961 behind the *Star-Bulletin*'s 28,698. The picture was helped by the *Advertiser*'s Sunday edition, the only one at the time, selling in excess of 22,000 copies. But the spread in the daily competition, reflected in advertising linage, would continue to be a vexing and, in time, dangerous problem for the *Advertiser*.

Research Fueled by "'Nippin' and 'Sippin'"

THE BUSINESS problems of the *Advertiser* seemed to have little or no effect on the makeup or mood of the newsroom. The 1930s brought in a number of talented journalists who worked hard and played hard. It was a time of wanderlust and the Far East was a powerful lure for many mainland newspeople who came to Honolulu, worked for a while, and went on to Japan or China, especially Shanghai, the "Paris of the Orient." Some came back and picked up as if they'd never been away.

One of the standouts among the bright writers was Bob Trumbull, born in Chicago in 1912 of show business parents and boarded with a Pittsburgh family until he finished high school during the Depression. A widowed grandmother in Seattle then housed him while he studied journalism at the University of Washington.

In the summer of 1933 he arrived in Honolulu on an ROTC training cruise. On the fourth day of a five-day stay, he visited Fred J. Green, the *Advertiser*'s business manager (who had also variously served as circulation manager and advertising director). Green's daughter, an actress, had starred in one of the senior Trumbull's companies, and she encouraged her father to give Bob a job. Green approached Editor Coll and offered to have the payroll cover a spot for Trumbull. Neither he nor Coll knew anything about Trumbull's ability, but Coll reluctantly took him on, at $12 a week.

Two years later Trumbull was city editor, succeeding Jack Ryan, a crack writer who, when working on a Newark, New Jersey, paper, was credited with breaking the Lindbergh kidnapping story. But Ryan was a heavy drinker and a contemporary recalls coming into the *Advertiser* office and seeing Ryan, "on one of his tears, balling up the night's copy and throwing it around the city room."[1]

At twenty-four, Trumbull was the youngest on the staff, often mistaken by visitors as the copy boy, but he was thoughtful, unfailingly polite, even courtly, and urbane beyond his years. He was dapper in his dress—unique today, coat and tie were standard—and, to look more mature, he affected a pencil mustache reminiscent of Adolph Menjou and Ronald Colman.

Trumbull had a staff of only seven or eight reporters, augmented by several deskmen who processed local and wire stories, photographers, and occasionally servicemen working part-time. He was a perfectionist and his writing and editing were models of precision. Under the pseudonym of Sol Pluvius, he wrote a daily weather column, surmounted by a lauhala hat, popular with readers for its homely humor. He and his wife Jean, who had been his college sweetheart, often hosted staffers at their Waikiki cottage, Hale Leaky Leaky.

Everyone worked a six-day week, competing with a larger and better paid *Star-Bulletin* staff. With no air-conditioning, the windows were always open, and buckets of water were kept on desks under overhead lights to lure flying termites.

"Boss" Coll, as the staff knew and addressed him, was the dominant presence, taking a close interest in the major stories. He departed from usual procedure by personally giving reporters assignments when politics was involved. City Editor Trumbull, who normally would have done this, was kept posted through a "rough liaison" with Coll in his corner office adjoining the newsroom. To Trumbull "every political reporter was a personal emissary for Coll. On their return from Iolani Palace [the seat of territorial government] or City Hall, they reported to the old man." But the reporting was "straight" and the "integrity level high."[2]

The *Star-Bulletin* was regarded as a Big Five paper, strongly supportive of the major corporations that ruled the economy. The *Advertiser*, while not trampling on Big Five toes, was seen as more independent, with a relationship closer to Walter Dillingham and his interests. Charlie Hogue, by then a senior journalist, wrote most editorials, but Coll also wrote some or dictated them.

Politics was always a hot subject and major responsibility for its coverage fell to Harry L. Stroup, an alumnus of the *Hilo Tribune-Herald* and the *Star-Bulletin*, who came to the *Advertiser* in 1932. After three years he joined a newspaper in Shanghai, then traveled the world, returning to the *Advertiser* in 1938. For the next eleven years he served as political reporter and sometimes city editor. (Because of a tight staff, almost everyone, it seemed, had a turn on the desk.)

Stroup was a crack political writer, with great contacts who trusted him for his fairness and sound judgment, and he often beat the competition. He additionally did a column under the pseudonym of "Kamaaina Campaigner," making insightful observations on the political scene. He was a whiz at pidgin, a less diluted patois in those days, and his column, "You Taleen Me," by "Joe Manuel, Da Raddio Cop," a fictional member of the Honolulu Police Department, had a loyal readership. His assignments at times went beyond politics. He worked on the Massie case and in World War II accompanied Ernie Pyle, the famous war correspondent, on his last assignment in the Pacific.

In war and peace, Honolulu had a reputation as a drinking town and Stroup and his colleagues had no difficulty in upholding it. If the "nippin' and sippin'" didn't interfere with one's work, no one thought about it. The office pub was Frankie's, across South Street. Pails of beer bought there and bottles of harder stuff were stashed in the *Advertiser* library, and there was a fairly constant need to hasten there for "research."

Frances Lycan, the flaming redheaded librarian, patiently put up with the alcoholic storage. But when some of the cabinets, including one marked Z for "zowie," started overflowing, she playfully rounded up a dozen bottles, put them in a cardboard box, and dumped it on Stroup's desk when he was out of the building. By happenstance, this was seconds before Publisher Thurston, on one of his rare trips to the newsroom, strode through, glanced at the bottles, presumably realized the prank, and marched on to the mechanical department without a word.

Librarian Lycan also had other ways of asserting herself. The library filed not only clippings and photographs, but metal engravings of people that could be reused without further expense and save the time required to make a fresh engraving from a photo. If Lycan didn't like a person in the news, she simply tossed his or her engraving into the wastebasket, a habit that not infrequently created consternation in the newsroom, especially on deadline.

Stroup left the paper in 1949, but in 1954, after serving as secretary to territorial Governors Ingram M. Stainback and Oren E. Long, he returned to head the legislative bureau, overseeing reporters Gardiner Jones and Brian Casey. A time clock put in by an efficiency expert offended his dignity, and after some months he left newspapering for good, for the political realm he had covered for so long, serving as the administrative assistant to Honolulu Mayors John H. Wilson and Neal Blaisdell. To the local press club, he remained one of their own, and they named him to the Hall of Fame.

In some ways the most colorful character in the cast was Edna B. "Ma" Lawson, a short woman with the bosomy figure of an opera star and a boyish bob, the society editor from 1932 to 1953. The first white girl born in Deadwood, territory of South Dakota, in 1898, she claimed to have been nursed by Calamity Jane, a famous frontier scout.

Coming to Honolulu in 1925, she taught at McKinley High School and the old Normal School, which preceded Teachers College, before joining the *Advertiser* in middle age. She was unfamiliar with journalism in general and a typewriter in particular. But she was enthusiastic and gutsy, an energetic worker whose day sometimes ran from 8 A.M. until midnight. She had devoted assistants in Ella Chun and Margaret Kamm, a highly regarded local actress.

She doubled as the drama, literary, music, and art critic, sometimes plunging beyond her depth but never losing her outward confidence. Says a colleague, "Edna B"—as she was affectionately known to her readers— "was the biggest fraud but we loved her. Once we swiped her book on music which she used in writing reviews. She was lost, devastated and furious. She lived at the Young Hotel and, when receiving guests, wore a black turban

and a long holoku-type dress. She was always flicking her eyes at you."[3]
Adds another:

> She was a great asset to the paper but something of a phony in regard to the
> cultural subjects she was supposed to cover. She once covered a piano con-
> cert and in her review stole freely from a stateside review of a violin perfor-
> mance of one of the numbers in the Honolulu concert. Unfortunately, her
> review told how wonderfully the pizzicato [string plucking] section had been
> performed by the pianist.[4]

Still, she was the town's social arbiter. She helped start the Honolulu
Community Theatre and was on the board of the symphony society. In 1949
the Honolulu Chamber of Commerce selected her as the first woman to
receive its "Man of the Week" award.

Lawson enjoyed dropping names of notables she met in covering the cultural scene, among them Yehudi Menuhin, Faith Baldwin, Lin Yü-t'ang,
Kathleen Norris, John Ford, Marian Anderson, and Artur Rubinstein.

A much younger, more modest, but far better writer than Lawson was
Naomi Benyas, the daughter of a prominent Honolulu physician and an
accomplished pianist, who filled in as an *Advertiser* reviewer of music and
theater. She went out as an inquiring reporter with chief staff photographer
Danny Morse and on boat day interviewed incoming celebrities, among them
Bette Davis, Clare Boothe Luce, and Ernest Hemingway, who said little.

The champion drinker on the staff was Walter J. "Doc" Adams, who did
feature stories and wrote a lively column five days a week. In his early to
middle thirties, he was a gregarious man who "knew everybody in town," got
to meet notable visitors, and had a presence about him. He was "the sweetheart of the staff and a wondrous drunk," right out of the Chicago epic, *The
Front Page*. He was "very funny and now and then would disappear" and
wind up in a bawdy house downtown chatting with the help.[5] Sadly, he
became a classic alcoholic and it got him in the end; he was found dead in a
San Francisco gutter.

One of the best-liked staffers was Andrew Mitsukado, who came aboard
full-time in June 1931 after serving as a sports stringer while attending the
University of Hawaii. He soon became Sports Editor Red McQueen's dependable right arm and, except for two years as an Army interpreter in the Tokyo
war crime trials, he served the paper for forty-two years, until retiring as
executive sports editor in 1973.

He covered everything—swimming, boxing, basketball, football—and
was responsible for giving rural high school sports their first real space.
Although he spoke Japanese well, he became skittish after an admiral on trial
in Tokyo ran into him in the men's room during a recess and told Andy his
translations were terrible. After that, he declined to interview visitors to the
Islands from Japan.

A later sports editor, Hal Wood, said of him: "He knew more sports figures and more sports figures knew him than any [other] person in Hawaii." A sellout crowd of six hundred honored him on retirement.

The paper had its own "celebrity," Jane Howard, a Radcliffe graduate, daughter of Roy Howard, editor of the *New York World-Telegram* and head of Scripps-Howard Newspapers and United Press. Predictably, during her stint from 1937 to 1939 Howard received special treatment. She explored Pan Am's trans-Pacific Clipper route to Hong Kong, with a side trip into China. There she flew to the provincial capital of Hankow, base of Chiang Kai-shek's resistance to Japanese invaders. Her father's stature opened doors and this gave the *Advertiser* good VIP copy. Howard interviewed Madame Chiang and then in Manila, where she was his house guest, U.S. Commissioner Paul V. McNutt. Out again in the fall of 1938, she reported from Japan, Manchukuo (Manchuria), and Korea.

The images of Hawaii that draw tourists also can lure working journalists. Alexander MacDonald, a Boston University alumnus who had begun newspapering as an eleven-year-old paperboy, was foreign news editor of the Bridgeport, Connecticut, *Times-Star* when, "on a bleak December day" he was handed a photograph of Waikiki Beach. "I studied the scene: the clear tropical sky, the waves curling in from the ocean, bathers lounging in the sand, in the background the dramatic profile of Diamond Head."[6]

Checking, he found there were English-language papers in the Islands. He quit his job and on January 19, 1933, arrived in Honolulu with $14 in his pockets. At the *Advertiser*, Editor Coll told him the staff was full but to try again in a few months. He landed on the *Star-Bulletin* at $25 a week, covering the waterfront, and lived in a $20-a-month beachside grass shack by the old Elks Club in Waikiki.

Nine months later, MacDonald joined a Bishop Museum expedition ship headed for a year in French Oceania, and the *Star-Bulletin* told him to consider himself permanently fired. When he returned to Honolulu, Coll met him at the dock and took him on as a police reporter, "6 P.M. to 2 A.M. every night except Sunday." On the side he wrote many articles on his South Seas adventures, colorfully illustrated by artist Jerry Chong, and in due course was named Sunday features editor.

Compared to the *Star-Bulletin*, which he had found "staid, humorless, tenaciously matter of fact," successful "with the business community and its conservative leadership," the *Advertiser* "sought more intimacy with its readers . . . It was a writer's paper." He had found the *Star-Bulletin* staff to be a teetotal lot," but

almost to a man, those on the Advertiser were two-fisted drinkers. Not that this was revealed in their output, though sometimes a staffer might slip out for a quick one at China Joe's, the bar and grill a few yards down Kapiolani

Boulevard. It was only after presstime that the city room gang routinely gathered for serious social drinking. Getting out the paper always came first.[7]

MacDonald fell in love with Betty Peet, whom he described as a tawny blonde, hazel-eyed and athletic, gifted with a talent for whimsy, and they were married July 3, 1937. During World War II he served in Navy intelligence, then with the Office of Strategic Services (OSS) in Asia and afterward founded the *Bangkok Post*. While in service he wrote a book, *Revolt in Paradise: The Social Revolution in Hawaii After Pearl Harbor*, which became a West Coast best-seller.

His bride Betty was the daughter of *Advertiser* sports editor Bill Peet; her godfather was the famed Walter Johnson of the Washington Senators. A University of Washington journalism graduate, she came home in 1935 and was told by her father it was time to go to work. He urged her to see Editor Coll as soon as she was settled, but, meanwhile, asked her to cover a swim meet that very night at the Natatorium. She earned her first byline but, in the process, misspelled Duke Kahanamoku's name. The next day, she called on Coll, got a job at $10 a week doing waterfront features, editing copy in cables from Japan, but especially enjoying turning out animal stories.

She wrote a sorrowful obituary on Daisy, the longtime zoo elephant, and discovered an arsonist mynah bird who swooped down, picking up lighted cigarettes, flying off with them to a dry coconut tree and loudly exulting as the tree burst into flame. Her story, with pictures, made page one. Then there was the bull terrier who in five minutes flat—she timed him—could husk a coconut, puncture the shell, and slurp down the milk. Part of *Advertiser* legend was her interview with an aged emu at the zoo. In 1937 she accepted a *Star-Bulletin* offer to be its society editor, and in the war she, like her then husband, was recruited by the OSS and later worked in Washington.

Another New Englander, William E. Hutchinson, who joined the *Advertiser* in September 1937, had worked on the *Boston Evening Transcript* until the urge to travel set in. A friend on the copy desk had worked for Ray Coll in Pennsylvania and gave Hutchinson his name. He wrote Coll, who replied that a job awaited him. He married his girlfriend, borrowed $300 from the *Transcript* to meet expenses, and took off with his bride for Honolulu.

He was an excellent deskman and probably one of the few anywhere to use a slide rule when making a page-one layout of where stories and photos were to be placed. He was responsible for a change in typography that gave the paper an appearance somewhat like that of the *New York Herald Tribune* and his old paper, the *Transcript*.

As news editor, he was dealing each night with dispatches coming over the wire. During 1940–1941 growing tension in Asia, fueled by Japan, dominated the news, and most, if not all, at the *Advertiser* expected war to break out—in the Philippines, if the United States was the target, or in Singapore or

Malaysia, if the first strike was against the British—but certainly not in fortress Hawaii.

When Hutchinson designed page one of the *Sunday Advertiser* of November 30, 1941, eight days before Pearl Harbor, his two top headlines dealt with the imminence of war. The larger headline conveyed that Japanese envoy Saburo Kurusu, who had been in Washington for talks with Secretary of State Cordell Hull, had been bluntly warned the United States was prepared for battle. The other headline, at the top of the page, above the *Advertiser* nameplate, proclaimed, "Japanese May Strike Over Weekend!" The story below it, from United Press in Washington, reported that "cancellation of [British] soldiers' leaves in Singapore coincided with a widespread belief that Japan may strike somewhere during the weekend." There was not the slightest intimation of Hawaii as a possible target, but that front page subsequently was cited by pseudohistorians theorizing that President Franklin D. Roosevelt knew Pearl Harbor would be attacked but kept it to himself. (In 1991, at the fiftieth anniversary of Pearl Harbor, the *Advertiser*'s 1941 front page was resurrected by both U.S. and Japanese television researchers and reporters looking for a startling peg for their broadcasts. One Tokyo TV crew calling at the *Advertiser* seemed determined to use the headline as proof of high-level American perfidy.)

In 1944 Hutchinson was recruited by the OSS and shipped off to India. He later joined the U.S. Information Service and remained for nineteen years, mostly abroad, before retiring to Maryland.

22

"If That's Anti-Japanese, Make the Most of It"

IN 1940 dual citizenship was a hot issue. Many Japanese born in Hawaii and thus automatically U.S. citizens were registered at birth at the Japanese consulate and also regarded as citizens of Japan. The *Advertiser* proclaimed it "an inexcusable, disagreeable situation, unacceptable to the American way of thinking."[1] The paper acknowledged that

> the very great majority of those Japanese born and raised here are loyal Americans. . . . The Hawaiian Japanese Civic Association, openly on record to aid the people it represents in ridding themselves of divided loyalty, is an outstanding example of what the younger Japanese stand for, [but] the American-born Japanese of maturity who deliberately holds on to his dual citizenship for business or political reasons or because of sympathy with an alien nation is and will continue to be the object of our censure. . . . If that's anti-Japanese, make the most of it."[2]

The issue became sharply focused when a deputy sheriff of the Big Island, Senji Abe, ran on the Republican ticket for a seat in the fifteen-member territorial Senate. Previously a clerk, then cashier and interpreter at the Hilo police court, he had been described by the *Star-Bulletin* in 1933 as "one of Hilo's most useful citizens." Island born, he had served in World War I and for fifteen years been a member of the American Legion. He had applied to Japan in the spring of 1940 for expatriation, but official approval was not received until three days before the general election, November 5.

The *Advertiser* had been hammering at Abe both because of dual citizenship and its feeling that he was running as a front for a politicized Hawaii county police department eager to stave off legislation creating a police commission. The chairman of the Hawaii county Republican committee, A. T. Spalding, in a letter to the *Advertiser*, contended that the newspaper was attacking Abe because of his racial origin and through him "the entire population of Hawaii of Japanese ancestry."[3] He added that the *Advertiser* was a Honolulu newspaper sticking its nose in a matter in which it had no business.

In an adjoining column the editor responded, "Since when is the Advertiser solely an Oahu newspaper? [It] stands for the best interests of all Hawaii." And, as far as it was concerned, "should the voters of Hawaii pause an instant in choosing the right men in this election"—including one of Abe's opponents—"their county will be branded immediately and decisively as unAmerican."[4]

Despite the commotion, Abe became the first American of Japanese ancestry elected to the territorial Senate, defeating a popular Democrat, Circuit Judge William Achi. He served in the regular and special sessions of the legislature in 1941. But in August 1942 he was charged under an army general order with possession of a Japanese flag, found among the props of a Hilo theater in which he had a business interest. Two days later the charge was dropped because the order had not yet officially taken effect. Returned to Abe, the flag was publicly burned outside the police station.

Abe subsequently was taken into custody, given a secret hearing without benefit of counsel, and, although never charged, was detained for two months on Sand Island and then seventeen months at Honouliuli, near Ewa Beach. Although he had been elected to a four-year Senate term, he resigned because of his inability to serve in the 1943 session.

The *Advertiser* called it "the right course" and said "the Republican party of the Island of Hawaii took the wrong course in the first place when it supported Abe and elected him to office. There was a lack of foresight among his supporters; they ignored the handwriting on the wall."[5]

Abe's three sons and three sons-in-law, all AJAS, served in World War II. In a 1968 *Advertiser* interview, Abe, seventy-three and blind, showed no rancor: "I can't kick too much about [being detained for nineteen months]. During a war period you have to expect anything. And of course times have changed."[6]

Along with its criticism of Abe, the *Advertiser* berated the Japanese-language papers for "not endorsing wholeheartedly the current movement to wipe out dual citizenship."[7] It charged, "In several editorials the Japanese newspapers have chosen to raise arguments that would support their followers in attitudes not 100 percent American."[8]

The tensions over dual citizenship by happenstance coincided with a significant national poll and local plebiscite. The poll, taken by Elmo Roper and reported in *Fortune* magazine, showed that if Hawaii were under attack only slightly more than half of the mainlanders queried favored a U.S. rescue effort, as against three-quarters supporting defense of Canada. To pro-Hawaii statehood forces this demonstrated an urgent need for early positive action by Congress.

The plebiscite, authorized by the 1940 territorial legislature, was on statehood. It was supported by sugar interests, the *Star-Bulletin*, and at least two Japanese-language papers, the *Hawaii Hochi* and the *Nippu Jiji*. But the *Advertiser* looked askance, arguing that because of the thousands of Japanese aliens in the Islands, plus the Japanese-language schools and the dangers inherent in Japanese propaganda, the Islands lacked the level of Americanism needed to merit statehood.

Calling only for eventual statehood, the plebiscite ironically was held with the 1940 election that Abe won. Sixty-seven percent of those who went to the polls voted "yes," with the Neighbor Islands' margin ahead of Oahu's.

The *Advertiser*'s view was that "few realists in the Territory expect [statehood] to be achieved for a long time to come."[9] The paper shared the line of Walter F. Dillingham and certain other leaders who wanted the status quo, politically, economically, and socially, maintained, since statehood, by widening the power base, would cut into their considerable clout. With war flaming in Europe and looming in the Pacific, the issue landed on the shelf until later in the decade.

In early 1941 Editor Coll and the *Advertiser* were cited for contempt of court by Federal Judge Ingram M. Stainback for printing a prejudicial headline and story reporting an "Espionage Investigation Launched Into Japan Case." Involved was the seizure of nineteen sampans by customs agents and the indictment of seventy-one persons and three fishing companies charged with conspiracy for false registration. There was no reference or charge of espionage in the case. Coll was placed on probation for sixty days.[10]

23

"Something's Going on out at Pearl"

THE *ADVERTISER*'S anti-Japanese attitude was a dominant feature of the paper's policy when the United States was suddenly catapulted into World War II.

For former Governor Lawrence M. Judd, it began as simply a frustrating Sunday morning. Up at 5:30, he couldn't find his *Advertiser.* A couple of hours later, still without his paper, he looked out from his hillside home and was puzzled by the noise and smoke and unusual movement of ships and planes in the distance at Pearl Harbor.[1] It was December 7, 1941.

Judd wasn't the only one without his Sunday paper. A gear on the *Advertiser* press had sheared the night before just as the Sunday edition run started, completely shutting down the machinery. And the distant commotion he viewed was the Japanese assault on Pearl Harbor. So absolute was the surprise that, as naval historian Samuel Eliot Morison wrote, "never in modern history was a war begun with so smashing a victory by one side."[2]

As soon as the *Advertiser* press failed, efforts were made by Henry Herrick, the department superintendent, and others to arrange for printing at the Japanese-language paper, the *Nippu Jiji,* on Bethel Street near Merchant, which had similar equipment. George Akeo, then a youthful *Advertiser* pressman, recalled making asbestos mats of the Sunday pages, which were taken to the *Nippu Jiji* by Herrick, production manager George Voorhees, and pressman Charlie Pedro.

By the time the curved metal plates for the press had been cast, by pumping molten lead into the asbestos mats, it was about 8 A.M. Strange noises were heard from outside. The Japanese pressmen and *Advertiser* people went out of the building to see what was happening. The December 7 *Sunday Advertiser* never went to press. Even if it had, its contents had been overtaken by one of the greatest, albeit tragic, news stories in American history.

Elaine Fogg, then working in the *Advertiser*'s circulation department, was waked at 6:45 A.M. by Bill Schiller, an assistant circulation manager, explaining the phones were blaring tirades from subscribers who wanted their Sunday paper and would she come in.

On arrival, she saw three musicians who had left KGU on the third floor and was told, "Something's going on out at Pearl." She and Schiller scrambled to the building roof for a look and found others already there. She remembers it vividly:

Great billows of oily black smoke were rising and spreading out over Pearl Harbor. There were planes darting in all directions. And the guns on Punchbowl had begun adding an authoritative voice to the improbable scenario.

Was this an unusually realistic alert or something more calamitous? While we were still deciding, a shell shattered a masonry wall at the rear of the building and gave the whole plant a mighty shake. Marion Mulrony [the KGU manager] had climbed about 10 feet up the radio tower [on the roof] to get a better look at what was going on. He had made his ascent one rung at a time. He came down like a fireman on a pole when the alarm sounds.

Fogg found herself on the news desk with Irva Edwards, a proofreader in the commercial printing department. "Neither of us belonged there, but the regular Sunday staff wasn't due in for several hours. Bob Trumbull [the city editor] and his wife were in the country for the weekend. So there we were; it was our maiden thrust into a news desk partnership that was to last many months."[3]

Another staffer, Jack Smith, later a popular columnist with the *Los Angeles Times*, was standing with friends in the yard of United Press correspondent William Tyree, after an all-night party, when they heard an explosion. Smith, his wife, and Harry Albright, an *Advertiser* reporter who months earlier had become a captain in Army public relations, drove off toward their homes downtown when Smith saw planes streaking toward Pearl Harbor. He observed that

somebody seemed to be shooting at the planes, since puffs of black smoke were appearing just below them. Captain Albright, assuming it was an exercise, stopped the car, got out in the street, arms akimbo, and said, "Damn those guys! I've told them and told them not to do things like this without letting me know." Albright dropped my wife and me off at our apartment near Queen's Hospital. I knew something was amiss, but couldn't define it. Then a friend hammered on our door and yelled, "The Japs are bombing us." I said, "I know it." Because I did.

My wife went to her job at RCA [Radio Communications of America] and I went to the Advertiser. We were all stunned. Harry Stroup and other reporters showed up and were sent out to Pearl Harbor.[4]

Stroup and writer LaSelle Gilman had a Pearl Harbor admission sticker on their car and got into the base during the final stages of the attack. At one point they ducked under the car, just before a plane's machine gun stitched a row of unfriendly holes in the roadway beside them. They got back to the office with an eyewitness account—to find there was no way of then printing it. Their bylined story ran the following morning, but it was largely gutted because of security considerations. Stroup said, "It was the biggest story of my life and I could only write what happened on the way there and back."[5]

City Editor Trumbull, who had raced to the office on hearing of the attack, quickly dispatched staffers on hand. In one of his recollections of that day, he said:

> Our photographer was out all morning shooting pictures of the civilian casualties. He brought them to me just before noon. Then I realized that for the first time here in Hawaii I was looking at pictures of civilian wartime casualties. Of course we couldn't print them. Some were terrible shots of people maimed and disemboweled. But for me, looking at those photos, I knew that we were at war.[6]

Bill Hutchinson woke just after 8 A.M. with a massive hangover. He had no car and public transportation wasn't working. He phoned his father and was driven to the *Advertiser* about nine o'clock. There he learned about the broken press gear and the never-published Sunday edition. "We all felt pretty hopeless and frustrated. Here was unquestionably the biggest story of our lives breaking all around us. We kept writing and editing copy for an extra, but there was no way to print anything." As it was, he didn't get home again for four days.[7]

Meanwhile, over on Merchant Street on that fateful Sunday, the *Star-Bulletin* was having a journalistic field day. Editor Riley Allen, who went in early every day, got an excited phone call from a circulation man near Pearl Harbor. He reported he had seen the Rising Sun insignia on the planes bombing the naval base. Once convinced, Allen summoned staffers and three hours later produced the first of three eight-page extras that day. Publisher Joseph R. Farrington later said, "Honolulu needed newspapers that morning as desperately as famished people need food."[8] In all, 126,000 papers were printed, triple the afternoon paper's usual circulation.

In the *Advertiser* newsroom frustration and dismay hung like black crepe even as the staff began gathering information and preparing stories and hoping for a Monday paper. Publisher Thurston arrived in the newspaper's parking lot shortly after the shell had landed near the plant. He soon began getting phone calls from the armed forces to shut down KGU, for fear the Japanese could follow its signal into Honolulu. Thurston, having heard from Governor Poindexter that he wanted to broadcast a proclamation of a state of emergency over KGU, told his callers he would take the station off the air after that but not before, since there had been no declaration of martial law.[9] The governor climbed the stairs to KGU and went on the air about 10:45 A.M., after which Thurston silenced the station.

Not long after, Poindexter reluctantly signed a second proclamation, declaring the Territory of Hawaii to be under martial law, with the Army's commander, General Walter C. Short, to serve as military governor, taking over the powers normally exercised by the civil governor, the legislature, and the judiciary, and thus controlling every activity in the Islands.

City Editor Trumbull sent Fogg to nearby Iolani Palace to get a copy of the martial law proclamation. While she was there "everything shook as a shell gouged out a crater in the mauka-waikiki corner of the palace grounds [where the archives building now stands]. I joined those running out to have a look at it and picked up a few pieces of shrapnel still so hot that they had to be tossed from one palm to another. . . ."

Soon after returning to the *Advertiser*, she got a taste of what military government would be. "A group of us went to Times Grill [next door] for what we considered a well-earned drink and a bite of lunch. We had been served just one drink before management got the official word: cease and desist providing alcoholic beverages.

> Soon sandbags began piling up at both front and rear doors of our building, accompanied in each case by a brace of young sentries who appeared to be as nervous as their wicked-looking guns. Makeshift blackout was being hurriedly applied to windows in key areas of the building.
>
> I returned from another assignment in the afternoon to find Wayne Damon [purchasing agent] and Allen Maguire [treasurer and business manager] sitting on a lower step of the waikiki-side stairway identifying employees as we came into the building. We were being issued "official" ID cards.[10]

Just ahead of Fogg a poorly dressed, slight little man, seeking entry, gave a foreign-sounding name which neither McGuire nor Damon recognized. They shook their heads. The man repeated his name, to no avail. Finally he wailed, "I'm Santa Claus." It developed that some weeks before Damon had hired him to play the role "beside the huge Christmas tree which stood in the lobby [as] part of an Advertiser–Junior League project to collect toys for needy children. Damon had never seen the little man except in full St. Nick regalia that made him three times life-size." Hearing the news, Santa had come to the office wanting to help. He got his ID card and that night, with photographer 'Colonel' [Kazuto] Shimagaki, manned an all-night coffee-and-soup station for those of us who remained in the building."[11]

The *Star-Bulletin*, with an idle press at night, briefly put aside its rivalry and permitted the *Advertiser* to print its December 8 issue in its building. By the following night an ingenious technician at Honolulu Iron Works had duplicated the *Advertiser*'s broken gear and the paper was back in business in its own plant.

But the December 7 jinx was still alive. Acting on a report from an unidentified Army source, the December 8 *Advertiser* blazoned a blockbuster page-one headline, "SABOTEURS LAND HERE!" Below it a story erroneously announced in large type that a party of saboteurs had landed on northern Oahu, wearing red disks on their shoulders, and the enemy paratroopers had dropped into Kalihi. The paper further reported renewed bombing attacks on

Oahu, red antiaircraft bursts from the direction of Hickam Field, and brief machine-gun firing heard along the waterfront.

The Army moved swiftly. Lieutenant Colonel Kendall J. Fielder, chief of intelligence (G-2) under General Short, knew "something had to be done to avoid unduly alarming the public. Things were chaotic enough without that."[12] Publisher Thurston and Editor Coll were summoned to Fielder's office at Fort Shafter. Albright and Hugh Lytle, former Associated Press bureau chief in Honolulu—both of whom would become *Advertiser* news executives after the war—sat in. Fielder lectured Thurston and Coll, told them that if there was a repetition the paper would be closed.

An agreement was reached "whereby they would publish no stories involving enemy action, sabotage, troop movements or other military matters without first checking with the G-2 section. This worked extremely well—all reporters and personnel were quickly briefed and throughout the war there was no real friction."[13]

Fielder's ultimatum had abundant muscle behind it. The Hawaii papers were not only under speedily imposed censorship but licensed as well, to publish only "under such conditions and regulations as shall be prescribed from time to time by the military governor," an extraordinary type of restraint that had ended in England in the seventeenth century and in the American colonies before the Revolutionary War. It flew in the face of the First Amendment to the U.S. Constitution, but the *Advertiser* management embraced it, along with self-censorship. It said in a December 13 editorial,

December 8, 1941. The *Advertiser's* first World War II headline was in error. No saboteurs!

The Military Governor has deemed it in the best interest of the Territory that newspapers and radio stations submit to censorship. The Advertiser, fully cognizant of the necessity of such action for the duration of military rule, is happy to comply. Other members of the press and radio field are meeting the situation with the same spirit. It is hardly necessary to detail to the reading public the need for such a move.

At the *Star-Bulletin,* Editor Allen, who had no enthusiasm for the military restraints, was reluctant to take on the responsibility of self-censorship and so, for a few weeks, two hastily recruited Army censors, ex-newsmen William R. Norwood and Kenneth Barr, scrutinized stories in the paper's newsroom.

Once the *Star-Bulletin's* cooperation was assured on security items, the censors moved to the two Japanese-language papers, the *Hawaii Hochi* and the *Nippu Jiji.* They had been closed December 11 but allowed to resume publication in early January 1942 as the military's only way of reaching Japanese who did not read English. That fall, the *Nippu Jiji* changed its name to the *Hawaii Times* and the *Hochi* to the *Hawaii Herald.* From time to time the military gave these papers editorials to run and insisted that they refer to enemy forces as "Japs," a term which the *Advertiser* frequently used after Pearl Harbor, but which the *Star-Bulletin* avoided.

Radio—stations KGU and KGMB on Oahu and one station each on Kauai and the island of Hawaii—was more closely monitored than the Honolulu dailies, the Neighbor Island papers, and the press associations. At the military's request, KGU began operating around the clock so that at night the pilots ferrying planes to the Islands would have a directional beam.

Once the ground rules with the military had been established, Lorrin Thurston quickly became a liaison between the military and the public. In November 1942 he was officially named by General Delos C. Emmons, the Army commander after Short, as public relations adviser to the military governor. The recently named territorial attorney general, J. Garner Anthony, a critic of martial law and censorship, felt "it was unfortunate that this newspaper thus foreclosed itself from being of any public service in criticizing the existing regime."[14]

Three days after Pearl Harbor the *Advertiser* had begun to adapt its schedules to the realities of war. It discontinued its nightly street-sale edition, the Bluestreak, because it was impossible to distribute it under martial law and blackout regulations. Two regular editions would be published, the first for home delivery at dawn and a street edition with news up to 6 A.M. for sale in the early daylight hours. And it advised readers that should newsprint and ink shortages develop on Oahu, curtailing the number of pages and the number of papers distributed, home-delivered copies would be given preference. It added that the Sunday society section and magazine were out until further notice and, if the just-arrived freighter had not brought them, the California-produced, sixteen-page comic sections would also be omitted.

The Army offered to make Thurston a colonel, but he declined. As it was, he could hardly have been more an advocate of military control. On September 4, 1942, the *Advertiser*'s editorial page declared that Hawaii was proud to serve as "a test tube and guinea pig" for martial law.

> For just about nine months it has followed obligingly the dictate of military rule—a rule as firm or firmer than any to be found in combat zones else-where. . . . The public has accepted military rule as a fact that is to be with us for no short time. It does not ask for its abolition or that Washington turn over all the duties of the military in government to civilian authority.

While the *Advertiser* had no criticism of local censorship, it complained a year after Pearl Harbor that mainland newspaper readers were getting far more news about the war than people in Hawaii and thousands of servicemen in the North and South Pacific.

The paucity of war news in Hawaii was unpopular, but no one can really say how the man in the street felt about martial law, except for those who wound up in the Army-run provost courts. Leaders of the establishment downtown supported military rule. Walter Dillingham, one of Hawaii's most influential figures, an *Advertiser* director and second largest stockholder, named by the Army to direct food production, told a board looking into the Pearl Harbor tragedy that the community was solidly behind whatever the military leaders felt should be done. The exception, he said, was the feeling "amongst some of our legal fraternity and colleagues that we ought to say, 'By God, we ought to maintain the rights of American citizens,' and all that sort of hooey that nobody cared a damn about."[15]

Some authorities did care, including Governor Poindexter's successor as of August 24, 1942, Ingram A. Stainback, Anthony, U.S. Secretary of the Interior Harold L. Ickes, and newly elected Congressional Delegate Joseph R. Farrington, whose *Star-Bulletin* could not have expressed his views without being closed down.

In the spring of 1944 when a high Interior Department official in charge of territories testified before Congress that conditions justified the complete restoration of civil authority to Hawaii, the *Advertiser*, in a signed editorial by Publisher Thurston, resorted to sarcasm:

> To hell with General Richardson and Admiral Nimitz and what they think is vitally necessary in Hawaii. The Department of Interior with the help of Governor Stainback under the guise of the inalienable rights guaranteed every citizen by the American constitution must be in a position to tell Admiral Nimitz and General Richardson to what extent, when, where and how, the Navy or Army can control any situation which might arise in Hawaii.[16]

When martial law was attacked in federal court, questioning the denial of habeas corpus proceedings and a provost court conviction, Judge Delbert

E. Metzger ruled the military's action was unlawful. The *Advertiser* promptly condemned him. The case eventually reached the U.S. Supreme Court, which decided on February 25, 1946, after the war, that Hawaii's Organic Act did not permit civilians to be tried by the military. While the Island press had not legally challenged military control over it, it was felt in some quarters that language in the high court's decision was broad enough to sustain the First Amendment.

After the U.S. Supreme Court decision the *Star-Bulletin* said, "War does not authorize or excuse the military arm of government in operating counter to the Constitution of the United States. That principle written into the laws of a free people has again been upheld by the highest tribunal in the land."[17] The *New York Times* declared that "military rule of Honolulu . . . was a sore point with the residents of Hawaii all through the war. They felt they were being deprived of constitutional rights for no good reason. After the battle of Midway, June 4–6, 1942, the Hawaiian Islands were never again remotely in danger of a Japanese attack. But their pleas went unheeded."[18] The *Advertiser* observed:

> Hawaii has been something of a proving ground for better application of democracy. Dark and anxious days that followed the outbreak of war . . . became a period of trial and error. From it we have learned what can and what cannot be done under martial law. . . . The military in their sometimes stern, sometimes harsh judicial manner, in their overall assumption of power of civilian courts, might be excused on the ground of expediency and lack of precedent to follow.

There was no mention of licensing or censorship.[19] Three weeks later, the *Advertiser* avowed that, contrary to the Supreme Court ruling, Hawaii's people liked the Army's rule. "They did it and we liked it."[20]

U.S. District Judge J. Frank McLauglin reacted sharply, declaring that Governor Poindexter had signed the proclamation handing over power to the Army only after being induced and "with the understanding that the effect of the proclamation would be for maybe 30 days. . . ." He charged that the military took power "in knowing disregard of the Constitution. They did it because Hawaii is not a state. They did it because they did not have faith that Americanism transcends race, class and creed."[21]

Years after the war, Jim A. Richstad, a former *Advertiser* reporter and editorial writer, had a lengthy interview with retired publisher Thurston, who said of the martial law period that "we were all so accustomed to working together that it didn't take long to learn what they wanted and what they didn't want."[22]

Alexander MacDonald, the *Advertiser*'s prewar Sunday editor, who entered naval intelligence, felt that media cooperation with the military paid off in economic terms: "Island newspapers took advantage of the times by putting out skeleton editions of eight to twelve pages, ascribing this move to lack of newsprint. . . ." But this "did not prevent either paper from publishing twenty- and thirty-page editions when some pretext for special advertising campaigns arose."[23]

The Army helped the papers get newsprint because their heavier press runs were necessary to provide daily information to the growing military and war-worker population and to print numerous service publications. As Thurston pointed out, the *Advertiser* alone printed twelve military papers and magazines, including the daily *Stars and Stripes* (with a peak circulation of 140,000) and the weekly *Yank* (123,000), both quartered in the *Advertiser* building and providing their own production as well as editorial staffers.

With a vastly expanded audience eager for whatever news it could get, the *Advertiser*'s daily circulation soared from 29,045 in 1941 to 139,435 in 1945, its Sunday issue from 41,795 to 86,660, and the *Star-Bulletin*'s daily from 45,414 to 153,405, although these dropped precipitously once peace came, servicemen were mustered out, and imported war workers left.

So pushed for press capacity was the *Advertiser* in the war years that it added an old press from St. Louis, literally shipped out in days in scores of crates. The paper made a great deal of money, as much as a million dollars a year, but the hefty excess-profits tax siphoned off most of it. Much of the rest went to dividends, with little or nothing put into a reserve fund for desperately needed postwar equipment.

Press licensing and censorship were ended by the Army on March 10, 1943. Martial law, however, continued until October 1944, and during this period, *Star-Bulletin* Editor Allen related, "Definite and extensive restrictions [remained] as to publication of certain classes and items of news, this through direct requests which in some cases amount to directives of the Army and Navy commands. . . ."[24]

As far back as December 1, 1942, Attorney General Anthony, in a report to Governor Stainback, said the military prohibited "certain news of general interest not related to the war. . . . Murders and rapes have occurred in Honolulu, yet the press is forbidden to publish these incidents. The press is denied access to police files." He cited prostitution as "a good illustration of how censorship works." For many months the local press carried not a word about the wide-open and flourishing brothels, some twenty to twenty-five primarily around River Street, in which some 350 women worked.

But Honoluluans were far less concerned with press problems than with getting on with daily living in a highly stressful environment. And this most did with dignity and fortitude.

The day after Pearl Harbor the *Advertiser* declared that "under the first baptism of fire Honolulu acquitted itself with a calmness. . . . Civilian defenders quickly took their posts, ambulances and fire engines arrived quickly on the scenes of disaster. It was fit tribute to the people of Honolulu. In the days ahead that shall be Hawaii's motto: 'Be calm.'"

But, understandably, rumors were rife. Word spread that an ad by the

Hawaii Importing Company that appeared in the *Advertiser* of December 4 and the *Star-Bulletin* the afternoon before gave coded instructions to the Japanese community. Naval intelligence put that one to rest on finding that for several preceding Decembers a similar ad had appeared.

The *Advertiser* told readers:

> You are going to live new lives and there may be many more days ahead fraught with danger. You may lose friends and loved ones. . . . None will go hungry. . . . Your menus may be skimpy, but with more robust foods. You are going to take this new Honolulu, this new America in stride—chin up in the best American style. An enemy has shown it can destroy. . . . The change in you is going to say, down to the last man: The destroyer shall be destroyed.[25]

People began digging bomb shelters, but it was a discouraging task, and the *Advertiser* reported that many were "in a state of suspended animation," since residents "can't get enough sand; can't get enough bags; can't get enough gumption."[26]

But even as daily life was being rearranged, the paper found time and space to dress down its afternoon rival. A *Star-Bulletin* editorial on December 30 had blamed Governor Poindexter for a "policy of delay and blunder" in the civilian defense system. Four days later in a four-column top-of-page-one editorial piously titled, "The Advertiser Regrets The Necessity of This Rebuke," it sharply lectured the *Star-Bulletin* that it was no time for censuring political leadership: "There is no place . . . for fly-speck heckling, finger-pointing clamor for readjustment or public criticism that is destructive to morale and harmful to cooperative effort."

The *Star-Bulletin* said it resented attacks against its motives and patriotism, "reaffirmed our inherent American right to expose conditions that require correction," and noted that its criticism had brought corrective action.

In mid-March 1942 an *Advertiser* editorial questioned whether Hawaii's defenses were strong enough to meet an all-out Japanese attack. Titled "Don't Let It Happen Here," it was reprinted in the *New York World-Telegram* at the top of its front page and heavily quoted by the *New York Times* and other papers. While military officials declined official comment, United Press reported that "it is widely accepted as a fact in Washington that Hawaiian defenses are stronger than before the Japanese attack on Pearl Harbor and that every effort is being made to further strengthen that stronghold as rapidly as possible."[27] Congressional Delegate Sam King shared that view.

The next month Thurston ran a double-paged signed message in *Editor & Publisher*, the industry's weekly journal, citing the upbeat attitude of Islanders, expressing thanks to the national advertisers "who have kept Hawaii on your schedules, in spite of everything," and saying that despite the multitude of problems, "We wouldn't leave Hawaii on a bet. It's still the best place in the world to live and work in, as far as we are concerned."[28]

In July 1942, after the stunning Navy victory at Midway assured that Hawaii was beyond the reach of enemy attackers, the blackout was reduced to a dimout, and the *Advertiser* cheerfully commented, "No more barking of shins, walking into doors, tripping over rugs or other such civilian wartime maneuvers."[29]

At the time, two widely read staff features were LaSelle Gilman's "Honolulu War Diary" and a series of columns by Earl A. Selle, appearing on the editorial page. Both were smooth writers.

Commenting on "loose-lipped rumor mongers," Gilman declared, "What this country needs is a good five-cent blackjack for use on such clatter boxes."[30] Quoting the *New York Daily News* disparaging the fact that five of seven candidates of Japanese ancestry had won in Island primary elections, he wished that "our Japanese community was far-sighted enough to keep its political-minded members under wraps during wartime."[31] But he was not reluctant to give deserved credit to the Japanese community, in this case to those joining the military governor's morale section to "aid in educating aliens and citizens in Americanism" and to encourage donations to the plasma bank. "Plasma is plasma and it doesn't matter what race, religion or sex it comes from."[32]

Selle's column, by contrast, was highly inflammatory. His China experience during the Sino-Japanese War left him with a low regard for all persons of Japanese ancestry. He wrote that Hawaii should "clean out its Little Japan," uprooting by law Japanese-language schools and "the so-called religion, Shinto," both of which had already been closed down. He saw the loyalty of young Americans of Japanese background as questionable.[33]

Selle's constant battering drew complaints to the point where Publisher Thurston wrote a signed commentary stating, "I personally have not and do not agree with many of Mr. Selle's convictions. . . . There is another side to the picture. . . . There always will be 'Jap haters'. . . . Prejudice, and not facts, largely guides their statements." And he predicted that Americans of Japanese descent who had "become full-fledged American soldiers" would set a record of which the nation would be proud.[34] Selle dropped the subject.

In late March 1943 a farewell ceremony was held for some twenty-eight hundred young Americans of Japanese ancestry (AJAS) who had volunteered for overseas combat duty. The *Advertiser* observed that "perhaps more truly than the average American soldier, those youths who stood, a bit self-conscious in their new uniforms, to hear an official goodbye, understood why they were going away and what their duty to their country is. . . ."[35]

The AJAS in both the 100th Infantry Battalion and the 442nd Regimental Combat Team quickly built an enviable record. In a press dispatch from Italy "officers said they never saw any troops handle themselves better" and quoted a Captain Tara Suzuki of Honolulu that "they are probably a criterion of the loyalty of all Americans of Japanese blood." Citing this in an editorial titled "Less Limelight, Please," the *Advertiser* said,

Such publicity may be interesting, but it does, in a subtle way, more harm than good. A great deal of praise has been written and published about the AJAs. The results include (1) an impression on many Mainland readers that the only fighting men from Hawaii are Japanese and (2) a distorted impression of their role in the war for the local Japanese themselves.

It took note of "Hawaii boys of Chinese or Portuguese or Scotch descent" in the armed forces "though you don't read very much about them. . . . Less pointed publicity about the boys of Japanese descent will be to their benefit in the long run.[36] The stories, of course, were not written by the AJAS. Hawaii residents of all races served with distinction, but by war's end the AJAS accounted for 80 percent of Islanders killed or wounded in combat.

For AJAS at home, the *Advertiser* continued to remind of the need and opportunities to actively show their patriotism. When Honolulu busmen engaged in a slowdown over a money issue, the paper said, "They have followed a course that can be regarded in no other light than as direct aid to Hirohito and his Tokyo butchers. This is particularly unfortunate because of the preponderance of young American-born Japanese among the bus drivers." It implied that they were strong enough to have blocked the slowdown, which the Army quickly reversed, and declared, "Americans are in no mood to stand for any nonsense or any hint of disloyalty."[37]

And while it agreed with President Roosevelt's 1943 report to the Senate that most AJAS sent from the Pacific coast to relocation centers were loyal to the United States, it said that they had brought much of the war-imposed hardship on themselves: "This has been because they have remained largely inarticulate in their Americanism, a criticism that rests upon those here as well as elsewhere. . . . This country wants its loyalties wholly free from adulteration."[38] It called for outlawing of Japanese-language newspapers, saying that while they had been useful in the early days of the war "in transmitting orders to aliens unfamiliar with the American language," that need had passed. "The aliens who read American know what is expected of them, and if they do not, they have means of learning." It viewed the papers as an un-American institution and asserted that "it cannot be argued that the abolition of foreign-language newspapers is an abridgment of free speech. . . ."[39] All but two Japanese-language papers had been closed and these had Americanized their names. The *Advertiser*'s call for abolition went unheeded.

In late 1943 daily and Sunday home-delivery costs were increased by twenty-five cents a month, because of greater expenses for newsprint, telegraphic news, and labor. Street sale rates remained unchanged, five cents a copy daily, ten cents on Sunday. To help conserve newsprint, smaller type was to be used for legal notices and advertisements.

On the personnel front, Irva Edwards and a skeleton staff on the news desk edited five editions a day. Postwar she edited features and the Sunday magazine and TV guide, and remained with the *Advertiser* until retirement in 1977.

One of the *Advertiser*'s ablest wartime reporters was Laurie Johnston, who also served as a correspondent for the British news agency Reuters and for *Time* magazine. She was one of the few women journalists in the Pacific accredited to both the Army and Navy. After the war she joined the *New York Times* as a reporter and feature writer. Her standout work at the *Advertiser* was recalled when in 1980 she won the Meyer Berger award, in memory of the *Times'* Pulitzer Prize winner, and the citation said that she "has maintained a verve and reportorial zeal that are the envy of many younger members of the profession. . . ."[40]

In November 1943 the paper was to lose one of its stars, City Editor Trumbull, to the *New York Times*. After Pearl Harbor, in addition to his regular duties, Trumbull had become a "stringer" for the *Times*, succeeding Vern Hinckley, the *Star-Bulletin*'s city editor. "When Pearl was attacked, the Times heard nothing from Hinckley; when they cabled asking why he hadn't covered for them the biggest story of the century, he replied he was 'too busy.' They summarily fired him."[41] Trumbull applied, with a recommendation from Coll, and got the job.

In his dual capacity Trumbull covered a press conference featuring three Navy fliers who had ditched their torpedo bomber in the South Pacific and survived thirty-four days at sea in a rubber raft before fatefully landing on a small Polynesian island. In record time—four weeks—Trumbull produced a saga of their experience, calling it *The Raft*. It became a Book-of-the-Month Club selection and won a Pulitzer Prize. Lewis Gannett of the *New York Herald Tribune* called it "one of the great stories of sea history."

Trumbull joined the *Times* full-time, changed his name from Bob to Robert, and built a distinguished career as a Pacific/Asia correspondent and bureau chief. He was one of the few newspeople who witnessed Pearl Harbor and then covered the Japanese surrender on the battleship *Missouri* in Tokyo Bay. After thirty-six years with the *Times* he retired to Honolulu in 1980 and for a while wrote a Sunday column on international affairs for the *Advertiser*.

The paper's wartime coverage was not just for its local audience. When ships and planes went to Pacific outposts the *Advertiser* went along, too—thanks to its Newspapers-for-Servicemen-Fund, cosponsored by the Junior Chamber of Commerce. When the six-man Marine crew of a large air freighter stepped ashore at Tacloban in the Philippines and yelled, "Honolulu Advertiser, Read All About The War," the troops there found it hard to believe. Two hundred copies were quickly snapped up.

Since its founding in April 1942 the fund had financed the shipment of almost a million *Advertiser*s to news-hungry servicemen. When U.S. occupation forces entered a prisoner-of-war camp in Japan they found well-thumbed copies of the *Advertiser*, dropped with food and medicine by B-29 crews. So it became the first American paper in Japan since the start of the war.

For servicemen in Hawaii and out front one of the *Advertiser*'s chief attractions was Miss Fixit's morale-boosting column. The demand was so heavy that one sergeant said she must be the most popular woman in the Pacific. It was written by Alicia Adams, who performed such services as arranging to have birthday cakes delivered to remote forward areas, finding scarce housing for service families, and returning lost wallets.[42]

The Vietnam War spawned a successor column, this one conducted by Tsuneko Ogure, who early on got the nickname of Scoops from her editorship of the Roosevelt High School paper. While at the University of Hawaii she became a fifty-cent-an-hour part-time *Advertiser* proofreader. At the time, she befriended a lonely GI from Schofield Barracks, James Jones, who later wrote the best-selling novel *From Here to Eternity*.

Feature stories she submitted landed her a full-time job at the paper and led to the second Miss Fixit column. In its kickoff on July 7, 1969, Scoops, then married to political reporter Brian Casey, "helped the recently arrived wife of an army man in Vietnam get in touch with a 'waiting wives' organization; assured a prospective bride that the odds were favorable for good weather at her planned outdoor wedding reception on August 9; told a perplexed working woman where to find day care for a 10-year-old niece visiting from the Mainland."[43]

She recommended an insect repellent that worked for an Ewa Beach woman who had complained, "Lately we haven't been able to make love because of mosquitoes." She was a good Samaritan, but focused on others who rendered good deeds and made them members of her Aloha Club.

On Christmas Day 1944 the paper, for the second time in twenty-two years, skipped publication to give workers a day of rest from "many months of increasing pressure resulting from the rush of war news."[44] KGU would present spot news during the break.

In February 1945 the *Advertiser* began getting the United Press teletype delivery of its full night leased wire news report, the first time any overseas paper received, with simultaneous speed and volume, the same news report as mainland dailies. Between thirty thousand and forty thousand words a night were pouring in at a cost of $5,917 a month, on a six-month trial.

With every plus, there seemed to be a minus. In May Thurston reported a critical shortage of newsprint for the *Stars and Stripes* and other company-produced publications. By the arrival of the next scheduled shipment about June 18, there would be only a three-day stock. George Voorhees, production chief, and Ted Oliphant of Honolulu Paper Company flew to the coast and fortunately were able to get an adequate supply.

The people at the paper were frazzled by the enormous load they were carrying, but they were bolstered by the conquest of Okinawa in June and the knowledge that while an invasion of the Japanese mainland would prove costly, the island empire was doomed.

As the war moved into 1945, the *Advertiser* zeroed in on "Honolulu's wretched housing conditions," both for the fifty thousand civilians brought in for war work as well as for many local residents. Economist Thomas Hitch has pointed out that the civilian and military influx between 1940 and 1944 jumped total employment threefold, from 184,000 to 591,000, and doubled the de facto population from 429,000 to 858,000.[45]

Even before the war Honolulu had a housing shortage, and after Pearl Harbor it was exacerbated by a scarcity of building materials. The *Advertiser* declared it was an ominous matter when people lived in congested houses, slept on floors, in garages, in musty attics and in dark cellars.

A long, signed editorial by Thurston on emergency housing said that at least twenty thousand units were needed immediately and the only feasible land able to hold them were golf courses and parks. But getting a consensus on proposed locations proved impossible. As *Advertiser* columnist "Sol Pluvius" observed, "Everybody wants more housing for Honolulu right away—right away from where they live."[46]

Meanwhile, *Advertiser* writer Gerry Burtnett was producing a series on housing that, together with editorials, began to generate attention. Burtnett conducted a Wake Up Washington fund and $2,500 in contributions bought six-column ads that appeared in the *Washington Star* and in the *Washington Post*. The ads stirred action. A U.S. House subcommittee came to the Islands, "heard dozens of witnesses, visited 'hot bed apartments' where 18 men in three shifts occupied one room . . . [and] estimated that housing had not been provided for 60,000 of the 107,679 newcomers to the islands, who had obtained shelter only through overcrowding and living in shacks."[47]

The National Housing Administration promised favorable action. And Governor Stainback said that if a requested $1 million from the federal government was slow in coming, he would ask the 1945 legislature to appropriate that amount from the territory's surplus.

Waikiki was also drawing attention, with the *Advertiser* deploring its "aura of Coney Island" and yearning for the day when the public beach could be restored from Kewalo Basin to the Elks Club at Diamond Head. That would involve acquiring parcels of land that wealthy people had bought and converted into private estates. A renewed beachfront was viewed as a proper memorial once the war was ended.[48]

In June 1945 the authorities decided that the rubber in gas masks could be better used and ordered the masks turned in. The *Advertiser* greeted this with:

Goodbye gas mask. We will not soon forget you. . . . Your fiendish proclivity in demanding a practice fitting at the exact moment when all the girls in the office were dolled up in new hair-dos; your inhuman ingenuity in refusing to adjust yourself to the necessities of optical aid; your ruthless battering of defenseless kneecaps in crowded places; your ability to stick together as if glued when you should have opened readily and your flabbiness around the edges when you were supposed to fit snugly; all these, and a hundred other foibles in which you gloried, perpetuate, if they do not endear, your memory.[49]

July 7, a Saturday, when the curfew was lifted, police expected exuberant commotion, but the *Advertiser* reported that "by 11:30 Honolulu began to openly yawn; it was past bedtime."[50]

Came August, a momentous month for the world, but with special meaning for Hawaii and its newspapers, which had recorded the forty-four months of war since Pearl Harbor.

Extra followed extra during the last week of fighting, climaxed by a V-J edition. Editorially, the paper called it "the supreme hour . . . the guns are silent . . . there will be no more blood spilled," adding, "it's a whale of a day to celebrate, isn't it?"[51]

And celebrate the people did. It was a day of history and happy hysteria.

Later in the month the *Advertiser* said dope sales had been a big wartime business in Honolulu and that taxis had served as vice shops on wheels, selling whiskey, women, and drugs.

In November suppressed tensions between servicemen and "locals" erupted as "one thousand sailors of the Honolulu air station armed with bayonets, clubs, rocks and hammers rioted through a nearby residential section [Damon Tract] for two hours . . . in what the sailors called retaliation for 'unprovoked attacks' by local Islanders."[52]

For several days thereafter there were further street fights and brawls, spotlighted on page one with the names of servicemen and civilians reporting

August 14–15, 1945. The end, after almost four years, of a bloody war that was started in Hawaii.

assaults or those charged or sentenced. The *Advertiser* declared, "The curbing of the rash of gang fights, beatings and rowdyism is going to take place only when the courts, military and civilian, and the police, military and civilian, really start working together." It called on Governor Stainback to "meet this serious problem" with active help from all the law enforcement agencies."[53]

But the community's criminal problems extended beyond the military and civilians. When thievery was uncovered among some police, the *Advertiser* reminded it should not reflect on the force as a whole, which "was giving excellent service." It praised Chief William A. Gabrielson for bringing "order out of chaos" in the department after the Massie case of 1931–1932: "He has done a good job, and the citizenry generally appreciates it."[54]

The paper reversed itself the next year. Gabrielson was forced out, although the Police Commission first tried to palm it off as voluntary. Soon after he went to Tokyo to serve on General Douglas MacArthur's police staff, he was the subject of thirteen local indictments alleging embezzlement, accepting bribes, and other crimes, some related to a major graft operation during wartime gambling. These were dropped when he refused to return.

The *Advertiser* said the press shared the blame in not telling the public at the outset that Gabrielson had been ousted: "Few in officialdom in the newspaper field can pretend ignorance of the truth in the Gabrielson affair. Yet it was kept 'hush hush' until [a city official] spoke up." The "whole affair is a sorry example of a prevalent bad habit: the failure to call promptly to account those who are remiss in a public trust until their offense grows to proportions that actually menace community welfare."[55]

24

The Battle to Salvage Circulation

WITH THE massive departure of military personnel and war workers, the circulation of the two daily newspapers plummeted. During 1946 the six-day *Advertiser* dropped 71,505 readers to a new total of 67,930. By 1950 it had further sunk to 46,933. While the *Star-Bulletin* lost 60,656 for a 1946 figure of 92,748, with continued decline to a 1950 total of 76,601, it maintained a hefty lead of almost 30,000 over its morning competitor. That was 16,000 more than its 1945 spread.

The *Star-Bulletin* had nurtured its home delivery during the war, but, because of blackout and curfew, that was harder to do for the *Advertiser*, which concentrated on street sales. Once papers were put out, they were scooped up by both military and civilians hungry for frontline dispatches, but street sales lacked the stability of home delivery.

In an effort to hold on to its war-born circulation, the *Advertiser* announced on March 5, 1946, that it would provide twenty-four-hour news service, giving the public in Honolulu the "round-the-clock" publication "already well established in Los Angeles, Washington and Boston, as well as in several smaller Mainland cities."

To do this the paper, as of March 11, would augment its two morning editions with afternoon and evening editions daily, with the *Sunday Advertiser* continuing on its current schedule. The morning home edition was to be delivered before 6 A.M., followed by a morning final on the streets and newsstands. An afternoon edition, at noon, would be for sale at the same locations, followed by an evening home edition, as of April 1. The news content would change from edition to edition "to keep pace with the hourly march of events both at home and on the national and international scenes."

Advertising, comics, and features, "available [from the *Advertiser*] to the evening reader audience in Hawaii for the first time," would run through all editions. Columnists included Thomas L. Stokes, Westbrook Pegler, Marquis Childs, Raymond Moley, Walter Winchell, Eleanor Roosevelt, Hedda Hopper, Leonard Lyons, George Dixon, and, from the staff, "Red" McQueen and Ray Coll, Jr.

Publisher Thurston said, "With the end of the war approaching, we realized that to keep jobs going and our splendid machinery running, we must look to additional work. The time seemed at last right to realize our long-standing ambition . . . to go into a full-fledged 'around-the-clock' newspaper service." Editor Coll called it "a new adventure" in the history of newspapers in Hawaii.

Hugh Lytle and Harry Albright, out of uniform, were named managing editors of the morning and evening editions, respectively. Both visited mainland newspapers that had a twenty-four-hour news service to get insights into their method of operation. Albright was a Californian who had come to the *Advertiser* in 1937. Lytle had arrived in Hawaii in 1938 to head the Associated Press bureau after having worked also with the United Press and on California newspapers. He was an Army reserve officer and on Pearl Harbor day, immediately after phoning the story to AP in New York, he donned his uniform and reported to Fort Shafter, serving there and as head of a unit that produced histories of Pacific combat operations on Kwajalein, Eniwetok, Okinawa, and the Philippines. He earned a bronze star during the battle for Okinawa. One of his sergeants was James McGregor Burns, who became a distinguished historian. A hard-working man, Lytle was something of a military ramrod, but his bite was milder than his bark and, underneath, he was warm and caring.

Fanfare greeted the first copy of the new evening home edition, autographed by Thurston and given to state archivist Maude Jones. The next copies were delivered to Mayor Lester Petrie and acting Governor Gerald R. Corbett.

But readers had their own ideas. They regarded the *Advertiser* as the morning paper and the *Star-Bulletin* as the afternoon. Getting the *Star-Bulletin* constituency to break long-standing habits and substitute the morning paper or add it to the one they'd long taken proved a mountainous obstacle.

Further, the *Star-Bulletin* had strongly penetrated the Japanese community, which regarded its editorial policy as more fair-minded than the *Advertiser*'s. It was a feeling evident in any ethnic analysis of *Advertiser* circulation. Even years later, a survey showed that 68 percent of Americans of Japanese ancestry read the *Star-Bulletin* occasionally and 43 percent regularly—in contrast to only 30 percent occasionally and 27 percent regularly for the *Advertiser*.[1]

At that time a new *Advertiser* management had been on the job and editorial policy had been greatly liberalized for some two decades. Why the continuing disparity in readership? The answer: while those in the younger generation most likely would not have harbored their elders' resentment against the *Advertiser*, they had grown up with the *Star-Bulletin*. They had read its news and sports pages, its editorials, its features, grown accustomed to the format.

In short, since newspaper readers are creatures of habit, the sins of a long-ago *Advertiser* were still being visited on the paper many years later.

On most days after the war the *Advertiser* equaled or even topped the afternoon paper in the range of news stories and often outperformed it in quality of writing, but the editorial page was sadly out of step with a Hawaii in transition.

Despite the *Advertiser*'s high hopes and heavy promotion, the afternoon and evening editions never caught on and in April 1950 were abandoned, with an accompanying effort to persuade readers the move was "designed to expand and improve the morning and street editions."[2]

There was no executive slot immediately available for Albright, so he went back to the Army for a while, then served for many years with the Board of Insurance Underwriters. He carried with him the memory of scooping the *Star-Bulletin* on the first day of the evening edition with the extra on a Hilo tidal wave: "So, although the PM edition would not stay the course, it had a sensational birth."[3]

The paper continued to cast about for answers to its circulation and advertising problems. It announced a new classified ad program for individuals—one line for one week for one dollar; for jobs wanted, desired salary must be stated; if room for rent, how much.

Not long after, still smarting from the rising circulation of the *Star-Bulletin* it once more produced a P.M. edition—the Red Streak—but three months later killed it. It next opted for the *Advertiser Shopper*, an ad-filled paper distributed free to nonsubscribers. At a board meeting Thurston reported on the "increasing acceptance" of the new publication. But that did not last, and it finally was discontinued for lack of interest by advertisers.

In September a new magazine was put into the Sunday paper, a twelve-pager focusing on life in Hawaii and Polynesia generally. But the daily circulation continued to go down, to 55,702 in 1947 and to a low of 44,924 in 1950.

A major handicap in those days was the fact of an early-rising, plantation-oriented society. Workers and supervisors were in the fields soon after sun-up. Downtown offices opened at 8 A.M., large stores at 8:30. Some businesses, including the *Advertiser*'s commercial departments, started the day at 7:45, ending it at 4:30 P.M., with forty-five minutes for lunch.

For a majority of people there was no time to read the paper before work. On the job, as many as ten individuals might peruse the office copy, but that counted for only one paper at the Audit Bureau of Circulation. With people returning home at 4:30 to 5 o'clock, and no television to compete, there was ample time to read the *Star-Bulletin* before the evening meal. That paper had an additional advantage: because of the time difference, by the time the home edition went to press, the day was finished in Europe and was well along in Washington and New York, the major centers of politics and business. The *Advertiser* was heavy on late-breaking local news, especially sports, but that was only a partial offset. And its promotion, while steady and worthwhile—ranging from swimming lessons for children to sponsoring art and science fairs—was not directly linked to generating new circulation.

25

A Blend of Photographers, Editors, and Managers

JUST BEFORE the war and into the 1950s the paper gained several photographers who would become living legends.

Kazuto Shimagaki was a roly poly little man with a game right leg, but "he went everywhere there was a news story. He climbed swaying Jacob's ladders. He clung from the rooftop of a 12-story Waikiki building. He 'mugged' thugs who spit at him in defiance—and he captured the grace and charm and loveliness of Shirley Temple when she visited here at age seven." He photographed the big ones—Roosevelt, Truman, Eisenhower—"but the little people, too, the humble people who were suddenly plunged into the news."[1]

He was born in a King Street tenement, and at age four polio left him with a limp. When he was eight he became a train "butcher," selling candy, magazines, and papers on the Oahu Railway and Land Company's run to Kahuku.

Photography intrigued him, and he came to the *Advertiser* a few months before the Pearl Harbor attack. He worked for three days and three nights 'round the clock, without sleep. His photos made front pages all over the world.

He was a nervy figure, brusquely ordering even generals into the poses he wanted. In World War II he earned the nickname of "The Colonel." He was undaunted by wealth or stature. Once, in his raspy voice, he instructed a prominent woman politician to stand facing him. She asked why. His reply, "So your double chin won't show."[2] She complied. His work was so good it landed in such national magazines as the *Saturday Evening Post* and *Collier's*.

He was gutsy. When he aimed his camera at a murder suspect at the police station, the man balled up a fist and yelled, "No pitchah." The "Colonel" retorted, "That's my business, getting a picture." At three feet he focused and snapped.[3]

And yet he was a kindly man, the first to collect for flowers for an ill colleague or to help one in need. In 1956, at forty-seven, he went into a diabetic coma, which ended his colorful career.

Then there was Yoshiaki Ishii, who bristled with energy, knew no fear, and tolerated no guff.

He was graduated in 1941 from Farrington High School and on December 7 of that year bought his first camera and went to Aiea Heights to record the devastation at Pearl Harbor. The Army confiscated his pictures, but he knew what his life's work would be.

While tooting a trombone in a taxi dance hall during the war, he devoted his off-time to amateur photography. He then spent a year in the *Milwaukee Journal's* darkroom before returning to snap tourists in Waikiki. In 1948, at half the income, he opted for a job at the *Advertiser.*

Despite resistance from society editor Edna B. Lawson, who believed the hefty Speed Graphics were forever, he introduced 35 millimeter cameras and color photography to the paper and was the first in the profession locally to use a fish-eye lens.

He covered everything from tidal waves and volcanic eruptions to the 1948 dock strike to the Olympic Games in Japan in 1964 and Mexico in 1968.

Ishii's favorite traveling companion was Scott Stone, the assistant city editor, who looked for and exploited opportunities to get them both out of town. Ishii accompanied Stone into offices of some of the highest officials in several foreign countries, where they met with kings, ministers, four-star generals. As Stone recalled, Ishii "could be as foul-mouthed as anyone alive, but he was invariably a gentleman on these occasions and became a favorite of almost everyone who met him."[4]

In New Zealand, when the governor general walked into a room where newspeople awaited, all rose in respect except a local reporter. Says Stone: "Ishii, who was as earthy as they come and generally disrespectful as a matter of style, leaned over to the reporter and hissed, 'Get off your ass or I knock your head.' The reporter got promptly to his feet."[5] In Antarctica, Stone

saw his innate sense of decency in action. We were with a group of reporters visiting a hut that had been used by the great explorer, Sir Ernest Henry Shackleton. Everything in the hut was perfectly preserved by the cold, and it was kept just as Shackleton had left it. When we reporters got back to our quarters, one of them slyly showed us a souvenir he had stolen from Shackleton's hut. We were all indignant, but Ishii was outraged. So that night he stole the souvenir out of the reporter's bag and took it back to Shackleton's hut and placed it back where it belonged.[6]

Ishii was a man of many parts. A baronial hallway outside Christchurch, New Zealand, was hung with coats of arms of a number of British noblemen. Stone "happened to recognize one and said, 'Look, Ishii, do you know what that is?' Ishii, this self-made man, looked up calmly and said, 'Yes, the coat of arms of James VI.' Then he went on to name most of the others, and accurately."[7]

Outwardly rough, Ishii won awards not only for spot news photos but human interest pictures as well. A series of photos inside Kaneohe State Hospital captured the stark mood of the institution, with symbolic bars and mesh screens setting the scene. The judges said, "Desperate loneliness emerges in one's response to the hospital views."

Early in his tenure at the paper, upset by the disparity in pay between some Oriental and comparable haole employees, he successfully led a movement for organization of a union by the Newspaper Guild. Ishii retired in March 1985, thirty-three years after his arrival.

Ishii was succeeded as chief photographer by Takashi Umeda, who started in 1956 and almost forty years later was still moving with zest and skill.

Umeda had studied photography in Los Angeles after military duty, then returned to the Islands. He won awards for a wide range of pictures, from day and night shots of volcanic eruptions to those of a man sobbing as fire destroyed his Maunakea Street cafe and a little boy clambering onto the hood of visiting President Lyndon Johnson's car to wish him aloha.

In 1965 he went six hundred feet underwater in a two-man research sub and accompanied his photos with a highly professional story. When Hurricane Iwa vented its fury on Hawaii in 1982, he was on the *Advertiser* team that

In 1968 a new "dress uniform" was sported by *Advertiser* photographers: *top*, Kenneth Kuwahara and Charles Okamura; *center*, Y. Ishii, chief photographer; and *bottom*, Leland Cheong and Takashi Umeda.

won national honors and reproduced 150 of their photos in a locally best-selling book.

News photography can take unusual twists, as it did one night in October 1976 for Umeda. As he arrived at a hotel to cover a fund-raiser, he heard muffled pounding in one of the elevators. Peeking through a one-inch crack between the stuck elevator doors, he saw U.S. Senator Hiram Fong inside. He carefully shot a picture of Fong through the tiny opening, then alerted hotel managers, whose repairmen rescued Fong, his wife, brother, and ten others after their fifty-minute stranding.

Another stalwart in the lens department was Gordon Morse, Honolulu-born, who became a reporter-photographer at the paper in 1952. His enjoyment of life was exuberantly mirrored in his stories and pictures. Nothing daunted him—or his wife. He was a cub reporter of three weeks when President-elect Dwight Eisenhower was to arrive in Hawaii on the cruiser *Helena*. At Morse's suggestion, his wife sent a special-delivery letter to await the general at the Kaneohe Marine Corps Air Station inviting him to their home for a relaxing dinner.

Eisenhower's personal secretary, a Navy lieutenant, phoned to say the president-elect already had a dinner engagement but would like to meet them and wondered how long it would take to get to their home in Wahiawa from Kaneohe. When he learned it would be an hour, he suggested that the Morses come instead to Kaneohe. They did and wound up at the dinner table with Eisenhower, Secretary of State-designate John Foster Dulles, Secretary of the Interior-designate Douglas McKay, Admiral and Mrs. Arthur Radford, Lieutenant General and Mrs. Henry Aurand, *Fortune* magazine publisher C. D. Jackson, and others.

Although a tyro, Morse was already an on-his-toes reporter. When he left for home, a covey of waiting reporters wanted to know what was going on. Morse, who had learned that Eisenhower had no objection to a story, snapped "no comment" and rushed with his wife to their car. The *Advertiser* on page one the next morning carried a two-column story, with all the details. What the Morses would not disclose was the content of a note the president-elect handed them as they were leaving.

When Morse went to cover a story, he was not easily dissuaded. Once he drove to Hickam Air Force Base to await a captain whose son had been killed by a homemade bomb. He was told to leave, declined, and was put under armed guard until the captain arrived and left. Air Force officials later apologized, stating the arrest was contrary to regulations.

On another occasion, when taking pictures at the scene of a fatal bus-trailer crash at Wilson Tunnel, he was manhandled by a Hawaiian Armed Services Police Marine sergeant. When he resisted, four Marines charged him, but were stopped by a civilian policeman from the Kaneohe district. A Navy spokesman said the sergeant acted contrary to instructions and sharp measures would be taken against him.

Morse left the *Advertiser* in 1967 for the Big Island, where he currently has a bed-and-breakfast operation but still enjoys his camera.

Photographers tend to regard themselves as a breed apart, but the zeal and professionalism of those at the paper were equally evident among fresh arrivals in the newsroom.

Gerry Lopez, a University of Hawaii graduate with war service in the Pacific, arrived at the paper in 1946, later worked elsewhere and returned in 1954 as a legislative reporter. He progressively became copy editor, news editor, then assistant managing editor. He decided the placement of stories and directed the news flow to the composing room, aided by a copydesk of eight staffers who edited stories for clarity and length and then wrote headlines for them. On Lopez' death from leukemia in 1982 at age sixty-four, City Editor Sanford Zalburg spoke of him as

> a skilled technician. He was steady and swift. Also he was very much a local boy. Most people thought he came from Hawaii instead of New York. He surfed and fished, talked pidgin. He was well aware of what was going on in the local community. He knew politicians of the day. All of this gave him an intimate sense of what was important for local people to read."[8]

Charles A. Ware, who was to spend thirty-five years at the paper, had worked in California prewar as a reporter-photographer, then saw Navy combat duty from Guadalcanal to the Aleutians. He arrived in 1948, was put on the city hall beat, and in the time following, except for two years with the Red

Advertiser copydesk in the 1960s. Here stories were edited and headlines written.

Cross, served successively as a jack-of-all-jobs—acting city editor, magazine section editor, Sunday editor, and assistant to the managing editor before becoming the ombudsman, one of about thirty in the United States, in essence serving as the readers' advocate on his own paper, sometimes in opposition to his colleagues. He was ideal for that duty, as a quiet, thoughtful man with dry humor and a keen sense of justice, maintained until his death in 1986.

In sports, the paper acquired two giants, Dan McGuire in 1946 and Monte Ito the following year.

McGuire was a peripatetic type who had served as a sports editor in the San Francisco Bay area and as a United Press war correspondent in the Pacific. He wrote a column for the *Advertiser* until 1950, when he became publicity director for the San Francisco Giants. He returned to the paper in 1965 and crafted a witty, award-winning column until his death in 1983.

A consummate Irishman, he got a tremendous play throughout the United States and even in Dublin for a piece suggesting that bartenders use green ice cubes on St. Patrick's Day. His column often featured Abercrombie, a cigar-chewing, hard-drinking dog-about-town who enjoyed left-handed martinis, with McGuire as the "Man in the Short White Jacket." Three times he won the accolade of Hawaii Sportswriter of the Year.

On McGuire's death, Bill Kwon, sports editor of the rival *Star-Bulletin*, said "nobody ever disliked Dan. He never hurt the English language or anyone

Advertiser **city room, 1976.**

in his 43 years in journalism. He gave our profession a good name."⁹ Others said they never knew anyone who got so much joy out of his job.

In Ito the paper gained a veritable bundle of energy. After graduating in 1931 from McKinley High School, where he won national awards for his work on the student paper, he wanted to be a newspaperman but found no openings and took a job in a grocery store.

In 1938 he was hired by the *Hawaii Hochi* and was acting editor when Red McQueen lured him to the *Advertiser*, where he covered every sport in Hawaii and in 1975 was the first to be named Hawaii Sportswriter of the Year by a national panel.

An avid golfer, as was McGuire, he was "commissioner" of the Dawn Patrol, a newspaper group of early-morning linksmen. On the side, for fifteen years, he wrote an *Advertiser* column on Japanese movies, a hobby of his. Even after retirement in 1976, and almost until his death twenty years later, he continued part-time as a golf writer. In 1972 he told columnist Bob Krauss:

> I've seen great changes in sports writing. In the old days, before television, we described football games play by play. Now the entire concept is different. The approach is more personal. Instead of describing the play, you talk to the quarterback about why he called it. The sports I like to cover best are golf and track. That's because I can get close to the players and talk to them.¹⁰

In 1948 the paper's commercial printing department attracted a widely recognized professional as its manager. Meiric Dutton had an impressive record in Sweden and on the U.S. mainland, ranging from directing the Ohio State University Press to serving as number two in the printing section of the World War II Production Board. An amateur historian, he did a series of articles and booklets on old Hawaii. He died in 1961.

In late August 1949 the *Advertiser* announced other executive changes. Jan Jabulka, business manager for ten years, returned to the newsroom as managing editor of the morning and afternoon editions, and Richard F. MacMillan, managing editor for the past year and a half, became night editor of the morning *Advertiser*, both under the general supervision of Editor Coll.

A few days thereafter, the editorial page was moved from the back page, where editorials had appeared for twenty-eight years, to a new inside location.

26

Fighting "Communism" and Farrington

POSTWAR, THE *Advertiser*'s editorial policy continued to be well received by the business community and tolerated by the old-line unions, but was heartily disliked, even hated, by more militant workers.

In 1946 the paper gladly supported an attack on the CIO by the Hawaii representatives of the American Federation of Labor, who declared, "We do not and cannot sympathize with the ulterior motives and misleading propaganda that is being disseminated to the sugar workers of the Territory by the imported ILWU leadership."[1]

This came during the industry-wide sugar strike, which the International Longshoremen's and Warehousemen's Union (ILWU) won. The AFL understandably was smarting under the fact that the CIO-affiliated ILWU was well on the way to gathering, by 1947, thirty thousand members on the sugar and pineapple plantations and the waterfront, a meteoric rise from the nine hundred of three years earlier.

An editorial adjoining that on the labor scene, headed "A Warning To Be Heeded," declared that when FBI Director J. Edgar Hoover "says the American government and the American way of life are at peril from Communism, the people of the country must accept this as being true."[2]

Some days later it got in a crack at Republican Delegate Joe Farrington and Democratic Mayor Johnny Wilson for accepting an ILWU endorsement, through the CIO's Political Action Committee (PAC), for the upcoming elections, which it said they didn't need. By so doing they were unwittingly contributing to a conspiracy "which is designed to first weaken and then destroy the American political party system." It concluded by quoting Stalin that the American Communist Party should form "a real revolutionary leadership capable of leading the millions of American workers into revolution."[3]

The ILWU called the *Advertiser* a mouthpiece for the sugar industry, a red-baiter, and anti-Semitic for printing a letter to the editor that asked, "Who are these 'Steins' and 'Golds' . . . that invade our home land and tell us they will not let us starve."[4] (The references were to Richard Gladstein, the ILWU West

Coast lawyer, and Louis B. Goldblatt, the international secretary-treasurer.) The union urged its members and the public to boycott the paper.

Advertiser Editor Coll went on radio station KGU and lashed back: "Now comes the ILWU with a doctrine of rule or ruin, long familiar of application in the dictatorial nations, Communist or Fascist, of Europe and Asia. Their credo is that if you cannot rule the opinion of the press, then destroy that press."

And he got in licks at the *Star-Bulletin:* "I think the public's attention should be called to the fact that The Advertiser is the only Honolulu newspaper that has dealt fearlessly and forthrightly with the current strike situation and its political and business implications. No other publication has come to actual grips with it as we have." He asked how Delegate Joe Farrington, publisher of the *Star-Bulletin*, could explain its "evasiveness."

And he warned, "Fires are being kindled to singe capitalism in these islands and eventually destroy it. Neither Delegate Farrington nor Citizen Farrington's investments will be safe if the flames are permitted to spread. . . ."[5]

Years later Mrs. Farrington would write, "Joe became the evil one. . . . The bombardment kept on. Our friends deserted us." To charges at the time that a deal had been made between the ILWU and Farrington's *Star-Bulletin*, she said, "There was no question about slanting our columns. It didn't mean we would support them in any way. It was merely fair news coverage. Joe never had a deal with them in his life."[6] To those at the polls who questioned his taking ILWU backing, Farrington responded that he didn't understand what they were talking about, that a bank takes money from a depositor and he takes a vote from a voter.

On the eve of the November 5, 1946, election, the *Advertiser* ran across the top of page one a forty-two-inch deep editorial headlined "Joe Farrington Vs. Hawaii's Business." It painted a dark picture of the future of Island enterprises, large and small, under the "ravages of the Wagner Act, which has taken away their rights of management and given special privilege to unscrupulous, irresponsible union leaders." It then asked, "What single thing has Delegate Farrington, or the newspaper he owns, done to help Hawaii and its business enterprises" to meet and solve their problems, "any one of which is more vital to them" than Statehood?

> Does Joe Farrington DO anything to give them comfort or relief? No. He talks about Statehood. . . .
>
> The man we were loyal to—is not loyal to us. He employs his newspaper solely to boost himself, to knock The Advertiser, to give aid and comfort to Harry Bridges' agents, who have brought ruin upon us, upon our employees, upon the people of all Hawaii. Why should we vote to keep him in office? . . .
> As Publisher he uses the Star-Bulletin to further the cause of those who, through the CIO's Political Action Committee, seek to enslave Hawaii's business by seizure of Hawaii's government."[7]

It implored voters to elect territorial tax commissioner William Borthwick, a Democrat, over Farrington. But Farrington won by 8,556 votes, and the feud between the *Advertiser* and Farrington/*Star-Bulletin* would continue. Meanwhile, the ILWU's satisfaction at the outcome of the delegate race was enhanced when thirty-five of the candidates it supported won seats in the legislature.

With World War II won, the "yellow peril" had given way locally to fear in some quarters of the "Communist peril," although a small faction in Congress exploited both to stall the statehood drive. The *Advertiser* was convinced of Communist infiltration, of increasing subversive activity, primarily linked to the ILWU. It declared that "nearly everyone in Hawaii knows that new charges of" such activity

> have been filed in Washington by official sources here. Reports of Communistic activity are known to be in the hands of the Secretary of the Interior. Doubtless, the same information is on file with the Secretary of State and the Federal Bureau of Information. But Julius Krug, Secretary of the Interior, links the matter with a "Territorial political controversy" and has returned noncommittal acknowledgements. There are too many rumors and hints of information to permit this situation to continue. . . . Someone better explain—fast.[8]

The *Star-Bulletin* took a calmer view. It wrote that "every locality seems to have its favorite monster—a half legendary Thing with which parents threaten naughty children and regale the gullible visitor. . . . We have our own spine-tingling monster here in Hawaii—a hydra-headed Thing called communism." It said it abhorred communism "but there is no need to let it take false, disproportionate, harmful dimensions in Hawaii."

> What is needed is plenty of commonsense thinking and acting. What is not needed is to permit the specter of communism to become so fantastically overdrawn that it hurts our best interests. We have just had an illustration of how an overdrawn bogey can hurt us. It has been used, successfully, as one of the reasons to block Hawaii statehood in the [U.S.] Senate. It has helped set the cause of statehood back for two years or more.[9]

But to the *Advertiser* the perceived danger was not overstated:

> We dislike Harry Bridges so roundly and distrust him so deeply that we want no part of him or his stooges controlling our political life. Harry and his nefarious C.I.O. are interlopers in these fair islands, preaching an alien ideology, to wit, class consciousness, class hatred and class strife, stirring up trouble by needless and disruptive strikes with a view to ruining private enterprise and setting up state socialism, with a dictatorship of the proletariat.[10]

With Thurston now chairing the Statehood Commission presumably he and Farrington would be making common cause in pursuing that goal, but that didn't stop the *Advertiser* from sending arrows flying at the *Star-Bulletin* publisher.

In April 1948, a year and a half after the *Advertiser*'s unsuccessful attempt to dump Farrington from the delegate's seat, it was doing a rerun just before the Republican territorial convention. It said Farrington had lost many Republican votes in the 1948 election because he failed to disavow the endorsement of the CIO's Political Action Committee, in which the ILWU played a key role.

The first responsibility of the Republican convention "will be to learn from Delegate Farrington just where he stands on the matter of American government. He cannot remain silent any longer, if he wants the party's support for reelection, and it is evident that he does."[11]

In responding with an "Open Letter to the Honolulu Advertiser," Farrington said the only surprise in the attack was that

> it appeared within less than four days after . . . Thurston arrived in Washington to join me in a series of conferences on statehood for Hawaii, to be among my guests at luncheon at the capital, and at supper in my home when my wife and children were hosts to many of our good friends in Washington, and to commend me warmly for my statement . . . before the Senate interior and insular affairs committee.
>
> I am sure that if Lorrin thought that I was a Communist sympathizer, a fellow traveler, and had any doubt about my supporting the American form of government, all of which you seem to have, he would have been unwilling to join with me in these conferences and to have accepted any of my hospitality. . . .

It turned out that Thurston had persuaded the Chamber of Commerce of Honolulu to send him to Washington to join the statehood campaign, a fact that Farrington said was fine with him. But he objected to the *Advertiser* editorially repeating allegations against him. He reiterated that the endorsement had been volunteered by the CIO-PAC, while his opponent Borthwick aggressively sought it. And he repeated his unswerving opposition to communism, declaring, "Its preachments of class and religious hatred are the antithesis of all we stand for in this country and particularly venomous in their application to Hawaii. It is our responsibility to expose this activity whenever it manifests itself in Hawaii and to correct the conditions on which it thrives."

But he vigorously objected to the *Advertiser*'s "practice of accusing your competitors and those who are in disagreement with you on other issues (than statehood) of being Communist sympathizers. . . . This is an old game that almost anyone can see through." He signed it with the name given him by the *Advertiser*, "Statehood Joe."[12]

Not long after, the *Advertiser* took on Mayor Wilson for his strong criticism of Senator Hugh Butler of Nebraska, who many regarded as deliberately delaying the statehood drive by wanting another on-the-scene congressional investigation of Hawaii's qualifications. In a letter to Butler, Wilson had said,

"We are amazed at your tactics. We challenge you to a plain showdown on this matter. . . ."[13]

When the *Advertiser* said Wilson had overstepped the bounds of propriety, the mayor quickly fired back with a letter that the paper declined to run. He then bought space in the *Star-Bulletin* for an ad shouting, "The Honolulu Advertiser Refused to Print this Letter." In it, he chastised the paper for having selected parts of his letter to Butler to publish and ignoring others, including this paragraph: "The American citizens of Hawaii have voted in a secret-ballot plebiscite more than 2 to 1 in favor of statehood. Yet you, in your appeal to the Senate against the floor vote on statehood, presented anonymous letters of opponents of statehood as a basis for your argument."

Wilson denounced Thurston as "Enemy No. 2 in our battle for statehood," next to Butler, and he charged "that the Honolulu Advertiser is today actually inviting recruits to Communism in Hawaii . . . [by] continuous and irresponsible red-baiting."

Thurston's bitterness against Farrington "is so great that you have preferred to sacrifice your chances for statehood in your desire to vilify him." Wilson blamed the paper "as second only to Senator Butler in responsibility for failure of [prostatehood] House Resolution No. 49 at the present session of Congress."[14]

The *Advertiser* snapped back, quoting a note its editor had sent the mayor:

> Your letter to the editor . . . seems as cockeyed to us as our editorial commenting on your letter to Senator Butler appears to be to you. For that reason, and because of excessive license in factual statement, I feel no obligation to publish your letter in its entirety, as you request, or in part. . . . Tell the little man at your elbow who writes so many letters to take an aspirin.

The paper declared it "believes Hawaii is ready for statehood now" and reiterated "its firm stand against Communism," saying it was "willing to leave to time the verdict on the wisdom of its unrelenting opposition to Mainland-directed Communist infiltration into Hawaii."[15]

A few days later it reported an issuance of pamphlets, "Communist propaganda . . . over the signature of 'The Communist Party of Hawaii,'" striving to enlist "the people of Hawaii in a revolution that would have as its objective the overthrow of American government."[16]

Moving to the national scene, it was pleased with the Republican nomination of Thomas Dewey for president and Earl Warren for vice-president and said "their election in November, while not a foregone conclusion, is high in the realm of possibilities."[17] A follow-up editorial observed that whether Dewey or Truman won, Hawaii would have a prostatehood figure in the White House. And it upped the odds in favor of Dewey, saying it seemed almost assured that he would be president.

Early in 1949 the *Advertiser* belatedly came around to seeing that Senator Butler, for whom it had made excuses, was indeed opposed to statehood for

Hawaii. This followed the Nebraska legislator's announcement that he planned a bill allowing the territory to elect its own governor and giving its congressional delegate a vote in the house, in lieu of full statehood.

But come May 1 there were greater and more immediate concerns. When the ILWU's effort to get Hawaii's longshore wages brought up to the West Coast level was rejected, the union struck the waterfront for 177 days.

The ILWU unloaded military and relief ships, and, under a dock-seizure law passed by the legislature, the government took over two stevedoring firms and unloaded cargo from East Coast and Gulf port ships. But Hawaii's economy was crippled. There were shortages of foodstuffs and supplies, and unemployment soared to 17 percent of the work force.

The *Advertiser* declared open combat on the ILWU, with a series of "Dear Joe" editorials beginning May 4. (The "Joe" was Stalin, not Farrington, as some surmised.) They were all written by Thurston, an avowed hater of the union leadership. His contention was that the longshoremen were engaged in a Stalin-like conspiracy to wreck the Island economy.

His first editorial, titled "What Are Your Next Orders, Joe? We Are Ready," read: "Strike the ships. Two thousand men can and have tied up a community of 450,000 people. Every man who strikes is tying up hopes, job security and welfare of 220 people. Good stuff? Five strikers tie up 1,000; 100 strikers, 22,000—and so on. Easy! Just like that. . . ."

The next day: "A Report to Joe . . . Progress!!," declaring

Things are going great down here in Hawaii, Joe. Employers are getting sore and Joe Public's wondering what to do. . . . The sugar gang is going nuts because before long all their warehouses will be full to busting and they'll have to shut down a bunch of plantation mills. . . . We're going to pull a stop-work meeting on 23 plantations later on in the month—to keep 'em worried. No kidding—we're going to have a first-class mess going. You'd really be proud.

Yet another: "We Got 'Em All Confused, Joe," proclaiming,

You'll get a kick out of this, Joe. Our underground tells us that the Chamber of Commerce directors was [*sic*] setting up a committee the other day to handle this strike problem and they couldn't decide on a name for it. Finally, one of 'em said, "Let's call it the C.A.I.B. Committee." You know—initials like all the New Deal committees. Translated it meant, "Christ, am I bewildered." Now the church people won't like that name. But you know, Joe, you're the only God we got. Don't we know you kicked all the churches out of Russia?[18]

And when Harry Bridges, ILWU international president, arrived in Hawaii, Thurston wrote, "Not since the day Kamehameha landed from Molokai, Joe, would Hawaii have been able to welcome such a complete and absolute dictator, who has almost secured the power of life or death, the well being, or lack of it, of every citizen, alien, or national, in the palm of his callous-less hand."[19]

The paper's opinion was carried over into the news columns: "A dramatic story of the ruinous suffering that can be brought upon a community by a handful of evil leaders who lead their followers blindly into a destructive blockade is told on the banners flown from brooms by women of Hawaii who are picketing ILWU longshore headquarters. . . ."[20]

Bitterness ran deep in the community, many siding with the *Advertiser*'s ongoing tirade. Some agreed with the paper that the strike went beyond normal trade unionism, that the ILWU leaders were hewing to a Communist line, a foreign ideology—and that led the CIO to expel the union.

It was true that Bridges was a devout Marxist, but he denied Communist Party leadership. Jack Hall, the regional director whom Bridges had hired, was also clearly aligned in those years with Communist philosophy.

In July Thurston cabled President Truman suggesting he visit Hawaii to see Americans under Communist domination. California's Senator William Knowland wanted Washington to mount a Berlin-type airlift. Hall declared, "We won't be smashed, no matter how much of their power is brought against us."[21]

Mid-day, October 23, 1949, the strike was settled. The union had won the wage increase it sought, but in two steps rather than one. Six months later, in April 1950, the House Un-American Activities Committee came to Hawaii to probe charges of communism, an event hailed by Thurston. Hall and thirty-eight others who were subpoenaed declined to testify; they were held in contempt and released on $200 bail. After a trial in January 1951, they were acquitted by federal District Judge Delbert E. Metzger.

But in August Hall and six others—soon to be known as the "Hawaii Seven"—were arrested and charged with violation of the Smith Act, which forbade advocating the violent overthrow of the U.S. government. After a turbulent thirty-two-week trial, they all were found guilty. When the verdict was announced, ILWU members stormed out of the courtroom in protest. The *Advertiser* termed it "one of the ugliest demonstrations of bad citizenry on record."[22]

The sentences of three to five years, plus fines, were appealed and reversed five years later by the U.S. Circuit Court of Appeals on grounds that advocacy was not the same as action.

The hostility between the *Advertiser* and the ILWU was always supercharged. In July 1950, soon after Communist forces invaded South Korea, triggering the United Nations' "police action," the *Advertiser* and KGU imposed self-censorship on news of ship, troop, and plane movements. Not long after, the paper castigated Neighbor Island newspaper publishers whose radio stations were permitting ILWU official Robert McElrath "to go on the air night after night to sneer at and denounce all the ideals that Americans cherish, bringing [Harry] Bridges and his fellow agitators . . . to Hawaii to spread their distortions of truth in such a manner as to build up local and industrial disturbance at a time when national union is essential to national defense." There is, warned the paper, "a limit to patience."[23]

Over time, plantations became more mechanized and ships containerized, and with a new generation of management and labor leaders, attitudes on both sides softened. When in June 1960 a seriously ailing, far less militant Hall left Hawaii to live in San Francisco, the *Advertiser*, once his arch enemy, but now under a new publisher (Thurston Twigg-Smith) and editor (the author), said, "It does not exaggerate to say that more than any other man, Hall helped bring industrial democracy to these Islands as they moved from feudalism and paternalism to the sophisticated and broadly affluent society of today."[24]

27

An About-Face on Statehood

WITH THE slow postwar return to normalcy, Hawaii once more could begin thinking about statehood. But heavy irony marked the *Advertiser*'s role in the final years of the campaign for that long-yearned-for status.

The Islands' battle to get their proper place in the American union went back more than half a century. Wallace R. Farrington, editor of the evening *Bulletin*, former editor of the *Advertiser*, and later governor, was advocating statehood as early as 1903, the year the legislature adopted a favorable resolution.

In 1919, Prince Jonah Kuhio Kalanianaole, delegate to Congress, put in the first of a seemingly endless series of statehood bills. Successors Victor S. K. Houston and Samuel Wilder King also favored statehood, but it was Delegate Joseph R. Farrington, *Star-Bulletin* publisher, who fought for it so vigorously he was dubbed "Statehood Joe." His editor, Riley Allen, kept the issue on the front burner during the years when the *Advertiser* was dragging its heels.

Even so, as one historian noted, "By 1927 even the strongly anti-statehood, anti-Japanese . . . *Advertiser* conceded that Hawaii exhibited almost all of the attributes which had helped other territories gain statehood"—in population, wealth, loyalty to the United States, taxes paid. But the paper warned that statehood could lead to "government controlled by an oriental power. . . . Such a power is Japan."[1]

That was the year that Lorrin A. Thurston made his position clear: "Do I object to statehood? Most assuredly not, so long as it remains an ideal, not a reality."[2]

Thurston's son and successor publisher, Lorrin P., also resisted change, despite a 1940 plebiscite in which the public favored statehood by a two-to-one vote. The argument was that the populace was not sufficiently advanced, but this really masked a fear that the non-Caucasian majority would take control of politics and much of business.

In October 1944, in an editorial "What We Need Before Statehood," the paper said the young people had to be educated in how state government is organized and operates and this was in the future.[3]

On Christmas Eve the following year it proclaimed the "time has arrived." But then it quickly hedged by seeing a lack of essential leadership in both the Democratic and Republican parties, "loosely-knit groups of factions, each with own interests . . . little more than convenient vehicles in which to transport their personal grindstones" and a public deficient in "an intelligent understanding of governmental administration."[4]

So when an eight-member bipartisan Statehood Commission was established in June 1947 many eyebrows lifted over the appointment of Lorrin P. Thurston. As one observer put it, he "was a surprise choice, as the influential *Advertiser*, which he partly owned, was unsympathetic to statehood, and many islanders felt he shared this opinion."[5]

Even as the *Advertiser* swung over to the statehood camp, it simultaneously was shrilly warning that Hawaii was in danger of being dominated by Communists, meaning leaders of the ILWU.

In April 1950, when the U.S. House Committee on Un-American Activities arrived in Honolulu to investigate communism, Thurston hailed it as a way to expose plans for a Red takeover of the Islands. And some southern members of Congress seized on the Communist issue to veil their opposition to statehood on racial grounds.

As it became increasingly evident that talk of ILWU rule of the Islands was one of the biggest obstacles to getting statehood, Thurston reversed his field. A July 1950 editorial charged delegates to the convention to draft a standby state constitution with dilatory tactics, but its president, Samuel Wilder King, defended the time spent on discussion.

In 1952 *Advertiser* staffer Buck Buchwach, who was to write many of the booklets and pamphlets for the Statehood Commission, joined the "Connally Cavalcade" to confront Texas U.S. Senator Tom Connally, an opponent of statehood. Buchwach, three other war veterans, and the mother of a soldier killed in the Pacific in World War II failed to convince Connally, but they received generous treatment in mainland media, including interviews in New York.

In 1954, pursuing an idea by Buchwach, a half-ton roll of newsprint, three miles long, was unfurled on Bishop Street to be signed as a statehood petition. It drew an estimated one hundred thousand signatures and a photo in *Life* magazine. It was then forwarded, with smaller rolls from Neighbor Islands, to Congress.

In 1955 Thurston was elected chairman of the Statehood Commission, and he was soon decrying charges that the ILWU controlled Hawaii's economy and political life and was telling mainland editors that communism was making no gains in the Islands. It was a clear 180-degree reversal.

But the poison had been spread, and columnist George Sokolsky, an avowed right-winger at Hearst's King Features Syndicate, wrote that with statehood Hawaii's two U.S. senators might well be "neither Republicans nor

June 1, 1949. Above: The ILWU, a bitter *Advertiser* target, parades a picket line in front of the newspaper building. *Below:* Harry Bridges, the ILWU's international leader, joins the AFL's Arthur Rutledge in support of the 1949 dock strike, which the paper relentlessly fought.

Democrats but Communists. For that lovely Polynesian area has become a pesthole of Communist infiltration and is controlled by Harry Bridges as though he was governor-general of the satrapy. . . ." Sokolsky accused the ILWU and United Public Workers of dominating even the radio stations and disparaged the population as being "mainly Orientals, with few emotional ties to the United States."[6]

Advertiser Editor Coll fired off a protest to Hearst, calling the column "100 percent non-factual." He took umbrage at the "libelous implication" of Communist control of radio stations and other communication—which included *Advertiser*-owned KGU, the NBC outlet in the mid-Pacific, and half-interest in KONA-TV—and declared Sokolsky "might as well have included us and the Advertiser as being dominated by the Communist unions."[7]

Thurston continued to downgrade any Communist peril. In February 1957 he told a San Francisco regional meeting of the Democratic National Committee that Communist strength in the Islands was slight and a few days later advised his fellow commissioners that overenthusiastic anti-Communists were impeding Hawaii's struggle for statehood.

In December he told the Hawaii Public Health Association that people who said that Communists controlled Hawaii or that the ILWU dominated politics were spreading "utter bunk" that made him "sick at heart." He also denied he was interested in becoming governor.

March 12, 1959. A half-century campaign brings sweet victory.

Thurston never explained his turnabout on statehood from vigorous foe to dedicated advocate. But Theon Wright, a former *Advertiser* staffer, says that although the reason for Thurston's shift remained unclear,

> one report, partially confirmed by [Congressional Delegate Jack] Burns, indicated that [Burns] had spent several hours with Thurston's editor, the late Ray Coll, and that it was Coll who persuaded Thurston that statehood was inevitable and the Advertiser should change its stance and support it editorially.
>
> Whatever the reason may have been, Thurston became one of the central figures in . . . the final—and successful—effort to achieve statehood for Hawaii.[8]

Burns opted for passage of the Alaska statehood bill before that of Hawaii, reasoning that once Alaska was accepted, Hawaii was a shoo-in. Thurston and many others viewed his position as naive, blundering, or even traitorous, and Thurston headed a delegation to Washington to try to get Burns to change. He stood fast, and his strategy proved out, with Alaska making it in 1958 and Hawaii the next year.

Late in life, Thurston said that while establishing the Pacific Area Travel Association, a tourism promotional consortium of countries in the region, gave him his greatest sense of pride, he also took considerable satisfaction from chairing the Statehood Commission.

But as statehood approached, he wryly recalled, Walter Dillingham told him to resign as commission chairman "or else." He said "he didn't want a goddamn Jap—to quote him exactly—to be governor or members of the Supreme Court, or the other official government offices . . . most of which has come true; and I hated it as much as he, but I'm still glad we got statehood."[9]

28

Sherman to Heloise: Gossip and Hints

IN OLDER days gossip and prattle were almost journalistic staples, sprinkled throughout the paper. As time passed they became increasingly confined to chit-chat columns, and in Hawaii the best-known of the three-dot writers was the *Advertiser*'s Eddie Sherman.

His items of one or two sentences conveyed the doings—and sometimes the undoing—of show-business, political, business, and sports types, visiting celebrities, and local jet-setters, actual or self-styled.

Sherman dished up a sometimes five-, sometimes six-a-week potpourri about life in the local fast lane. What his column lacked in substance, it made up in brashness, in a mix of Winchellese and Hollywoodese.

Eddie came to the *Advertiser* in 1955, after traveling a rough road from his Boston childhood. His divorced mother was unable to support him, and he spent his formative years, from six to thirteen, in a charity home for boys. Small but scrappy, he found an outlet in boxing and scored wins until a shoulder injury knocked him out of the ring and, later, out of the Coast Guard.

He wound up as a sheet-metal worker at Pearl Harbor in 1942, alongside another Massachusetts boy, Ed Sheehan, who would become a more serious wordsmith. After the war, Sherman began to yearn for the bright lights, the entertainment world. After a brief stint hosting radio station KGU's "Breakfast in Waikiki" he met Jack DeMello, destined to become a top Island composer-musician, and together in 1947 they played at the old and ornate Lau Yee Chai in Waikiki in a corny production titled the Coconut Willie Revue.

But Eddie's dreams were bigger. In 1949 he went back to the mainland, got some gigs as a standup comic, but five years later returned to the Islands, played the nightclub circuit, then sought to persuade his friend Buck Buchwach, the *Advertiser*'s city editor, and Thurston Twigg-Smith, managing editor, to let him do a show-business column.

After he submitted several samples, he was told they'd try one column a week, at thirty-five cents an inch, which came out to about $25 a month. He knew little about writing, nothing about newspapering, but he had a quick mind, an abundant supply of chutzpah, and the ability to vacuum up endless titillating trivia, a must since he needed up to fifty items for a single column.

He soaked up as much as he could about reporting and soon was doing two, three, and finally six columns a week. As soon as a column was finished, after hours on the phone, reinforced by notes from a night-before swing of the "in" spots, the copy went to Buchwach, who cleaned up any untidy grammar and excised or softened items that had the smell of libel.

The Sherman column soon became the best-read feature in town. In 1958, when he married Peggy Ryan, a film dancer, he was making $65 a week at the paper and another $250 hosting, and hustling commercials for, the Eddie Sherman Movie on TV. (Some critics suggested that he plugged advertisers in his column, but both he and Buchwach denied it.)

He got to know every Hollywood celebrity who came to Honolulu, and he enjoyed visions of one day being among them. He became a good friend of Marlon Brando, Mike Todd, Robert Cummings, Rita Moreno, Mitzi Gaynor, June Allyson, and John Ford, among others. As the *Beacon* magazine said, "Calls from any one of scores of the great and near-great of Hollywood, seeking advice and counsel, are not uncommon, and many of Honolulu's most affluent political and business leaders are not above a quiet chat with Eddie. Viewed from this angle, Eddie has made it."[1]

In 1960 he tried several times for a raise but was told that the paper was having financial problems. He phoned *Star-Bulletin* Editor William Ewing,

Three-dot columnist Eddie Sherman.

who quickly signed him on with a hefty pay boost. But half a year later Eddie was back at the *Advertiser*, this time with more money, an office, and a secretary. He told friends he'd returned home.

On the side, he dug up and polished a ten-year-old manuscript into a novel, *Mention My Name in Hawaii*, which made it to the bookstore shelves. Asked to review it, Scott Stone, former assistant city editor of the *Advertiser*, panned it as one of the worst books he'd ever read. Unfazed, Eddie wrote a column item giving Stone "a great big orchid lei for his rave review."[2]

Despite his oversized ambition, his yearning for a magic formula that would propel him to riches and mainland fame, there was an underlying warmth and kindness. He helped many a struggling entertainer on the way up—and comforted many on the way down. He admitted that he was not the most incisive critic, for no matter how bad an act was he tried to find something good to say. And whenever a worthy cause needed a champion, Eddie rarely said no—whether it was MC-ing one of the early March of Dimes telethons, or raising $5,000 in dimes and dollars for the crippled boxer Toy Tamanaha, when his wife and daughter were struck by a car, or conceiving and conducting the Kui Lee cancer research fund, which reached $150,000. When *Advertiser* correspondent Bob Jones wrote Eddie from Vietnam that GIs there were thirsty, Eddie's item sent thousands of Coca-Cola cans to them.

In September 1973, after seventeen years of giving readers the scoop, Eddie Sherman went after the pot at the foot of the rainbow. In his final *Advertiser* column, addressed to his son Shawn, he wrote that he was leaving "the greatest adventure of my life up to now" to "look for change and challenge—to try something new."[3] Seven hundred friends turned out for a farewell roast and toast.

He set up a show-business booking agency, and he and Peggy also became interested in the Kohala Plastics plant, one of five businesses set up with loans from the state's Kohala Task Force and the County of Hawaii to offset the loss of a Big Island sugar company. The Shermans were among the guarantors of the $300,000 state/county loan. When the bubble burst, they filed a petition in federal bankruptcy court, listing liabilities of $339,973 and assets of $17,650.

They moved to Las Vegas, where Peggy taught dancing and Eddie got into time-sharing sales. He later returned to Honolulu alone and began writing a popular three-dot column for a free-distribution weekly.

In seeking a successor, the *Advertiser*, in advance of Sherman's departure, placed an ad in *Editor & Publisher*, the national weekly journal of newspapering, and carried a Sunday story seeking applicants. It called the job "one of the most challenging and stimulating" on a newspaper and explained: "The 'three-dot' columnist talks to presidents and paupers, dines with movie stars and prisoners, hunts down items from Kakaako to Karachi, and chronicles the revealing tidbits that many people turn to when they get their morning newspaper."

The paper wanted "a tenacious reporter, a vigorous digger, a person who enjoys people and their activities. He should be an energetic prober, a good listener, an honest evaluator, an articulate questioner—and have the capacity to produce from his daily contacts a column jampacked with items which would appeal to any reader."[4]

The *Advertiser* heard from 132 applicants, from New York to Seoul. Chosen was Tom Horton, thirty-three, columnist for the *Sacramento Union;* his wife, Karen, the *Union's* city hall reporter, was taken on as a feature writer.

An Oklahoman whose parents moved to California when he was twelve, Horton had been with the *Union* for thirteen years, finally writing a column, hoping to match a *Union* alumnus named Herb Caen, the longtime San Francisco star.

Horton was an essayist rather than a three-dotter, and he was a smooth writer, which Sherman never pretended to be. Horton began his first column, with the heading "Tom who?," this way:

How can he write a daily column about Hawaii without knowing anybody in Hawaii, dot-dot-dot? It's easy, really. You type with your fingers crossed, hoping you don't write makai when you mean mauka; you wake in the middle of the night screaming 'items, items!'; you do a quick read and a fast 20 questions on everybody from the guy trying to sell you matching Aloha shirts and muumuus to the car-wash girl trying to scrape off the last of the California bugs, hoping somebody will say something funny, foolish or frightening so the next morning everybody can read it and marvel, 'Now here's a guy who really KNOWS Hawaii.'

On arrival Horton found a personal message, which read, "You'll be working for a lo—— newspaper, but good luck." Horton wrote that he couldn't make out the key word. "It's either lovely or lousy." The personal greeting was signed by Frank F. Fasi, the mayor of Honolulu.[5]

Horton did the column for two and a half years. He was anchored in a fixed position on page three of the first section, a choice location. Over time, in the view of the *Advertiser's* editors, he began to suffer from a malady that seems to inflict many columnists, a feeling that the paper exists to provide them space to do entirely as they wish.

The *Advertiser* had a couple of ground rules. The columnist, after turning in his copy, was to be reachable for a little while so anything that seemed unclear or questionable could be checked out. Another rule: the columnist should leave political items to the paper's writers who cover politics full-time, and who are far less likely to be conned by a politician or his or her people, especially around election time. At any rate, Horton disregarded both rules. He had a political item in a column, left the office after turning in his copy, which was standard, but could not be reached at his usual phone numbers before it was time to send the column to the composing room to be set into type. So the political item was edited out.

The next morning, he charged in with blood in his eye and demanded to know why his column had been tampered with. The explanation failed to satisfy him. There were several subsequent disagreements, and he announced that he was quitting.

On Friday, February 20, 1976, under his column heading there appeared a single sentence: "Tom Horton has resigned for personal reasons." A facile writer, he quickly connected elsewhere, doing a column for *Honolulu Magazine* and, with his wife, editing the Aloha Airlines in-flight magazine and some travel guides.

It took until August to find a new columnist. George Daacon, twenty-nine, had become addicted to three-dot columns in Chicago and other newspapers when he was a boy in a Wisconsin town. On arrival at the *Advertiser*, he told Bob Krauss, "Everything I learned I got out of three-dot columns. I've never been to journalism school. But I've read 10 to 15 columns a day for years."

When he was twenty-three, "a friend in Vancouver [B.C.] hired me to sell advertising for a shoppers' news. I also wrote two columns. After about three months I figured it looked so easy I could be in business for myself."

He started his own throwaway paper, which lasted four months. He began driving a truck, but sent one-liners to Vancouver columnists and bombarded the newspapers with letters filled with snappers. So much of his material was used, he said, he called on the editor of the newspaper in nearby New Westminster, the *Columbian*.

"They looked at me sort of funny, a truck driver wanting to be a columnist, but they gave me a month's trial. I drove a truck and wrote three columns a week," then was hired to do a daily column.[6]

From three years on the *Columbian*, he was hired by the *Vancouver Sun*. Seven months later he read an item in Irv Kupcinet's column in the *Chicago Sun-Times* about an *Advertiser* opening. He wrote to Buchwach, then executive editor, and was hired. He anticipated no problem getting material:

> Honolulu is a fantastic three-dot column town. There's a lot of activity, celebrities, movement in and out, a lot of money in this town. . . . Essays? I'll do that as little as possible. I'm not comfortable doing that. I figure, if an item can't be done in two sentences, then it belongs someplace else in the newspaper.[7]

He wrote a breezy column and had a good following, but he wouldn't leave well enough alone. In the late spring of 1979, he wrote management to advise that he was about to engage in an outside business, putting together tours to Las Vegas.

Buchwach told him this would create a conflict of interest and that it violated the *Advertiser*'s code of ethics and its contract with the Hawaii Newspaper Guild, which prohibited staffer activities that could adversely affect the paper's reputation with its readers and news sources. It was explained that his credibility would be undercut, since he would be suspected of publicizing people who joined his excursions.

Daacon persisted, went to the top of the ladder, to the publisher, who referred him back to Buchwach. Daacon insisted he was going ahead with his "moonlighting," and he was discharged on June 30. He went to the guild, which showed no sympathy. Buchwach wryly observed that Daacon left the way he arrived—"fired with enthusiasm."

An overture to conduct the column was made to *Advertiser* feature writer Pierre Bowman, who thought about it, then said no. Daacon went into real estate and the *Advertiser*, as it had in the past, beat the bushes for a successor.

Among the last of some three hundred applications was one from thirty-year-old Don Chapman, an Oregonian who before getting into workaday journalism "played bass fiddle and guitar in bands, did some farming, sold shoes, drove a bus, and worked as a delivery boy for a drugstore. I had thoughts of becoming a Lutheran minister and attended a seminary for two terms, but decided one night while walking in the rain that I wasn't meant to be a priest."[8]

He began newspapering in Pendleton, Oregon, where his big story "was passage by the city council in Stanfield of an ordinance that levied a fine on owners of dogs who had sex in public." On the side he learned to rope steers.

He moved around, was a social worker and school teacher in a tough black neighborhood in St. Louis, then took journalism courses and was writing sports in San Jose when his letter to the *Advertiser* rang the bell. He arrived starry-eyed, with his St. Bernard named Bozo, and did his first column October 29.

A lead item in his kickoff titled "Smoke detector alarm" revealed a four-month-old "friendly neighborhood bet" between Clare Boothe Luce and Betty (Mrs. Adrian) Perry. Both were trying to quit smoking cold turkey, and the first to cave in would pay the other $10,000. Chapman invoked "one loud chorus of 'Smoke better not get in your eyes.'" The size of the wager was a sufficient inhibitor; neither woman smoked again, neither paid.

Chapman did a workmanlike job, but over the years he gradually seemed to run out of steam. In December 1991 his column was moved from the paper's second page to a space created alongside the comics, to run three times a week. And on June 10, 1992, after nearly thirteen years, Chapman wrote his finale, citing his record of "about 2,700 columns, 40,500 items, 80,000 names and 121,503 dots." He mentioned some of the biggies he'd met—Ray Charles, Jack Lord, Jack Nicklaus, Jim Nabors, Tom Selleck, Dolly Parton, Arnold Palmer among them—but said his greatest satisfaction came from being part of the team that carried the *Advertiser* from a poor second to the *Star-Bulletin* in readership to number one in circulation. "Today, the Advertiser boasts a circulation of 107,600; the afternooners 87,300." Chapman's departure was taken in stride by both paper and readers. No replacement was sought.

But some columns seem to go on forever. There was the dazzling case of Heloise, of whom *Time* magazine wrote:

Her normally brown hair sprayed soft silver for the occasion, the job applicant presented herself at the desk of George Chaplin, editor of the Honolulu
Advertiser. . . . Housewife Heloise Cruse admitted that she knew nothing
about journalism, but Chaplin was undone by the sight of that sterling coif-
fure topping 62 inches of feminine aggression. "It was obvious," he said later,
"that if I didn't say yes, I was going to spend the rest of my working days saying no to her." So began, in improbable fashion, one of the most improbable
success stories in the annals of U.S. newspapering.[9]

What *Time* had overlooked was the pivotal role played in the acquisition
of Heloise by Publisher Twigg-Smith. While at the American Press Institute
seminar in Reston, Virginia, he had been impressed by a similar and successful
Washington Star column. By happenstance, soon after his return to Honolulu,
Heloise breezed into his office. He immediately saw her as a readership
bonanza and sent her to me. I was skeptical, put off by her lack of experience,
her appearance, and her assertiveness, but Twigg-Smith persuaded me to
yield to her tenacity and give the column a try. His judgment was on the mark;
she was an instant hit.

The thirty-nine-year-old wife of a lieutenant colonel at Hickam Air Force
Base and the mother of two, Heloise was a Fort Worth native who was gradu-

Heloise Cruse started her nationally
syndicated household hints column at
the *Advertiser*.

ated from the Texas School of the Arts, then took business courses and became a licensed bookkeeper. With her husband Marshall she moved around, to military posts in Japan, Okinawa, Mexico, Canada, China.

She admittedly had been no great shakes as a housekeeper, conceding, "I didn't know you had to clean a john until six months after I got married."[10]

But she was not lacking in confidence or vigor. Asked at a party one night what she'd like to do, she replied in her Texas drawl, "I'd like to have a column in a newspaper." A man snorted, "Who do you think you are . . . Abby or Walter Winchell?" He bet her one hundred to one she couldn't do it.

Her column, on a thirty-day trial basis, first appeared in the *Advertiser* on February 15, 1959. It was called "Reader's Exchange," and while she printed letters on personal problems, she let other readers provide answers. She focused on housekeeping, cooking, cleaning, and gardening.

The column quickly developed into a bible of household hints. Its magic was that Heloise never wrote a kind word for a product or a recipe she hadn't personally tested. Her readers quickly identified with her. She saved them time, energy, drudgery. She was "testing, testing, testing, whitening clothes, waxing floors, taking spots off furniture, trying new methods and sampling new products. Once a week she [was] guest speaker at a women's club."[11]

The mail started flooding in—she soon needed a part-time staff of seven, working in her home—and her advice went out. Anything she liked became a sellout. Typical example: a reader praised a particular bug-killer. Heloise published the letter, noting, "I know. I bought it too. Amazing, isn't it?"

Upshot: the distributor, who normally ran a one-man office, had to get four assistants to take orders, while a phone answering service took on three more women, and two telephone men were installing additional lines. Meanwhile, buyers flocked to retail stores throughout the community.[12]

When she brought out a forty-eight-page booklet on household hints, more than fifteen thousand copies were sold, many autographed by her in supermarkets.

At a May 1961 lunch eight hundred female fans saluted her, along with Mayor Neal Blaisdell and more than a dozen top corporate executives. She was exuberant and flamboyant, changing the color of her hair about once a week, ranging over nine colors, with blue her favorite, explaining she'd been doing it for years, long before turning columnist. Her fans ate it up.

Managing Editor Buck Buchwach proposed national syndication. She asked him if he would try for it, insisting that, if it came about, she would pay him a commission on the income generated. Buck canvassed the field and worked out a favorable agreement with King Syndicate in New York in September 1961. Newspapers began to take on the column. The *New York Journal-American* plastered its two hundred delivery trucks with $4\frac{1}{2}$-by-$9\frac{1}{2}$-foot posters, "Happy Hints for Housewives. Read Heloise daily." The *Chicago American* followed suit.

Soon there were 65 papers, and Heloise's office, formerly the master bedroom of her Foster Village house, overflowed with mail. The newspaper list continued to expand—to 260, including 10 in Canada, Germany, and Japan.

Four months after syndication, Heloise's offer of a booklet on laundry—how to wash clothes white and save time and money doing so—brought one hundred thousand airmail letters, with surface mail still to come. Honolulu Postmaster George Hara called it the largest single delivery of mail in Hawaii's history. *Newsweek* magazine described the column as "one of the hottest properties in the newspaper business."[13]

Late in 1962, Colonel Cruse was transferred to the Pentagon, and Heloise set up shop in her new house in Washington. The syndicate added to her fame with a 250-page book of selected household hints, published by Prentice-Hall. Soon she was up to five hundred papers. The column was a gold mine, but along the way Heloise forgot Buchwach, who simply shrugged it off.

A quiet man, Colonel Cruse took in stride his wife's success, as well as the mail that avalanched all over the house and the staffers who assisted Heloise. With typical astuteness she added "Heloise" to the name of her look-alike daughter Ponce, and when she died in 1977 the column continued apace with a new twenty-six-year-old conductor. Thirty years after its start, "Heloise" was still a winner.

29

Advertiser's Dilemma: Hope versus Reality

IN APRIL 1953, on the eighth anniversary of noted war correspondent Ernie Pyle's death, Roy W. Howard, chief of Scripps-Howard newspapers and a friend of Thurston, placed a spray of flowers on the grave in Punchbowl national cemetery. Editor Coll recalled war-weary Pyle's sadness and silence when he passed through Honolulu on his way to the western Pacific, where a sniper killed him on an Okinawan island.

Thurston entertained his friend Howard and may have shared with him his longtime hope that he could work out some arrangement with the *Star-Bulletin* on joint use of facilities. At the January 27, 1954, board meeting he reported on a conference he'd had with representatives of Arthur Little & Company, then conducting a management survey for the *Star-Bulletin*, on possible combination of certain mechanical equipment of the two papers.

Sometime later, with Thurston absent, the board agreed that a definite plan should be adopted. On his return, Thurston felt a third party might accomplish something, and Walter Dillingham was authorized to seek anyone of his choice to try to bring about a combination.

No one seemed to understand or acknowledge that they were pursuing an illusion. After the *Advertiser*'s bitter attacks on *Star-Bulletin* publisher Farrington and the enmity they engendered, that paper had no thought of engaging in any deal that would benefit Thurston.

With *Advertiser* equipment deteriorating, the paper in November 1954 bought five used press units from the *Mobile Press-Register* for $320,000. They provided a total of ten units in the pressroom, enabling a more flexible operation.

The next month Thurston reported to the board on "the present favorable advertising picture." But this was more an expression of hope than of reality, since for every new line of advertising garnered by the *Advertiser* the *Star-Bulletin* gained several.

But on the editorial side the staff could take some small comfort from a letter addressed to Thurston and Coll from John A. Burns, chairman of the Democratic Party of Hawaii, praising the paper as "fair and objective" in its coverage of the 1954 campaign.

The Sunday paper continued as the mainstay, saving the six weekday issues, which lost money, and on March 1, 1955, the *Advertiser* produced a 126-pager, one of the biggest in a long time, including a 16-page school section, a 10-page garden section, a new Bob Krauss column titled "The Night Side," a new weekly boys' and girls' page, and a weekly column by Art Buchwald.

Later in the year, it increased the daily street-sale price to ten cents from five, which had held steady since the paper went daily in the 1880s. The newsprint price had gone from $40 a ton in 1940 to $146 in 1955, a jump of 150 percent in fifteen years. And since 1948 the yearly cost of publishing the paper had risen $710,000, with each day's paper costing $7,000 to $8,000.

As its centennial in July neared, special sections were planned to cover century-old firms, sugar, pineapple, utilities, armed services, the visitor industry, and growth in other fields.

Despite its weakness on the business side, the *Advertiser* had an enterprising editorial staff. On May 31, 1956, the paper carried the first color news photo to appear in the next day's issue of an Island daily. It had been taken by photographer Y. Ishii at 11 A.M. the previous day at Punchbowl's memorial day

July 1956. *Advertiser* executives and directors. Publisher Lorrin P. Thurston is flanked on his left by editor Raymond S. Coll, on his immediate right by Walter F. Dillingham and Robert S. Thurston. *Back row, from left:* Wayne Damon, secretary; Allan McGuire, business manager; William O. Paine, radio station KGU manager; S. N. Castle; Reginald P. Faithfull; George Voorhees, production director; and Thurston Twigg-Smith, managing editor.

observance. The picture was of two mothers of Medal of Honor winners, dedicating a great wreath to the memory of all who sleep in the national cemetery. Previously, such photos either were prepared long in advance of publication or ran two or three days after being shot.

Coll, visiting New York for his first time in twenty years, was interviewed by the *World-Telegram*. He said that Hawaii's residents of Japanese or Chinese ancestry were "fully American. . . . They are, in a sense, the new Pacific Man."[1]

The one hundredth anniversary of the *Advertiser*, July 2, 1956, was marked by an open house, with guests greeted by Thurston, Coll, and Vice-President Dillingham. Thurston, in a signed editorial, bemoaned the passage of "kamaaina leaders," with "millions of dollars worth of Hawaiian stock . . . being voted by trust company officials [on behalf] of children and grandchildren" of "men of courage, vision and ability."

Trust estate earnings, he wrote, were rarely "being put back into our Hawaiian economy." The same, he said, was true of resources of federal credit unions and the territorial employees' retirement system.

Also "sad to note . . . the famous names of pioneer business men are steadily disappearing from the directorates of our large local companies."

He saw leadership, money, time, and energy having to come from the mainland—as witness the Castle & Cooke investment in macadamia nuts, Hawaiian Pine's building of its own can factory, the start of three television stations, and the buyout of local companies by mainland investors, opportunities that "many kamaaina descendants overlook or are unable to finance."

In September the *Advertiser* campaigned for use of the Ward Estate's twenty-two-acre Old Plantation on Ward Avenue, being condemned and bought by the city, for a new Bishop Museum as a repository of Polynesian culture. But museum director Alex Spoehr was reluctant to move, and the city planning commission, committed to building an auditorium on the site, with a $2 million bond sale to buy the property already advertised, let the idea die.

At the end of the year the paper called 1956 "the greatest peacetime year in the history of the territory" and saw 1957 moving to even higher levels. But the *Advertiser* was in a critical cash position and sought to renegotiate loans with the Bank of Hawaii and Bishop National, then at $325,000, with a view of going to $500,000. Both banks accommodated, agreeing to a $250,000 loan each.

Robert R. Midkiff, a vice-president of Hawaiian Trust Company, was elected a director, and Thurston continued to seek a partial combination of the papers' mechanical facilities, but without success. When Joe Farrington died in June 1954, Thurston renewed his efforts, but again to no avail. Farrington's widow, Betty, was even more disdainful of Thurston than her late husband had been.

On the technological front, Hawaii continued to benefit from developments. Moments after a new 2,400-mile trans-Pacific submarine telephone cable was dedicated, United Press sent the first of two newsphotos to the

Advertiser from San Francisco and Washington, D.C., by direct phone line, a transmission requiring ten minutes. Previously telephotos had been sent by radio. The first photo was of the dedication ceremony; the second of Admiral Rawson Bennett announcing progress of the Navy's earth satellite program.

At the 1958 stockholders' meeting in April, Thurston reported that economies effected in the last half of 1957 made prospects for 1958 look good. Although cutbacks temporarily put the paper in the black, they did more harm than good because the drop in quality took its toll in advertising and circulation with the net result that the spread between the *Advertiser* and *Star-Bulletin* widened. During the years of distress, modest quarterly dividends were declared, giving an impression of stability, especially to the small stockholders.

But in reality the paper was in a bad way. Except for some Linotypes, no new machinery had been bought for thirty years, and a survey showed a minimum of $1.5 million in new equipment was needed.

Circulation and advertising were also in deep trouble. Between 1950 and 1958 the *Advertiser*'s circulation increased by only eight copies, while the *Star-Bulletin* picked up thousands. In sum, the *Star-Bulletin* had twice the circulation and twice the advertising volume and was generating new ad space at a four-to-one rate over the *Advertiser.*

30

From War Service to Family Paper

IN MANY ways modern-day Hawaii began with World War II, which brought fundamental and interlinking changes on an enormous scale. It broke down the conservative haole oligarchy that had controlled the islands for decades. It propelled society toward racial equality. It helped advance the cause of statehood. It paved the way for Democratic Party ascendancy. It opened a new era in unionism. And, in time, it was to bring a sweeping transformation of the Honolulu newspaper scene, especially at the *Advertiser*, where top management and policy were lingering in the past.

When, fresh from wartime service, Thurston Twigg-Smith, a fifth-generation Islander, grandson of Lorrin A. Thurston and nephew of Publisher Lorrin P. Thurston, arrived at the *Advertiser*, he was unaware of the crucial and controversial role he would play in shaping the paper's future.

Twigg-Smith's mother, Margaret, was the sister of the publisher. His father was William, a New Zealand painter who migrated to Honolulu via the Chicago Art Institute. In addition to recording island scenes in pencil, charcoal, and oil for the Hawaiian Sugar Planters' Association and himself, he served as a long-time manager and flutist with the Honolulu Symphony Orchestra.

Thurston Twigg-Smith was born in Honolulu on August 17, 1921. After graduating from Punahou, he studied mechanical engineering at Yale, got his degree in early June 1942, married the next day, and soon found himself a combat field artillery officer. He landed in Normandy on D-Day-plus-six and fought through five campaigns in France and Germany. At war's end his battalion was in Magdeburg on the Elbe River, where, with other units, it was halted under the agreement that let the Russians get to Berlin first.

He was separated from service as a major in 1946, returned home, joined the National Guard to form the 483rd Field Artillery Battalion and was soon promoted to lieutenant colonel. He had an affinity for the military and was torn between becoming a career soldier, taking a plantation engineering job, or working on the paper. But he had a strong sense of family responsibility and sought the counsel of Jan Jabulka, who had resumed duties as the *Advertiser's* general manager after serving in Australia as a World War II correspondent for the paper.

Jabulka liked Twigg-Smith, perhaps saw his potential, and persuaded him to join the staff as an advertising salesman. After a couple of years at that, he became a circulation district manager for a year. His gravel-voiced supervisor, David Medeiros, recalled that "Twigg worked in Kalihi-Palama, a rough area at the time. But he went around, to pound on doors. He worked hard. I really give him credit."[1]

His next stop was the national advertising department, managed by his uncle, Robert Thurston, who wanted to groom him as his successor. The assistant manager, Margaret Kinney, was helpful but feared he would take away her opportunity to move up. When the ILWU waterfront strike in 1949 dried up advertising, the paper at times running as few as four pages, Kinney suggested that Twigg-Smith opt for editorial experience. Jabulka agreed, so he went up to the second floor to Editor Coll's department, where he remained for the next ten years.

For him this was a whole new world, peopled by an unfamiliar cast led by two managing editors, Hugh Lytle and Harry Albright, and City Editor Howard Case, a legendary figure on the Honolulu newspaper scene.

Although a gentle man at heart, Case exuded enthusiasm, matching the Hollywood version of a city editor—"two telephones going at the same time; always moving at a sprint pace; painting every little incident larger than life."[2]

As a 1912 cub reporter on the *Star-Bulletin*, he covered his first stories on foot, but

> we also got around on street cars. You jumped in on the side. They were open, clean, fast. It wasn't until the early 1920s, after I got married, that we paid $50 for a second-hand model-T Ford.
>
> By that time a policeman at King and Fort Streets was directing traffic from under an umbrella. We called him the hula cop from the way he motioned cars to stop and go. Three cars at the intersection was a traffic jam.[3]

A mainland colleague later described him as naive but resourceful, "the type of reporter who would caress Galli-Curci on the cheek while interviewing her or ask the Prince of Wales for a nip from his flask—and get by with it. Generals, admirals and mess-boys all look alike to Case."[4]

He started a column, "Down to Cases," in which he wrote lively doggerel, employed puns, and jested at the solemn and pompous.

In 1946 he came over to the *Advertiser* as city editor, lured by Coll's offer of $30 a month extra for his "Down to Cases" column. A few months later, still the reporter, he covered the second Bikini A-bomb test.

He retired in 1959, but continued to write his column, and when its fifty-first anniversary was marked in April 1970 it was believed to have set a national record for longevity.

In 1973, at age seventy-nine, four years before his death, Case was enshrined, along with Ray Coll, in the Honolulu Press Club's Hall of Fame. He was deservedly called the "dean of Hawaii's press corps, a walking encyclopedia of Island history, a newspaperman's newspaperman."[5]

When Twigg-Smith arrived, the newsroom had about twenty cityside reporters and photographers, far fewer than the *Star-Bulletin*. Their desks and typewriters were decrepit. When one elderly reporter who had a World War I–vintage typewriter died, his machine was immediately seized by a much younger colleague. Pencil stubs were often taped together. Company-paid travel was rare, except for coverage of volcanic eruptions—and, even then, staffers carried their sleeping bags and bunked in with the Big Island correspondent, whose wife fed them.

Many *Advertiser* newspeople "moonlighted" as stringers for Time-Life or Reuters or such newspapers as the *New York Times*, *Chicago Sun-Times*, and *Wall Street Journal* or freelanced magazine articles and books to bring in needed extra income.

There was no clock-watching and no overtime. What had to be done was. Election-night coverage was primitive. Reporters phoned in voting results, and they were counted on a hand-cranked adding machine. Niihau, the Robinson family–owned island off Kauai, always came in first, with a predictable ballot count of forty-nine for Republicans, two for Democrats.

Although undermanned and underfinanced, the staff competed strongly against the *Star-Bulletin*. There was a high level of esprit, the feeling that *Advertiser* people were more idealistic, harder working, and enjoyed more latitude than their rivals. The budget was low, but energy and endurance were high.

There was a lively mix of old-timers and young eager beavers. The turnover was fairly active, but the *Advertiser* was a beacon. Some people left two or three times but then came home.

Twigg-Smith had never written a news story, but he quickly learned and found the atmosphere and camaraderie exciting. His first major assignment was the 1950 Constitutional Convention, an experience that led him to cover the legislature. Several years later he was named night editor, with responsibility to format the next morning's paper. Given "dummies," blank pages on which to locate stories and photos, he was helped by his engineering training and his ever-present slide rule.

Subsequently, for about a year he wrote editorials under Lytle, who had yielded his managing editorship to Richard F. MacMillan, a former *Chicago Sun-Times* sports writer who joined the *Advertiser* in 1945. MacMillan was "a warm, sometimes crusty, witty companion who enjoyed good talk, bright writing and an occasional warming glass," the last a bit of understatement.[6]

Lytle served as editor of the editorial page for thirteen years, 1947–1960. Unabashedly an ultraconservative, a self-described red-baiter, a militant opponent of gun control, he was to the right of Coll, but none of his fulminations were killed. He left the paper to become Governor William F. Quinn's press secretary, but after six months, observing that they didn't think alike, he opened his own public relations agency.

From the editorial page, Twigg-Smith returned to newsroom jobs. He enjoyed his work but was still attracted by the military. At the outbreak of the Korean War he felt his National Guard battalion was likely to be called up. He took leave, went off to Fort Sill as a lieutenant colonel for an advanced refresher course, finished first in his class and was offered a post as gunnery instructor. With a wife and child, he was tempted by an Army career and its higher pay but decided, after consulting with Jan Jabulka, by that time executive editor, to stick with the paper, despite a lack of encouragement from his uncle-publisher.

When MacMillan left in 1954, Editor Coll named Twigg-Smith managing editor. His staff, though small, had several stars. One was a Bronx boy, Sanford Zalburg, who was graduated from the University of Missouri's journalism school (but lacked the $5 to buy a diploma) and worked briefly on papers from Florida to Alaska before coming to the Islands in 1950. Earlier he had spent six years in uniform, half in the Canadian army, half in the U.S. infantry. He was a D-Day veteran, hitting the Dog White sector of Omaha Beach at H-hour plus thirty minutes.

After some months at the paper, Zalburg left to cover the Korean War for Reuters, then worked out of Tokyo for the *Pacific Stars and Stripes*, returning to the *Advertiser* in 1953 and six years later making it to the city desk. He held that post until mid-1972, when he went back to reporting for eight years before retiring in 1980.

In his almost thirty years on the paper he was considered by even his competitors as Hawaii's ablest reporter of his time, a lively and innovative writer, a stickler for accuracy and fairness, a craftsman with a sense of history.

In 1969, on the twenty-fifth anniversary of the historic Allied landing in Normandy, he wrote a strong exception to a UPI story about GIs "storming ashore." Those weren't

> the fellows I knew—the doughs, the footsloggers, the infantry. They didn't "storm ashore". That's crap. They dragged themselves ashore, many of them. They waded through the water. They were seasick and scared and dead tired. Some of them were soaking wet from the spray and the turbulent sea. . . .
>
> What won the beach was not the battleships firing 14-inch shells, nor the bombers unloading 500- and 1,000-pound bombs. What won the beach was a few brave men.
>
> I can't help but remembering D-Day and Omaha Beach even after 25 years, no matter how I'd like to forget it. I left my youth there.[7]

In 1976 Zalburg took a year's leave to write a book about Jack Hall, the late ILWU leader, and the Islands' labor movement. When he returned to the paper he was astonished at the change in the city room: the immaculate desks, the ultramodern red cushioned chairs, the sleek black IBM Selectrics instead of the old battered Underwoods, the video display terminals.

> It has changed beyond belief and I was feeling old and sickhearted and then I heard a familiar sound—the buzzing of a mosquito. It was one of the old breed, too, a relative of those pesky mosquitoes that used to hang around the city room. At that very moment there were a number of people in the room, all of them younger, plumper and sweeter than I. But that saucy fellow settled on my arm, ready to take a nip. Nice to know I'm not completely disowned in my old city room.[8]

When in 1980 he composed his swan song, he asked himself if his years in journalism had been worth the effort since "the day after your story appears in the paper, the housewife uses the page to wrap garbage in."[9]

He recalled the day when, in a sour mood, he had discouraged an applicant on the phone from becoming a reporter. He also remembered that soon thereafter he did a piece about the Gouveia sisters, who lived in Palolo Valley in the early 1950s: "One of the sisters had read something I had written and phoned me from a neighbor's house. She didn't have a phone. She said she and her sister were living on welfare and the monthly check wasn't enough." She asked if he would come and talk with them and he said sure. Sandy Zalburg wrote a story.

> Suddenly, things began to happen. A Marine went out to their place with a sickle and lawnmower and cut the grass. A carpenter came by with his tool chest and some lumber and fixed the rickety steps. No one told them to do it. They just wanted to. Someone left a bag of groceries. Someone left an envelope with a ten-dollar bill. Maybe the same things would happen today. I don't know. Maybe the town had more heart then.
>
> A few days later the sister called me and said thanks: "I knew if you put it in the paper, it would help us," she said. "That's what papers are for—to help people."
>
> I've never forgotten. And that's what I should have told the young man who called me. I should have said that every now and then you can help people. And in this terribly screwed-up world they need all the help they can get. You can help people understand things, and not only the news. You can explain. You can explore. You can entertain. You can teach. You can bring joy or comfort: a laugh, a tear, perhaps, as Emily Dickinson said, "help one fainting robin unto his nest again." And maybe even on occasion produce a bag of groceries. That's what makes it worthwhile to work on a paper.[10]

A week after Zalburg retired, Scott C. S. Stone, who had come to the paper from the *Dayton Daily News* and served for ten years as military reporter and then assistant city editor, wrote of Zalburg's "singular dedication to journalism, his unselfish aid to other newsmen, and his ongoing search for truth behind the rhetoric."

From the *San Diego Evening Tribune*, Laurel Murphy, for two summers an *Advertiser* intern, wrote, "I can trace my birth as a reporter to the one exact moment in the city room when Sandy Zalburg, then city editor, commented, 'The kid can write.' . . . He was irascible. He was tenacious. He was also an inspiration. In short, though my career has led me to four other journals since, Sandy Zalburg was and remains the best newspaperman I have ever met."

In October 1951, a year and a half after Zalburg's arrival, Bob Krauss made his debut. A Nebraskan, son of a circuit-riding Lutheran minister, a World War II Navy combat veteran, he got a journalism degree at the University of Minnesota and after briefly reporting for a small South Dakota daily headed for Hawaii. He planned to work a year or two and then go on. "I had absolutely no intention of staying in a little place like this out in the middle of the Pacific that nobody had ever heard of. But it was romantic and I jumped at the chance to come."[11]

Krauss was assigned to the territorial government beat, then moved to the waterfront, meanwhile starting a daily column titled "In One Ear." It was soon popular for its human interest and down-to-earth humor, built around the foibles of his family and people in general. The Linotype operators vied to see who would put his column in type, so they could read it first.

Krauss had a pixie-like quality and enjoyed the zany, the tongue-in-cheek. He was great on stunts, most of which landed on page one. Thor Heyerdahl could have his *Kon-Tiki*; Krauss and TV's Kini Popo heroically sailed their raft

Longtime local features columnist Bob Krauss.

the length of the Ala Wai Canal. Then the two of them, with an ex-Army mule, spent eight days traveling around Oahu to check on native hospitality. They carried no money or blankets, but were lavished with food and drink and well housed. At the end of the journey, Governor Samuel W. King hailed them at Iolani Palace.

There was a lot more, never predictable. Krauss conducted a reducing contest by printing a diet—"Calorie Counters Anonymous"—in each day's column. Oahu Prison inmates tried it. Restaurants cried for advance copies. It became an attraction at dinner parties.

Time magazine picked up on his next venture—his five-day demonstration of caring for four preschoolers in Kailua, an unfamiliar exercise in running a home and a family. *Time* reported that Krauss had "never cooked, changed a diaper, made up a feeding formula or burped a baby."[12] But he managed to successfully substitute during the day for the children's mother, the wife of a Coast Guard officer.

The surrogate's summation: "To me, the hardest part of being a mother is boredom. You wash the same dishes every day, fold the same clothes, dust the same bookcases and change the same diapers." Asked if he'd ever repeat the experience, he winced, "Not unless you can catch me and tie me down."[13]

The readers loved it and produced an avalanche of letters to the editor.

But he had his serious side, too. With Dr. Kenneth Emory, the noted anthropologist, he explored an ancient burial cave at Kealakekua Bay on the island of Hawaii and accompanied him on other expeditions.

When, during a 1963 recession no one felt that Honolulu money could be raised to save the crumbling four-master sailing ship *Falls of Clyde*, a famous relic of the early U.S.-Hawaii trade, from becoming a Vancouver logging camp breakwater, Krauss took it on. In a matter of days, his column brought in $35,000. Thanks to him, the restored vessel is now a part of the Hawaii Maritime Museum.

He raised $8,000 to rescue the Ulu Mau Village, an authentic reminder of old Hawaii in Ala Moana Park. When the double-hulled *Hokule'a*, a voyaging canoe reminiscent of early Hawaiian craft, retraced migration routes, Krauss was aboard on the Tahiti-Raiatea leg. Over the years he visited and wrote about close to forty atolls and islands in the Pacific. He went in by boat to Kalalau Valley on Kauai's Na Pali coast to locate a mysterious hermit, who turned out to be a former medical man living in a cave and who, during a day of talk, reminded Krauss of an Old Testament prophet.

Humanitarian needs always found him ready. In three days he pulled in $3,000 to send a six-year-old Hawaiian lad to Philadelphia for open-heart surgery. To generate funds for the March of Dimes, he spent two days in an iron lung; he was appealing for $2,000 to buy a lung but quickly raised twice that.

When a Denver couple was shot at the Pali by a sniper, Krauss garnered $10,000 to pay their hospital bills and airfare home. And when five hundred natives on a Micronesian atoll lacked medical facilities, he helped send a pre-fab dispensary and crates of medical supplies via Coast Guard cutter.

While in Micronesia, at the Kwajalein missile base, he was put under house arrest by the Army. But his column on the affair led to a relaxation of restrictions on newspeople.

Like many journalists, he was a statehood fan, and a column urging action in Washington, sent to colleagues on papers in thirty states, stimulated some thousands of letters to Congress—and brought him a territorial Senate commendation, introduced by Senator Frank F. Fasi.

In 1964 the Sales and Marketing Executives of Hawaii selected him as "Salesman of the Year," an award previously given to the likes of Henry Kaiser, former Governor William F. Quinn, Duke Kahanamoku, and the Rev. Abraham Akaka. Asked to speak at the ceremony as his editor, I said that

> he operates a rather quiet corner where in this frantic, frenetic world one can find a smile or a grin or a bit of inspiration, where one can find a wise essay on one man's family or on the whole human family, or a series of anec-dotes or an exhortation to help a good cause and thus help one's spirit. And sometimes one can find, too, a bit of nonsense, which we all need now and then. He is a talented, thoughtful newsman [who proves] you don't have to be born here to be a true kamaaina.[14]

On Christmas 1965 Krauss arrived in Vietnam to join Bob Jones, the *Advertiser*'s military reporter, in coverage of the war there. Both were with the troops of Hawaii's 25th Infantry Division at Pleiku, the hot spot in the cen-tral highlands. Krauss next went to the Da Nang area to cover the Kaneohe Marines fighting there. To him, he reflected later,

> the war seemed unreal. Going on patrol in Vietnam is like hiking to Manoa Falls. There's the same humidity, the same dense foliage. Even the fruit trees are the same—mango, coconut, guava.
>
> But in Vietnam there were mines on the trail. Razor-sharp pungee sticks in the mud. Snipers in the leafy branches. That's the difference between war and peace, the knowledge that you may die at any moment. How do [I] explain that to shoppers at the Ala Moana Center . . .?

War was "a vastly complicated human experience that revealed man's noblest nature and his absolute worst."[15]

U.S. Senator Dan Inouye called Krauss and Jones "frontline combat cor-respondents in the best Ernie Pyle tradition." And he added that the *Advertiser* "is perhaps the only metropolitan paper in the 50,000 to 100,000 circulation class with two full-time reporters covering the battlefields."[16] The U.S. com-mander in Vietnam, General William C. Westmoreland, wrote in a note of appreciation to the paper that Krauss and Jones were reporting "thoroughly and accurately."[17]

In 1973 Krauss, Twigg-Smith, and three others retraced by foot and sailing canoe a three-hundred-mile trip around the Big Island, starting at Kailua-Kona, taken by missionary William Ellis in 1823. Krauss kept readers posted with a daily account. In the next two years he and Twigg-Smith led similar expeditions around Lanai and Tahiti, with Molokai to follow.

In 1978 when the *Advertiser* cosponsored an attempt by an Outrigger Canoe Club crew to paddle the English Channel, Krauss covered it as a sequel to the paper's Cook 200 Progress Edition and the bicentennial of Captain James Cook's Western discovery of the Hawaiian Islands. After the channel crossing, the canoe was donated to the people of Middlesbrough, where Cook was born 250 years before.

On another trip, the columnist helped raise funds and accompanied teachers and Hawaiian kids to a Navajo reservation in Arizona in a cultural exchange with Indian schoolchildren.

The *Advertiser* early on had become Krauss' home. When he first arrived, he found it "a warm place, an understanding place, and there was a lot of freedom." There was a sense of tradition and pride. He enjoyed working with Jack Burby, "one hell of a writer," and he respected Gardiner B. Jones, "a damned competent political man," and Buck Buchwach, "one of the really competent journalists."[18]

But he was upset with the lingering aroma of the past. Some Oriental staffers in the 1950s were paid less than haole counterparts. So Krauss joined the photographer Yoshiaki Ishii and reporters Jack Burby, Brian Casey, and Ron Bennett to successfully push for a National Labor Relations Board election and establishment by a 32-to-6 vote of a union, affiliated with the American Newspaper Guild. "Boss Coll was terribly hurt, took it very personally, as a reflection on him. But we got the wages equalled."[19] Subsequently employees of the display and classified ad departments joined, with the business office, circulation, and maintenance departments following. The mechanical departments were already unionized, so contract negotiations became a way of life at the paper.

Because of a personal experience Krauss also found fault with the paper's unbelievably early presstimes. One Sunday he was asked to check on a strike of Honolulu Rapid Transit workers. He went to the bus company quarters, on the site of the present municipal office building, and stuck around. Unexpectedly, about 5 P.M. the strike was settled. Krauss hot-footed it back to the city room, to find everything closed down.

He got an engraver, Louie Souza, to phone Editor Coll, who called the managing editor, Dick MacMillan, who raced down and stopped the press to insert two or three paragraphs on what should have been a banner story.

Krauss loved to write and he loved Hawaii—and this spilled over from his newspapering into books. In 1960 he brought out *Here's Hawaii*. James Michener, who did the introduction, called Krauss "a tonic to our islands, a brash wonderful wit. He has an inborn feeling for the rare and exotic nonsense that flourishes in the Fiftieth State. Hawaii is his land. With joy and outrage Krauss has made the islands his domain. . . . One gets a true picture of what life is like."[20]

Here's Hawaii became an Island best-seller, as did many of the dozen books that followed in Krauss' four decades on the paper. The young eager beaver who arrived in "a pork pie hat, unbuttoned sports coat and loosely knotted tie" had come to resemble "a white-haired sea captain with mutton chops and mustache."[21] But what remained unchanged was his zest for life in Hawaii and his need to translate that into the printed word.

One of the paper's most versatile members was Gardiner Jones, who served three stretches totaling fifteen years. He was an enthusiastic professional, a thorough researcher, and a sharp writer, adept at producing series on front-burner topics.

He was born in Manila to an Army father, served in the Air Force in World War II in Europe, then got a journalism degree from the University of Minnesota and worked five years for United Press in the Midwest before becoming an *Advertiser* reporter in 1951.

Over the years, he held diverse positions—political reporter, feature writer, travel editor, city editor, Sunday news editor, editor of the editorial page, then associate editor. While at the *Advertiser* he won five awards from the Honolulu Press Club, including the Paul Beam Memorial Award for three consecutive years for overall excellence in journalism.

When society editor Edna B. Lawson retired in April 1953, her assistant, Druzella G. Lytle, succeeded her but soon changed that title to women's editor. An alumna of Occidental College and the University of California, she was lively and likable, well organized, and soon improved the pages under her control.

Her first husband, John Terry, a *Star-Bulletin* alumnus representing the *Chicago Daily News*, was killed in 1944 covering the American invasion of the Philippines at Tacloban. Three years later she married Hugh Lytle, then at the *Advertiser.*

She expanded her staff and added food, fashion, child care, and medical coverage. Her team soon started winning not only local but national honors. Among other awards, the women's pages were ranked second best in the *Advertiser*'s circulation category by the University of Missouri Journalism School.

At the awards ceremony in 1962 Dru cited two problems of editing an Island women's page: providing good coverage of the many layers of Hawaii social life and keeping up with new mainland trends.

Another women's section stalwart was Mary Cooke, a Punahou graduate who cut her journalistic teeth as a barefooted cub on Kauai's weekly *Garden Island,* wearing a beat-up shirt and sailor pants. She was always accompanied by her poi dog, and one day, while she was covering a Board of Supervisors meeting, her canine and one owned by a *Star-Bulletin* correspondent started a fight that ended only when a supervisor hurled a spittoon at them.

The young writer digressed into play-scripting, won a national award for a children's drama, then in 1950 arrived at the *Advertiser*. She believed in hands-on journalism. When Oahu Sugar Company was retiring the last of its women field workers (the "hoe hana" women), Cooke put on their garb, including Japanese slippers, and spent a day working alongside, while she gained insights into their daily lives.

Once, on a Canadian vacation, she came across a group of long-forgotten Hawaiians living on an island near Vancouver. There were twenty-five to thirty families, descendants of sailors who had worked for the Hudson's Bay Company. Her story "started the editor's phone ringing" and resulted in a delegation's "first trip home in 130 years."[22] The tab was picked up by the *Advertiser*, an airline, and a hotel.

In 1959 Cooke was among four *Advertiser* staffers who won all five first-place awards in the annual Honolulu Press Club competition, the others being photographers Gordon Morse and Robert Young and reporter Jack Teehan, who earned two.

Her 1966 feature on how thirty charter members of the Outdoor Circle battled successfully between 1913 and 1926 to ban billboards won national acclaim. And her historical novel on the missionary period became an Island best-seller.

While a tenacious digger, she was cheery, gracious, and unruffled, unfailingly poised whether interviewing a yardman or the queen of England, Pat Nixon or ballet stars Rudolph Nureyev and Margot Fonteyn.

In 1978 she became food editor and wrote a popular column, "Coping with the Cost," on how to stretch the kitchen dollar. After thirty-one years at the paper, she retired in 1987, commenting on the "growth, happiness and satisfaction" provided by her career.

Business and financial affairs are often complex, but the job of a newsperson covering them is to make them easy to digest for the general reader.

From 1956 to 1963, except for a spell of editorial writing, that task fell to Edward J. Greaney, Jr., an Islander educated at Punahou, the University of Hawaii, and the Wharton School of Finance and Commerce at the University of Pennsylvania. He was soft-voiced and slow-spoken but resolute in searching out the facts.

His column, as he wrote near the end of his tenure, permitted him "to earn his livelihood interviewing taro farmers and ukulele makers, members of the [U.S.] cabinet, heads of Westinghouse, General Electric and Chrysler." (One indelible memory: driving the chairman of General Mills to the doctor's, after an interview, in his $15 auto.)[23]

He wrote of the varied backgrounds of outstanding business leaders:

For instance, neither of the two major banks here are headed by college men. The president of Hawaiian Telephone started out as an apprentice switchman at age 15. The president of Honolulu Rapid Transit began as a timekeeper.

Others have been men of academic stature who have been successful in business as well. The most notable example is Hung Wo Ching, president of Aloha Airlines. He holds a Ph.D. in economics and has taken sabbaticals from his career to pursue further learning at Harvard.[24]

Greaney left after seven years to take a state post, subsequently to become Governor George Ariyoshi's press secretary and later U.S. Senator Spark Matsunaga's.

After several successors, the post gained genuine stability with the coming home in August 1971 of Kit Smith, after working at the Los Angeles bureau of *Business Week*.

His family had moved from the Islands when he was finishing Punahou at seventeen. At Princeton he majored in music, with a minor in economics. "I played the trombone at all the football games. From there I went into the Navy, where they put me in charge of teaching illiterate recruits how to read. I begged for sea duty so they put me aboard a destroyer out of Long Beach. My job was gunnery officer, but I got a bigger kick out of putting out news releases, my secondary assignment," which earned him a commendation.[25]

That tipped him toward journalism and Stanford, where he earned a master's degree in communications and embarked on his life's work.

He found Hawaii business in the big leagues, with four locally based companies on the New York Stock Exchange. He quickly got on top of the local situation and won the respect of the heads of large and small enterprises as a thoughtful, thorough journalist who placed the highest premium on fairness and accuracy. Year after year went by without the need for a single correction.

No modern newspaper can function without an art department—to retouch the photos, draw maps and diagrams, and come up with sketches to match a story. In 1958 when then chief artist Jerry Chong asked the Honolulu Academy of Arts to recommend a part-time helper, Adam Nakamura got the job. He was quiet but talented. He drew acclaim for his pencil sketches of everything from sports to celebrities to his favorite, wildlife. Less mentioned was Nakamura's virtuosity as a slack-key guitarist. On his death in 1990, the paper said, "Adam enjoyed life and his pen could translate the beauty of life onto paper like nobody else."

Can a Reporter Protect a Source?

A NEWSPAPER needs sources that it can trust to provide reliable tips and leads or, even better, detailed accurate information. In 1957 the *Advertiser* was embroiled in a legal dispute over identification of a source, a dispute with significant ramifications. Reporter Alan Goodfader, who joined the *Advertiser* in 1956 from a small New York state newspaper, got a tip that Nesta Gallas, City and County personnel director, might be fired. He knew of friction between Gallas and some on the five-member Civil Service Commission, but none would confirm his tip. He approached Gallas, but she seemed unaware of any impending effort to dump her.

Then, on the night of December 16, 1957, before a commission meeting, Goodfader saw a light burning in Gallas' second-floor office at City Hall. Anticipating possible fireworks, he called the paper and asked for a photographer, who soon arrived.

The reporter's hunch proved out. In quick order, once the meeting began, three of the five commissioners summarily discharged Gallas. Some time later, charging conspiracy, she filed a $183,000 suit against the city for back pay and damages, and it came to trial in 1962.

Goodfader, called as a witness by Gallas' lawyers, was accompanied to court by *Advertiser* general counsel J. Russell Cades and colleague Harold S. Wright and by national and local representatives of the American Newspaper Guild. When asked who had tipped him that Gallas was in jeopardy, Goodfader replied that his source was confidential and he could not reveal it. Circuit Judge Edward J. Crumpacker ruled Goodfader had to disclose or be cited for contempt.

The *Advertiser*'s attorneys argued that forcing a reporter to identify his sources undercut his ability to serve the public. Cades' brief cited the case of the *New York Herald-Tribune*'s television columnist, Marie Torre, who served ten days in jail in 1958 for refusing to disclose a source of information. The judge agreed to suspend a contempt citation pending an appeal to the territorial Supreme Court.

Hawaii's high court subsequently ruled, four to one, that there was no statutory privilege locally allowing newspeople to withhold such information.

The case went back to Circuit Court, this time with Judge Allen Hawkins presiding. Gallas' attorneys opted not to question Goodfader as to his source. Had they done so and he had declined to give a name, the judge would have had no choice but to hold him in contempt of court.

A bill was introduced in the legislature to allow print and electronic reporters to protect news sources, except in cases of bad faith and/or malice, but it soon died. Gallas lost her case, including an appeal.

A similar case arose in 1983 when former State Senator D. G. (Andy) Anderson was charged with renovating two Waikiki buildings without the necessary building code permits.

During the controversy extending over months, *Advertiser* reporter Gerald Kato wrote at least three stories on the subject. He quoted Anderson that he was frustrated by city hall delays and had moved ahead on renovations without permits. "We have," Anderson said,

> taken the worst corner of Waikiki [at Seaside and Kuhio Avenues] and spent a million dollars to clean out porno houses and bathhouses that were run-down and filthy, and we have done it properly. If City Hall wants to pass my application around from desk to desk I'm not going to stand still for it. They can cite me and I'll face that hurdle when it faces me.[1]

Anderson's trial in September 1984 was stalled when Kato was suddenly subpoenaed by the prosecution to testify about conversations he had had with Anderson and to verify "admissions" by Anderson in his articles. He refused, and *Advertiser* attorney Jeffrey Portnoy declared people would shy away from interviews if they knew everything they said might be disclosed in court. The "chilling effect," he said, threatened the First Amendment guarantee of a free press.

District Judge William E. Smith ordered Kato to appear in court and testify. Portnoy appealed, but the State Supreme Court refused to set aside Smith's ruling, thus facing Kato with the likelihood of a contempt citation and possible jail term. But the high court left open the way for an appeal on specific questions and responses should Kato be cited, and it quoted a 1972 U.S. Supreme Court ruling that called for case-by-case review and for a lower court to forgo a contempt citation until it had exhausted all other means of getting the information it wanted from a journalist.

A showdown was averted when Anderson pleaded no contest to the charges, telling reporters, "I think if Gerry Kato were not in an awkward spot I probably would have pursued it to the end."[2]

An *Advertiser* editorial the next day suggested Anderson's "altruism" was "less than convincing" in the light of Anderson's ignoring six warnings in six months over not having the required permits. It said a reporter's job is to "serve the public by providing accurate information on government activities and not serving as agent of either prosecution or defense attorneys." It added Anderson had never complained that Kato's stories were inaccurate.

As a result of the Gallas and Kato cases, reporters came under pressure to seek sources who do not demand confidentiality or who agree, if a reporter is called to testify, to waive such protection—and to recognize that saying their stories speak for themselves may not serve as an adequate defense against contempt proceedings.

Years later a Circuit Court judge for the first time in Hawaii conclusively ruled that reporters had a qualified privilege. The case concerned unpublished photographs that an injured individual sought and that the *Advertiser* refused to voluntarily produce. Circuit Judge Wendell Huddy in 1995 ruled that the reporter's privilege held unless the person seeking information showed it was critical to his or her case and could not be obtained from other sources. In effect, the judge was saying that the ruling in the Goodfader case was no longer good law.[3]

32

A New Hand on the Editorial Helm

IN SEPTEMBER 1958, with the sale to the *Times-Picayune* of the New Orleans *Item*, which I had edited for nine years, I was invited to come to Hawaii and discuss the editorship of the *Advertiser*. I did, the board approved, and I agreed to come December 1.

In World War II I had been the founding editor and officer-in-charge of the *Stars and Stripes, Mid-Pacific*, the armed forces newspaper printed at the *Advertiser*, and I had met Thurston and Coll. Also in the years since the war I had written many prostatehood editorials, and these, coming by clipping service, had reached the *Advertiser*.

With the exception of Twigg-Smith, the board consisted of ultraconservatives, most advanced in age, but the paper was in such deep trouble they were willing to take on a moderately liberal editor with experience in fighting battles on papers second in advertising and circulation.

I accepted the title of associate editor for three months, until March 1959, when Coll would formally retire, but was given immediate authority. In Coll one could still sense the fire and force that had marked his earlier years, but he had stayed on too long and been overtaken, as had Thurston, by the powerful changes in the Islands' political, economic, and social structure.

I quickly formed a team with Twigg-Smith and Buck Buchwach, then city editor. Both were topflight journalists but had been fettered by top management's outdated policies. Buchwach, an honors graduate of the University of Oregon journalism school, had been with me on the *Stars and Stripes*, then joined the *Advertiser* on his discharge from the Army. He began as a military reporter and for four years was a familiar figure on Oahu posts as he drove "Buckety Buck," the green and white surplus Jeep he'd bought. He was a highly intelligent, lively man, small in stature, big in humor. He enjoyed celebrities, became friends of many. (Years later, after he had a heart bypass by Dr. Michael DeBakey in Houston, Frank Sinatra sent his private plane to fly Buchwach to relatives in Oregon to recuperate.)

The three of us worked well together. Years later, Twigg-Smith told an interviewer: "George and I became great pals. I respected what he was doing and he respected my perception of the problems the Advertiser was having."[1]

Still, Twigg-Smith felt that with Coll in his mid-eighties Thurston had brought in an outside editor to sidetrack him: "I think by that time [Thurston] really didn't want to share the limelight. . . . I remember when I became a trustee at Punahou [in 1954 at age thirty-three] he was very upset. His father had been a trustee, but they never asked him."[2]

With the editorial department in new hands, Twigg-Smith felt he could be more useful on the business side, so he went downstairs, expecting to be assistant to the publisher. But Thurston had other ideas, assigning his nephew as assistant to the business manager, Allan McGuire. Since the post was a nonentity, Twigg-Smith managed to take charge of promotion, sorely needed because the *Advertiser*'s daily circulation was 46,693, less than half of the *Star-Bulletin*'s 97,495.

When I came to the paper, I knew the daily was sick but felt the *Sunday Advertiser*, a strong product that had had the field to itself since its founding in 1903, would provide the time to build the daily. The immediate goal was to improve the content and layout daily and Sunday while seeking more circulation and advertising through aggressive promotion.

Because of the paper's perilous condition, Thurston virtually gave me carte blanche. The editorial policy, which had ranged from ultraconservative to reactionary, was transformed into one in rhythm with the new Hawaii. For the first time in Island history the Democratic Party had taken control of the territorial legislature in 1954 and would gain the governorship in 1962. There was a new wave of liberalism and idealism and the *Advertiser* was in tune.

On the editorial page, columnists Westbrook Pegler, George Sokolsky, and Victor Riesel were replaced by Doris Fleeson, William White, and Marquis Childs. Cartoonists Herblock of the *Washington Post* and Fitzpatrick of the *St. Louis Post-Dispatch* were added. Locally, Professor Dan Tuttle, a University of Hawaii political scientist with keen insights into Island government, agreed to write a Sunday column, which quickly developed a wide readership.

But the paper could not afford $50 a week for the *New York Times* news service by mail; the *Star-Bulletin* grabbed it and was soon getting the material by wire, as it does to this day.

Usually, redesign of a newspaper is done over time to avoid jarring the readers, but the *Advertiser* had to move rapidly. Use of photographs was doubled or tripled. Larger body type enabled easier reading. In my second or third week I handed Andrew Mitsukado, who did sports layout, a copy of the lively *Sunday Miami Herald* sports section and suggested he use it as a model. He did the very next Sunday, with football coverage regionalized, with many more action pictures and snappier headlines.

The paper got into two-fisted investigative reporting. Jack Teehan, a decorated World War II B-52 pilot who came from New Hampshire to join the *Star-Bulletin*, saw the "new" *Advertiser* as a "big, shining white light" and joined its staff. In 1959, he inventoried state property at Iolani Palace, the capitol, at the end of the last territorial legislative session before statehood and found missing items included three Senate office rugs, a number of desks and filing cabinets, ten desk lamps, more than forty pencil sharpeners, six electric fans, $3,000 worth of fountain pens, 103 dictionaries, and, ironically, 150 sets of the Revised Laws of Hawaii. Page-one stories and editorials ("You Can't Ignore Thievery") led Governor Quinn to order an inquiry. As it began, rugs and other large items magically surfaced, including fans and lamps deposited in the driveway of the attorney general's investigator. *Newsweek* quoted a scoffing Democratic Senate leader, Matsuki (Mutt) Arashiro, who cited what he called an old Island custom of departing legislators' sacking the capitol: "Who," he said, "wants to use something that has been used by someone else?"[3]

The *Star-Bulletin* was smarting at being licked on such a story of political mischief, and when investigator Everett N. Afook announced he had found the last missing chair among *Advertiser* belongings in the Iolani Palace newsroom, the afternoon paper jumped into action. It gleefully blazoned the story under the headline "Last Missing Chair is Under A Newsman."[4] The AP picked up the details and flashed them to numerous Honolulu radio stations. But the egg turned out to be on the faces of Afook and the newspeople who spread the story.

The *Advertiser* had bought the chair with other office equipment from Honolulu Paper Company. When asked by the AP for a statement, the *Advertiser* said Afook and others could have been saved from rushing into print with a "flat misstatement of fact if they had simply contacted the paper, which would have gladly shown them the bill of sale for the chair."[5]

The upshot of the commotion was tighter property controls and a reminder that one of the major roles of a newspaper, as stressed by Jefferson and Madison, was to keep a keen eye on government. Attorney General Jack H. Mizuha took note of this on calling the *Advertiser*'s probing "a great public service."[6]

Teehan moved on to a traffic-safety series that stimulated passage of a driver point-system law. He then spent seven days at the Kaneohe hospital for the mentally ill and wrote a series that sparked a state Senate investigation, resulting in more funds and jobs for the hospital and a decent burial for 648 former patients whose cremated remains had been stored for years in shoeboxes.

For ninety consecutive days the paper published on the editorial page a photo of a rear-end collision, representing one in every four traffic accidents, and bringing an 18 percent reduction in such mishaps. The National Trucking Association awarded the paper first place in its annual safety contest for the year's most effective overall campaign.

For six weeks cartoonist Harry Lyons teamed up with news photographers to go after chuckholes in the streets with chuckles—Lyons sketching in a cartoon figure, Peter Puka, golfing, swimming, sighting submarines in the holes. Repair crews went into quick action.

The paper also brought about improved rules for admitting emergency cases in Honolulu hospitals. This was after a bride falling from her groom's car had been shunted among three hospitals, each worried about her credit standing, before dying after surgery.

In stories and editorials the paper explored the benefits of a proposed united fund and contributed to its establishment soon afterward.

After an unusual number of attack and rape cases, a campaign was mounted for more street lights and police, leading to a $1 million lighting program in metropolitan Honolulu and a pledge to add seventy police officers.

Police reporter Terry McMurray revealed that bars in the town's best hotels were selling liquor to minors, including a thirteen-year-old who accompanied him in his field work. The story cost the *Advertiser* all of its liquor advertising for a few months, but no one in the ad department complained to the editor.

The paper blew the whistle on the lack of fire-warning systems in public schools. It campaigned for and got an overpass at Nanakuli so fourteen hundred schoolchildren could safely cross crowded Farrington Highway. It published a five-part series that played a pivotal role in Windward Oahu getting its first hospital, Castle Memorial. At the start of the series the state resisted the project and any grant of government aid; after it, it relented.

City hall got its share of attention and within a matter of months in 1960–1961 a variety of issues hit the headlines.

One controversy jumped out of plans for the city's new auditorium on the old Ward Estate property. The design of a local architectural firm called for a concert/theater hall and a sports arena with adjacent exhibition space.

Mayor Neal S. Blaisdell said that would cost too much and brought in a Los Angeles architect, who scrapped the concert hall and proposed a single multipurpose structure to embrace everything from boxing, basketball, and wrestling to symphony, ballet, and road shows.

A circular arena would offer 9,400 seats for sports, 7,500 for conventions, and, once a portable stage was set up and large drapes dropped from the ceiling, 3,300 for symphonies and other cultural events. The acoustics, it was pretended, would be as good as any theater's. And anyway, said the mayor, ignoring his own citizens' advisory committee, any separate hall would be way in the future.

The *Advertiser*, in an editorial titled "How To Botch a Job," criticized Blaisdell's attitude toward the committee, verging on "indifference, if not outright resentment."[7] The group's chairman, attorney J. Russell Cades, who coincidentally was the paper's general counsel, resigned and formed a private-sector committee, including architects Vladimir Ossipoff, Alfred Preis, and Roger Benezet, and continued fighting for a separate cultural facility.

The dispute reached the point, said the *Advertiser*, "where tempers are high, backs are up and personal pride is involved." Given "the mayor's well-known capacity for setting his jaw," the paper urged that he show "a greater respect for conflicting views."[8] Cartoonist Lyons brought his light touch to bear with a drawing of basketball players racing through the Honolulu Symphony Orchestra during a Beethoven concert.

A few weeks later Blaisdell came around to endorsing the separate concert building, and both he and the paper were urging the legislature, which had earlier appropriated $850,000 toward the project, to come up with additional funding. Olive branches were exchanged, with the mayor saying, "I know, of course, I can count on the Advertiser's support of the community effort" and with the paper praising him for acting constructively.[9] The legislature granted $1.5 million, and in September 1964 the new international center—later to be named for Blaisdell—was formally opened.

But that was not to be the mayor's only battleground. Almost as acrimonious was the multimillion-dollar Queen Emma slum clearance project on Lunalilo Freeway, off Nuuanu Avenue, the beginning of a massive community face-lifting.

Of the six bidding groups, the city's Honolulu Development Agency by 1960 favored a combine headed by developer Joseph R. Pao, a close friend of the mayor. Under federal regulations three consultants reviewed the plans, but their report was bottled up by the redevelopment agency. The *Advertiser* phoned the overseeing federal office in San Francisco and warned that if the critique was not released within an hour, a blistering front-page editorial would follow. The findings were yielded, showing criticism of the developer's design as creating a wind tunnel.

At about this time, the *Advertiser* got a tip that Mayor Blaisdell and Pao had made an unpublicized visit to Las Vegas ten weeks earlier. The paper confirmed the report, then had reporters simultaneously contact Blaisdell, who was on an official trip to Tokyo, and Pao, who was in town. Blaisdell said sure, he and his political adviser, Angel Maehara, and Pao and their wives had spent a weekend in Vegas, but saw nothing wrong with it. At the time "I didn't even know [Pao] had a bid in there" for the Queen Emma project.[10] He added that he was unaware that his Los Angeles architect for the international center was also associated with Pao.

Meanwhile, at the same hour, Pao denied the Vegas trip. After his comment and the mayor's appeared in the next morning's *Advertiser,* Pao did an about-face, explaining he had been trying to spare his friend any embarrassment. The paper's reaction:

> It is bad enough for the mayor of a city to go weekend-ing in Las Vegas with
> a businessman who at the time is bidding on a multimillion-dollar job to be
> let by an agency whose commission that mayor has appointed. . . . What's
> involved here is a sense of propriety, a sense of official morality. . . . We are
> not suggesting that the businessman ever asked the mayor to lift a finger in
> his behalf or that the mayor ever did. But if the mayor doesn't clearly see the

implications that could flow from his super-quiet Vegas trip, then he better borrow a civics book and carefully begin reading.[11]

The paper suggested that the redevelopment commission resign; it blamed the mayor for putting on "the shoulders of nonprofessionals . . . responsibilities requiring the talents of a mortgage banker, a city planner, an appraiser and architects."[12]

The commission remained, but the Federal Housing and Home Finance Agency forced the commission to reverse itself when it refused to accept the favored bid, as well as five others. The upshot was that new proposals were called for, another combine was chosen, and it selected the noted Detroit architect Minoru Yamasaki to design the complex that now graces the site.

On the heels of the Queen Emma strife came three more shockers.

Advertiser reporter Robert Monahan uncovered several instances of city engineers making money on the side by checking and certifying construction plans for private builders.

Advertiser reporter George Eagle "lifted the lid on the city garbage dump and sniffed more than the usual aroma. Deliberate undercharging of some private rubbish collectors who used the dump [had] cost the city up to an estimated $125,000 a year in fees since 1957."[13] In a follow-up the paper said, "It doesn't ring right for the chief of the refuse collection division to be the major stockholder of a [competing] private garbage firm," which had originally given him fifty shares as a gift.[14] The mayor, who earlier had twice given his garbage manager a clean bill of health on conflict-of-interest questions, finally fired him.

Advertiser reporter Bud Bendix covered irregularities in city purchasing procedures in dealing with Windward Roofing Company, where the mayor's brother was sales manager, which had gotten "an undue share of city roofing and repair business—without the required competitive bidding."[15] When the city finance director earlier complained about this, his reward was a reprimand from on high.

The paper wrote, "We'd much prefer to publish editorials praising rather than criticizing Mayor Blaisdell—and we'd very much like the mayor to give us an opportunity to do so. Until he does, he can count on our continued raising of questions and pointing out facts."[16]

In 1965, in Blaisdell's final term, the chairman of the City Planning Commission, George Centeio, slammed through rezoning to allow multistory apartment buildings abutting Diamond Head. The *Advertiser* took on protection of the famous landmark as a crusade, supporting residents and community groups, and the day was won. Heat was put on Centeio, and the day after he quit his post the paper, in one of its briefest editorials ever, titled "Public Service," said, "George F. Centeio, for more than 11 years a member and several times chairman of the City Planning Commission, yesterday rendered what we believe to be his greatest contribution to that body. He resigned."[17]

Blaisdell, the last of the kamaaina mayors, was a warm and pleasant man, easy to like. But he often did business—and permitted those around him to— in a relaxed way that invited abuses. It was a time of great growth, following the attainment of statehood and the opening of the jet age, and things could get out of hand.

But despite sometimes strong disagreement with Blaisdell, the *Advertiser* supported him on several occasions for reelection because there were also substantial achievements. His fourteen-year administration saw adoption of the first city charter, the city's first general plan, adoption of a sign ordinance at the behest of the Outdoor Circle, the start of planning for the redevelopment of Chinatown, and groundwork studies for a mass-transit system.

Blaisdell made his mark nationally as president of the U.S. Conference of Mayors and internationally as a founder of the Japan-America Conference of Mayors and Chamber of Commerce Presidents and as the establisher of sister-city relationships in Japan proper, Okinawa, Taiwan, and France.

In the moves for better understanding the mayor had the full support of the paper, which had greatly stepped up its own coverage of Asia, with editors and staffers regularly going out into the region for firsthand, in-depth reporting.

Strong backing was given to the concept of an East-West Center, and when President Eisenhower stopped in Honolulu on returning from a nine-day Far Eastern trip, a chest of ten thousand pennies that the *Advertiser* had helped to raise from public school students for the center was presented to him.

The paper also wrote to sixteen hundred dailies on the mainland seeking funds needed to start construction of the long-delayed USS Arizona Memorial at Pearl Harbor. Thousands of dollars poured in and, due to a Los Angeles editorial quoting the *Advertiser,* Elvis Presley starred in a Honolulu benefit concert that led to federal and state appropriations putting the fund over the top. The completed memorial was dedicated May 30, 1962, and on that day a Navy League of the United States "meritorious citation" credited the paper with the success.

In 1959 the paper had gained an extra and valuable dimension when Harry Lyons, a Scarsdale, New York, boy who said he failed out at Maine's Colby College, arrived as editorial-page cartoonist.

Earlier he had done a hitch in the Marines, part of it on Oahu, where he painted a mural in a Camp Catlin mess hall. As a free-lance cartoonist in New York he hit national magazines but yearned for a more laid-back life. He had a keen sense of what's funny, and his work, a gag-cartoon style, reflected that. Krauss quoted him as once saying,

> I don't think a hell of a lot of people have a good sense of humor. I'm not sure what it is. Bob Hope said an orange is not funny, but an egg is. I know what he meant. An egg is off center. It rolls crazy. That's humor, looking at something from a different point of view. . . .

> I wish people didn't take themselves so seriously. We're here for 70 years. Why not have a few laughs along the way? I don't mean to get thrown in jail. You should pay your bets, not only financial. But Walter Hagen said, "Don't forget to smell the flowers."[18]

Harry often lampooned politicians, but they usually loved it and saw him as a friend socially.

His cartoons were properly treated as art, collected by Mayor Frank Fasi, Kennedy press secretary Pierre Salinger, federal Judge Sam King, entertainment stars, and scores of Islanders who bid for them at charity auctions.

Lyons drew with unbelievable speed, but only after hours of thought and targeted doodling. Early each afternoon he showed three rough-cartoon versions to the editor and editorial-page editor. Among them they settled on one, which might be related to the next morning's lead editorial, to give it a supporting punch.

Once decided, Harry whipped out the cartoon and hastened to the bar at next-door Columbia Inn for a round of Beefeaters on the rocks. He knew he drank too much and that he shouldn't let his weight run, but his attitude was what-the-heck.

In 1979 he decided to take a year's leave, with syndicated cartoonist Ranan Lurie coming to Honolulu to fill in while he plopped down on the beach at Kailua-Kona. When the time was up, he proposed remaining in Kona and sending cartoons by plane. The editors deemed this unworkable and urged him to return, but he loved the Kona life and finally resigned. When he died ten years later at age fifty-nine Krauss called him "Hawaii's most successful leprechaun."

In June 1981 a Chicago-born artist, fresh from fifteen years in Asia, sat down at the cartoonist's drawing board. Dick Adair was a Navy journalist aboard the USS *Yorktown* in the 1950s, then studied art in Los Angeles, on the side designing sets and dancing with a Spanish-American ballet troupe. Next to Mexico for more study, more dance, and writing the national ballet company's first full-length jazz performance.

Still more study and working as a cruise ship deckhand led to Tokyo, then Vietnam, where he was an artist-correspondent for the armed forces newspaper, *Stars and Stripes*. A text-and-sketchbook on wartime experiences and life in Saigon earned a foreword by the AP's Pulitzer Prize-winner, Peter Arnett.

Adair next moved to the Philippines for seven years as artist, writer, and maker of documentary films before settling in Honolulu. At the *Advertiser* he was soon winning local and national awards while applying his wit and satire to editorial-page cartoons.

33

The Saga of Sammy Amalu

IN MAY 1962 a series of bombshell stories, exuding money and mystery, stood Honolulu on its head, and for days spun it around. It began, as far as the public knew, with a larger than usual eight-column, double-deck headline in the *Advertiser.*

SHERATON OFFERED $34 MILLION
FOR HOTEL HOLDINGS IN ISLANDS

Two days before, at a cocktail party at the Royal Hawaiian Hotel, I had asked Sheraton's Hawaii vice-president, Richard Holtzman, "What's new?" He answered, "As a matter of fact we've had an offer from a syndicate in Switzerland to buy our Waikiki hotels."

Advertiser financial editor Edward Greaney went the next day to get details, and the following morning the *Advertiser* spread the blockbuster across page one. The International Trade Exchange Central of Zurich was willing to pay a $16 million profit for the Royal Hawaiian, Princess Kaiulani, Surfrider, and Moana Hotels. There would also be a long-term management contract for Sheraton, which had bought the properties only three years before for $18 million.

It quickly turned out that exceedingly handsome offers had also been made for the George Murphy ranch on Molokai, the Makaha lands of Chinn Ho's Capital Investment Company, and a number of other properties, bringing the total to more than $50 million. It was to be the biggest realty transaction in Island history.

Holtzman had his doubts about the deal. But Ernest Henderson, Sheraton's president in Boston, felt that stockholders' interests had to be kept in mind, and he sent his vice-president/finance, Richard P. Boonisar, to Honolulu to pursue the transaction.

It was the talk of the town, "Christmas on the real estate market," as Krauss later wrote.[1] But much of it was also wrapped in secrecy. The syndicate was represented at a Sheraton meeting by one tight-lipped D. Franklin Carson, who called himself a "proregent" or royal courier, but looked "more like a teen-age surfer than business executive."[2] Boonisar insisted on reaching a superior and was able to talk by phone locally with a man who spoke Oxonian English but would not appear in person. The identity of the Swiss principals remained a mystery. Henderson had not heard of the company, nor had bankers in Zurich or firms on Wall Street. UPI called it "the deepest financial mystery since Captain Cook first introduced money to Hawaii."[3] But the syndicate had Harold C. Schnack as its local attorney and Ann Felzer and Milton Beamer as its Realtors, and Felzer had given Capital Investment her own check for $10,000 as good faith for the $10.2 million Makaha offer.

After days of exciting headlines and endless conjecture, rumors surfaced that Samuel Crowninburg Amalu, a Punahou alumnus and son of famed beach boy Charles K. Amalu, might be involved. Carson denied knowing Amalu and deplored the "journalistic intrusion into our private affairs," indicating his principals might not want to do business in such a prying community.[4]

But three days later Amalu and Felzer left for the mainland, presumably to close the deal in New York with Sheraton. It was then that the past cropped up, and Amalu was arrested at the Hilton Inn at the Seattle airport on a complaint of San Francisco attorney George T. Davis, who had an option on the Molokai ranch and to whom Amalu had given two bum checks, totaling $30,200, the previous December.

That was the end of the mythical syndicate and its phony deal, with Carson revealing that he and two of his California surfing pals, just arrived in Hawaii, had been picked up near the airport by Sammy Amalu and hired, but never paid, as proregents. It was also the beginning of fresh trouble for Hawaii's greatest con man and past and future free-lance *Advertiser* columnist.

Newcomers to Hawaii in the 1960s wondered who was this Sammy Amalu, where had he been, what had he done, what made Sammy run? The answer involved a bright, charismatic man with a considerable knowledge of Hawaiian history and lore, an inventive flair, a lighthearted air, a glib tongue, and poetic pen. He enjoyed creating commotion, he loved attention, and, in building his hoaxes, he came to regard fact and fiction as interchangeable. He was a claimant to royal heritage and wished to be called His Highness Samuel Crowninburg-Amalu, High Chief Kapiikauinamoku, and Prince of Keawe. But he said "it is not enough to bask in the ancient glories of Hawaii" and sought a broader stage.[5]

In January 1946 the *Advertiser* and the *Star-Bulletin* carried long, detailed accounts of the marriage in New York, in the Cathedral of St. John Divine, of Samuel Amalu and of Maria Anastasia di Torlona, daughter of a Philadelphia socialite and a prominent European financier. The bride wore a white satin gown embroidered with seed pearls, and her veil was held in place by a diamond-festooned coronet from a collection of the late czarina of imperial Russia.

Sammy, the story recounted, had attended Punahou (where the 1935 yearbook dubbed him the "future czar of Hawaii") and the Universities of Hawaii (which he'd left after his freshman year) and Waseda and Doshisha in Japan and had studied at Oxford when he was a U.S. Army captain in World War II. (Actually, he had been booted out with a medical discharge for alleged homosexuality, which he denied. He had enlisted as a private but was soon seen wearing a captain's bars and later said he had been an honorary lieutenant colonel.)

The couple, the story said, had met at a White House reception for the Norwegian crown prince and renewed their acquaintance at the United Nations conference in San Francisco. After the honeymoon they planned to divide their time between their Long Island home and his Virginia farm. Subsequently there were reports of a child and a divorce, but the original stories bore neither a United Press nor Associated Press logo, and a *Newsweek* story about Sammy in 1962 said "no such wedding ever took place."[6]

In 1952, after living for several years in the Philippines, Sammy, alias Albert Spencer, was jailed for two to six years for writing $4,410 in checks on a nonexistent San Francisco bank and about a year later was deported to the United States.

His next endeavor, and possibly his first gainful work ever, began in 1955 when he wrote the first of scores of columns for the *Advertiser* on Hawaiian genealogy. They were titled the "Song of Eternity" and carried the byline of Kapiikauinamoku. Krauss wrote later that the series "created a flurry of interest long before the Hawaiian ethnic identity movement got under way because it related a genealogy of the Hawaiian people beginning with the gods."[7]

Twigg-Smith, who was managing editor at the time, knew Sammy from their Punahou days, admired his writing ability, and ran the columns because they were "beautiful stuff."[8] At one point, he said, someone at the Bishop Museum phoned, "wanting to know the source of this because the material was so great. I got the feeling they lost interest when they heard Sammy Amalu wrote them." The museum's senior anthropologist, Dr. Kenneth Emory, said the columns could have come from standard sources, with nothing new except that "Sammy keeps trying to relate himself to God."[9] Even so, the Rev. Abraham Akaka of Kawaiahao Church gave Sammy high marks as a genealogist. The columns were widely read, and they marked the start of Sammy's intermittent career as a free-lance columnist for the *Advertiser.*

But he could not stay in one place for long, and in 1956 he was in Denver, scheduled to wed Jane Tomberlin, an attractive, red-haired socialite, the former wife of a millionaire oil man, whom he had met in a hotel elevator there and started romancing. But he failed to show at the appointed hour, and the bride-to-be, after declaring "I'm damned mad," brought out the champagne for her guests.[10] Sammy appeared two days later, explaining he had been kidnapped to a Texas ranch by his relatives seeking to prevent the marriage.

The revived ceremony was then held in Colorado Springs, with press dispatches calling him a prince who held an executive position with companies in Hong Kong and Singapore. Immediately after the rites, Sammy tossed $10 in dimes out of his hotel windows, declaring, "It's an old Chinese custom."[11] But even before the planned honeymoon to Hawaii began, the FBI arrested Sammy on interstate fraud charges, having to do with $600 in elastic checks he had passed in Texas and Colorado hotels, and possibly with four bad-check warrants held by Honolulu police.

At his trial, his new wife tearfully said they had lived together only thirteen days in their nine-and-a-half-month marriage and that the union had never been consummated. She dropped an annulment suit, but divorced him at his urging as he began serving up to four years in the federal penitentiary at Leavenworth, Kansas. Three years later he was returned to Colorado on probation and told to get a job. He said he would probably end up dishwashing since he didn't know of any bank that would take him on as a teller.

Sammy's next hoax was his most audacious—the $50 million Hawaii property scam of spring 1962. He might have come out unscathed after having his fun puncturing some oversized local egos had he not, six months earlier, given those bad checks to attorney Davis. For that misdeed he spent a year in the San Francisco county jail. On a trip to the coast, managing editor Buchwach visited Sammy and was told by a guard: "If they elected the jail boss, Sammy would be running this place . . . and sometime I think he is." Buchwach called him "the only truly unique character I've ever met."[12]

Sammy's thirst for check-writing remained unquenchable. A month after his release from jail, he wrote on the same day, May 22, 1963, two rubber checks—one for $26,000 to pay for a Cadillac, another for $73,000 for seven British-made automobiles. His guilty plea to grand theft brought a sentence of six months to ten years in a minimum-security facility in Vacaville, California. But after he hoodwinked a prison cook into trying to cash $200,000 in checks at a local bank, he was transferred to Folsom, a high-security prison. Sammy needed an outlet of expression, so he started sending columns, in the form of letters, to *Advertiser* publisher Twigg-Smith and thus became America's only federal prison columnist writing for a metropolitan daily newspaper. Twigg-Smith agreed in the hope that this might contribute to Sammy's rehabilitation, and for a while the brightly minted columns passed muster by the prison authorities. But when Sammy turned penologist and started doing sharp-edged critiques of Folsom's operation, he was muzzled.

A somewhat mellower attorney Davis came to the *Advertiser* to see Twigg-Smith. He said Sammy was being denied his constitutional right of free expression and that he, Davis, would carry a legal test all the way to the U.S. Supreme Court, charging only out-of-pocket expenses. Twigg-Smith had a better idea. He asked Clare Boothe Luce, who lived part-time in Honolulu, to intercede with her friend, Governor Ronald Reagan. As a result, Sammy was permitted to resume his column, but leaving prison matters to the warden. Shortly thereafter, with Luce's backing and the governor's help, after six and a half years behind bars, he was released on probation. He was not bitter: "Do you know how much it costs to hire a butler. I have my meals served to me here. We have a swimming pool, a golf course and a counselor to talk to. This isn't a bad life."[13]

He needed a job and once again Twigg-Smith came through for him, with Sammy to write a regular *Advertiser* column, not as a staffer but as an independent contractor. By this time he had developed quite a following among those who enjoyed his exuberant and flowery style, his wit, his irreverence, his flights into fantasy, and his confidence in writing with great authority on any and every subject.

Lack of facts was never a handicap, and people enjoyed his commentaries—titled "The Special World of Sammy Amalu"—for what they were, one unconventional man's view, real or concocted, of life and its vagaries. But each of his swinging columns had to be carefully scrutinized by an editor, and a fair number never saw print, because libel was a stranger to Sammy's lexicon.

In 1976 an embolism paralyzed him from the waist down, but he continued to write until July 1984, when he acknowledged in a court case that he had accepted $500 from the late Robert V. Toledo to write favorably about the local dairy industry. Buchwach immediately suspended him for violating the paper's code of ethics, with final action awaiting Twigg-Smith's return from a mainland trip. Twigg-Smith, although sorry for Sammy, let the suspension stand, despite a belated and obviously organized flood of letters pleading for Sammy's return. On February 23, 1986, at age sixty-eight, Sammy Amalu died.

Sixteen years before, he had written his own obituary in a lengthy column that ended thusly:

> Sing no sad songs over my mortal dust. Tell me no gentle lies to wash more chaste the wanton waste of my days. . . . I have known laughter. I have known tears. I have tasted victory. I have sipped of failure. Is not all this enough? Say only this of me when I am no more: He lived his brief hour nor begrudged the dissonance of his days. He was numbered among the transgressors yet never once despaired his claim to Heaven's domain. He was a child of princes, and the dust of his flesh was fashioned of Hawaii's soil. Say only this of me and no more.

In its history, the *Advertiser* has had its champs and its chumps—but only one Sammy Amalu. He was, in truth, *sui generis*.

34

An All-Out Try to Rescue the Paper

AT THE start of the 1960s, as the town began noticing the paper's revitalization, Twigg-Smith and an assistant, former Sunday Editor Richard Habein, started a sizzling promotion campaign to attract more circulation, an essential forerunner to increased advertising. A rental condo was given away in a contest titled "Income for Life." Other contests bore such names as "Tangletowns," "Lucky Bucks," "Prizewords," "Safety Jingle," "Skil-Words." Prizes, ranging from cash to round-trip flight tickets to Europe and Tahiti or boat trips to the mainland (scrounged from airlines and a shipping company), went to winners.

These attention-getters were bulwarked by a phone room—a hard-sell telephone crew soliciting ninety-day subscriptions, with part of the proceeds going to a cooperating charity, such as the Red Cross and the Diamond Head School for Blind and Deaf Children. Premiums were handed out for new subscriptions—alarm clocks, radios, recordings of Japanese, French, or Spanish language lessons.

Given this intensive promotion, the circulation director, Milan Leavitt, was able to push daily street sales and home delivery from 46,967 in December 1958 to 62,381 in February 1960 and almost to 70,000 in 1961. The Sunday paper, 82,125 in the last quarter of 1958, climbed 10,000 by the same period in 1959. And for one Sunday it reached 100,000, which was enough to generate punchy full-page ads trumpeting the achievement. Much later Twigg-Smith and I were to learn that to reach that figure the circulation department had, in the vernacular, "eaten a lot of papers," paying for them with promotion funds.

The *Star-Bulletin* smarted under the feverish action. The widely touted figures of both the *Advertiser*'s daily and Sunday issues, the subject of a laudatory feature in *Editor & Publisher*, the national weekly of newspapering, was too much for *Star-Bulletin* management to take. They hit back where it hurt—grievously hurt. On November 1, 1960, they brought out their own Sunday paper and forced every reader to take it, as a condition of having the daily delivered. On their very first Sunday they automatically had a circulation of 111,180, a spread of close to 20,000 over the fifty-six-year-old *Sunday Advertiser*, long the savior of the six anemic daily issues.

The *Advertiser's* circulation gains had attracted some advertising to the extremely lean daily, but not nearly enough. And now the new *Sunday Star-Bulletin* was siphoning both lineage and circulation from the *Advertiser's* long-established flagship. By early 1962 the *Sunday Advertiser* had dropped more than 11,000 copies, to 80,941, while the *Star-Bulletin* increased to 115,792.

To make matters worse, the *Advertiser* lacked a dynamic advertising director. The incumbent, Frank Addleman, a Hearst alumnus who joined the paper in 1953, was pleasant but ineffectual. Instead of spending most of his time on the street, calling on major accounts, he holed up in his office, tinkering with a calculator.

Meanwhile, Twigg-Smith was still boxed out of the power structure by Lorrin Thurston, with no prospect of moving up and with the paper in danger of dying. He was distressed, as were his mother and his retired uncle Robert, whose assets consisted almost entirely of *Advertiser* stock.

Early in 1960, when Thurston and McGuire pushed for a cutback in the promotional spending that was bringing circulation and advertising gains, Twigg-Smith told me, "It's absolutely hopeless. The only way to resolve this is for me to get control of the stock" and go all-out to try to rescue the paper.[1]

He got a list of stockholders and methodically approached the larger ones. "I found most of them very willing to see a change made, but not all of them willing to put their hands up when it came to a vote."[2] From those family members loyal to him, Twigg-Smith could count on 25,564 shares, about 12,000 short of the 51 percent needed of 75,456 outstanding.

Walter F. Dillingham, longtime *Advertiser* director and vice-president, controlled 8,865 shares owned by the B. F. Dillingham Company, and while he favored a change, he did not want to take a public position, and Twigg-Smith was unsure that in a showdown he could count on him.

Reluctant to take chances on uncertain supporters, Twigg-Smith asked stockbroker George Kellerman to start buying shares, and to finance the effort he obtained a bank loan of $100,000. He gained additional financial support from Zadoc Brown, who acquired 1,200 shares, and Chinn Ho, who bought personally and advanced Twigg-Smith money to buy more. Brown later joined Chinn Ho on the board and remained a loyal supporter until he resigned in 1984 due to ill health.

George Voorhees, who had designed the newspaper building and was with the paper for thirty-three years, twenty of them as head of commercial printing, and retired composing room superintendent William Hoffman were among the *Advertiser* people who sided with Twigg-Smith and sold him their shares.

I was strongly on Twigg-Smith's side, but since Lorrin Thurston had hired me, I asked for more time to try to persuade Thurston to get an abler advertising director. I had had several meetings with Thurston on needed changes, and when he told me he needed an understudy, I responded that he had a natural in his nephew. I tried, without success, to get him to give Twigg-Smith a substantial, deserved pay raise. And I kept pecking away on our weakness in advertising sales. When, finally, he told me he appreciated my thoughts but didn't want to hear any more, I walked directly from his office to Twigg-Smith's and told him he could count on the 4,367 shares of stock held by me and my father in South Carolina.

That brought him to within some 3,000 shares of gaining control, at which point he appeared stalemated, apparently unable to acquire more. He made several fruitless visits to Dr. Leona Bilger, a University of Hawaii chemistry professor who had inherited 4,000 shares from her close friend, the late Northrup Castle, a longtime *Advertiser* board member. She disliked Thurston and promised to back Twigg-Smith but said she intended to keep her stock.

At the time, any available stock had been selling for $14 to $16 a share. As a last resort, Twigg-Smith offered Bilger $10,000 for a year's option to buy her stock at $40 a share. She accepted, he exercised the option, and he and his supporters were over the top.

While Twigg-Smith was working to gain control what was Lorrin Thurston doing? Wayne Damon, corporate secretary, later informed Twigg-Smith he had told Thurston that stock was being bought up: "I think it's Twigg and George that are buying this stuff" and Thurston had responded: "Oh, hell no, they couldn't. . . . They wouldn't do anything. Don't worry about it, Wayne, don't worry about it."[3]

A week or so before going in to see Thurston, Twigg-Smith had told Allan McGuire, the business manager, what was about to happen and sought his support. He got an extremely nervous response: "Oh, Jesus, don't do that. We can work this thing out."[4]

In February 1961 Twigg-Smith went to the publisher's office and broke the news to Thurston, who refused to believe it and said Chinn Ho and I would have to personally tell him it was so before he'd be convinced. He rejected a letter that Twigg-Smith had prepared for his signature, in which he would retire, become chairman of the *Advertiser* board of directors, and continue to receive his current salary.

The next day Chinn Ho and I accompanied Twigg-Smith to Thurston's office. His face dropped, and he was understandably distraught. I told him that we wanted to see him maintain his stature in the community, but that certain things had to be done at the paper if it was to have a chance to survive.

He said you just don't throw someone out who's worked for forty years. (His obvious feeling of a conspiracy seemed to mirror his quotation from King Lear, in his senior-year sketch in the 1916 Punahou yearbook: "I am a man sinned against more than sinning.") He could not accept the reality of the *Advertiser*'s condition.

It was an emotional session. After Twigg-Smith and Chinn Ho left, I remained behind. Thurston wept and I wept too, at the sadness of the situation, of his failure to understand that he had let the paper go downhill for years. He signed the letter of resignation.

Part V

1961–1995

35

Twigg-Smith Takes Over as Publisher

ON MARCH 21, 1961, at the annual stockholders meeting, Lorrin Thurston announced a company reorganization plan leading to his retirement at the end of the year.

He would remain until then as president of the parent firm, whose interests included the *Advertiser*, a commercial printing division, radio station KGU, and half-interest in KONA-TV.

Twigg-Smith would immediately become *Advertiser* publisher, with full responsibilities for the daily and Sunday papers, and executive vice-president of the parent company. He was popular plant-wide as publisher. He was down-to-earth (even copy boy Robert Chang called him Twigg). He was fully supportive of his editors, and, on most days, he saw the editorials and the stories, like any reader, when the paper was delivered to his home. The staff, top to bottom, respected and admired him. The result was a congenial, family-like environment.

Thurston, in addition to the presidency, would remain as board chairman until year's end if he conducted himself in accord with the new management's policies and then continue at his regular salary of $2,400 a month as a TV-radio consultant until reaching the age of sixty-five in December 1964.

He would also get $125 a month for a one-year rental of an office outside the *Advertiser* building and could remain for six months in the company-owned house on Makiki Heights he had occupied since 1945, with an option to buy it after an independent appraisal. Originally he had bought the house, then sold it to the *Advertiser* for $110,000, its approximate cost, and was enabled to rent it at $150 to $175 a month. He paid for a cook, but the cost of other servants was absorbed by the company.

When the board moved to sell the property, Thurston contended there had been a gentlemen's agreement with *Advertiser* directors in 1945 that he could buy it back at a depreciated price. There was no record on the books—and the board approved acceptance of an offer, which Thurston declined to match, of $217,000 plus $13,000 for the leasehold portion.

Defying an eviction order, Thurston sued, seeking to get the house for $60,338.24. In September 1963 Circuit Judge Ronald Jamieson ordered Thurston to vacate the property and pay the paper $1,400 a month in rental since November 1, 1962. The judge called Thurston's claim of a "secret" oral agreement with the board "absolutely incredible," declaring that if such an arrangement had been true it would be a fraud on the company and its stockholders.

The hullabaloo over the house had led to the board's termination of Thurston's consultancy and his resignation as a director, completing his disassociation from the paper. He moved to his home in Kona and a few years later sold twenty-seven acres of nearby oceanfront property, once the home of King Kamehameha, for $7 million.

One of Twigg-Smith's first acts as publisher was to successfully ask the banks to extend a loan of $111,000 because of the paper's inability to pay. He then sold some outside stock the company owned and this with borrowing on executives' insurance policies held by the company enabled him to pay off its existing debt. He had sought to sell the paper's half share of KONA-TV but was unable to at the time. The banks flatly told him, no more loans. Equipment replacement needs remained at $1.5 million.

He immediately began calling on advertisers—Sears, Liberty House, McInerny, Andrade, the Ritz, Reyn's, Sumida Dry Goods, RCA, and many others. In April Addleman was out as advertising director, succeeded some weeks later by Joel Irwin, who had worked on the *Cincinnati Enquirer* and the *New Orleans Item*.

Irwin had been in Honolulu in World War II as an Army officer with the *Stars and Stripes*, which was printed in the *Advertiser* building, and he and I had worked together in New Jersey and New Orleans.

Thurston Twigg-Smith, reporter, city editor, managing editor, assistant to the business manager, then publisher from 1961 to 1993.

Twigg-Smith later said that with Irwin's arrival "we really breathed new life into the advertising department. So, during the fall of 1961, due to his really good sound sales programs, we were making nice gains, especially on Sunday."[1]

Irwin disliked the rate discount program he inherited and began to dismantle it, only to be faced by a step-up in *Star-Bulletin* discounts, especially in classified advertising and legal notices, and by its acceptance of ads from accounts that the *Advertiser* had cut off because of nonpayment.

The *Advertiser*'s practice before Irwin arrived and the *Star-Bulletin*'s afterward proved costly to both papers. A later chart by Twigg-Smith showed that from the time the *Advertiser* circulation began climbing in late 1958 until December 1961 the paper's income dropped by some $150,000, but the *Star-Bulletin* showed a decline of approximately $550,000. *Advertiser* dividends were suspended in 1960.

With Irwin, some encouragement was derived from the trend toward later store openings and school schedules, which meant a bit more time for morning newspaper reading. But no one underestimated the vast chasm between the two papers in advertising and circulation.

Meanwhile, Thurston was actively maneuvering to somehow regain control. His wife Barbara phoned Twigg-Smith and said she and Lorrin were proposing a voting trust of all family holdings to protect against any outsider "raider" seeking to acquire the paper. She suggested that her husband and the Twigg-Smith brothers, Thurston and David, serve as trustees—who, although she didn't say it, would have the power to do whatever they wished with the paper and its management. The Twigg-Smiths, finding it incredible, quickly agreed and documents were drawn up and signed.

It developed that the Thurstons assumed that David Twigg-Smith would vote with Lorrin, which would have meant a quick ouster of Thurston Twigg-Smith. This assumption was a gross error, and the dismayed Thurstons found their stock in the control of their opponents, who, over Thurston's protest, enlarged the trust to include other interested stockholders.

Foiled in his attempted coup, Thurston filed suit to have his fellow trustees removed. After seven weeks of hearings, which regurgitated history, Judge William Z. Fairbanks threw out the case, calling it a family generational dispute and citing Twigg-Smith's control of majority stock.

At the time of Thurston's ejection, the *Advertiser* had less than six days of operating cash. Twigg-Smith, who obtained some relief from the banks, concluded that the paper's salvation lay in achieving a joint operating agreement (JOA) with the *Star-Bulletin*. In such the ownership and editorial staffs and policies of the two papers would be separate and independent, but an agency would be set up to consolidate and oversee the commercial and production functions, cutting costs to both papers and consumers.

Sporadically, the *Advertiser* had entertained hopes of a JOA with its rival as far back as the 1940s or early 1950, along the lines of the first such venture, in Albuquerque, New Mexico, in 1933, subsequently emulated in some twenty other U.S. cities ranging from Nashville and Salt Lake City to San Francisco and Charleston, West Virgina. In each case a once-weaker second paper was enabled to survive. By contrast, in some metropolitan areas, among them Atlanta, New Orleans, Minneapolis, Portland, and Des Moines, a single owner had merged two papers into one. For Honolulu a JOA was clearly preferable.

But Thurston, who in print had so consistently denounced Joe Farrington, *Star-Bulletin* publisher and congressional delegate, stood no chance of getting a deal. Yet he was on sound ground on at least one matter: the *Advertiser* building, built by his father, the publisher from annexation until his death in 1931, was large enough to comfortably accommodate both newspapers.

Twigg-Smith lost no time in calling on Betty Farrington, who had succeeded her late husband as publisher. She was outwardly cordial and listened to his proposal. But as he later recalled, "I don't think she trusted the *Advertiser* because of Lorrin's relationship, although she knew he was out."[2]

So nothing happened and the battle dragged on well into the summer of 1961. Then in August a rumor reached Twigg-Smith that the *Star-Bulletin* was up for sale. He called retired Army General Edmond Leavey, a trustee of the Farrington Estate, which owned the paper, and with whom he was friendly. Leavey, the husband of a sister of the late Joe Farrington, confirmed it.

Circumstances fortuitous for the *Advertiser* lay behind the decision to sell. The *Star-Bulletin* was about to lose the site of its printing plant, at Kapiolani Boulevard Extension and Hotel Street, to land acquisition for a new Civic Center. In an unusual arrangement, the editorial and most of the production facilities of the *Star-Bulletin* were on Merchant Street, with the asbestos page "mats" rushed by motorcycle to the printing plant blocks away. The loss of that plant faced the Farrington trustees with the need to resettle the entire newspaper in a structure costing up to $7.5 million. Beyond that, their bylaws prevented capital expenditures of such size without a 75 percent approval of the two camps, Farrington's and Leavey's, each owning 50 percent. Those obstacles, coupled with the decline in the profit picture from the costly battle with the *Advertiser,* persuaded the trustees to sell, a decision unsuccessfully challenged in court by Betty Farrington, trying to save her job.

In his conversation with Leavey, Twigg-Smith broached the idea of a joint operation and noted that a prospective buyer who knew such was available might pay a higher price for the *Star-Bulletin.* Leavey was intrigued and, at his suggestion, Twigg-Smith phoned the trustees' broker, Vincent Manno, in New York, who was immediately interested and offered to send prospective buyers to talk with him.

In the next few months no fewer than eight newspaper representatives, including ones from Scripps-Howard and the Ridder chain, talked with Twigg-Smith. All were receptive. In late November 1961 Manno would recommend that *Star-Bulletin* trustees accept the offer of the "Chinn Ho hui."

Chinn Ho, whose Capital Investment Company owned 2,000 shares of *Advertiser* stock, had become a director on April 19, 1960. He soon had a firsthand look at the paper's condition and became a Twigg-Smith supporter. In August he acquired more stock as part of the Twigg-Smith takeover plan. In October, seeing the possibilities of acquiring the *Star-Bulletin*, he resigned from the *Advertiser* board.

On November 20 his company wrote Twigg-Smith, as the key player in the *Advertiser* voting trust, offering 4,282 shares to the trust at $20 a share. Nine days later, Mrs. Thurston wrote Twigg-Smith a letter of objection, saying her husband had made an offer to Chinn Ho to buy his stock. Twigg-Smith and his brother David, over Thurston's objection, determined that, pursuant to the voting trustee agreement, the Chinn Ho stock should be offered to Advertiser Publishing Company. Both the Bank of Hawaii and the First National Bank (which succeeded Bishop Bank and preceded the First Hawaiian Bank) agreed to lend the *Advertiser* funds for the purchase. The board approved, with Thurston and Reginald Faithfull opposing and Dillingham abstaining.

Chinn Ho originally had joined a group headed by Carlton Skinner, an investor and former governor of Guam, and on behalf of the members offered Manno $11 million for the *Star-Bulletin* and put up a $275,000 deposit. But Skinner and several associates dropped out, and Chinn Ho (everyone called him that, never Ho), while traveling in France, called Twigg-Smith to say he wanted to pursue the deal and to ask Twigg-Smith if he could think of someone who could help organize a group. When Twigg-Smith suggested trust company executive Robert Midkiff, his Yale roommate, Chinn Ho said, fine, please ask him to start on it. Midkiff went to his cousin J. Ballard Atherton, manager of the telephone company and chairman of the trustees of the Atherton Trust, the largest minority stockholder in the *Star-Bulletin* with 75,000 shares.

Atherton was interested, as was his brother, Alexander S. Atherton, an assistant vice-president of Hawaiian Trust Company. Midkiff then successfully approached John T. Waterhouse, vice-president of Alexander & Baldwin; state Senate President William H. (Doc) Hill, who also headed the electric company in Hilo; and former Judge William H. Heen, a onetime power on the political scene. All were receptive to the concept of a partial consolidation with the *Advertiser*, which Midkiff would get Twigg-Smith and Brown to explain to them. In the ten days or so that the maneuvers took, Chinn Ho continued his trip around the world, calling Twigg-Smith almost daily, from Paris, Rome, Athens, Bangkok, and finally Hong Kong. By the Hong Kong calls, Midkiff was able to tell him the group was assembled. He was elated and asked Midkiff to advise broker Manno of their great interest. Midkiff did so and got the Bank of Hawaii to agree to short-term financing once Manno had recommended that the *Star-Bulletin* trustees accept the group's bid of $13.5 million. Chinn Ho's company would finance 25 percent and the Atherton interests, 40 percent.

Chinn Ho had several reasons for wanting a substantial part-ownership of the *Star-Bulletin*. He saw it as profitable for his company. He wanted to gain further stature in the business community and bring "local boys" into a closer relationship with the Big Five and other kamaaina corporations. And, of greatest interest to the *Advertiser*, he favored a JOA to avoid the death of the morning paper or the possible acquisition of the two papers by a mainland chain, in either case making Honolulu a one-newspaper-owner community.

Once negotiations for a joint operation began, Midkiff was quickly out as spokesman for the *Star-Bulletin* group, which felt he favored too generous a share of the net profit for the *Advertiser*.

The bargaining started in March 1962, with the initial session at the Hawaiian Trust Company. Those present included Manno, who had come out from New York; Thurston Twigg-Smith; Porter Dickinson, *Star-Bulletin* advertising director; Alexander (Pug) Atherton; a friend of Atherton's, Tony Peterson, general manager of the joint operation in Salt Lake City; attorney Martin Anderson; and this writer.

When the question of the Sunday paper was raised, Twigg-Smith said the *Advertiser* had traditionally produced it and should continue to. Manno exploded and flatly declared it would be a *Star-Bulletin* product. In the resultant turbulence it appeared negotiations might end then and there, but someone wisely suggested a lunch break.

When talks resumed, the *Star-Bulletin* retreated from its demand to put out the Sunday paper and said the *Advertiser* could have it if it picked up the tab. Next arose the division of net profits once the two papers set up an agency to oversee the production and commercial departments. Twigg-Smith blandly suggested a 50-50 split. Manno banged the table and said the only possible deal would be on *Star-Bulletin* terms. He mentioned an 80-20 arrangement, and Twigg-Smith said 20 percent would not even cover editorial costs. That led to talk of an additional editorial allowance and rental credit for use of the *Advertiser* building.

At that point negotiations were recessed to resume in New York City in April during the convention of the American Newspaper Publishers Association. Twigg-Smith and general counsel J. Russell Cades were on hand for the *Advertiser*, Chinn Ho, Porter Dickinson, Alexander Atherton, and attorney Martin Anderson for the *Star-Bulletin*.

It developed that at a cocktail party the *Star-Bulletin* people had been told they should have their name on the Sunday edition, so they reneged on letting the *Advertiser* have the masthead to itself. They insisted that the paper be called the *Sunday Star-Bulletin and Advertiser*, thus establishing an equity in it, while requiring the *Advertiser* to pick up the cost of staffing it. Attorney Cades was so annoyed he walked out of the room. The only consolation was the *Star-Bulletin*'s willingness to let the *Advertiser* have the Sunday editorial page, a condition that would have been immediately challenged had the *Star-Bulletin* team included an editor.

Meetings that were spread over five days and nights, sometimes until 2 A.M., brought agreement in principle despite heated disputes over revenues and managerial appointments in the proposed Hawaii Newspaper Agency.

Twigg-Smith put up a spirited battle but had no choice but to yield on a number of points. Beyond that, he felt he was sitting on a time bomb. In June the Audit Bureau of Circulation would be issuing its figures for the three months ended March 31. With all *Advertiser* promotions abandoned for lack of funds, circulation in March had dropped to 67,109 from 70,097 the previous September. Also, the paper had lost its circulation director, with Milan Leavitt resigning because of his concern that if a joint operation was achieved, the *Star-Bulletin*'s circulation manager would likely oversee that function for both papers.

Always hanging over the *Advertiser*'s head like a Damoclean sword was its financial weakness, vividly demonstrated in its disparity with the *Star-Bulletin* in the preceding ten years' earnings before taxes:

Year	Star-Bulletin	Advertiser
1952	$ 267,735.07	$ 183,312.56
1953	284,159.41	52,822.26
1954	408,906.85	(46,864.55)
1955	617,538.54	109,166.34
1956	606,256.50	140,910.04
1957	684,672.91	(47,514.34)
1958	1,086,760.14	191,927.62
1959	1,407,977.55	56,981.17
1960	1,005,074.08	(110,615.40)
1961	944,512.43	(72,395.35)

In sum, as *Advertiser* lawyers would later state it, "By 1962 the money had run out, the newspaper was continuing to lose money, the *Star-Bulletin* started a Sunday edition which was growing stronger and weakening the Advertiser's only hope. And, at the same time, there was no financing for needed equipment or operations."[3]

Twigg-Smith's fear was that once the *Star-Bulletin* owners saw the Audit Bureau of Circulation figures they would focus on the fall-off and decide to sit back and let the *Advertiser* bleed to death. He saw it as imperative that a joint operation be achieved by May 31.

On May 28 the lawyers' final version of the joint operating contract was submitted to the *Advertiser*'s board of directors for ratification. Thurston said he hadn't seen the document and wanted to read it in full. This done, he resisted approval. A recess was called; attorney Cades took him to lunch and persuaded him to change his mind and sign. Thurston later said, "I was faced with the dilemma of assisting [Twigg-Smith] by voting for the agreement because I knew the joint publishing thing would be successful for the company or get my dander up and get sore and hurt the company. So I went along with him."[4]

The next day the stockholders approved. The agreement was for thirty years, and until the *Star-Bulletin*'s net income was $13.5 million, the amount the Chinn Ho group had paid for the property, that paper would receive 80 percent of the profit and the *Advertiser* 20 percent. For the following five years the split would be 60-40 and thereafter 55-45. Each paper would receive an $800,000 editorial budget plus automatic adjustments for editorial wage increases. Either paper from its profits could spend more than its editorial budget and the *Advertiser* soon did. As the dominant "partner," the *Star-Bulletin* would have the greater say in the circulation and advertising departments, but the *Advertiser*'s existence and restoration to health were assured.

On June 2, 1962, the first issue of the *Sunday Star-Bulletin and Advertiser* appeared, front-paging a joint statement by Twigg-Smith and Chinn Ho, the new *Star-Bulletin* president. They explained the joint operating agreement and pledged two separate and independent editorial voices, with "vigorous competition in information and ideas."

The joint Sunday paper began with a circulation at the 150,000 level, which over the years would grow above 200,000.

The two papers formed a jointly owned third company, the Hawaii Newspaper Agency, Inc. (HNA) to handle their noneditorial functions under Philip M. Knox, a veteran Hearst executive from the *San Francisco Examiner*.

Porter Dickinson and A. K. Wong of the *Star-Bulletin* were named president and secretary-treasurer respectively and Allan McGuire of the *Advertiser*, vice-president. They and David Twigg-Smith and, as a neutral member, James H. Tabor formed the board of directors.

Joel Irwin left the *Advertiser* to become HNA's advertising director, but some months later was succeeded by Carl Barrea, who had headed the *Star-Bulletin*'s ad department, and left for a newspaper promotion job in New York City. Al Fink, the *Star-Bulletin*'s circulation director, was named to that post at the agency.

When McGuire left as *Advertiser* treasurer he was succeeded by Wayne Damon, who had joined the paper in 1935 and became assistant treasurer in 1942.

The *Advertiser*'s antiquated press would be removed to make way for modern printing and mailroom equipment in a new adjoining building, with the papers meanwhile being printed in the *Star-Bulletin*'s plant. The *Advertiser*'s share of the cost of the modernization was to be about $1.8 million.

On March 11, 1963, the *Star-Bulletin* moved into the *Advertiser* building, renamed the News Building, on King and South Streets and Kapiolani Boulevard. Henry (Tony) Messina, the *Advertiser*'s former production chief, now doing that job for the agency, had chalked out places for *Star-Bulletin* Linotypes and other machinery, and the move was accomplished so smoothly that not a single edition was missed.

Papers began to be produced in part by women punching tapes that were fed into automatic Linotypes, which set type without the traditional operators.

The Hawaii Newspaper Agency took over the expense of stock market reports, the Sunday TV section, the library, election returns, and the Sunday syndicated magazine, *Family Weekly*, soon superseded by *This Week*.

The beneficial effect of the new plan on the *Advertiser's* editorial department was almost immediate. News columns were increased by sixteen a day; working conditions were greatly improved by installation of proper lighting and, within a year, air conditioning; a program was developed for replacement of typewriters, desks, chairs, and filing cabinets; new cameras and lab equipment were bought.

A full-time bureau was set up, for the first time, on Kauai, augmenting those on Hawaii and Maui, and the windward Oahu bureau was strengthened by giving its chief, Gordon Morse, a part-time assistant.

The *Washington Post–Los Angeles Times* News Service was taken by mail and in 1966 by teletype, the Harris Poll was added, a part-time Washington bureau was established, and the paper was enabled to send staffers to cover Hawaii servicemen in Vietnam. By 1964 more than $860,000—by far the largest annual budget ever—was being spent on editorial operations. Competition with the *Star-Bulletin* was not only maintained but intensified because of the *Advertiser's* heightened resources. For a staff enabled to do a more effective job, it was a truly exciting time.

Once the new presses were in, the *Advertiser* sold six of its ten outmoded units, acquired secondhand in the 1940s and 1950s, to a newspaper in Seoul, South Korea, retaining four units to print the Sunday comics.

36

Staff Talents Cover a Wide Spectrum

MORE THAN thirty years after his arrival from the *Portland Oregonian*, Ferd Borsch was still writing lively sports. He had been hired by phone in 1961 to begin with coverage of the new Hawaii Islanders baseball team in spring training in Ontario, California. So it was that Borsch earned and cashed five paychecks before meeting any of his new co-workers.

Red McQueen was sports editor, Andrew Mitsukado, assistant sports editor and makeup editor, and Monte Ito and Kenny Haina were full-time staffers. Borsch warmed at once to the *Advertiser* as "a happy and professional place to work."

He was awed by McQueen, who "started his newspaper career in the Golden Era of sports, when Babe Ruth, Walter Johnson, Red Grange, and Knute Rockne became legends on the field, and Grantland Rice, Henry McLemore, Ring Lardner, and Red Smith became legends in the press box. Red [McQueen] too, was a legend."[1]

Borsch, bubbly, ever smiling, who always saw the best in people, served under all the sports editors who followed McQueen. He especially enjoyed his association with Hal Wood, 1965–1975,

> the last of the old-time sports editors. He came after some 20 years as West Coast sports writer and editor for United Press International, working out of San Francisco. He did everything—ran the office, made out the schedule, wrote a daily column, covered the breaking stories. When we came up short on manpower, he also did some makeup. His forte was golf and he covered the west part of the PGA tour every year.

A Dakotan, his family had been in newspapering since 1805.

Borsch's true love was and is baseball, and he covered every Islander home game—more than two thousand in all—in the team's twenty-seven seasons. More recently he reported on University of Hawaii baseball, with fill-ins on small-college basketball, high school sports, lots of interviews. A third of a century after he came, this mobile baseball encyclopedia strode through the city room, a booming-voiced veteran with stardust still in his eyes.

In 1963 the *Advertiser* acquired Sidney William (Bill) Cook, who was among daily journalism's early planning and urban affairs writers. A Louisianian, he had worked with United Press in New Orleans and Kansas City and on an El Paso paper. Four years later Cook wrote that when he began specializing "there probably weren't enough urban affairs writers to form a crowd in a phone booth. Today there are about 500—which might be regarded as a barometer reading of the seriousness of the urban crisis."[2]

He pushed for better zoning. He blew the whistle when part of a Palolo Valley hillside subdivision began slowly sliding away. He supported the Outdoor Circle and other environmental activists.

It was hardly surprising when Governor Burns lured him as his staff expert on housing and as chairman of the Hawaii Housing Authority Commission. When Cook left government after three years to become an ad agency executive, Burns hailed him for playing a major role in drafting sorely needed housing legislation.

In January 1966 the *Advertiser* opened a bureau in Vietnam, with Bob Jones as its chief. Five weeks later the thirty-year-old reporter was hit in his back, one leg, and both hands by mortar fragments while covering an operation against Viet Cong forces. Even so, he was able to get off a story to the paper before entering a military hospital.

Three months later a band of rioting Vietnamese teenagers threatened to set him ablaze with gasoline they carried in five-gallon cans. Jones, on advice of a Vietnamese friend, was wearing a card saying "Bao Chi," meaning "Press," but the teenagers, yelling a synonym for "bad," ripped off the card and tore it to pieces, and one opened a gasoline can. One youth told Jones, "You go quick, they burn you." A young apprentice Buddhist priest came out of the crowd, grabbed the reporter's hand, a Vietnamese expression of friendship, walked him two blocks away, apologized in broken English for the mob's behavior, and left.

In May, Denby Fawcett, twenty-four, joined the *Advertiser* bureau, specializing in feature stories in and around Saigon. Jones, whom she later married, returned to Hawaii in July to join a TV station, and Fawcett took over the bureau.

Others from the *Advertiser* also did stints of varying length in Vietnam: Sanford Zalburg, Bob Krauss, Scott Stone, Leonard Lueras, and Eric Cavaliero, turned free-lancer.

Cavaliero, a Britisher who had served in the Royal Air Force, came to the *Advertiser* in 1965 as a reporter and church editor—and was quickly dubbed Eric the Cleric. In his four years in Honolulu he had some memorable assignments: covering Duke Kahanamoku's funeral, with the eulogy by Arthur Godfrey; flying to Molokai with ex-King Leopold of Belgium and his wife and Pan Am's Sam Pryor; reporting the return of the three Apollo 11 astronauts; coming upon former South Vietnamese President Nguyen Van Thieu, in Hawaii to visit President Johnson, enjoying a swim at Fort DeRussy, a diminutive figure in the middle of a hollow square formed by tough-looking, water-treading bodyguards.

In early June 1966 he went to the airport to cover the arrival of Jackie Kennedy and her children, Caroline and John, Jr. It was a highly competitive media event and reporters were there en masse. A collective groan went up when the third or fourth person off the plane was Buck Buchwach, *Advertiser* managing editor and a close friend of Kennedy relative Peter Lawford. Buchwach had great quotes, but no one else could get near the party.

The media and a spokesperson for Mrs. Kennedy soon agreed that if she would make herself available once, she would be assured privacy. The result was that her planned three-week stay was extended by about a month and on July 25 she wrote to the editors of both the *Advertiser* and *Star-Bulletin* to thank them "for all that you have done to make this vacation such a perfect one for my children and for me. I had forgotten, and my children had never known, what it was like to discover a new place, unwatched and unnoticed."

Another star in the 1960s and until the mid-1970s was Gene Hunter, who, as Krauss once observed, had as colorful a past as the gangland characters about whom he wrote. A high school dropout, he was a printer's devil at fourteen earning fifty cents a week and Cokes. He bummed around the West Coast, got tattooed in his two hitches in the Navy, served at Pearl Harbor briefly in World War II and again in the Korean War, and began writing with stories for pulp magazines.

Hunter came to the *Advertiser* in 1958 from the *Los Angeles Times*, soon returned to the mainland, then came back in 1963. City Editor Zalburg called him a superb reporter. "He would take a few notes on a scratchpad, come into the office, sit down at the typewriter, have a quick look at his notes and then, as fast as he could type, write a smooth, well-balanced, readable story. He did it seemingly effortlessly."

He was equally skilled at rewriting others' copy. "He knew how to organize an ineptly done story, how to write a crisp lead, how to cut out the trivia and get to the heart of things—how to make a story flow."[3]

A friendly but fearless man, Hunter gave Honolulu its first full report on organized criminal operations here, and yet he had the respect of the underworld as well as of the police. He was a relentless searcher after facts, but he was always fair.

In 1970 his seven-part series naming syndicate leaders and how they operated was chosen from three hundred entries by the Pulitzer Prize jurors, composed of editors, for the award for the year's best investigative reporting in the United States. But the advisory committee of academics and publishers, which has final say, overruled the decision and gave the prize to a Chicago paper for stories on ambulance chasing. Over the years, a number of other *Advertiser* stories were nominated for Pulitzers, but none came this close.

Said Hunter, "It's like being invited to spend the night with Racquel Welch and then being turned away by the butler. For me it was heartbreaking. No paper in Hawaii has ever won a Pulitzer Prize."[4]

Much of his information on organized crime was picked up while having a beer in out-of-the-way bars. Krauss tells how Hunter, homeward bound, "stopped in a bar in Kaneohe where the bartender introduced him to a lieutenant of crime boss Alema Leota. Since Hunter's series naming Leota as an underworld kingpin in Hawaii, the two men have met." Hunter said Leota

> assured me there were no hard feelings. Before he got killed, Chocolate Joe Kang called me and said he didn't care what I wrote about him so long as it was the truth.
>
> When Francis Lloyd Burke was killed in October 1970, his widow called me to complain about the way I handled the story of his funeral service. I apologized. We got to talking. She sounded like a pleasant person and agreed to meet me. She wound up giving me an exclusive account of her husband's life, with some sidelights about what it's like to be married to a man like him.[5]

Hunter had no illusions about eliminating organized crime groups: "As long as they provide illegal services that people want—gambling, narcotics, prostitution—you'll have the syndicate. So long as the market exists, somebody will run the store."[6]

The paper recognized him with the title of associate editor, but he always regarded himself as Gene Hunter, reporter. In March 1976 he died at fifty of a heart attack. Before going, he asked that $200 of his insurance money go for a party for friends at Columbia Inn, the popular watering hole next-door to the paper.

As the paper neared its 113th anniversary in July 1969, it remarked on its "youth," referring to the fact that eighteen of its reporters, two copy editors, and three photographers were twenty-nine or younger, with an average age of twenty-three.

City Editor Zalburg exulted: "Who else has such a roomful of cheerful, bright-eyed young people with verve, dash, energy and ability?"[7]

Interestingly, they had accumulated considerable experience, in jobs ranging from correspondents on papers in the Orient, South America, and Europe to those of junior executives, bricklayers, and doormen. Among them were a champion bridge player, a woman skydiver, a motorcyclist, and a surfer.

Gerry Keir, at twenty-five one of the youngest politics writers on a major American daily, had come to the Islands in 1966 as an Army officer with bachelor's and master's degrees in journalism from Michigan State. While in school at Lansing, the state capital, he freelanced for some Michigan papers. Summertime he worked on his home sheet in Springfield, Massachusetts.

His Army hitch over, he joined the *Advertiser* in 1968 as a general assignment reporter, working his way into political coverage, in three years becoming chief of the paper's five-person legislative bureau.

Of him Managing Editor Buchwach said, "In the 25 years I've been in Hawaii, I haven't [known] any political writer who has so quickly grasped the essence of the political scene and who has been so quickly accepted and saluted for his integrity and impartiality."[8]

In 1970, still a "new boy" at the capitol, Keir won an American Political Science Association national award for his notable reporting of the legislature's handling of an abortion bill.

Keir in those early years enjoyed "the intrigue and the digging" that went with covering the political scene. "It's got some fascinating people in it and the decisions that they make have such a real effect on the quality of life around here and on everybody's pocketbook. I feel I can do something worthwhile for the community by doing an accurate job of reporting on the government." He enjoyed writing and found "less tedium and monotony in journalism than in any other field I've ever considered."[9]

Another comer was Wayne Harada, who cut his teeth as editor of his grammar school paper in 1956, before going to Farrington High School and the University of Hawaii, where he majored in journalism.

After serving as a stringer and a reporter-columnist for the *Advertiser*'s Sunday youth tabloid, he was hired full-time in 1964, beginning a more than thirty-year record as the paper's first and only entertainment editor. Ironically, the *Star-Bulletin*, which provided his four-year university scholarship, had no opening for him.

When he was twenty-seven the *Advertiser* described him as "probably the most young-at-heart show business critic in the U.S."[10] After one downside review, entertainer Don Ho had another description: "The Kamikaze Pilot."

In those years he was called "hip in a jolly personal way. Beads are his bag and oftentimes you'll see him dashing about the city room in a tropical bush jacket and mod apache tie."[11]

He enjoyed the shows, the performers, and the opportunity "to see or recognize true talent in a person and see this talent grow and be nurtured. You see the development of a star."[12]

He covered the full spectrum of show business—from stage productions to opera, from nightclubs to visiting musical attractions, from TV filming in Hawaii to reviewing recordings. He also reported on theatrical endeavors in New York, Los Angeles, Las Vegas, London, Vancouver, and Toronto and got newsy items phoned in by such friends as Wayne Newton, Paul Anka, David Copperfield, and Charo.

Over the years, he was an Island correspondent for *People Magazine* and the trade journals *Billboard* and *Hollywood Reporter*.

Still another "kid" whose work would bear the imprint of excellence to come was Janice Wolf, a petite blond who arrived in 1968 as a cadet reporter fresh off the plane from the University of Michigan.

A bit later she pioneered what was called the "human affairs beat," one of the few if not the only one in the country at that time. It involved writing about the disadvantaged, what she called "the forgotten people"—the elderly who were alone, the poor, the disabled, the homeless. She would spend a night on the street with a bag lady and a man from Saturn. To better understand and communicate how the system treated drunks, she got drunk, was dumped on the doorstep of Queen's Hospital emergency room, and ultimately spent five miserable days drying out at the Salvation Army.

The tragedy that perhaps most influenced the way she reported was the gang rape and robbery of a Finnish woman on a Nanakuli beach. Her coverage brought thousands of dollars to help the foreign victim and, after several defendants were acquitted, played a part in changing Hawaii's rape law.

She wrote a column called "Sunday's Child" to help find adoptive and long-term foster homes for the State's hard-to-place children. Each week she focused on a particular child—his or her looks, needs, background. The result: safe and nurturing homes found for dozens of children, many abused or neglected, some badly handicapped.

In the 1970s, thanks to Senior Family Court Judge Betty Vitousek, she became the first reporter to cover that court from the "inside." It was a time when confidentiality barred scrutiny of the cases, and the way they were handled, giving the court a bad image.

Wolf spent months in Family Court, through countless divorce contests, child abuse proceedings, mental commitment hearings, and criminal trials. Early skepticism by attorneys, fearful their clients' confidentiality would be breached, faded away.

Her multipart series, first of its kind in the Islands, demystified and humanized Family Court. At Judge Vitousek's request, it was reproduced as a booklet and widely distributed on the mainland. Wolf made a bit of personal news in 1970 when she was covering an airport conference with then Canadian Prime Minister Pierre Trudeau. With TV cameras whirring, other newspeople asked him about his recent trip to Southeast Asia; she wanted to know what it was like to be the world's most eligible bachelor. His response was to ask her for a date. Then married, she turned him down, an event reported around the world.

She stayed at the *Advertiser* until 1982, then entered law school, in time became the state courts administrator, which she left to enter private practice.

Starting in the 1970s, the editorial department campaigned to bring on Island journalism students, both from the University of Hawaii and mainland schools, as summer (or legislative) interns, hoping that after college they would return as full-time staffers. The project paid off handsomely, providing both talent and the insights of a local background. Former interns currently on the staff: Vickie Ong, Andy Yamaguchi, Debra Yuen, Curtis Lum, Bart Asato, Esme Infante, Darren Pai, Stephen Downes, Mike Gordon, Wade

Shirkey, Jan TenBruggencate, John Bender, Suzanne Roig, Linda Dalrymple. Some others peeled off after a time for other publications, local or mainland, or other professions (e.g., attorneys Laurel Loo and Bruce Voss). Some have shown administrative capabilities, but with several exceptions have preferred frontline reporting or photography to supervisory desk jobs.

37

A Policy Shift from Conservatism

ON OCTOBER 29, 1962, the *Advertiser* carried a "We Endorse" editorial, supporting Governor Quinn for reelection, Representative Inouye for the U.S. Senate, Spark M. Matsunaga for one House seat, and, with qualifications, Thomas P. Gill for the second.

On the previous Friday, Twigg-Smith, out of respect for Walter Dillingham, visited him at his La Pietra home and let him read the forthcoming editorial, which explained that while the paper respected the candidacy of his son, Ben Dillingham, Inouye, in his three years in the U.S. House, had sustained "the high hopes of Hawaii . . . in a manner both admirable and productive."

It was an emotional session in which the elderly Dillingham unsuccessfully pleaded for a reversal of the paper's position. He asked Twigg-Smith to meet with his older son, Lowell, at his office at the Ala Moana Building, and again the meeting was moving but without change.

On November 1 Frank Hicks, chairman of the Republican Party's Oahu County Committee, strongly attacked the *Advertiser* as having a "left-wing outlook" and "a left-wing editor." Twigg-Smith called the charge "absurd," noting that the paper not only endorsed Republican Quinn but Republicans Ward Russell, Wadsworth Yee, and Lawrence Kunihisa as well as Democrat Vincent Esposito for the state Senate. Quinn lost to John A. Burns, but Inouye, Matsunaga, and Gill won.

Walter Dillingham resigned, ending a fifty-year association with the paper, during which, he said, he had lent "personal financial assistance to keep the Advertiser alive as an independent statewide voice."[1] He said that while he had a "deep interest" in the Senate campaign of his son Ben, the "determining factor in my decision . . . is the disregard by the management of the policy-making responsibilities of other officers and directors of the company." At a press conference, speaking through his son Lowell, Dillingham said he felt that political endorsements were a business, not an editorial policy, and should not be made without prior consultation with the directors.

Twigg-Smith, expressing "sadness and regret" at the eighty-seven-year-old Dillingham's departure, said,

> For decades past The Advertiser was a Republican newspaper which in recent years had been moving toward independent political leanings.
>
> The present editor, George Chaplin, accepted employment in 1958 on the condition that he could edit a completely independent newspaper, beholden to neither political party, to no special interest. He has done so and as a result the stature of The Advertiser has risen. . . . When the Inouye-Dillingham endorsement decision was faced, this newspaper, were it to remain true to its policy of independence, had to take a clear-cut stand. We did so, in good conscience, based on our conviction of what was best for Hawaii.[2]

The Dillingham interests owned 8,865 shares, or 12 percent, of *Advertiser* stock, and Dillingham said there was no intention of disposing of it. Bayard Dillingham, Walter's nephew, was elected to the newspaper's board to represent the family's holdings.

On November 4, 1962, just before the election, Lorrin Thurston bought an ad in the *Advertiser*, titled "Ben Dillingham or Dan Inouye." He said that Ben Dillingham was the man to vote for, the better "pilot" of the two. "Through no fault of his own, Dan hasn't got the broad background of business experience and understanding of Hawaii's and our nation's problems to make a good senator."

Concerning the *Advertiser*'s endorsement of Inouye, he said that as the major stockholder he "was not consulted by Thurston Twigg-Smith and George Chaplin before the editorial came out." He added, "While I personally recommended George Chaplin to the Board of Directors to become Editor of the Advertiser, which I realize now was a sad mistake for the Advertiser, I did so with no understanding of any kind that the Directors or I had to accept his policy decisions—or else."

In the 1964 national election the *Advertiser*'s editorials critical of Barry Goldwater were too much for Ben Dillingham. He labeled this writer a "Fabian Socialist—vicious, dangerous, ugly, the most dangerous man in the community."[3] He charged that similar "Fabian Socialist" views were held by columnist Walter Lippmann, Ambassador Adlai Stevenson, Secretary of State Dean Rusk, former Secretary Dean Acheson, and the late Eleanor Roosevelt. He stated that his views of the *Advertiser* and its editor were not based on the paper's opposition to him in the 1962 campaign.

The *Advertiser* responded that Dillingham's "unfounded smears and juvenile bombast during each political season simply reaffirm this newspaper's good judgment two years ago in endorsing Dan Inouye for a U.S. Senate seat."[4]

While heated political battles were standard fare in the Islands, on one subject—civil rights—there was far less disagreement.

On May 17, 1964, the tenth anniversary of the U.S. Supreme Court decision striking down public school segregation, Civil Rights Sunday was observed, by proclamation of Governor Burns. A civil rights conference was set up and, in cooperation with it, the *Advertiser* helped prepare eighty thousand postcards to be sent by Islanders to mainland families and friends, urging them to write to their U.S. senators to support the pending civil rights bill. The *Advertiser* also wrote to more than sixty leading mainland newspapers exhorting their readers to join the campaign.

Later that month the National Association of Real Estate Boards fought against the civil rights legislation, and the president of the Honolulu board indicated his group would go along. The *Advertiser* wrote two strong editorials, leading the local board to support the "objectives and intent" of the legislation, opposing its national body.

The paper hailed the decision of the Bishop Estate and real estate dealers to no longer permit racial discrimination in Kahala leaseholds, and it editorially urged the Pacific Club, without success at the time, to forgo exclusion of prospective members on the basis of race. Editorials reminded the club that, under the existing policy, not a single member of Hawaii's congressional delegation, nor the chief justice of the state Supreme Court, nor a vice-chancellor of the East-West Center would be regarded as qualified for membership. Some time later, due to a group that included publisher Twigg-Smith, Henry Clark, Robert Midkiff, Buck Buchwach, and the writer, the club democratized its policy.

A Joint "Op," a Strike, and a Would-be Buyer

WITHIN DAYS after the joint operation was announced in June 1962, inquiries were begun by both the Hawaii attorney general's office and the antitrust division of the U.S. Justice Department, which had two field agents in Hawaii studying interlocking directorates of major corporations.

The state requested several modest changes, mostly in the handling of classified ads, and the papers assented; the federal concerns appeared deeper.

Twigg-Smith had retained attorney Victor H. Kramer, of Arnold, Fortas, and Porter in Washington, a nationally respected antitrust expert who for twenty years had been chief trial lawyer for the Justice Department's antitrust division. Kramer advised the *Advertiser*, which feared that Justice's field agents might recommend prosecution without adequate research, to seek a meeting with the assistant attorney general in charge of the antitrust division and provide all requested information.

The session in Washington was set up in early September, chaired by Assistant Attorney General Leo Loevinger and attended by a number of his attorneys and by Kramer, Twigg-Smith, and me, along with attorney Livingston Jenks, sent by the *Star-Bulletin* just to observe.

A lengthy discussion was followed by seven penetrating questions in writing, six of them asking for detailed facts and figures on every aspect of the *Advertiser*'s past operations. The seventh asked if Twigg-Smith objected to the government's getting topflight publishers to go to Hawaii and check out the publisher's statement that a dissolution of the mutual plan would mean the *Advertiser*'s demise.

Twigg-Smith said he would welcome such a study, and when asked to suggest names, he listed such distinguished publishers as Arthur Ochs Sulzberger of the *New York Times*, Ralph McGill of the *Atlanta Constitution*, Lee Hills of the *Detroit Free Press*, John S. Knight of the *Miami Herald*, and Barry Bingham of the *Louisville Courier-Journal*.

It took two weeks to research, assemble, and submit the information sought by the Justice Department. No further word was heard from it. But uncertainty remained, and in March 1969 a U.S. Supreme Court ruling in a

Tucson, Arizona, case put the joint newspaper operations in more than twenty cities, including Honolulu, in jeopardy.

Since the first joint venture was formed in Albuquerque, New Mexico, in 1933, no administration, Republican or Democratic, had sought a breakup. But in Tucson, when one paper, which had been a loser but had been made profitable by a JOA, was sold to the other, the Justice Department sued under the Sherman Antitrust Act and the District and Supreme Courts ruled there was a violation.

The only relief for the JOAs lay with Congress, and two days after the final court action Senator Inouye was joined by twenty-four colleagues in both parties, and later eight more, in sponsoring the Newspaper Preservation Act. In the lower chamber, Hawaii Representative Matsunaga took the lead, with an identical bill and more than one hundred cosponsors.

In addressing the Senate on January 29, 1970, Inouye said that without a protective law the "obvious and clear effect" of the Supreme Court ruling "would be to put one paper in each [affected] city, with its independent news and editorial voice, out of business." He then cited an anomaly: "If the two papers in the same city," one of them in failing condition,

> had fully merged and operated under single ownership, then such actions would not be illegal. The one owner would set his advertising and circulation rates for both morning and afternoon papers . . . and divide the profit any way he saw it. . . . No competition at all is preferred to competition in the area most vital to our democratic form of government—the free interchange of ideas and points of view. . . . It is obvious that this does not make good sense.

In the Islands the proposed legislation was supported by resolutions of the legislature, the Honolulu City Council, all Neighbor Island councils, and by letters and statements from the business community and unions, including the local unit of the Newspaper Guild, which took a position opposite that of its national office.

Advertiser executives, who felt survival of the paper was at stake, sought the support of hundreds of daily newspapers across the United States, made calls on key members of Congress, and, with a number of other joint-plan newspapers, engaged Washington attorney Morris J. Levin as a coordinator and lobbyist.

Twigg-Smith and Roy Kruse, administrative officer of the Hawaii Newspaper Guild, testified at congressional hearings. Opponents included many suburban papers, some law professors, and the American Newspaper Guild.

Once the legislation reached the floor in Congress, the votes were lopsided in favor—63 to 14 in the Senate, 292 to 87 in the House, with President Richard M. Nixon signing it into law on July 24, 1970.

The act required that at least one of the papers entering a JOA not be likely to remain or to become financially sound. It permitted papers in a joint plan to set advertising or circulation rates, as a single owner of two papers could—but it expressly forbade predatory actions.

The effect of the legislation was to validate the Honolulu and other existing JOAS. But Hawaii, like other states, had its own antitrust laws—and although federal statutes dealing with newspapers, which are in interstate commerce, supersede any conflict in state language, the Honolulu dailies anticipated political harassment.

To discourage capricious use of the state antitrust laws, which although failing would be costly in terms of time, energy, and money, the newspapers sought passage of a state statute copying the federal law. Such a bill was introduced in the 1970 legislature and passed in 1972. The question of its effectiveness was left to an uncertain future.

When the two Honolulu dailies inaugurated their joint operating plan, the Newspaper Guild's national publication said other publishers might benefit from a similar "easy does it approach."[1] And any employee concerns were seemingly allayed when no cuts in staff were made.

But in the concentration of energy by both papers in making the new commercial and production arrangement work there was insufficient two-way communication between management and the unions. Tensions developed that might otherwise have been averted, and at 6:30 A.M. on June 21, 1963, after negotiations on a new contract collapsed, Honolulu suffered its first, and so far its only, daily newspaper strike.

Last-ditch efforts by two federal mediators and separate meetings two days after the walkout between Governor Burns and unions and management were unavailing. Eight hundred and fifty members of the Newspaper Guild, the typographers, the machinists, the photoengravers, the pressmen, the lithographers, and the International Longshoremen's and Warehousemen's Union, which had circulation workers, hit the sidewalks for forty-four days because of differences over wages, sick pay, vacations, and holidays. The giant presses were stilled, and Honoluluans were deprived of in-depth news and commentary. (The two remaining dailies were small, bilingual, primarily in Japanese, with some news in English.)

On June 15, Twigg-Smith had mailed a memo to his employees, including those in commercial printing. In it he said *Advertiser* pay rates, as well as holidays and vacations, compared favorably with the average of the thirty-one largest cities on the mainland. "While Honolulu is a much smaller city and our circulation and revenues are less, we have used this 31-city average as a guide in an effort to set a fair wage." On sick leave, because of a no-waiting period in the previous two years, "the cost of one or/and two-day absences has skyrocketed." So a two-day waiting period was proposed before payments would begin.

Although each union had its spokesman, the real labor leadership in the strike was provided by Jack Hall of the ILWU. His union's publication declared that "our wages are far below those that prevail in West Coast cities—our closest neighbors. . . . Employees in Hawaii must work up to two hours a week longer than most newspaper employees for their weekly wages and . . . living costs in Hawaii are as high or higher than in any other metropolitan area."[2] There were further statements and at times personal name-calling but no movement.

Picketing of the News Building was peaceful, with teachers, longshoremen, and musicians, some playing instruments, occasionally joining the twenty-four-hour line to show support for what one called the city's first strike to include white-collar workers.

In the third week of the impasse, *Time* magazine characterized it as "a contest of wills between hard-headed financier Chinn Ho, who dominated both papers, and Jack Hall, the tough boss of militant unionism in the islands."[3] Hall was quoted as saying the strike "will give the impetus to organization of many more white collar workers here" and Chinn Ho as declaring "he would hold out against the unions for six months if necessary."[4]

In a statement to a weekly paper, the *Leeward Press*, Chinn Ho denied dominating both papers. In actuality he no longer had any *Advertiser* stock and was not the major stockholder in the *Star-Bulletin*, but he did chair its board and enjoyed serving as a spokesman for the paper.

Off-the-record, separate meetings were conducted by federal mediators and representatives of the papers and the union, and then union and management spokesmen began meeting directly. In time, a feeling of optimism was evident on the picket line, fueled by scuttlebutt that Chinn Ho and Hall had met one night in Hall's kitchen, that a bottle was brought out and some time later a deal was struck.

The rumor was unconfirmed, but on August 2 the newspapers and unions announced agreement on a compromise on key issues for a three-year contract. But as United Press reported, one union—the typographers with 118 members present—"threw a scare into everyone" when it "first rejected the offered settlement and then by 10 votes accepted it in a second balloting."[5]

It took time to reactivate machinery, and publication did not resume until August 7, with both papers printing a detailed review of the news missed by the public. An *Advertiser* story estimated the strike had cost retailers between $10 million and $20 million. People were hungry to read and to buy, and there was a sharp, if temporary, increase in advertising and circulation.

Subsequent years saw some negotiations going down to the wire, but with the help of mediators and state officials any further strikes were warded off. In November 1968 the typographers flexed their muscle with a work stoppage over a disciplinary action taken against one of its members, but that was resolved after eight hours. The only casualty was the next morning's *Advertiser*, with a drastic shrinkage from a scheduled sixty-four-pager.

In early November 1963 James Copley of San Diego, owner of a chain of conservative papers in California and Illinois, came to Honolulu to seek to buy the *Advertiser*. He asked for a meeting and he, several of his executives, and his local attorney, Harold Conroy, had a discussion at the Surfrider Hotel with Twigg-Smith, his brother David, and me.

Twigg-Smith said the majority stockholders had no interest in selling, whereupon Copley met with the major stockholders of the *Star-Bulletin* and got a similar turndown.

Copley then aggressively sought a strong minority position in the *Advertiser*. In the weeks that followed the Dillingham interests sold him their 8,805 shares for a reported $440,000, or $50 a share, and he acquired an option on Lorrin Thurston's stock at $75 a share, which first, however, had to be offered to the *Advertiser* voting trust, which still had seven and a half years to run. Thurston had assured him that $75 was beyond the Twigg-Smith ability to pay. At the same time, in simultaneous offerings to each member of the Twigg-Smith family he made an offer of $75, which all rejected.

The offering of the Lorrin Thurston stock to the voting trust was then made, and the family of Thurston Twigg-Smith and uncle Robert S. Thurston bought 5,200 of Lorrin's shares for $390,000, giving them majority control without dependence on other stockholders. The remaining 13,221 shares of Thurston's stock were purchased by Copley for about $1 million.

By mid-January 1964 these acquisitions, together with some other, small blocs of minority stock, gave Copley 34 percent of the *Advertiser*, plus the hope that in time he could get the paper. He named Jack A. Heintz, his publisher in Springfield, Illinois, to be his Hawaii representative and, with attorney Conroy, to serve for him on the *Advertiser* board. Heintz also was appointed a trustee of the *Advertiser* voting trust to succeed former Publisher Thurston.

Thurston, who no longer had a connection with the *Advertiser*, praised Copley as a publisher who might make the paper one of which the community "can again be proud and willing to subscribe to." He said that "the policies of the present editor and publisher . . . bear little resemblance to the Advertiser I took over from my father." He opined that the paper "has lost most of its close contact with things Hawaiian," that primary news was "very poorly handled and slanting of the news seems commonplace." Twigg-Smith, he added, has "little regard to the public trust."[6]

Copley said he hoped to help "enhance the Advertiser's future and to give its readers a great newspaper which will keep pace with Hawaii's own unlimited future."[7] But no ideas or suggestions were advanced, either then or in the months ahead.

By September 1966 Copley, despite continued flashing of big money, realized he had no chance of acquiring the *Advertiser* and sold his stock to the *Advertiser* voting trust—with 7,835 shares going to the Twigg-Smith family for $700,000, giving it 81 percent control of the Advertiser Publishing Company, Ltd., and the remaining 8,944 shares to the company itself. In payment, the *Advertiser* gave Copley radio station KGU and a reputed $1 million from its share of proceeds from the 1965 sale of KONA-TV.

The Copley sale stimulated *Time* magazine to devote most of a page to *Advertiser* history, past and contemporary, and to observe that "Copley may not have appreciated Twigg-Smith's stubborn heritage" and his desire to carry on the family paper, which, with its Inouye endorsement, had arrived in the "new" Hawaii.[8]

The paper's voting trust, no longer serving a purpose, was dissolved a month after the Copley stock was acquired.

In 1978 the Twigg-Smith family finally acquired full ownership of the *Advertiser* by merging two holding companies, Persis and Asa Hawaii Corporation. Asa had owned more than 96 percent of Persis, the paper's parent company. As a result of the consolidation, minority holders in the former Persis firm exchanged their stock for $375 a share. The new entity retained the title of Persis, which, interestingly, was the name of the first missionary girl born in the Mission House on King Street—a reminder of Twigg-Smith's roots and his sense of history.

39

Historic Stamps, Art, and Journalism

THURSTON TWIGG-SMITH'S primary concern was newspapering, but he had other *Advertiser*-linked interests, among them art and historic Island stamps.

In 1961 he had established the Contemporary Arts Center of Hawaii in the courtyard of the newspaper building, featuring exhibitions of the work of major local artists, ranging from paintings to ceramics, weaving, photography, and advertising art and design. A *New York Times* article credited the center with bringing Hawaii and its artists into the international world of contemporary art.

Years later, Twigg-Smith's cultural contribution was reflected in the acquisition of the former Spalding estate in Makiki Heights and the opening there of the Contemporary Museum, which accumulated more than fifteen hundred works by some five hundred artists.

Twigg-Smith was recognized nationally with memberships on the national committees of the Whitney Museum in New York and the Yale Art Gallery in New Haven, Connecticut, and a trusteeship of the Museum of Contemporary Art, Los Angeles.

He also treasured old Hawaii stamps, probably because the *Advertiser*'s founder, Henry Martyn Whitney, was in 1851 the first postmaster in royal days, and some of the early stamps—a series called the Numerals—were printed in the paper's composing room.

In January 1972 the *Advertiser* acquired and added to its own holdings the world's outstanding collection of such stamps from owner Alfred J. Ostheimer III, a local resident and nationally known insurance executive.

In 1974 Twigg-Smith was approached by the Honolulu Academy of Arts and obtained for $365,000 a collection of local stamps contributed to the academy by the late Frank Atherton. Because of donor restrictions on sale of the Atherton stamps, it was necessary to obtain court approval. Twigg-Smith said the *Advertiser*'s ultimate aim was to get its collection into some form of public ownership. A few months later, the *Advertiser* stamps were awarded the "grand prix international, western hemisphere" at Interphil, a worldwide philatelic show, the largest ever held in the United States. It also won prizes in exhibitions in Basle and Amsterdam and was displayed in the Courts of Honor of fourteen international stamp shows around the world.

Hawaii was the only state that had had its own stamps—and individual collectors around the world and such institutions as the Smithsonian were eager to obtain the rare emblems of the past. Noting the paper's role in Island history and culture, Twigg-Smith said it could once again act as a catalyst in preserving a community asset.

But the younger stockholders in Persis, the family corporation that owned the *Advertiser*, who had contributed more than $25 million in years past to various charities across the United States, were now more interested in money than in financing an irreplaceable historic treasure. They wanted a tax credit. Twigg-Smith had held talks for years with the Smithsonian Institution, which wanted to exchange an $8 million tax credit for the stamps, a precedent used by the institution in the past. Congress approved it in 1993, but President Bush vetoed the bill that contained it. Efforts to revive the credit in the 1994 Congress failed.

Finally in November 1995 the stamps were put up for auction in New York. The collection's showpiece, a Hawaiian two-cent Missionary cover, sold for a record-breaking $2.09 million; an unused two-cent Missionary stamp brought $660,000. Both were record prices. The Smithsonian successfully bid just under $1 million—half of which was contributed by Persis—for eleven stamps and postal envelopes. When the sale ended three days later, it had produced $9.8 million, a record total for a stamp auction in the United States.

When there was an appropriate news peg, the paper would run stories about its stamps and art, but its promotional activities went far beyond. There were a series of T-shirts featuring historical events, aloha shirts with montages of *Advertiser* headlines over momentous news, and a variety of books. One, *A Day in the Life of Hawaii*, sold eleven thousand copies in three weeks, four thousand of them on a Saturday morning drive-through in the company's large parking lot.

Almanacs, tax guides, runs-for-fun, a yearly statewide spelling bee, annual banquets for high school valedictorians and outstanding student athletes, a Christmas fund for the needy which grew to more than $100,000 a year, local sponsorship of the Jefferson Awards that annually honored up to ten Hawaii residents who had rendered selfless service to the community (several over the years selected for national recognition)—there seemed no end to the *Advertiser*'s lively promotions.

The paper's 125th birthday was celebrated with a six-by-twelve-foot cake and an open house that drew thousands eager to see all aspects of newspaper production. And to recreate the journalistic lifestyle of yore, printer Raybern Freitas and his family moved into the historic Mission House, with its replica of the original *Advertiser* press, to live as people did when the paper was first printed in 1856.

The sparkplug for all the razzle-dazzle was Buchwach, who had a master showman's flair. He was assisted by Marcie Farias, his secretary, who became promotions manager. The job was a lighting rod for zany visitors. During one week, three different men came up to her desk, announced they were Jesus and had a message for Buchwach. One came straight from the airport with suitcases. Another arrived on a skateboard toting his belongings in a pillow case. And the third showed up empty-handed but proclaimed his divinity. Farias managed to shunt each aside.

The paper's open-door policy for visitors soon produced another bizarre twist. Fifteen yellow-suited members of the "Revolutionary Communist Party" charged into the editor's second-floor office and locked the door, meanwhile chanting "Down with Teng Hsaio-ping. Long live Mao Tse-tung."

When the startled editor looked up, a spokesman said they were upset because the media hadn't covered their press conferences. They left behind a written statement opposing Vice-Premier Teng's visit to Washington. At the *Star-Bulletin* the group got into a shouting and shoving match with Managing Editor John E. Simonds, who suffered scratches on his arm.

Some years later, security guards were hired, at first only for duty at a side entrance after normal hours, later for all entrances.

There was rarely a dull day in Hawaii or its media. In 1977 considerable hullabaloo was created by a TV broadcast and the publication in a Maui bimonthly of a report that Larry Mehau, Big Island rancher, former Honolulu policeman, and vice-chairman of the state Board of Land and Natural Resources, was the "godfather" of organized crime in Hawaii. There was no evidence then or subsequently to support such a charge, but several newspapers and television stations and UPI distributed it. The *Advertiser* tried to reach Mehau, who was on the mainland but, being unsuccessful, held off on printing a story.

On his return several days later, Mehau denied the allegation and quickly filed a $51 million libel suit against thirteen defendants. The *Advertiser*, in publishing this action and what led to it, ran a front-page box explaining its delay:

> Our function is to gather news and present it clearly and swiftly. But inherent in this is the responsibility to be fair. . . . Aside from the question of possible libel, there is the necessity to abide by The Advertiser's written code of ethics [which] requires that before publishing such grievous accusations, especially in the absence of any tangible evidence or police documentation, we reach the individual and give him or her the opportunity to respond simultaneously with the publication of the allegations.[1]

In following years, political opponents sought to besmirch Mehau, a friend of Governor George Ariyoshi, but neither they, nor reporters, nor even federal investigators ever produced visible evidence of illegality. The *Advertiser* took some criticism, including from a few of its own staffers, for its delay in printing the Mehau story, but no newspaper ever expects to be free of flak.

During the 1970s the paper was often attacked on the air by popular disc jockey J. Akuhead Pupule, the pseudonym of Hal Lewis. On the mornings of September 28 and 29, 1978, an election year, Aku charged that the paper had commissioned a political campaign poll but, not liking the results, had purposely not published them so as to influence the upcoming primary. The paper, as it turned out, had received the poll results from SMS Research, Inc. at 1 P.M. on Friday, September 29, and published them the following morning. Aku and his station, KGMB, publicly apologized.

The Honolulu Community Media Council, after a study some weeks later, concluded that the *Advertiser*'s pre-election polls were conducted in a responsible manner in keeping with the council's guidelines.

The *Advertiser* had begun sponsoring polls in 1974 after Gerry Keir, then city editor, spent the 1973–1974 school year on a fellowship studying polling techniques at the University of Michigan and its renowned Survey Research Center. In announcing the program, the paper said it sought to examine what people are worried about, how they feel about government and politicians, and how that climate was affecting that year's election.

The initial survey measured voter attitudes toward politicians' honesty and ability; sentiment about such then-current issues as the H-3 freeway and population growth; and general feeling about local political institutions. The polls were not designed to foretell election outcomes but to provide a "snapshot" of people's sentiments at the time the surveys were conducted.

Keir for a number of years prepared the polls, and SMS Research, Inc., was hired to conduct them. Jim Dannemiller of SMS, the former director of the Office of Survey Research at the University of Hawaii, described Keir as the ablest and best-trained Islander in the field. Media critic Bob Dye, writing in *Honolulu Magazine* in April 1981, said Keir's work "has done much to quash reporting of vest-pocket polls leaked to influence elections and rendered harmless the results of straw polls. Because of the Advertiser's willingness to spend money required to do serious polling, voters now get information which at least approximates that used by contenders for major political office."

In 1983 Keir went back to the mainland to learn more—with a six-month fellowship at the Syracuse University Communications Research Center. He coauthored a college text on reporting techniques, focusing in part on survey and other social science tools.

Over the years the poll has had a good to excellent track record, although it missed the mark in several races, including the 1988 mayoral contest between Frank Fasi and Marilyn Bornhorst, which Fasi won handily in contrast to the survey's showing of a "statistical tie." Also there was a subsequent Democratic gubernatorial primary battle between Cecil Heftel and John Waihee in which the poll failed to perceive the softness of Heftel's lead, which evaporated under Waihee's massive campaign effort in the final days.

Fourteen years after its debut, the *Advertiser* Poll gained a cosponsor in KHON-Channel 2 News and took on the name of Hawaii Poll.

In the political season of 1978, having forgone editorial endorsements for several years after the Nixon-McGovern presidential race, the *Advertiser* felt "a critical situation" called for a resumption. It regarded the outcome of the race for governor between incumbent Ariyoshi and Mayor Fasi as pivotal to the future of the Islands.

A lengthy Sunday editorial described Ariyoshi as "quiet, reserved, unpretentious," Fasi as a mud slinger, lusting after power, "flashy, boisterous, boastful." Fasi was a believer in "confrontation politics, skilled in divide-and-conquer tactics"; Ariyoshi, favoring consensus, was "more in rhythm with the aloha spirit." It contended that while Ariyoshi was not without his flaws, he came through overall as an honorable man more to be trusted than Fasi, who the paper opposed in each of his numerous campaigns for governor, all unsuccessful.

Strong editorial positions were not confined to political races. They were just as readily taken against the University of Hawaii basketball coach and players appearing in an auto dealer's TV commercials and against real or potential conflicts of interest of a former head of the State Department of Agriculture and the city's auditoriums director.

On ethics in government, while spotlighting real or potential abuses, the paper was steadily calling for tougher standards for public servants, a recurrent need in Island governments.

The *Advertiser* wrote its own code of conduct, obliging its staff to forgo conduct that would adversely affect the reputation of any employee or of the paper for truthfulness, independence, fairness, and honesty and to avoid both conflicts of interest and the appearance of such.

In mid-summer 1978 with the upcoming election contests augmented by voter decisions on results of the constitutional convention, Managing Editor Buchwach posted a newsroom bulletin urging staffers to "be as fair as you can and keep your cool" in the face of certain maligning of motives by those whose disfavor is incurred. Writers were cautioned to not let their reporting be affected by whatever editorial positions the management might take. The bulletin became an election-year standard that continued even after the Buchwach era.

40

Right-to-Print Hits Official Snag

THE 1970S generated considerable Hawaii news of major import. Abortion was legalized, public workers won the right to collective bargaining, delegates met in the state's third Constitutional Convention, and voters approved its establishment of an Office of Hawaiian Affairs.

With the Vietnam War boiling, University of Hawaii students took over the ROTC quarters for almost a week. The city acquired the formerly private bus system, the bicentennial of Captain Cook's arrival was celebrated, the *Hokule'a* sailed to Tahiti and back, and the first 747 airliner arrived, harbinger of a tourism boom.

Former Governor Burns, whom the *Advertiser* had supported, based on his record once he was in office, died, and his successor, George Ariyoshi, began his second term with the first-ever woman lieutenant governor, Jean King. Hawaiians launched a campaign for the Navy to give up Kahoolawe. And to cap the decade, Hawaii was the first state to ratify the Equal Rights Amendment.

In 1970 the *Advertiser* played a key role in proposing and providing detailed coverage of the Governor's Conference on the Year 2000, an exercise in anticipatory democracy, soon emulated by the states of Washington and Iowa, the commonwealth of Puerto Rico, and Malaysia.

That same year, Honolulu became one of the few U.S. cities to have a media council, designed to provide a mechanism to remedy wrongdoings by or against print and broadcast organizations.

An Episcopal clergyman, Claude F. DuTeil, upset at a clash over news coverage between Mayor Fasi and the *Star-Bulletin*, had visited editors of the two dailies. Both suggested a community media forum, and after a seminar involving various segments of the city, a thirty-three-member council, with media types a small minority, chaired by retired Family Court Judge Gerald Corbett, was established.

Although only one mainland media council remains, the Honolulu program has continued through the years, receiving, analyzing, and passing judgment on complaints that readers and listeners voiced to papers and radio-TV stations without getting what they felt were satisfactory responses. Protests from media were rare. When complaints to the council seemed justified, it had only the power of persuasion, but this sensitized the media, which wanted to avoid even mild public censure.

But, of course, many complaints surfaced outside the council. An example: the battle of words that Clare Boothe Luce and the *Advertiser* engaged in on the Vietnam War.

A long letter from Luce lumped the paper with "the anti-war media [which have] spared no ink in destroying America's regard for its Vietnam allies," and in painting "the Saigonese as soft, deceitful and corrupt . . . [and] the South Vietnam leaders [as] powerful thugs and money-mad opportunists. . . . Never in American history has the media reached such depths of high-minded hypocrisy. . . ."

In an adjoining editorial the paper said,

> In their search for scapegoats to blame for the collapse of American policy in Indochina, it is not surprising that unregenerated hawks like Clare Luce vent their frustrations on the media.
>
> There is room for rational debate on what happened in Indochina and the pro's and con's of the media's role there and in the U.S. during the war. But Mrs. Luce does not give it to us in a long and bitter polemic that, when it comes to the Advertiser, is both inaccurate and intellectually dishonest.[1]

To provide more divergent viewpoints, whether on the war or on domestic issues, a new editorial-page feature, "Other Voices," was unveiled, with this explanation:

> The Advertiser's image seems to be liberal and establishment. If we are biased—and everyone is no matter how hard he tries to be fair—it is in those directions.
>
> For that we don't apologize. Newspapers should have a point of view and editorial opinions to back it up. But we also want to make sure that other points of view get heard.

To that end, space would be offered to the underrepresented, including "such people as senior citizens, immigrants, women, the poor, the far right and left, the military, racial groups and maybe Republicans as a minority group in a Democratic state."[2]

The early contributors included Max Roffman, veteran labor leader active in senior citizen programs; the Rev. Ryo Imamura, director of the Buddhist Study Center; academician Joan Abramson, author of a recently released book on sex discrimination detailing her case at the University of Hawaii, which had fired her in 1973; Professor Ted Becker, a political scientist; and Samuel M. Slom, state chairman of Young Americans for Freedom.

To further remind readers that freedom of the press belongs to them and that a newspaper's right to print flows from the individual's greater right to read, the *Advertiser* began an extensive series titled "Free Press/Free Society." The articles were written by a cross-section of people on all islands, "expressing their own views of the role and performance of an unfettered press in a land of liberty." Each guest writer was urged to not hesitate "to express any criticism you might have of the press—or to make suggestions for improvement."

The aim was to contribute to a "better understanding of the relationship of the First Amendment, the press and the reader."[3]

The resultant series, which ran for weeks, received the charter E. W. Scripps award of the Scripps-Howard Foundation for "outstanding service to the cause of a free press," presented at a New York ceremony by Leon Jaworski, who had been the special Watergate prosecutor in the final crucial months of the Nixon administration.

The press' commitment to a free flow of information not infrequently collided with the government's dislike of giving out embarrassing information, as witness the State Health Department refusal to let an *Advertiser* reporter see files on lower Waikele Stream, where children swim and fish.

The reason was simple: the popular swimming hole is downstream of the city's Mililani sewage treatment plant. For two years both state and city officials knew of the failure to meet federal standards for pollution in dumped wastes, which contained unsafe concentrations of viruses linked to polio, diarrhea, and a type of meningitis.

The *Advertiser* went to court, and Circuit Judge Arthur Fong ordered the opening of the files: "I think the more we shine the light on people who represent us, we'll be better off." The state's attitude was "let's hide it" and "that's what Watergate was all about."[4]

This was not an isolated case. Not long before, an *Advertiser* staffer discovered that city workers had illegally paved a private bus company's parking lot with government materials and equipment. The information was shared with the City Department of Public Works, which said it conducted an investigation that unearthed no wrongdoing or any sign of paving activity. But the reporter proved tenacious. Upshot: five municipal employees pleaded guilty to first-degree theft.

Skilled investigative reporters are among the rarest and most valuable practitioners in journalism. The job requires a skeptical mindset, often assuming the worst rather than the best in people; ears and eyes alert for any hint of wrongdoing; the ability to develop contacts and sources based on integrity and trust; a willingness to dig relentlessly for solid facts and, once these are in hand and checked out, to collate them in straightforward, lively prose in balanced, fair-minded fashion.

Jim Dooley, son of a San Francisco editor, graduated from the University of California at Davis in 1972 and joined UPI in Honolulu. When it appeared the news service wanted him to move to Buffalo, New York, he accepted an *Advertiser* offer in 1974.

More than any other newsperson in Hawaii, Dooley for years shone a bright lamp in the dark corners of government and high-level private-sector abuse. His aggressive but careful reporting uncovered one smelly situation after another that, were it not for him, would have slid by without public awareness. In essence, he validated the belief of the First Amendment champions Jefferson and Madison that the press had the responsibility to be a watchdog on those in power.

These were but some of Dooley's revelations:

- The spread to Hawaii of Japanese organized crime, specifically the *yakuza*.
- Political corruption and criminal activity in the city's $50 million Kukui Plaza redevelopment project.
- Cronyism and bid-rigging in the award of $11 million in consulting contracts at U.S. naval shipyards around the country.
- Insider abuse and lax government oversight of the industrial loan industry.
- Secret land investment partnerships involving prominent public officials and businessmen.
- Teamsters Union internal warfare over control of Hawaii's film industry.
- Japanese acquisition of golf course and resort properties in the United States as well as widespread involvement of Japanese organized crime in the golfing business.
- Widespread irregularities in state government procurement practices during the Waihee administration.
- Purchase of homes in a city-sponsored housing development by some city officials and members of Mayor Frank Fasi's family.

For several years another staffer and talented writer, Walter Wright, also engaged in investigative reporting, with his disclosures ranging from financial scandals to an inside view of the Islands' marijuana industry.

Neighbor Islands Make News Too

THE NEWSROOM'S primary focus has always been on Oahu, where 80 percent of Hawaii's people live, but the Neighbor Islands are very much a part of the *Advertiser*'s territory.

Longtime staff correspondents—Hugh Clark on the Big Island, Jan TenBruggencate on Kauai, and Ed Tanji on Maui—provided informed coverage despite the size of their beats. While purely local material ran only in the Neighbor Island edition, that of wider interest made the Oahu edition as well.

Clark, a Californian who jumped into journalism while a high school student and later at Humboldt State University, worked on papers in his home state, then in Idaho and Texas and in Hilo for five years as news editor of the *Tribune-Herald* before joining the *Advertiser* in November 1971.

In earlier years the paper had been represented by Ron Bennett, later a Honolulu city hall reporter; Terry McMurray, who became for many years the *Advertiser*'s Honolulu Police Department reporter; Walt Southward, who put in seven years before going into public relations; John Knox, later on the Honolulu staff; and briefly by Hal Glatzer.

The primary founder of the Big Island Press Club, Clark was in the forefront of the battle for press access to public information, battling efforts of the Police Department and other agencies to restrict the flow of news. The Press Club honored him in 1970, 1975, and again in 1987, when he organized a day-long seminar on constitutional and openness issues. And on a National Endowment for the Humanities fellowship he spent two months in 1979 at Tufts University in Massachusetts at a "Free Flow of Ideas" seminar.

Clark's major stories included the November 1975 earthquake, tidal wave, and volcanic eruption—a three-ring disaster; the 1977–1978 Madamba underworld murder and subsequent trials; and the continuing 1983 Kilauea eruption. Nature's power was brought home to him personally when, after filing a story on a 1973 earthquake, he returned to his home to find it in shambles. He managed a few hours' sleep, got up and resumed work.

Jan TenBruggencate, who became an *Advertiser* staffer in 1970, was born in the Netherlands, moved to Canada in 1949, to Hawaii in 1956, and grew up on a Molokai pineapple plantation, where his father was an agriculturist. As a youngster, he and a neighbor boy started a mimeographed paper that went two issues before folding. In his early days on the *Advertiser* his beats ranged from the military to religion, and in October 1971 he took over the Kauai bureau.

He was deeply interested in ecology and, in addition to his standard coverage of Kauai affairs, he got deeply involved in environmental and science stories, soon receiving awards and invitations to lecture. The information he provided readers on the delicate Hawaiian environment was before the subject became popular and no one else in the state was writing about it. It led to an every-Sunday column, "Environmental Update," which has appeared since 1987.

After Hurricane Iwa, TenBruggencate wrote the text and took some of the photographs for an "instant" booklet that the paper helped sponsor, promote, and sell. He wrote the text, with the late chief artist Adam Nakamura's illustrations, for an *Advertiser*-published book *Wildlife of Hawaii*. And he wrote much of the text for the color publication *Kilauea: The Flow to the Sea*, cosponsored by the paper.

In his view, the *Advertiser* has sought to make itself a part of people's lives and to make them a part of the paper's life. As an example of its emphasis on Hawaii's uniqueness, he cited the *Advertiser*'s assignment of four staffers, including two photographers, to cover a volcanic eruption in the 1970s, with the *Star-Bulletin* depending solely on its Big Island correspondent.

Ed Tanji, after an army stint in Vietnam and then getting a journalism degree from the University of Hawaii while serving as an *Advertiser* copy editor, became Maui bureau chief in 1974.

In late 1975 Hawaiian activists Walter Ritte, Jr., and Dr. Emmett Aluli invited him for drinks to voice their concern over the Navy practice bombing of Kahoolawe. His reporting of their feelings and of Mayor Elmer Cravalho's consistently voiced objections to the military use of what they described as a Hawaiian island contributed to a bombing ban and Kahoolawe's return to native control.

In 1977 Tanji's story on how a Makawao subdivision could force a chicken farm to close led to a state "Right to Farm" act, requiring residents moving next to existing farms to be warned of a potential nuisance from operations and assuring the farmer's right to continue normal practice. When the intent of the act was raised in a court case, Judge E. John McConnell, a former deputy attorney general advising the Land Use Commission, commented, "Why don't you ask Tanji back there. He's the one responsible."[1]

Another story, in which Tanji first reported the uncovering of a thousand burials in the Honokahua sand dunes, stopped construction of a hotel there.

He was red-faced the day in June 1979 when Mayor Cravalho, under months of federal fire on the Lahaina sewage system, surprisingly resigned. A press conference had been scheduled, but the mayor's staff said it was to deal with the county budget. So Tanji went off on a story in distant Hana, figuring he could pick up the details later in the day. When he called, Cravalho laughed and asked, "Where were you?" Tanji recalled, "He definitely got a kick out of my situation."[2]

Tanji's philosophy of journalism, which he attributed to Buck Buchwach, was that having fun went hand in glove with chasing big stories.

Before the 1974 general election, the *Advertiser*'s editorial page solemnly noted a poll "showing that most Hawaii voters are skeptical and distrustful of the honesty and ability of those who run government here," paralleling national trends. And it deplored widespread voter apathy. Tanji, in a report on Maui, said the political races there were "generating all the excitement of a cockfight featuring two egg-laying hens."[3]

For a good many years, starting in the 1970s, *Advertiser* news executives, the publisher, and Clark, TenBruggencate, and Tanji met annually with leaders of a different Neighbor Island. State Editor Jim Richardson said these gatherings offered a new perspective for most of the paper's management team.

42

Technology Brings a Host of Changes

WHILE THE staff sought ways to improve statewide coverage, it also moved ahead on the technological front. In July 1973, in the start of a new era, the traditional clatter of Linotypes spewing individual lines of hot metal type suddenly died, replaced by a photo-chemical process that reproduced stories and photographs onto paper.

Retrained compositors made up pages by pasting in the stories and pictures. The pages were then converted into curved aluminum plates ready for the presses, which had been adjusted to accommodate them.

A pivotal player in this transition from hot to cold type and the rise of the computer was Mike Middlesworth, brought in as managing editor when Buchwach moved up to the newly created executive editorship.

A veteran of a dozen years on papers in Indiana, Michigan, and Oklahoma, Middlesworth had developed an expertise in the new technology. The overall objective, he said, "was to put in place a system that would permit the building of pages on computer terminals in the newsroom," to include not only news stories but illustrations and ads, a process called pagination.[1] By the late 1980s the newsroom was producing full pages, including four-color illustrations.

The old system, in the early 1970s, required some 350 printers. This figure dropped within two decades to 75, bringing a substantial payroll saving to management.

About the time the technological changes were beginning, there was a major corporate development. Twigg-Smith in November 1973 advised stockholders that the agreement for joint operation of the *Advertiser* and *Star-Bulletin* had been extended for fifty years, to expire at the end of 2042. To achieve this, the *Advertiser* had to waive a 5 percent increase in its share of annual net proceeds, originally scheduled to jump from 40 to 45 percent. The thirty-year contract negotiated in 1962 was to expire in 1992, and *Advertiser* executives feared that as the date neared, the Hawaii Newspaper Agency, in which the *Star-Bulletin* had the majority voice, would let *Advertiser* circulation sharply slide—thus cutting any bargaining power the morning paper had in renewal of the agreement.

Advertiser personnel felt Twigg-Smith had negotiated a prudent deal. So did the shareholders, since the new pact enabled the paper to reduce equipment it was obligated to furnish the joint facility and to sell the remaining matériel to the *Star-Bulletin*. The cash generated enabled the *Advertiser* to distribute two extraordinary dividends of $14 a share each, in addition to a regular $1 dividend.

Twigg-Smith, writing to stockholders, said: "With the amended agreement we look forward not only to an improved product and the extended assurance of two independent editorial voices in Honolulu, but also to a stabilized ongoing business, with the expectation of stabilized earnings for the foreseeable future."[2]

The joint operation from its first day had created considerable public confusion, fueled in part by the name of the *Sunday Star-Bulletin and Advertiser,* required by the *Star-Bulletin* as a condition of entering into the mutual production plan. From the outset, the *Advertiser* produced and bore the cost of the entire Sunday paper except for the agency-produced TV section and other supplements. The *Star-Bulletin* periodically pushed for inclusion of its own editorial page, never granted, and for production of some of the news content.

In January 1974, with the contract extended, the *Advertiser* acknowledged that Sunday readers would benefit from utilization of the *Star-Bulletin* staff, and agreement was reached for it to put out the feature sections. But the spot news and editorial and sports sections remained strictly the *Advertiser*'s. And for the first time the AP and New York Times News Service augmented the dispatches of the UPI and the *Washington Post–Los Angeles Times* service.

Still, a goodly number of people felt there was a single owner of both papers and that there was no editorial competition, both of which were untrue. In addition, the very idea of a joint operation had its critics, including the U.S. Justice Department, which in time reversed its position, and even a few newspapers, such as the *New York Times*. After one of several *Times* editorials, Twigg-Smith was moved to respond with a letter to the editor. The *Times*, interestingly, wanted him to trim certain sentences, but after some back-and-forth the following was printed, under the heading "Newspaper Competition."

To the Editor:

The suggestion in your Jan. 31 editorial and in previous editorials that the Newspaper Preservation bill could provide "a shield to established publishers against the entrance of new journalistic competitors" ignores the realities.

With no such statute at present, what is keeping new ventures out of the daily field in New York, especially in the afternoon? Why is there only one morning newspaper in the entire state of Michigan—population in excess of eight million? Why, in no major U.S. community in many years, has any newspaper which died been succeeded by a newcomer?

The answer is economics. The death of the World-Journal-Tribune represented the end of what had once been eight independent New York City newspapers. Less dramatic perhaps, but equally tragic, have been the deaths of scores of dailies throughout the nation.

Fewer than sixty cities now have more than a single editorial and news voice, and in 22 of these the editorial diversity is assured only because of a merger of commercial departments of two separately owned papers. Should the Newspaper Preservation bill, which passed the Senate, fail to pass the House the financially weaker paper in each of these 22 communities will be faced with disaster.

To my knowledge only one joint operating venture has been voluntarily severed, and that in Chattanooga. The reports are that, as a result, both papers moved from the black into the red.

You interpret the recent Federal Court order in the Tucson case as providing "considerable latitude for united operation without any necessity for a new law" and as laying down "healthy guidelines."

Your view is not shared by those who are under the gun. It would be sad, indeed, if it took the death of one of the Tucson papers to prove you wrong.

On another aspect, your editorial says . . . "the sheltered environment of a carefully divided market is a poor spur to editorial ingenuity or creativity."

Editorial ingenuity and creativity have flourished far more in our "sheltered environment" than was ever possible when The Advertiser was a dying No. 2 newspaper.

As a result of our joint commercial agency, Honolulu today has two vigorous, highly competitive editorial voices—both of which have won numerous national awards and also have made more contributions to a better Hawaii than otherwise would have been possible.

In an increasingly complex world, the great need is for more dialogue, more diversity of ideas and opinions—not less. That end, in the 22 joint-plan cities, will be infinitely better served by House passage of the newspaper bill than by the Tucson court decision which you commend.

Thurston Twigg-Smith
President and Publisher
The Honolulu Advertiser
Honolulu, Feb. 6, 1970

In following years, as more and more newspapers died, it became clear that in some twenty cities two separately owned and editorially independent papers remained alive only because of a joint operation. Cities as large as Baltimore, Houston, New Orleans, Miami, and St. Louis were down to a single daily and in a number of other cities with two papers there was a single owner of both and thus a single viewpoint.

43

Mayor Fasi's Battle with the Press

FOR THE two Honolulu daily newspapers, but especially the *Advertiser*, the late 1960s and 1970s were marked by assaults by Mayor Frank F. Fasi and a small but tenacious group of legislators led by Senators Duke Kawasaki and Neil Abercrombie and Representative Stanley Roehrig of Hilo. Their goal ranged from a series of restrictions on the papers' functions to a breakup of the joint operating agreement.

During the first six years of the arrangement, when Fasi was a city councilman, his relations with the *Advertiser* were generally cordial. On the eve of his 1968 election as mayor, he wrote to convey his appreciation "for the extensive, impartial coverage that your newspaper gave to the mayoralty race. . . . I think your staff has done a remarkable job in bringing the news to the readers as they perceived it happened and no candidate for any office can ask for more than that."[1] Earlier he had said the *Advertiser* was fair to him, even though it had endorsed Andy Anderson for mayor.

But once in the top city office, when the paper did not editorially agree with all of his actions, he saw it, and the *Star-Bulletin* as well, as organs of evil. He began a bitter ongoing campaign against the papers that seemed to emulate Vice-President Spiro Agnew's castigation of the national TV networks.

The *Advertiser* came to regard Fasi as a churlish authoritarian who threw verbal tantrums if things didn't go all his way. Over the years, at least two city hall reporters, fed up with his tongue-lashings, asked to be moved to other beats.

Possibly laying groundwork for the first of his races for governor, he stumped the state, speaking to service clubs, to the military, realtors, even to high schools. With the Honolulu papers covering him, his audience was their full readership.

He pounded away at a single theme: that the *Advertiser* and *Star-Bulletin* had since the establishment of the joint plan in 1962 "knowingly and maliciously" violated the antitrust laws while "ripping off" the public with excessive ad rates.[2] He used the airways; for a while he produced his own monthly paper, *The Honolulu News*, ironically edited by two former *Advertiser* staffers, Jack Teehan and Brian Casey; he wrote a regular column for the weekly *Sun Press*, as did his public relations director, Jim Loomis, under the pen name of "Kimo," and for a time authored a weekly column for the *Star-Bulletin*, often devoted to criticizing the *Advertiser*.

He charged "monopoly," but the *Advertiser* responded that he was conveniently overlooking competition for advertising dollars from five TV and some twenty radio stations, plus magazines and neighborhood, bilingual, and tourism papers. Undaunted, Fasi, always the eager wordsmith, came back with, "You guys make the members of the OPEC monopoly look like a bunch of pikers."[3]

The *Advertiser* was never slow to respond: "We don't expect that providing the truth will have any effect on Mayor Fasi's paranoid-like view of the media. But we continue to believe that the public welfare is always best served by setting the record straight."[4] He was accused of "mixing considerable fiction and fantasy with a few facts."[5]

Twigg-Smith pointed out that advertising rates were lower than those in most comparable cities and called Fasi a local version of Agnew, who "made some political hay—for a while—by accusing the press of bias and indecency and worse."[6]

At times, Fasi overextended his eagerness to zap the *Advertiser*, which saw him as akin to "an old snake oil salesman at a carnival."[7] In a talk to a Rotary Club on Maui he charged the *Advertiser* had suppressed a poll showing him leading Ariyoshi and state Senator Andy Anderson in a three-way race for governor. When the *Advertiser* called it "an outright falsehood," since it had not yet done polling in that race, and threatened legal action, Fasi recanted and publicly apologized.[8]

Openly resentful of reportage he disliked, in December 1973 he excluded the *Star-Bulletin*'s City Hall reporter, Richard Borreca, from his press conferences and the next month barred *Advertiser* reporter Douglas Carlson.

Both papers went to court seeking relief. After federal District Judge Samuel P. King issued a preliminary injunction sought by the *Star-Bulletin* against Fasi's tactics, he defiantly invited representatives of three TV stations and a radio station for "personal interviews on a collective basis." When the *Advertiser*'s Carlson sought to attend, he was turned away. The paper went to federal District Judge Martin Pence, who issued a declaratory judgment that Mayor Fasi had violated the First (free press) and Fourteenth (equal protection) Amendments to the U.S. Constitution. City attorneys acknowledged that barring Carlson had been an unconstitutional act.

But the mayor sought to turn defeat into victory by announcing that he had made his point, then opened his press conferences to all newspeople. At the same time, he continued his war against the papers in the legislative arena.

He proposed a law to give the state Public Utilities Commission control of the two dailies' advertising and circulation rates and had his administration draft a bill to accomplish this. At Fasi's request, it was introduced by Representative Clarence Akizaki. The state attorney general's office gave its opinion that the bill was unconstitutional, leading to Fasi's observation that it would have been only a partial remedy anyway, and what was needed was repeal of the state's Newspaper Preservation Act, which was identical with federal law.

Other antipress bills went into the hopper at each legislative session, and even when killed some reappeared the next year. One would have established a "media responsibility commission," appointed by the governor, to accept complaints and, if it deemed it appropriate, to levy fines against the offending media. Another would have required the newspapers to file annual financial statements and to submit all advertising and circulation rate changes to the attorney general for approval. A third would have created a state-subsidized newspaper. A fourth would have required registration of and financial disclosure statements by reporters covering the legislature. Still another would have mandated the media to file "advocacy impact statements," disclosing research sources and the probable effect of "any identified editorial statement of opinion, reaction or conclusion." That was too much even for Fasi to stomach and he testified against it.

At each session, especially in the Senate, Twigg-Smith testified at hearings and usually found himself tangling with Kawasaki, who dominated committee questioning and statements. The *Star-Bulletin* largely confined itself to sending written testimony. None of the antipress bills got enough votes to pass.

One unrelated piece of legislation did get through the legislature in the mid-1970s that unintentionally had substantial impact for a time on the papers and their readers. The purpose of Act 45 was to prevent abuse of police records of innocent persons by prospective employers, insurers, and credit bureaus. But as written it was a masterpiece of ambiguity, and police on all Islands interpreted it to mean they could release no information on any arrest until there was a conviction. This closed files previously available to the press and thus to the public. Grand jury indictments also were kept secret. Day after day, *Advertiser* police reporter Terry McMurray could only write that police had said it had been a routine twenty-four hours.

A circuit judge provided a preliminary injunction, and a federal judge issued a restraining order restoring the flow of information. The Honolulu Police Department urged repeal of the statute, and some months later the legislature complied.

Throughout the 1970s Fasi was unswerving in his determination to bring about a dissolution of the joint operation of Honolulu's two major dailies. As the decade neared an end, he finally had a City Council that was willing to try.

Thursday, July 8, 1982, was, for most people in Honolulu, just another summer day—hot, but with a redeeming trade wind. The news in that morning's *Advertiser* was pretty routine, with one exception: a Hawaii jury, after first leaning eight-to-four for conviction, had acquitted union organizer Henry

Huihui of all four extortion counts accusing him of threatening two electricians with physical harm. Otherwise, there were no eyebrow-lifters. The summer doldrums appeared to have settled in.

But in a fourth-floor courtroom in the fortress-like Federal Building on Punchbowl Street at Ala Moana Boulevard, a drama of great import began to unfold.

Judge Jesse Curtis of Los Angeles, a white-haired veteran of twenty years on the federal bench, was hearing opening arguments in the newspaper antitrust case initiated in 1979 by Mayor Fasi. The outcome could determine whether Honolulu would continue to have two major daily papers—or just one.

The jury had been seated the day before. Judge Curtis had questioned more than sixty prospective jurors on whether they had any "ill feeling or grudge" against the *Advertiser* or *Star-Bulletin*. After attorneys' challenges were exercised, an all-woman panel of eight—six regular jurors and two alternates—was seated in the box where they would spend their daytime hours, mostly Monday through Friday, for the next three and a half weeks.

The defendants were the parent companies of the two dailies and the Hawaii Newspaper Agency, which performed all the noneditorial functions of the separately owned and editorially independent publications.

The city's suit, based on its purchase of legal advertising, contended that the 1962 agreement by which the *Advertiser* and the *Star-Bulletin* entered into a joint operation violated the Newspaper Preservation Act of 1970 and federal antitrust laws. It argued that the *Advertiser* in 1962 was not financially unsound and that the joint operation set noncompetitive ad rates. A third contention, that the papers had ceased to be editorially independent, was summarily dismissed by the judge.

Mayor Fasi acknowledged that it was not until January 1979 that he had a City Council majority that would bring his long-threatened suit, which sought triple compensatory damages, amount unspecified, and a breakup of the joint arrangement.

Impressive legal teams went to work. The city employed on a contingency basis San Francisco antitrust lawyer Josef D. Cooper, aided by two mainland associates. The lead counsel for the defense was Martin Anderson, aided by two other *Star-Bulletin* lawyers, David Reber and Lani Ewell, *Advertiser* attorneys William Cardwell and William Swope, and for the newspaper agency, John S. Smith of Rochester, New York.

Although the trial was in 1982, it was to deal with events that took place twenty years before, at a time when several of the jurors were children. Each day it was the duty of jurors to put aside any consideration of the *Advertiser* and Honolulu of 1982 and focus on the newspaper and community of two decades earlier. It would not be an easy task.

At the outset, opposing counsel presented diametrically contrary views, Cooper contending that in 1962 the *Advertiser* was a healthy, growing, financially sound newspaper, Anderson arguing that the *Advertiser* would have failed without the partial consolidation.

Defense witnesses, led by Twigg-Smith, day after day recounted the history and the headaches of the *Advertiser*. Rudolph Peterson, retired president of the Bank of America and, earlier, of the Bank of Hawaii, testified he would not have favored a long-term loan to the paper because it was considered financially unhealthy. An Occidental Life Insurance Company executive told how the paper's request for a loan to buy equipment was turned down, because it was "on the edge of the cliff" and the loan would soon be in default.

April 14 and November 4, 1984. Like his predecessor Harry Lyons, Dick Adair found Frank Fasi an ever-present subject.

For the city, a mainland circulation consultant testified the *Advertiser* was closing the gap with the *Star-Bulletin* and would in time be the dominant paper. His views were echoed by Milan Leavitt, who quit as *Advertiser* circulation director in 1961.

Both sides had expert witnesses. For the city, Marvin Stone, a Denver certified public accountant who had testified in mainland newspaper antitrust cases, saw the *Advertiser* becoming an attractive money-maker. He provided figures growing out of a 3,500-hour study and billed the city $300,000.

The newspapers' expert witness was James Rosse, a Stanford economist, who testified he knew of no case where a newspaper as far behind as the *Advertiser* was in 1957 had ever recovered. His testimony reflected 2,500 hours of study, which brought the defense a bill for $250,000.

Closing arguments by attorneys were presented on Friday, July 30, and Judge Curtis then gave final instructions to the jury, repeating and expanding on his instructions at the outset of the trial:

> The decision as to whether the Honolulu Advertiser was likely to remain or become financially sound is a business judgment, the kind of judgment which businessmen in management positions are called upon to make in directing the affairs of their respective enterprises.
>
> The soundness of such decisions when made in good faith and with a reasonable basis cannot ordinarily be challenged in a court of law. If, after considering the facts in this case, you find that the managing officers of the Honolulu Advertiser entered into the joint operating agreement in the honest belief that otherwise the Honolulu Advertiser wasn't likely to remain or become financially sound, you must find that the defendants are qualified for the exception provided in the Newspaper Preservation Act and render your verdict in favor of the defendants.

The judge further told the jury that "it must analyze the facts as they would have appeared to a reasonably well informed observer in 1962."

On the newspapers' request for a directed verdict on the merits and a ruling that the city had waited too long after the joint plan was established (seventeen years) to bring its lawsuit, the judge said he would rule later. He set October 12 as the deadline for both sides to file legal briefs on the issue of the city's long delay.

The jury deliberated for eight hours, until 9 P.M., and then was released for the weekend. At 3:58 P.M. on Monday the jury forewoman said the panel was hopelessly deadlocked. Judge Martin Pence, filling in for Curtis, who had had to return to Los Angeles, announced a hung jury and dismissed the jurors.

Talking with reporters outside the building, jurors said that first they were four-to-two in favor of the newspapers but finally split three-to-three. They couldn't agree on the *Advertiser*'s financial condition in 1962 or on the credibility of the expert witnesses. One said, "If we could only bring them back" to testify—referring to the newspaper officials and board members who had died in the two decades between the start of the joint plan and the trial itself.

Twigg-Smith said that without information from departed witnesses "I can't blame [the jurors] for being confused." He observed that the case had cost the newspapers close to $2 million, and he speculated, with later confirmation by city counsel, that the city spent some $500,000, excluding its contingency-fee lawyers, who would get paid only if the city won.

Legal briefs, essentially repeating arguments voiced during the trial, were filed in October. On February 10, 1983, Judge Curtis filed his twenty-seven-page decision, ruling in favor of the newspapers both on the merits of the case and the unreasonableness of the city's seventeen-year delay in bringing its suit.

As to the latter, he said the statute of limitations, which began to run in 1970, on passage of the Newspaper Preservation Act, and expired in 1974, was "to protect against the prosecution of stale claims and to prevent prejudice occurring from the loss of records, dim memories and the death of witnesses."

As to the merits, he upheld the joint newspaper operation and the *Advertiser*'s entitlement to a limited exemption from the antitrust statutes. He noted the paper's "serious financial trouble for many years" and the evidence that the management in good faith believed the joint plan was necessary to preserve a separate editorial voice in the community.

He took note of the fact that in 1960 the *Advertiser* "suffered a net loss of $110,615, whereas the Star-Bulletin had a net income of $888,591; in 1961 the Advertiser suffered a net loss of $72,395, whereas the Star-Bulletin had a net income of $896,973."

The judge was unimpressed with the testimony of the two expert witnesses, which had cost the parties more than a half-million dollars, saying "they have largely neutralized, if not destroyed, the persuasiveness of each other's testimony."

Regarding the jury, he stated "that no jury composed of reasonable people who understood and followed my instructions could come to any other conclusion" than it had "in the light of the evidence taken as a whole."

Reaction to the decision was unsurprising. Twigg-Smith, *Star-Bulletin* publisher Philip T. Gialanella, and Hawaii Newspaper Guild executive Roy Kruse, were pleased. State Senator Duke Kawasaki, who had long sought repeal of the state's Newspaper Preservation Act and was a courtroom observer throughout the trial, called it a bad decision by a biased judge.

On March 10, 1983, the City Council voted eight-to-zero to not appeal Curtis' ruling, but the battle was not yet over. At 11:45 P.M. on Monday, March 14— fifteen minutes before the deadline—four opponents of the newspapers asked the federal courts for permission to file an appeal.

Kawasaki, former Mayor Fasi (who for one term lost his seat to Eileen Anderson), state Senator Lehua Fernandes Salling of Kauai, and tire dealer Lex Brodie asked for standing as buyers of "expensive" advertising. It was left to Judge Curtis to decide whether the foursome could contest his decision in the 9th Circuit Court of Appeals.

On May 16 Judge Curtis ruled that Fasi and the others could intervene in place of the city, and with a new attorney, rather than Cooper, they did so. The newspapers reacted by filing in federal court a claim against the group for $685,000 in trial costs that had been waived for City Hall. On September 17 Curtis ruled that if their appeal failed, Fasi, Kawasaki, Salling, and Brodie would indeed be liable for that amount.

Fasi called the ruling "blackmail," but he and his cointervenors lost their enthusiasm for the appeal and they asked the appellate court to dismiss it with "prejudice," meaning there would be no reinstatement of an appeal or refiling of the original suit by any of them. This was conditioned on the newspapers' willingness to not press for collection of trial costs. The papers agreed—and thus ended, presumably for good, the challenge to the legitimacy of the joint operation.

But it would not inhibit Fasi's cries of "monopoly" and his attacks on the *Advertiser* and *Star-Bulletin*, which continued in the years that followed.

44

A New Publisher and a New Mood

BETWEEN MAN and nature Island newspeople in the 1980s were kept on the run. Hurricane Iwa battered Kauai, damaged parts of Oahu, and subjected the *Advertiser* to seven hours of power outages and surges, delaying paper deliveries until late the next morning and into the afternoon.

An Aleutian earthquake triggered a tsunami alert, which fizzled after creating massive traffic jams in low-lying neighborhoods. And on the Big Island Kilauea volcano began a years-long eruption.

When the pesticide heptachlor was found in milk, the state yanked dairy products off Oahu store shelves. Ailing Philippines President Ferdinand Marcos, with his wife Imelda and entourage, arrived after being toppled by Corazon Aquino, and generated headlines for the three years before his death. St. Francis Hospital surgeons performed Hawaii's first heart transplant.

The islands' usually serene skies turned tragic. An Aloha Airlines plane lost a stretch of its fuselage in flight, killing an attendant and hurting sixty-one passengers, but was safely landed on Maui. Another Aloha craft disappeared and was found splashed on an East Molokai ridge, with all twenty aboard dead. And a hole that ruptured the fuselage in a United flight soon after liftoff from Honolulu sucked out nine passengers.

There was also bad news on the ground. Citizens saw crime as a major and growing issue, the number-one concern in the *Advertiser*'s Oahu public opinion polls. They called for an improvement in the criminal justice system, with more police officers and a strong prosecutor being elected, rather than appointed, for the first time.

The *Advertiser* said "Hawaii has coasted on its incredible beauty and the unbelievable aloha spirit for so long . . . but there are challenges for tourism ahead, and the crime problem is only one of them."

Increased petroleum costs, which substantially boosted air fares to the Islands, were an added burden. "If the potential visitor . . . gets the impression that it will not only be cheaper, but safer, to go somewhere else, it will take more than flowery advertising to bring him here."[1]

Some years later, people told the paper's pollsters that traffic and transportation had moved to the top of their worries list, followed by housing, education, crime, and the need for jobs.

The *Advertiser* contended that rush-hour traffic headaches weren't curable by just more buses and more freeways. At "some point we have to decide not whether we need a rapid transit system, but how and when we can afford it."[2] The paper saw rapid transit as desirable now and inevitable someday for the central Honolulu corridor and was greatly troubled when the proposed system landed on the shelf.

Like many, perhaps most, of its Oahu readers, the *Advertiser* was disenchanted by the quality of its municipal government. It said the City Council "lacked leadership, style, vision and island-wide perspective." It scored "secret dealings, pettiness [and] foot-dragging" and the politicos' disdain for "the attitude and input of community groups."

The council's chairman, Rudy Pacarro, had been elected outright in the 1982 primary election for lack of an opponent—and the paper, calling him "a central figure in the mixture of conniving and chaos," said that didn't mean he should be named chairman again. "Nor does it mean that the people of Honolulu have to put up with another four years from much of the same old gang doing favors for friends and other special interests."[3]

The need, it said, was for a new City Council that would modernize and sanitize the legislative branch at City Hall. A petition for a recall election failed for lack of sufficient names. But in the next few years, either by failing to run or by defeat at the polls, Pacarro and the other five targets were off the council.

In the 1982 state election the *Advertiser* continued to endorse Governor Ariyoshi, who won over Republican Andy Anderson and Frank Fasi running as an independent Democrat. And two years later it backed Eileen Anderson for mayor of Honolulu in her defeat of Fasi, who failed to take her campaign seriously. It then supported her for reelection, but Fasi, running hard, retrieved the office.

In the 1986 primary, the paper sought reform at the state level:

> For, while the Burns-Ariyoshi years brought largely positive or at least sincere governance, the very length of their tenure also had a side effect: It produced a network of wheeler-dealers interested in gains for themselves, legal and illegal rather than the public good. . . .
>
> That "old boy network" must be cut off from the Capitol if Hawaii is to attain the degrees of reform and the fresh start it needs.[4]

Seeking that, the paper endorsed Congressman Cecil Heftel, something of a maverick, over Lieutenant Governor John Waihee. A supporter of Waihee quickly bought an ad accusing the paper of being influenced by its president's contribution to the Heftel campaign.

Twigg-Smith promptly replied that the paper, as a matter of policy, had not made corporate contributions to candidates or officeholders, but that executives and editors had been free to contribute to candidates of their choice. He said that in his "commitment to the democratic election process" he had contributed to candidates of all parties—in the current campaign including Heftel, Waihee, Anderson, and many others.

As a result of the criticism, however, he instituted a new policy "that executives, managers and editors of the Honolulu Advertiser will not financially support any incumbent officeholder or any candidate running for public office." The objective was to preclude any appearance of conflict and to "maintain our integrity by providing objective, unbiased reporting in our news columns and to continue independent viewpoints on the editorial page."[5]

Despite this flap, when Waihee won the primary, the *Advertiser* preferred him in the general election to Republican Andy Anderson. And four years later it endorsed him for reelection, which he won, for having brought a new activism to state government. Disappointingly, this second term was marred by scandal.

But at the paper political and all other kinds of news took a back seat to an electrifying announcement on Sunday, May 4, 1986. Philip T. Gialanella, who only three weeks before had left the *Star-Bulletin* and the Gannett Company, had now joined his arch rival, the Honolulu *Advertiser*. He was to be both publisher of the *Advertiser* and president of the media division of Persis, the newspaper's parent company. The latter post involved overseeing a number of recently acquired small mainland newspapers and a cable company in the Seattle area.

Even though Twigg-Smith would remain as president of Persis and the *Advertiser*, and chief executive officer of both, with Gialanella reporting to him, the staff was instantly apprehensive. It feared that what had been the somewhat informal environment of a family newspaper would yield to an impersonal corporate atmosphere.

Twigg-Smith, at sixty-six, saw Gialanella, ten years his junior, as a natural successor in due course, since none of the Twigg-Smith children showed any interest in newspapering. To him it was a prudent move to bring aboard "the consummate newspaper operator."[6]

And that, everyone in the business, locally and nationally, acknowledged. Phil Gialanella was like a major character in a Horatio Alger story. The son of Italian immigrants in Binghamton, New York—his father was a shoemaker— he began working as a teenager in the mailroom of the local Gannett paper. With money saved, he earned bachelor's and master's degrees, taught high school English for a year, but couldn't shake off the spell of newspapering. On Gannett papers in New York, New Jersey, and Connecticut he rose from promotion director to vice-president/general manager to president/publisher.

He arrived in the Islands in 1971 at age forty-five as executive vice-president of the Hawaii Newspaper Agency and then president, a post he continued to fill after being named publisher of the *Star-Bulletin*, which Gannett had acquired that same year from local owners. He additionally took on regional duties for Gannett and then became in 1982 the president of *USA Today*, the nation's first truly national newspaper, all the while maintaining his Hawaii ties.

Why did he come to the *Advertiser?* Al Neuharth, the chief of Gannett, wanted Gialanella to take on top-tier duties on the mainland—but Gialanella loved Hawaii and the idea of heading one paper and a small mainland group appealed to him. He was already wealthy and wanted to enjoy life.

Despite a publisher's power, he avoided the social whirl, had a close circle of friends, mostly Oriental, most notably Chinn Ho. He respected and liked Twigg-Smith but never invited him to his house. He wore expensive but informal clothes and shunned socks—and didn't care what anyone thought about it.

When asked by *Honolulu Magazine* in a July 1986 interview what exactly would he be doing as *Advertiser* publisher, he gave a self-effacing answer:

> George Chaplin, Bucky Buchwach and Twigg-Smith are probably the three biggest reasons why the Advertiser is here today. Those guys went through hell to bring this paper to this point in time. They took the paper when it was losing money, there was even a question as to whether they'd even be able to continue publishing. It was done with three people making these contributions, both on the news side as well as on the business side. Twigg, as publisher, made as many contributions to the news side as George and Bucky. What we've done now is just add a fourth to the equation.

He was, of course, infinitely more than that. Recognizing his talent and dynamism, Twigg-Smith let him largely run the operation, most obviously the day-to-day functions.

Gialanella had a unique management style; he liked keeping his top managers off balance with frequent criticism. By design, he was aloof from the run of employees but expected loyalty from key subordinates and gave it in return. He was able, he was tough, at times to the point of what seemed to some to be ruthlessness, and he maximized the bottom line, bringing to the business side of the *Advertiser* all he had learned in his years with Gannett. As to those who grumbled about his bottom-line orientation, his expressed view was that a paper had to be a financial success if it wanted to maintain its independence.

Concurrent with Gialanella's arrival at the *Advertiser* were several other major personnel changes.

At seventy-two, I was to retire as editor-in-chief on December 1, the twenty-eighth anniversary of my appointment as editor, to be succeeded by longtime friend and colleague Buck Buchwach, sixty-five, the executive editor. *Advertiser* editorial policy, which Twigg-Smith said would remain unchanged, would be reviewed by a newly named editorial board consisting of Twigg-Smith, Gialanella, Buchwach, editorial-page editor John Griffin, and this writer.

At Persis, Paul deVille, long active in its real estate activities, would head a new investment division, and Twigg-Smith's brother David would be vice-president for strategic planning.

During my remaining six months on the job, Gialanella left the editorial department strictly alone, made no suggestions, asked for no reports, allowing me the essentially free hand I had enjoyed during my many years with Twigg-Smith.

Once I left, that abruptly changed. Marked-up *Advertiser*s often accompanied by blistering memos about stories he saw as falling short were routinely sent to editors, although in personal discussions he tended to be pleasant. He made frequent story suggestions, often good since he was "plugged in" to the community. He disliked small talk and seemed uncomfortable, almost shy, among people he didn't know.

Editorials for the next day were discussed with him at four o'clock the afternoon before, and although they usually passed muster, he was not bashful about making changes in content. It was said that while he might not know what he liked, he clearly knew what he disliked.

Despite Mayor Fasi's bashing of the newspapers, Gialanella, possibly because of their common ethnicity, felt he could bring him around. Within months, the illusion ended in a shouting match on a golf course.

As long as expenses were under control and his views were carried out, Gialanella was at one with the staff in wanting a good newspaper. In 1988, UPI, an *Advertiser* staple since the early 1900s, but which of late had rapidly deteriorated, was replaced by the Associated Press news and photo service.

Even more important, in symbol and fact, was the *Advertiser*'s moving into first place in daily circulation, something unimaginable in, say, 1958, when the paper had less than half the *Star-Bulletin* count, 46,874 to 99,961.

The *Star-Bulletin*'s dominance had continued for years, reaching a peak in 1973 of 131,529 to 77,123. From then on, the *Star-Bulletin* declined, suffering from the inroads throughout the United States of TV news against afternoon newspapers and, *Advertiser* people believed, a steadily improving morning product.

In November 1988 the *Advertiser* had jumped to 97,179, compared to the *Star-Bulletin*'s 96,347. Thereafter the spread widened substantially—103,877 to 87,021 in 1992 and on to 107,038 versus 82,859 in 1994. The Sunday paper continued to hover around the 200,000 mark.

Three months after Gialanella's arrival, he and Twigg-Smith were ready to make a number of supervisory changes. In the upper brackets, Mike Middlesworth, for thirteen years managing editor, was named to the new post of business manager, to oversee newsroom budgeting and electronic operations and perform some corporate duties for the Persis papers in the northwest. He was succeeded by Gerry Keir, then forty-two, city editor since 1974, who would report to Buchwach.

Every paper needs at least one character, and on the reporting level, the staff gained a writer with a Damon Runyan touch who brought a special flair. He could inject satire or humor into almost any story. He could handle the serious but enjoyed the offbeat, the little dramas of human life.

Will Hoover's prejournalism experience helped. He'd been an award-winning song writer, a theatrical photographer, a bartender, a beauty salon chain operator. He had the knack of making people talk. Once a murder suspect stammered out a confession; a woman told him she'd revealed more to him in minutes than to her husband in thirty years.

An Iowan, he had freelanced for a dozen years before going to the *Des Moines Register* for eight years. In Honolulu he quickly settled in, and his byline guaranteed a good read. He appeared by invitation on the TV show "Magnum P.I.," reportedly the only journalist to do so, after a story he did on real detectives in Honolulu intrigued the producer.

He interviewed Ferdinand and Imelda Marcos and covered the former's wake. And on the twentieth anniversary of Martin Luther King's death he questioned the convicted assassin, James Earl Ray, who gave the *Advertiser* the only advance copy of his forthcoming book on the tragedy. Hoover's series that followed gave readers the first look at Ray's detailed account of what happened on April 4, 1968, plus an inside view of the prisoner himself.

On December 1, as scheduled, Buchwach realized his dream of going through all the chairs from reporter to editor of the *Advertiser*, the first in the paper's history to do so. He was not in good health—like others in his family he had coronary ailments—and he wanted only a couple of years in the top spot.

He was, as former City Editor Zalburg described him, "a tremendously gifted editor. He was able to catch instantly the flavor, pitch and value of a news story. He also knew instantly what makes right or wrong with a story and how to mend it. Almost automatically he made sound news judgments. He had a sixth sense that told him what can 'grab' the reader. All these assets had been honed to a hard edge."[7]

Buck, as everyone, including the copy boys, called him, brought liveliness, excitement, vitality to his job, while meeting his responsibility to the writing of history-on-the-run.

He enjoyed celebrities and gravitated toward them. As an *Advertiser* reporter he interviewed seven U.S. presidents and such other notables as General Douglas MacArthur, Madame Chiang Kai-shek, Admiral Chester Nimitz, and foreign leaders Syngman Rhee, Anthony Eden, and Robert Menzies.

He drove Jackie Kennedy around town in his red convertible, was a guest at Frank Sinatra's home, and had lunch cooked for him by Shirley Temple.

He traveled on every kind of transportation, from Henry Kaiser's hydroplane to the nuclear submarine *Nautilus*. He held hands with Helen Keller, was kissed by a flock of film stars from Rita Hayworth to Dorothy Lamour.

But he never forgot who he was and his work proved it, even or especially when he was on vacation. Bob Krauss has cited notable examples:

Buchwach was in Paris in 1967 when an anti–Hubert Humphrey student riot broke out. He picked up an anti-Humphrey "Paix in Viet Nam" placard and waved it while escaping unscathed to cable a story.

He was in Chicago when President John Kennedy was killed, immediately booked a flight for Washington and covered the funeral.

In 1960 he interviewed convicted killer Caryl Chessman on death row at San Quentin. Chessman told Buchwach he'd like to go to Hawaii "to get away from everything."

Buchwach was at the door of the U.S. House of Representatives in 1954 waiting to see an old friend, Rep. Walter Norblad, when shots rang out.

A few minutes later, Rep. Walter Judd, a doctor, came out with blood on his hands. Five congressmen had just been shot and wounded by fanatical Puerto Rican assassins.

Buchwach got an exclusive interview with moon walker Buzz Aldrin at Cocoa Beach during Aldrin's last unrestricted weekend before the historic moon space shot.

In 1963 Buchwach sent in stories about four major football games in five days: the East/West Shrine game in San Francisco, the NFL game between the New York Giants and Chicago Bears in Chicago, the Sun Bowl game in El Paso and the Cotton Bowl game in Dallas.

As a reporter, Buchwach covered the world as if it were Kalihi. As an editor, he deployed his reporters like a general on the battlefield, and was at his best on election day. . . .

One year Buck won four of the top eight writing awards in the Honolulu Press Club's annual statewide contest. He was honored by the American Political Science Association and other organizations. But his greatest prize— the one he coveted most—was passing the *Star-Bulletin* in daily circulation while he was still active.

That achieved, at the end of December 1988 he stepped down, to be succeeded by Gerry Keir, forty-five, a twenty-year veteran at the paper. Twigg-Smith called Keir "the best man anywhere to lead the Advertiser into the 21st century," and Gialanella said he was "a first-class newsman . . . more than ready to move the Advertiser to new heights."

Keir had joined the paper in 1968 after two years of working weekends while on Army duty as a captain at Schofield Barracks. In time he moved up from general assignment reporter to politics editor and chief of the state capitol bureau to city editor, 1974–1986, and managing editor, 1986–1988.

He covered national political conventions, including the Democratic in Miami Beach in 1972, marked by massive anti-Vietnam War demonstrations. His astute reporting brought him a fax from Buchwach telling him he'd done a good job and that "in violation of all Nixon wage-price guidelines" Buck was ordering a $50 bonus.

At the capitol bureau he had earned a reputation for fairness, intelligence, and hard work. He gained the respect of those in the legislature, in the governor's office, and in executive posts of all the counties.

As managing editor he proved he was "computer friendly," worked closely with the executives of other departments, while protecting editorial integrity. And, he was appreciated as the able overseer of the paper's public opinion polling.

On his first day as editor, under a Focus section headline, "Blending Change and Tradition at The Advertiser," Keir wrote that the *Advertiser* remained "a locally-owned paper with its roots deep in this community," and with no planned shift in editorial policy, while staying abreast of change:

> We aim to tell you the most important stories with the detail and expertise that you can find nowhere else, and to supplement that with easy-to-read, time-saving news briefs from the Islands, the nation, and the world. We want to help you see how Hawaii fits into the Pacific Rim and the rest of the world.[8]

He promised fair news coverage, with quick correction of errors, and urged readers to say what they liked and didn't like about the paper—which had just named two women as managing editors, Anne Harpham for news, Susan Yim for features and design.

And in praising predecessors Keir noted that "the editors on our staff have lived here an average of 21 years apiece. Our many talented reporters, photographers, copy editors and artists are still on the job—people such as senior political pundit Jerry Burris, master storyteller Bob Krauss, columnists Wayne Harada and Don Chapman and many others." And the editorial-page editor, John Griffin, was hailed as "a talented professional with more than three decades of experience in Asia and the Pacific."[9]

For Keir, as he had been for Buchwach and earlier for me, Griffin was a strong right arm, a warm, knowledgeable, sensitive overseer of the *Advertiser*'s opinion columns, the heart of the paper. He was a quiet, studious man, a facile writer, with a strong sense of justice and a deep affection for Asia.

In earlier days he suffered from restlessness—here for a while, then off, then back. From the Navy Air Corps here in the 1940s he left to start college, returned to the University of Hawaii in 1950, joined the *Star-Bulletin* (copy boy and up to labor and politics beats), then a year at Bristol University in England, back to the *Bulletin*, next to the Associated Press in Asia, then to the *Advertiser* in 1962 covering politics, next to the Peace Corps, back to the *Advertiser* as associate editor, off on a South Pacific fellowship. It took until the 1970s for him to settle down.

He admitted to friends that when away, even as an AP correspondent chasing big stories in Asia, he felt something was lacking because what he was covering was not about "his" community.

When he took over the editorial pages it was somewhat reluctantly, since he had the typical reporter's aversion to writing opinion rather than straight facts. But he soon realized that the editorial page could help influence events in a place he cared deeply about. The point was driven home in the mid-1960s when the paper's editorial campaign helped save Diamond Head from high-rise development. And at times the paper had had influence on elections and key city and state decisions.

Griffin enjoyed election nights for two reasons. One was watching the newsroom function as a smooth, effective team under Buchwach's planning. The other was the rush he had on deadline, turning out two or three editorials on the results, from president to governor to mayor to other important races or trends. Sometimes he had to sweat out the results, holding and changing editorials right to deadline when the outcome hung in the balance.

But he found it all satisfying, especially in the days of the "ohana" with Twigg-Smith as leader and *Advertiser* editorial executives Buchwach, Griffin, and this writer.

Everyone at the paper knew of Buck's heart problems—his several major and minor attacks, his two bypass surgeries, about which he was totally fatalistic, never showing the slightest concern. But still it came as a shock when, after collapsing at home and being taken to Queen's Hospital, he died at 11:47 P.M. on September 3, 1989. Despite the late hour, the *Advertiser* was able to squeeze in a front-page bulletin. Buck would have been unhappy if the competition had gotten first crack at his departure.

Colleagues and officials had kind words to say about Buck, Mayor Fasi among them. But as to the *Advertiser*, a few months earlier, Fasi said it was "not even good wrapping paper for garbage." He put on a $10,000 TV and radio

Three Advertiser editors: George Chaplin (1958–1986), Buck Buchwach (1986–1988), and Gerry Keir (1988–1995).

blitz against both dailies and their "biased stories and editorials," said he hoped to "hurt them in the pocketbook" and pledged to go "round after round until I die."[10]

The same year, an editorial declared that Ferdinand Marcos' desired return from Hawaii to the Philippines to die should be decided by President Corazon Aquino. An accompanying cartoon depicted Aquino's late husband, Benigno, sprawled in a pool of blood at the bottom of airliner steps and quoted Marcos' son, Ferdinand, Jr.: "No civilized nation would deny a citizen the right to die in his homeland."[11]

Marcos loyalists in the Islands—believed to be about half of the Filipinos in residence—exploded in outrage. Several hundred assembled in a restaurant parking lot, with effigies of Editorial Page Editor Griffin and cartoonist Dick Adair. Their plan to burn the figures ran afoul of police, who explained it would be unlawful as a fire hazard. So they pulled out knives and a jagged-tooth handsaw and set about hacking apart the effigies, which were then trampled on and tossed into an outdoor barbecue pit, topped by two wooden crosses.

Letters to the editor were divided, some praising the editorial and cartoon, others branding them as vicious.

45

Nearly a Century Ends in a Sale

AS HAWAII entered the 1990s and looked toward the twenty-first century, absentee ownership of Island enterprises—including the *Star-Bulletin,* television stations, three of the Big Five companies, major department stores, many hotels, large drugstores, and some supermarkets—was an accepted reality.

But the *Advertiser* was seen as an exception, an Island-rooted, community-minded business that had been in the hands of one missionary-descended family for almost a century.

So it came as blockbuster news on September 3, 1992, that the Twigg-Smith family, through its Persis Corporation, would be selling the *Advertiser,* including building and land, to the Gannett Company, the nation's largest newspaper chain, for some $250 million.

Late the day before, Twigg-Smith conducted a newsroom meeting with *Advertiser* staffers and told them first: "As an old newsman who worked the streets and edited news before the age of computers, I can't recall a more difficult [story] to write." Then he read the lead of the news that would break in the morning.

Boards of both companies had approved the sale plan that would go to *Advertiser* stockholders on October 26, with the deal to be closed no later than January 31, 1993. Gannett would sell the *Star-Bulletin* to comply with antitrust laws barring the company from owning both Honolulu dailies.

The usually noisy newsroom was pin-drop silent as the incredulous staff hung on to Twigg-Smith's every word. "This wasn't an easy decision to make even for an old gaffer like me," he explained, "and the root of it is that matter of age, that Big 71 I passed two weeks ago." The decision was based entirely on that, and on the diverse interests within his ever-growing family, and "how best to plan for the future of the Advertiser."

> This paper has been in our family for nearly 100 of its 136 years and I've been associated with the businesses in this building for 55 of those 136 years, the past nearly 47 with the Advertiser. . . . I had hoped for years that some member of the family would want to be the candidate to succeed me and be put forward by his peers the way I was after World War II. Not so. . . .

> So what to do? It seemed to me that now was pretty much my last
> chance to make sure the Advertiser and all of your jobs would continue in
> full force. And although we've fought the Gannettoids for years it finally
> dawned on me that our best chance for the long term lies in joining them.
> They liked the idea and here we are. . . .
>
> I guess my greatest satisfaction has been being here to see the Advertiser
> become number one. And that's crowned now by knowing that we're turning
> the mantle over to a good and capable bunch of guys who'll keep it that way.

He said he would remain as *Advertiser* chairman because Gannett wanted him around for his community involvement. But he would have no hand in
operations. I remained as editor-at-large on the same basis.

With Twigg-Smith in the newsroom were Gannett executives headed by
the chain's chairman and chief executive officer, John Curley. He had changed
into an *Advertiser* aloha shirt moments after breaking the news to *Star-
Bulletin* employees. The *Advertiser* would become the eighty-third paper
owned by Gannett, whose other properties included the national *USA Today,*
the newspaper magazine *USA Weekend,* ten TV stations, fifteen radio stations,
and leases for outdoor ad displays in eleven states.

Mayor Fasi, perennial critic, said the deal "just goes to show you how
profitable having a monopoly can be. In 1962 The Advertiser was nearly
broke. Now I see Gannett thinks it's worth $250 million."[1]

On October 26 *Advertiser* stockholders, all family members, unanimously
approved the sale. Remaining obstacles—an Internal Revenue Service ruling
that the sale doesn't violate tax-free exchange rules, and sale by Gannett of
the *Star-Bulletin*—were soon cleared.

On January 30, 1993, sales of both the *Advertiser* and *Star-Bulletin* were
complete. The *Star-Bulletin*'s new owner was Liberty Newspapers, an
Arkansas limited partnership headed by Rupert E. Phillips, a Florida newspaper investor-broker. Documents were signed without fanfare in a downtown
law office. Persis shareholders were getting $100 million in Gannett stock,
and Gannett was taking over about $150 million in Persis liabilities, largely
incurred in acquiring a number of mainland newspapers and some real estate.

Several major changes in operation were involved:

- The joint publishing plan, due to run for fifty years, was cut back to twenty,
  with automatic five-year renewals unless one of the papers objected twenty-
  four months before expiration of the agreement.
- The Hawaii Newspaper Agency, in which both papers had had a voice,
  would be managed solely by Gannett.
- Gannett gained the right to terminate the *Star-Bulletin*'s Saturday paper
  or have it switched to morning publication if economics dictated it.
  Liberty could sell the *Star-Bulletin* but only with Gannett's consent.
- The previous formula for sharing net profit between the two papers—60

percent for the *Star-Bulletin*, 40 percent for the *Advertiser*—was superseded by an infinitely less attractive schedule of payments to the *Star-Bulletin*'s new owner.

Liberty's share of profits would step up incrementally from $1.4 million in 1993 to $2.5 million in 2012, the year of the contract expiration. An *Advertiser* story said, "The amended joint operating agreement shows the Hawaii Newspaper Agency handling the non-editorial functions of the two newspapers may have a $60.8 million profit this year excluding newsroom, working capital and other expenses. The profit is projected to increase to $153.6 million in 2012, according to the forecast."[2]

Twigg-Smith said, "It's a good deal all the way around," ensuring two separately owned, editorially independent newspapers for the next twenty years.[3]

John Morton of Washington, a highly regarded newspaper financial analyst, said shifting to the *Advertiser* side of the News Building "was a smart move on the part of Gannett. Obviously the Advertiser had been catching up with the Star-Bulletin and put Gannett in a tough position. The logical way out of this was to buy the Advertiser."[4]

He predicted that the *Advertiser* might take on a slightly different look in keeping with Gannett theories about graphics and organization of news stories. And he noted that Gannett newspapers are expected to subscribe to News2000, a company program telling how newspapers can better serve readers.

Once Gannett took over the *Advertiser*, Philip Gialanella retired as publisher but would continue to help Persis with its mainland properties—three dailies and two weeklies in the state of Washington and one daily near Knoxville, Tennessee. He was succeeded by Gannett's Richard Hartnett, who would also retain his duties as head of the Hawaii Newspaper Agency.

In the fall of 1993 Gialanella was diagnosed as having a brain tumor. He underwent surgery, but died January 28, 1994. In May Persis sold its mainland papers.

Predictably, the transition from a family paper, locally owned, to a chain operation was not without trauma. There were substantial changes in the approach to news coverage and in newsroom management itself. The staff found itself using Gannett's News2000 plan, which blueprinted a new philosophy of reporting approach, news gathering, and news values. Since most papers everywhere were losing circulation, this was an understandable effort to find ways to stem the tide by better covering their communities.

But the *Advertiser* was, in fact, growing, presumably a reflection of reader satisfaction. Still, editors consulted social trends, opinion surveys, and U.S. Census data, and staffers were encouraged to ask people at random about their problems and concerns and whether they felt the paper was mirroring those in its coverage. As a result, the *Advertiser* overhauled the beats its reporters covered and made other changes. It was an unsettling time in the newsroom. This was furthered by the fact that twice a year a panel of editors from Gannett papers met at corporate headquarters in Virginia and, using the chain's standards, graded papers' performance.

It was a body blow to the *Advertiser*'s proud staffers and to their morale when their publication, in the first evaluation in early 1994, was ranked the worst of Gannett's eighty-three papers by News2000 criteria. The editors worked at shoring things up and there was progress, with the *Advertiser*'s News2000 score gaining every six months; but by mid-1995 it was still rated lowest among Gannett's dozen or so big-city papers.

Yet, within months, a national panel of outside editors, judging the annual "Best of Gannett" contest for 1995, gave the *Advertiser* the top awards for public service and spot news among the chain's "Metro" papers—in such cities as Detroit, Cincinnati, Des Moines, Louisville, and Nashville. The public service recognition was for news stories and editorials in an ongoing investigation into abuses in the state prison system. The spot news prize was for coverage of the fiftieth anniversary of the victorious end of World War II.

This acknowledgment of quality journalism provided balm for the staff's bruised self-esteem. But there was still the disquieting reality of longtime stability yielding to a revolving door. Editorial Page Editor John Griffin retired at sixty-five, as he'd long planned to do. He was succeeded by Jerry Burris, respected city editor and a veteran political writer and columnist. Mark Matsunaga was named city editor, but after a year went back to reporting. Griffin's wife, Susan Yim, managing editor for features, resigned to freelance and travel with her husband. Anne Harpham, managing editor for news, moved to a nonmanagement post.

Brought in from mainland papers were a city editor (Dan Nakaso from Hearst's *San Francisco Examiner*), a managing editor (M. J. Smith from the *Hartford Courant*, a Times-Mirror paper), and an executive editor (John Hollon, from Gannett's paper in Great Falls, Montana).

Finally, in September 1995, Editor Gerry Keir called the staff together and stood on the newsroom steps to the library—site of many retirement speeches and the place where Twigg-Smith had announced the sale of the paper. Keir said he, too, was leaving. He thus ended a twenty-seven-year career with the *Advertiser* to become senior vice-president for corporate communications at the First Hawaiian Bank.

In December, to succeed Keir, Jim Gatti, a fifty-two-year-old veteran newsman, came from Gannett's *Detroit News*. He had served there as city editor, national editor, and news editor, then as deputy managing editor heading the news operation. Commenting on Hawaii's East-West location, he pledged to continue "to reflect this community's needs and concerns."

All of the new editors and Publisher Larry Fuller, who had a solid newsroom background, cared about the paper. But clearly the *Advertiser* had shifted from almost a century of ownership by a local family to an outpost of American corporate journalism. One era had ended and another had begun.

Appendix

Thank heaven the day at length has dawned when the Hawaiian Nation can boast a free press, untrammelled by government patronage or party pledges, unbiased by ministerial frowns or favors—a press whose aim shall be the advancement of the nation in its commercial, political and social condition.

The day that witnessed the abolition by Liholiho Iolani of the tyrannous system of tabus, which had crushed with despotic power from the most ancient days, the liberties of this people will not be longer remembered than that which witnessed the advent of free thought and free principles throughout the group.

That such a press, truly independent and free, has long been needed here, all must admit; but to establish one on a permanent basis, and to conduct it in such a manner as to give general satisfaction and produce good results in a community made up of such various elements as ours, is an undertaking of so great risk that few have been willing to attempt it.

It is needed in the family to enliven the social evening circle. It is needed in the counting room of the merchant whose eye glances instinctively to the marine and commercial news. It is needed in the farm house and on the distant plantation to convey thence whatever is transpiring at the metropolis and throughout the kingdom.

It is needed by the wealthy shipowner abroad who seeks reliable advices from his cruising vessels. It is needed in the palace and the government halls, that the rulers of the nation may feel the throbbing of the public heart and guide their councils with discreetness. And lastly, it is needed by the intelligent native who is seeking to extend the sphere of his knowledge by the acquisition of our noble mother tongue.

We want a medium for expression of public thought—some mirror to portray our national features—some fit representative to bear to the enlightened nations of the earth the badges of our dignity and worth, not of our ignorance and vulgarity, and that will command from them respect and esteem.

The time has come when the attempt shall again be made, when the reading, thinking laboring portion of the community, who are the life and soul of the nation, shall have an organ adapted to their necessities, breathing their thoughts, carrying the spirit of enterprize [*sic*] to every portion of the king-dom and breaking through the crust of indolence and lethargy which is fast burying this nation and must soon seal its fate, like the mighty stream of lava rolling down the sides of Moana Loa, which turns the hitherto impenetrable forest into a dreary waste.

We therefore issue this morning the pioneer number of the *"Pacific Commercial Advertiser,"* a paper destined, we trust, to exert more than an ephemeral influence on the industrial and social condition of our community and nation. The principal objects of this paper have been set forth by the pub-lisher, some weeks since, which will be found on the first page. They certainly embrace a wide field, scarcely occupied at present, which will furnish materi-al to fill the medium-sized sheet on which *The Advertiser* is printed.

The main objects of a newspaper should be to encourage every branch of lawful industry—to be the exponent and leader of public opinion on the great questions of the day—to aim to make that public opinion powerful and irre-sistible—to second the government in all its honest efforts to improve physically and mentally the condition of the body politic—to frown with imperious scorn on every attempt to infringe popular rights and on every act that tends to violate the confidence reposed by the nation in those elevated to authority—in a word the public welfare—these we conceive to be the end and aim of a public press.

But the community such as this made up of inhabitants from every portion of the globe, from the frozen shores of northern Russia to the most southern portion of Africa, America or Australia, what can be looked for but diversity of thought and opinion on every subject that may be embraced in the columns of a newspaper, whether it be on morals, politics, religion or reforms.

One perhaps desires a paper to commence a fierce attack on the govern-ment and every member of it; another would have excluded from its columns everything that bears the semblance of the teachings of morality and religion, and devoted wholly to commercial intelligence; while a third would frown on every item that causes mirth and on notices of public amusements, but would have its columns wholly devoted to morality and religion.

In the outset of our enterprise, we might as well have a distinct under-standing with our patrons. To each and all of them we respectfully say, that in the form and style and general management of this paper and its contents, we must be left to our judgement, to act with entire independence.

To commence on any other basis, would be but to render our sheet what every former attempt has been, the tool of a party or the mouthpiece of a min-ister. Suggestions will always be cordially received; dictation never. To be entirely independent in what we have to say is all we seek, to show when occasion demands it, that the political wisdom of the nation is not all cen-tered within the radius of the flickerings of the foreign office candlelight, or how far the financial prosperity of the country is dependent on the move-ments of the Lord Treasurer.

"The days are rapidly passing away," says the London Times, "when any Newspaper of character can avow itself as the unflinching advocate of any party or any person—of anything, in fact, except that which ought to be the object of all periodicals as well as all permanent writing—the truth, the whole truth, and nothing but the truth. To give true narrative of passing events and to make on those events just, natural and pertinent reflections, is all to which we aspire, it being a matter to us of the purest indifference what party, what clique or what individual reputation may be damaged or promoted by our faithful and fearless discharge of the duty we undertake."

This is what we shall aim at—to give a truthful record of the present, and to point out the errors of the past, that they may afford experience for the future. If the policy of the government is clearly detrimental to the public interests, or the acts of its officials open to animadversion or reprehension, the errors of the former will be plainly pointed out, and the shortcoming of the latter fearlessly exposed and condemned.

As this paper is established for the public good, so its columns will always be open to a free and temperate discussion of matters of general interest. Correspondents will always be welcome, but they will bear in mind that brevity will be a chief recommendation to notice. We cannot allow anyone to monopolize our columns, however important the subject may be. Neither can personal abuse be allowed by us, nor our paper be prostituted to become the vehicle of petty individual disputes or party bickerings.

Doubts have been expressed to us in regard to the propriety of publishing a portion of our issue for the Hawaiian race. It may be that such a publication is not demanded by them but we think it is, and are willing at our own risk to make the trial. The truth is, the experiment of a sterling weekly paper, partly in English and partly in Hawaiian, ought to have been made by the Government years ago, instead of wasting its funds in foreign publications of doubtful utility.

The intellectual eyes of the native race have been opened for years, but beyond a few elementary columns, and some charitable attempts to provide newspapers for them, they have been and still are left to grope about, seeking light but finding little or none. There are intelligent natives here and throughout this group, who are desirous of knowing what is transpiring throughout the world, and who, finding their own dialect too limited, are striving to learn the English language. Such are willing to pay for a paper adapted to them, cost what it may. And though the experiment may not return to us its cost, yet, if at the end of the year our native list of subscribers is no larger than today, we shall rest satisfied with our efforts in their behalf.

Thus is our little bark launched on the uncertain tide of life. What she is—whether a full clipper of the most approved model, in hull, spars, sails and rigging, whether in short she is such a craft as is needed for the trade, or not, 'tis yours, also to help freight her with the produce, the wares and merchandise which you may have to dispose of.

It will be our duty to stand by the helm and ever keep a watchful eye to windward and with the compass and chart of experience to steer her over the shoals and reefs and breakers that may lie in our track. We cannot expect always to sail smoothly under our perpetual trade breeze, with studding-sails fore and aft. There are often squalls and gales slumbering unnoticed on the horizon of the most tranquil sky, while reefs and shoals are to be met in every voyage.

Notes

Part I. 1856–1880

1. A "Reliable Domestic Newspaper" Is Born

1. Henry M. Whitney, *Advertiser*, January 1, 1900.
2. *Polynesian*, May 3, 1856.
3. *Advertiser*, April 14, 1903.
4. Meiric K. Dutton, *Henry M. Whitney, Pioneer Printer-Publisher & Hawaii's First Postmaster* (Honolulu: Loomis House Press and Hale Pai a Lumiki, 1955).
5. *Advertiser*, April 14, 1903.
6. Ibid.
7. *Advertiser*, January 1, 1900.
8. Dutton, *Henry M. Whitney*.
9. Whitney, letter to cousin, June 2, 1851. Private collection.
10. J. F. Wooley, postmaster, "Postoffice Department of the Hawaiian Monarchy and Republic of Hawaii," *Thrum's Hawaiian Annual for 1931*, p. 34.
11. Whitney, letter to R. C. Wyllie, minister of foreign relations, November 22, 1854. Hawaii State Archives.
12. Whitney, letter to Keoni Ana, minister of interior, December 8, 1854. Hawaii State Archives.

2. "New Type, a New Press, a New Building"

1. Eleanor H. Davis, *Abraham Fornander, A Biography* (Honolulu: University Press of Hawaii, 1979), 118.
2. Davis, *Abraham Fornander*, 118.
3. Thomas F. Thrum, *Hawaiian Annual of 1877*.
4. Edward Scott, *The Saga of the Sandwich Islands* (Lake Tahoe, Nev.: Sierra-Tahoe Publishing Co., 1968), vol. 1, 55, quoting from the *Sandwich Island Gazette*.
5. Riley H. Allen, "Hawaii's Pioneers of Journalism." Paper read before the Social Science Association of Honolulu, January 7, 1929. Hawaiian Historical Society Annual Report for the Year 1928, 69–103.
6. Helen G. Chapin, "Newspapers of Hawaii, 1834 to 1903: From 'He Liona' to the Pacific Cable," *Hawaiian Journal of History* 18 (1984): 65.
7. *Advertiser*, January 1, 1900.
8. Joseph O. Carter, *Advertiser*, July 2, 1906.

9. Henry M. Whitney, "Historical Sketches," Hawaiian Gazette Co., Ltd., 1899.

10. Ibid.

11. Ibid.

12. *Advertiser*, October 3, 1861.

13. Rubellite Kinney Johnson, *Kukini 'Aha'ilono* (Honolulu: Topgallant Publishing Co., 1976).

14. Gavan Daws, "Honolulu: The First Century: Influences in the Development of the Town to 1876" (Ph.D. diss., University of Hawaii, 1966).

15. *Advertiser*, March 5, 1857.

16. *Advertiser*, January 22, 1870.

17. W. N. Armstrong, *Advertiser*, November 5, 1898.

18. Henry M. Whitney, letter to R. C. Wyllie, minister of foreign relations, March 18, 1861.

19. Henry M. Whitney, "Historical Sketches" (Honolulu: Hawaiian Gazette Co., Ltd., 1899).

20. *Advertiser*, February 22, 1981.

21. Henry M. Whitney, *Advertiser*, July 5, 1860.

3. "Going to Sea without a Passport"

1. *Advertiser*, March 8, 1860.

2. *Advertiser*, June 21, 1860.

3. *Advertiser*, August 17, 1867.

4. *Advertiser*, June 8, 1867.

5. *Advertiser*, April 23, 1857.

6. *Advertiser*, October 9, 1856.

7. *Advertiser*, December 18, 1869.

8. Gavan Daws, *Shoal of Time: A History of the Hawaiian Islands* (Honolulu: University of Hawaii Press, 1968).

9. *Advertiser*, August 23, 1860.

10. *Advertiser*, February 10, 1859.

11. *Advertiser*, August 15, 1861.

4. "We Shall Not Flinch from the Issue"

1. *Advertiser*, July 24, 1856.

2. *Advertiser*, September 25, 1856.

3. Johnson, *Kukiki 'Aha'ilono*.

4. *Advertiser*, July 2, 1856.

5. *Advertiser*, December 30, 1865.

6. *Advertiser*, December 11, 1869.

7. Daws, "Honolulu," 536.

8. *Advertiser*, September 14, 1869.

5. Amid the Press Battles, a Shocker

1. *Advertiser*, August 6, 1857.

2. *Advertiser*, August 20, 1857.

3. *Advertiser*, August 18, 1859.

4. *Advertiser*, February 24, 1859.

5. Privy Council Records, January 1859. Hawaii State Archives.

6. *Polynesian*, October 6, 1860.

7. *Advertiser*, July 10, 1862.

8. G. M. Robertson, interior minister, letter to Henry M. Whitney, February 6, 1864. Hawaii State Archives.

9. *Advertiser*, February 13, 1864.

10. Henry M. Whitney, "The PCA in Hawaii Nei," series, Hawaiian Gazette Co., 1899.

11. *Advertiser*, April 15, 1865.

12. *Advertiser*, April 1, 1865.

13. *Advertiser*, October 28, 1865.

14. *Advertiser*, September 8, 1866.

15. *Advertiser*, September 22, 1866.

16. *Advertiser*, July 10, 1869.

17. *Advertiser*, April 13, 1867.

18. *Advertiser*, October 29, 1866.

19. *Gazette*, August 11, 1869.

20. *Advertiser*, November 21, 1868.

21. *Advertiser*, March 17, 1869.

22. *Advertiser*, April 17, 1869.

6. Praise and Presses, Letters and Lava

1. *Advertiser*, April 5, 1860.

2. *Advertiser*, May 5, 1860.

3. *Advertiser*, June 25, 1857.

4. *Advertiser*, July 2, 1857.

5. *Advertiser*, July 2, 1857.

6. *Advertiser*, March 20, 1862.

7. *Advertiser*, May 1, 1862.

8. *Advertiser*, January 21, 1864.

9. *Advertiser*, April 16, 1868.

10. W. Storrs Lee, *The Islands* (New York: Holt, Rinehart, and Winston, 1966).

7. "No Opening Offered" for Mark Twain

1. *Advertiser*, January 1, 1900.

2. *Advertiser*, November 30, 1915.

3. Walter Francis Frear, *Mark Twain and Hawaii* (Chicago: The Lakeside Press, 1947).

4. *Advertiser*, August 11, 1866.

5. *Daily Hawaiian Herald*, October 17, 1866.

8. "Scheme to Crush the Advertiser"

1. *Advertiser*, January 1, 1857.

2. L. D. Timmons, "Cotton A Possible Hawaiian Industry," *Thrum's Annual*, 1898.

3. Rossie Moodie Frost, "King Cotton, the Spinning Wheel and Loom in the Sandwich Islands," *Hawaiian Journal of History* 5 (1971):119.

4. F. G. Krause, "Cotton Culture in Hawaii," *Thrum's Annual*, 1911.

5. L.D. Timmons, "Cotton in the Hawaiian Islands," *Thrum's Annual*, 1910.

6. *Advertiser*, November 25, 1858.

7. *Advertiser*, July 28, 1866.

8. *Advertiser*, November 28, 1868.

9. *Advertiser*, May 4, 1867.

10. *Advertiser*, April 3, 1869.

11. *Advertiser*, September 5, 1868.

12. *Advertiser*, February 20, 1869.

13. *Advertiser*, September 12, 1868.

14. *Advertiser*, July 30, 1870.

15. *Advertiser*, November 6, 1869.

16. *Advertiser*, October 16, 1869.

17. *Advertiser*, November 6, 1869.

18. *Advertiser*, September 3, 1870.

19. *Gazette*, September 7, 1870.

20. Whitney Collection, Hawaii State Archives.

21. Ethel M. Damon, *Sanford Ballard Dole and His Hawaii* (Palo Alto, Calif.: Pacific Books, 1957), 96.

22. Frear, *Mark Twain*, 163.

9. "Press Has All the Freedom It Could Desire"

1. *Advertiser*, June 6, 1909.

2. Ibid.

3. Ralph S. Kuykendall, *The Hawaiian Kingdom, Vol. II, 1854–1874, Twenty Critical Years* (Honolulu: University of Hawai'i Press, 1953), 227.

4. *Advertiser*, October 1, 1870.

5. Ibid.

6. *Advertiser*, October 8, 1870.

7. *Advertiser*, November 5, 1870.

8. *Advertiser*, November 26, 1870.

9. *Gazette*, November 21, 1883.

10. Riley H. Allen, "Hawaii's Pioneers of Journalism," paper read to Hawaiian Historical Society, February 5, 1929.

11. Henry L. Sheldon, letters to the Rev. Samuel C. Damon, June 24, 1864–January 17, 1865. Samuel C. Damon Papers, 1830–1890, Hawaiian Mission Children's Society Library (HMCSL).

12. Henry L. Sheldon, letter to Damon, September 7, 1864. HMCSL.

13. Henry L. Sheldon, letter to Damon, January 17, 1865. HMCSL.

14. Ibid.

15. *Advertiser*, February 8, 1873.

16. *Advertiser*, October 8, 1870.

17. *Advertiser*, May 21, 1871.

18. Ibid.

19. *Advertiser*, June 24, 1871.

20. *Advertiser*, September 16, 1871.

21. Kuykendall, *The Hawaiian Kingdom*, II, 174.

22. *Gazette*, October 11, 1871.

23. *Advertiser*, April 15, 1871.

24. *Advertiser*, April 13, 1872.

25. *Advertiser*, August 3, 1872.

26. *Advertiser*, March 29, 1873.

27. *Advertiser*, July 5, 1873.

28. *Advertiser*, July 26, 1873.

29. *Advertiser*, August 2, 1873.

30. *Advertiser*, October 11, 1873.

31. *Advertiser*, October 18, 1873.

32. *Advertiser*, October 10, 1874.

33. *Advertiser*, March 7, 1874.

34. *Advertiser*, March 4, 1871.

35. *Advertiser*, December 14, 1872.

36. *Advertiser*, July 1, 1871.

37. *Advertiser*, July 29, 1871.

38. *Advertiser*, April 30, 1870.

39. *Advertiser*, January 31, 1874.

40. *Advertiser*, August 14, 1875.

41. *Advertiser*, January 1, 1876.

42. *Advertiser*, March 24, 1876.

43. *Advertiser*, April 10, 1875.

44. *Advertiser*, January 10, 1880.

45. *Advertiser*, October 11, 1879.

46. *Advertiser*, February 10, 1877.

47. Henry L. Sheldon, letter to Dr. John Mott-Smith, August 1, 1877. HMCSL.

48. *Advertiser*, November 17, 1877.

49. *Advertiser*, June 8, 1878.

50. *Advertiser*, February 2, 1878.

51. *Advertiser*, November 22, 1879.

52. Henry L. Sheldon, letter to the Rev. Samuel C. Damon, October 4, 1878. HMCSL.

53. *Advertiser*, August 2, 1879.

54. *Advertiser*, July 16, 1878.

55. Ibid.

56. *Advertiser*, February 1, 1879.

57. Ibid.

58. *Advertiser*, October 25, 1879.

59. *Advertiser*, November 1, 1879.

60. *Advertiser*, August 7, 1880.

61. Sanford B. Dole to J. H. Black, May 13, 1880, letterbook, HMCSL.

62. Black to Dole, June 1, 1880, HMCSL.

63. Dole to brother George, June 14, 21, 1880. HMCSL.

Part II. 1880–1898

10. "To Be Invariably Loyal to His Majesty"

1. David Graham Adee, "Memories of Honolulu," *The Republic* (Washington, D.C.), May 28, 1884, 467.

2. *Advertiser*, July 4, 1861.

3. *Advertiser*, March 20, 1862.

4. *Polynesian*, October 4, 1862.

5. *Advertiser*, October 9, 1862.

6. *Advertiser*, October 5, 1872.

7. *Advertiser*, September 4, 1880.

8. Ibid.

9. *Gazette*, September 8, 1880.

10. *Advertiser*, September 25, 1880.

11. Letter, Sanford Dole to *Advertiser*, August 15, 1881.

12. *Advertiser*, February 4, 1882.

13. *Saturday Press*, June 10, 1882.

14. *Advertiser*, February 19, 1883.

15. *Saturday Press*, August 25, 1883.

16. *Saturday Press*, September 29, 1883.

17. *Advertiser*, October 19, 1883.

18. *Advertiser*, October 16, 1883.

19. *Advertiser*, Centennial Edition, July 1–7, 1959.

20. Kathleen D. Mellen, *An Island Kingdom Passes: Hawaii Becomes American* (New York: Hastings House, 1958), 167.

21. *Advertiser*, Centennial Edition.

22. *Advertiser*, June 21, 1884.

23. *Advertiser*, June 19, 20, 1884.

24. *Advertiser*, June 23, 1884.

25. *Advertiser*, June 19, 1884.

26. *Advertiser*, June 29, 1884.

27. *Advertiser*, July 1, 1884.

28. Ibid.

29. *Bulletin*, quoting Adee, "Memories of Honolulu."

30. *Bulletin*, July 15, 1884.

31. *Advertiser*, October 2, 1884.

32. Letter, Robert Creighton to W. L. Booker, May 7, 1886, quoted in Ralph S. Kuykendall, *The Hawaiian Kingdom, Vol. III, 1874–1893, The Kalakaua Dynasty* (Honolulu: University of Hawai'i Press, 1967), 281–282.

33. Letter, Gibson to H. A. P. Carter, Foreign Office Miscellaneous and Consular Letterbook #19, Hawaiian Legation, Washington, D.C., 1873–1887, Vol. I.

34. Jacob Adler, *Claus Spreckels: The Sugar King in Hawaii* (Honolulu: University of Hawai'i Press, 1966), 17.

11. "Laws of U.S. Are Good Enough for Hawaii"

1. Henry M. Whitney, historical sketch of *Advertiser*, printed by Hawaiian Gazette Company, 1891.

2. Letter from Henry N. Castle to unidentified recipient, 1883, in *Letters of Henry Northrup Castle 1882–1895* (London, 1902).

3. Letter, Castle to sister Helen, September 21, 1884.

4. Letter, Castle to his brother, W. R., 1889.

5. Letter, Castle to sister Helen, January 16, 1890.

6. *Advertiser*, August 31, 1891.

7. *Advertiser*, December 22, 1891.

8. *Advertiser*, August 30, 1892.

9. *Advertiser*, January 13, 1893.

10. *Advertiser*, January 18, 1893.

11. Ibid.

12. *Advertiser*, January 23, 1893.

13. *Advertiser*, February 2, 1893.

14. *Advertiser*, February 6, 1893.

15. *Advertiser*, November 16, 1893.

16. *Advertiser*, January 2, 1894.

17. *Advertiser*, January 31, 1894.

18. *Advertiser*, June 2, 1894.

19. *Advertiser*, January 8, April 2, 1894.

20. Letter, Castle to wife Mabel, November 6, 1894.

21. *Advertiser*, November 23, 1894.

22. *Advertiser*, January 2, 1896.

23. Ibid.

24. Thornton Sherburne Hardy, *Wallace Rider Farrington* (Honolulu: Honolulu Star-Bulletin, Ltd., 1935), 19.

25. *Advertiser*, June 30, 1896.

26. *Advertiser*, July 11, January 7, 1895.

27. *Advertiser*, July 30, 1895.

28. *Advertiser*, July 27, 1895.

29. *Advertiser*, March 12, 1896.

30. *Advertiser*, February 21, 1895.

31. *Advertiser*, November 17, 1896.

32. *Advertiser,* November 20, 1896.
33. *Advertiser,* November 26, 1896.
34. *Advertiser,* January 17, 1896.
35. Minutes of *Advertiser* annual stockholders' meeting, May 21, 1896. Persis Company files.
36. Minutes of *Gazette* company board meeting, June 25, 1897. Persis Company files.
37. *Advertiser,* August 4, 1897.
38. *Gazette* company minutes, June 25, 1897.
39. *Advertiser,* January 2, 1895.
40. *Advertiser,* February 11, 1930, Albert P. Taylor's recollection.
41. *Advertiser,* March 10, 1898.
42. *Advertiser,* April 26, 1898.
43. *Advertiser,* November 24, 1897.
44. *Advertiser,* June 2, 1898.
45. Ibid.
46. *Advertiser,* June 23, 1898.
47. *Advertiser,* July 13, 1898.
48. *Advertiser,* August 13, 1898.
49. *Advertiser,* August 12, 1898.

Part III. 1898–1931

12. An "Itching for Printer's Ink"

1. Lorrin A. Thurston, *Advertiser,* February 11, 1930.
2. Lorrin A. Thurston, *Writings of Lorrin A. Thurston,* ed. Andrew Farrell (Honolulu: Advertiser Publishing Company, 1936).
3. Ibid.
4. Andrew Farrell, Preface to Thurston, *Writings.*
5. Daws, *Shoal of Time,* 242.
6. Albert P. Taylor, *Advertiser,* February 11, 1930.
7. *Advertiser,* November 15, 1899.
8. *Advertiser,* August 20, 1914.
9. *Advertiser,* February 11, 1930.
10. Ibid.
11. *Advertiser,* February 7, 1901.
12. *Los Angeles Times,* March 5, 1901.
13. *Advertiser,* March 25, 1971.
14. *Advertiser,* January 1, 1900.
15. *Advertiser,* January 26, 1900.
16. *Advertiser,* February 18, March 25, 1901.
17. *Advertiser,* October 10, 1905.
18. *Advertiser,* October 22, 1905.
19. *Advertiser,* November 13, 1905.
20. *Advertiser,* January 3, 1902.

21. *Advertiser*, January 21, 1906.

22. *Bulletin*, October 10, 1903.

23. *Advertiser*, April 14, 1903.

24. *Advertiser*, April 10, 1904.

25. *Advertiser*, September 5, 1907.

26. *Star*, November 2, 1907.

27. *Advertiser*, September 7, 1908.

28. *Advertiser*, February 11, 1907.

29. *Advertiser*, June 13, 1908.

30. *Advertiser*, September 27, 1909.

31. *Advertiser*, June 30, 1912.

32. *Advertiser*, September 25, 1909.

33. *Advertiser*, December 13, 1909.

34. *Advertiser*, December 9, 1913.

35. *Advertiser*, April 14, 1913.

36. *Advertiser*, September 5, 1949.

37. *Advertiser*, November 20, 1957.

38. *Advertiser*, December 16, 1911.

39. *Advertiser*, March 28, 1913.

40. *Advertiser*, November 1, 1914.

41. Ibid.

42. *Advertiser*, May 10, 1912.

43. *Advertiser*, February 23, 1910.

13. "From Street Cars to Volcanoes"

1. Russell Apple, *Hawaii Tribune-Herald* (Hilo), January 22, 1989.

2. *Advertiser*, September 17, 1923.

3. Bob Krauss, *Advertiser*, March 1, 1978.

4. Ibid.

5. Thurston, *Writings*, 105–106.

6. *Advertiser*, April 2, 1901.

7. *Advertiser*, October 14, 1903.

8. *Advertiser*, October 31, 1903.

9. *Advertiser*, April 28, 1905.

10. *Advertiser*, February 21, 1920.

11. *Advertiser*, November 4, 1908.

12. *Advertiser*, November 5, 1908.

13. *Advertiser*, January 5, 1909.

14. *Advertiser*, January 17, 1920.

15. *Advertiser*, February 21, 1920.

16. *Advertiser*, November 1, 1920.

17. *Advertiser*, November 4, 1926.

18. *Advertiser*, November 3, 1926.

19. *Advertiser,* July 23, 1923.

20. Ibid.

21. *Advertiser,* October 12, 1925.

22. *Advertiser,* October 3, 1926.

23. *Advertiser,* December 2, 1930.

24. *Advertiser,* July 17, 1927.

25. *Advertiser,* January 12, 1923.

26. Bill signed by Governor Farrington, April 29, 1925.

27. *Advertiser,* October 15, 1911.

28. *Advertiser,* October 26, 1911.

29. *Star,* October 27, 1911.

30. *Advertiser,* March 11, 1923.

31. *Advertiser,* April 25, 1922.

32. *Advertiser,* August 13 and 14, 1922.

33. *Advertiser,* November 25, 1922.

34. *Advertiser,* February 22, 1927.

35. Governor Wallace R. Farrington, report to U.S. secretary of the interior, 1927.

14. Laborers "Cannot Run These Islands"

1. *Advertiser,* July 3, 1900.

2. *Advertiser,* May 25, 1905.

3. *Advertiser,* May 21–26, 1905.

4. *Advertiser,* May 23, 1905.

5. *Advertiser,* January 20, 1906.

6. *Advertiser,* May 23, 1905.

7. *Advertiser,* January 16-22, 1906.

8. *Advertiser,* January 14, 1909.

9. *Advertiser,* August 4, 1909.

10. Hearings of U.S. Senate Subcommittee on Immigration, Washington, D.C., 1920.

11. *Advertiser,* May 10, 1909.

12. Lorrin A. Thurston, paper to Social Science Association, April 6, 1906.

13. *Yamato Shimbun,* April 1906.

14. C. J. Henderson, paper to Social Science Association, May 9, 1949.

15. *Advertiser,* January 27, 1920.

16. *Advertiser,* January 30, 1920.

17. *Advertiser,* February 2, 1920.

18. *Star-Bulletin,* February 13, 1920.

19. *Advertiser,* February 3, 1920.

20. *Nippu Jiji,* February 21, 1920.

21. *Advertiser,* January 24, 1920.

22. *Planters' Monthly,* 1882.

23. *Advertiser,* April 23, 1920.

24. Report of U.S. Senate Committee on Immigration (Washington, D.C.: Government Printing Office, 1921).

25. *Star-Bulletin*, April 1, 1921.

26. *Advertiser*, April 1, 1921.

27. *Advertiser*, September 18, 1924.

28. *Advertiser*, September 11, 1924.

15. "Blood Calls for Blood"

1. *Advertiser*, October 6, 1915.

2. *Advertiser*, March 1, 1917.

3. *Advertiser*, April 17, 1917.

4. *Advertiser*, April 9, 1918.

5. *Advertiser*, November 19, 1917.

6. *Advertiser*, June 23, 1917.

7. *Advertiser*, June 27, 1917.

8. *Advertiser*, May 14, 1919.

9. *Advertiser*, June 3, 1919.

10. *Advertiser*, June 1, 1919.

11. *Advertiser*, April 9, 1917.

12. Lorrin A. Thurston, paper to Social Science Association, February 13, 1910; *Advertiser*, June 28–July 11, 1910.

13. *Advertiser*, April 9, 1914.

14. *Advertiser*, June 8, 1917.

15. *Advertiser*, October 3, 1918.

16. *Advertiser*, July 8, 1928.

17. *Advertiser*, November 15, 1918.

18. *Advertiser*, September 27, 1919.

19. *Advertiser*, February 8, 1911.

16. "Talking through the Air"

1. Lorrin A. Thurston, *Advertiser*, February 13, 1930.

2. *Advertiser*, November 28, 1965.

3. *Advertiser*, May 23, 1922.

4. *Advertiser*, March 5, 1929.

5. *Advertiser*, November 28, 1965.

17. "Where America and Asia Meet"

1. *Hilo Tribune*, December 17, 1920.

2. Walter J. (Doc) Adams, *Advertiser*, July 12, 1934.

3. Raymond Coll obituary, *Advertiser*, April 10, 1962.

4. Nan Coll, interview, Watumull Foundation Oral History Project, May 10, 1972.

5. Charles E. Hogue, *Advertiser*, September 19, 1949.

6. *Advertiser*, December 1, 1924.

7. *Advertiser*, April 15, 1959.

8. *Advertiser*, March 31, 1984.
9. Ibid.
10. *Advertiser*, July 29, 1946.
11. Honolulu Press Club resolution, July 30, 1946.
12. *Advertiser*, November 18, 1984.
13. Ibid.
14. *Advertiser*, March 12, 1923.
15. Ibid.
16. *Advertiser*, August 21, 1923.
17. *Advertiser*, May 20, 1927.
18. *Advertiser*, September 18, 1926.
19. *Advertiser*, June 28, 1924.
20. *Advertiser*, October 30, 1910.
21. *Advertiser*, February 12, 1930.
22. *Thrum's Annual*, 1931.
23. *Advertiser*, May 13, 1931.
24. *Star Bulletin*, May 12, 1931.
25. *Advertiser*, July 2, 1936.
26. Rev. Henry P. Judd, Thurston eulogy.
27. *Advertiser*, July 2, 1931.

Part IV. 1931–1961

18. A Son Inherits the Publishership

1. *Advertiser*, July 2, 1931.
2. Circuit Judge William Z. Fairbanks, June 30, 1962.

19. Race, Murder, and the Press

1. *Advertiser*, September 19, 1928.
2. *Advertiser*, October 4, 1928.
3. Ibid.
4. *Advertiser*, October 4, 1928.
5. *Advertiser*, November 17, 1929.
6. *Advertiser*, November 22, 1929.
7. Ibid.
8. *Advertiser*, September 14, 1931.
9. Ibid.
10. *Advertiser*, October 15, 1931.
11. *Advertiser*, November 17, 1931.
12. *Advertiser*, December 3, 1931.
13. *Star-Bulletin*, December 12, 1931.
14. *Advertiser*, December 11, 1931.
15. Nan Coll, interview, Watumull Foundation Oral History Project, May 10, 1972, and author's telephone conversation with Robert Van Dyke, September 10, 1992.

16. *San Francisco Examiner*, January 12, 1932.

17. Admiral William V. Pratt, January 8, 1932.

18. *Advertiser*, January 9, 1932.

19. *Advertiser*, April 30, 1932.

20. *Advertiser*, May 5, 1932.

21. Ibid.

22. *Advertiser*, May 7, 1932.

23. Richardson report, April 4, 1932, in *Honolulu Star-Bulletin*, April 6, 1932.

24. Pinkerton report, October 5, 1932, in Peter Van Slingerland, *Something Terrible Has Happened* (New York: Harper and Row, 1966), 324–326.

20. Editorial Policy Gets "Help" from the Big Five

1. *Advertiser*, November 21, 1932.

2. *Advertiser*, April 17, 1935.

3. *Advertiser*, February 9, 1931.

4. *Advertiser*, March 9, 1933.

5. *Star-Bulletin*, August 28, 1935.

6. E. J. Eagen, report, NLRB, 1939.

7. James H. Shoemaker, Bureau of Labor Statistics report, 1939.

8. *Advertiser*, December 18, 1940.

9. Edward D. Beechert, *Working In Hawaii, A Labor History* (Honolulu: University of Hawai'i Press, 1985), 271.

10. Joseph Barber, Jr., *Hawaii: Restless Rampart* (New York: Bobbs-Merrill, 1941), 88–89.

11. Ibid., 89.

12. Ibid., 90.

21. Research Fueled by "Nippin' and Sippin'"

1. Alexander MacDonald, letter to the author, June 26, 1991.

2. Robert S. Trumbull, interview with author, 1986.

3. Betty MacDonald McIntosh, letter to author, August 4, 1991.

4. Alexander MacDonald, letter, June 26, 1991.

5. Edward P. Morgan, letter to author, June 25, 1991.

6. Alexander MacDonald, *My Footloose Newspaper Life* (Bangkok: Post Publishing Company, 1990), 19.

7. Ibid., 58.

22. "If That's Anti-Japanese, Make the Most of It"

1. *Advertiser*, October 3, 1940.

2. *Advertiser*, October 30, 1940.

3. A. T. Spalding, letter to *Advertiser*, November 4, 1940.

4. Ibid.

5. *Advertiser*, February 6, 1943.

6. *Advertiser*, June 16, 1968.

7. *Advertiser*, October 11, 1940.

8. *Advertiser*, October 14, 1940.

9. *Advertiser*, July 5, 1942.

10. *Advertiser*, March 1, 1941.

11. *Advertiser*, September 3, 1941.

23. "Something's Going on out at Pearl"

1. Lawrence M. Judd and Hugh W. Lytle, *Lawrence M. Judd & Hawaii: An Autobiography* (Rutland, Vt.: Charles E. Tuttle, 1971), 235–236.

2. Samuel Eliot Morison, *History of United States Naval Operations in World War II* (Boston: Little, Brown, 1948), 3:125.

3. Elaine Fogg Stroup, memo to author, September 1988.

4. Jack Smith, letter to author, March 6, 1989.

5. *Advertiser*, December 3, 1960.

6. *Advertiser*, January 29, 1976.

7. William Hutchinson, letter to author, November 13, 1991.

8. Farrington file, Hawaii State Archives, quoted in Paul Alfred Pratte, "A History of the Honolulu Star-Bulletin and its Antecedents from 1820 to 1966" (M.A. thesis, Brigham Young University, 1967).

9. Interview with Lorrin P. Thurston reported in Jim A. Richstad, *The Press Under Martial Law: The Hawaiian Experience*, Journalism Monograph no. 17 (Lexington, Ky.: Association for Education in Journalism, 1970).

10. Elaine Stroup, memo to author, September 1988.

11. Ibid.

12. Interview with Colonel Kendall J. Fielder, in Jim A. Richstad, "The Press and the Courts Under Martial Rule in Hawaii During World War II: From Pearl Harbor to Duncan v. Kahanamoku" (Ph.D. diss., University of Minnesota, 1967).

13. Ibid.

14. J. Garner Anthony, *Hawaii Under Army Rule* (Palo Alto, Calif.: Stanford University Press, 1955), 38.

15. Hearings, Joint Committee on the Investigation of the Pearl Harbor Attack, 79th Congress, S. Con. Res. 27, Part 28, p. 1444.

16. *Advertiser*, April 27, 1944.

17. *Star-Bulletin*, February 26, 1946.

18. *New York Times*, February 27, 1946.

19. *Advertiser*, February 26, 1946.

20. *Advertiser*, March 16, 1946.

21. Congressional Record Appendix, July 31, 1946, A4931.

22. Richstad interview with Thurston, 1965, in Richstad, "The Press and the Courts Under Martial Rule in Hawaii During World War II," 173–204.

23. Alexander MacDonald, *Revolt in Paradise: The Social Revolution in Hawaii After Pearl Harbor* (New York: Stephen Daye Press, 1944), 250.

24. Riley Allen, "Memorandum on Newspaper Censorship in Hawaii," June 5, 1944. Hawaii War Records Depository, Hamilton Library, University of Hawaii.

25. *Advertiser*, December 9, 1941.

26. *Advertiser*, January 13, 1942.

27. United Press, Washington, D.C., March 15, 1942.

28. *Editor & Publisher*, New York, April 25, 1942.

29. *Advertiser*, July 19, 1942.

30. LaSelle Gilman, *Advertiser*, April 8, 1942.

31. Ibid.

32. Gilman, *Advertiser*, August 16, 1942.

33. Earl A. Selle, *Advertiser*, March 6, 1943.

34. Lorrin A. Thurston, *Advertiser*, March 21, 1943.

35. *Advertiser*, March 30, 1943.

36. *Advertiser*, October 18, 1943.

37. *Advertiser*, July 3, 1943.

38. *Advertiser*, September 16, 1943.

39. *Advertiser*, November 12, 1943.

40. *Advertiser*, May 19, 1980.

41. Alexander MacDonald, letter to the author, June 26, 1991.

42. *Advertiser*, February 24, 1984.

43. Ibid.

44. *Advertiser*, December 24, 1944.

45. Thomas Kemper Hitch, *Islands in Transition: The Past, Present, and Future of Hawaii's Economy* (Honolulu: First Hawaiian Bank, 1992), 135.

46. *Advertiser*, April 19, 1945.

47. Gwenfread Allen, *Hawaii's War Years* (Honolulu: University of Hawai'i Press, 1950), 330.

48. *Advertiser*, January 24, 1945.

49. *Advertiser*, July 3, 1945.

50. *Advertiser*, July 8, 1945.

51. *Advertiser*, August 15, 1945.

52. United Press, November 13, 1945.

53. *Advertiser*, November 23, 1945.

54. *Advertiser*, January 9, 1945.

55. *Advertiser*, December 9, 1945.

24. The Battle to Salvage Circulation

1. *Advertiser*/SMS research survey, February-March 1980.

2. *Advertiser*, April 22, 1950.

3. Harry Albright, letter to author, September 5, 1992.

25. A Blend of Photographers, Editors and Managers

1. Sanford Zalburg, *Advertiser*, August 23, 1956.

2. Ibid.

3. *Advertiser*, August 23, 1956.

4. Scott Stone, letter to author, July 20, 1993.

5. Ibid.

6. Ibid.

7. Ibid.

8. *Advertiser*, February 20, 1982.

9. *Star-Bulletin*, June 15, 1983.

10. *Advertiser*, July 23, 1972.

26. Fighting "Communism" and Farrington

1. *Advertiser*, October 2, 1946.

2. Ibid.

3. *Advertiser*, October 11, 1946.

4. *Advertiser*, September 30, 1946.

5. Ray Coll, on KGU, October 10, 1946.

6. Bylined story by Mrs. Joseph Farrington, *Star-Bulletin*, August 21, 1969.

7. *Advertiser*, November 4, 1946.

8. *Advertiser*, October 24, 1947.

9. *Star-Bulletin*, June 4, 1948.

10. *Advertiser*, April 18, 1948.

11. Ibid.

12. *Star-Bulletin*, April 22, 1948.

13. *Advertiser*, June 4, 1948.

14. *Star-Bulletin*, June 14, 1948.

15. *Advertiser*, June 16, 1948.

16. *Advertiser*, June 24, 1948.

17. *Advertiser*, June 26, 1948.

18. *Advertiser*, May 12, 1949.

19. *Advertiser*, August 6, 1949.

20. *Advertiser*, June 10, 1949.

21. Jack Hall, *Advertiser*, July 22, 1949.

22. *Advertiser*, June 24, 1953.

23. *Advertiser*, July 9, 1950.

24. United Press, July 10, 1965.

27. An About-Face on Statehood

1. Roger Bell, *Last Among Equals: Hawaiian Statehood and American Politics* (Honolulu: University of Hawai'i Press, 1984), 55.

2. Ibid.

3. *Advertiser*, October 12, 1944.

4. *Advertiser*, December 24, 1945.

5. Bell, *Last Among Equals*, 123.

6. George Sokolsky, syndicated column, November 24, 1956.

7. Ray Coll, letter to Hearst, December 3, 1956.

8. Theon Wright, *The Disenchanted Isles* (New York: Dial Press, 1972), 201.

9. Lorrin P. Thurston, 1980, deposition preceding the city's antitrust trial against the *Advertiser*, *Star-Bulletin*, and Hawaii Newspaper Agency.

28. Sherman to Heloise: Gossip and Hints

1. *Beacon* magazine, February 1963.
2. *Advertiser*, November 1, 1972.
3. *Advertiser*, September 23, 1973.
4. *Advertiser*, July 29, 1973.
5. Ibid.
6. *Advertiser*, August 29, 1976.
7. Ibid.
8. Bob Krauss column, *Advertiser*, October 22, 1979.
9. *Time* magazine, June 23, 1961, p. 48.
10. Mary Cooke, *Advertiser*, September 27, 1952.
11. Cooke, *Advertiser*, May 14, 1961.
12. Cooke, *Advertiser*, March 10, 1960.
13. *Newsweek*, April 16, 1962.

29. Advertiser's Dilemma: Hope versus Reality

1. *Advertiser*, September 1, 1956.

30. From War Service to Family Paper

1. David Medeiros, *Advertiser*, June 17, 1979.
2. Elaine Stroup, memo to author, 1988.
3. *Advertiser*, June 26, 1972.
4. V. Y. Dallman, *Star-Bulletin*, February 8, 1925.
5. Bob Krauss, *Advertiser*, June 26, 1972.
6. *Advertiser*, July 19, 1973.
7. *Advertiser*, June 6, 1969.
8. *Advertiser*, October 14, 1977.
9. *Advertiser*, March 1, 1980.
10. Ibid.
11. Krauss, memo to author, June 20, 1986.
12. *Time* magazine, May 21, 1956.
13. Ibid.
14. *Advertiser*, February 1, 1964.
15. *Advertiser*, January 24, 1973.
16. *Advertiser*, April 8, 1966.
17. *Sunday Star-Bulletin & Advertiser*, February 20, 1966.
18. Krauss, memo to author, June 20, 1986.
19. Ibid.
20. Ibid.
21. Interview by Ron Jacobs, *Hawaii* magazine, April 1991.
22. *Advertiser*, July 4, 1972.
23. *Advertiser*, January 11, 1963.
24. Ibid.
25. Quoted by Bob Krauss, *Advertiser*, July 3, 1972.

31. Can a Reporter Protect a Source?

1. *Advertiser*, July 26, 1983.
2. *Star-Bulletin*, September 27, 1984.
3. Circuit Judge Wendell K. Huddy, April 8, 1994.

32. A New Hand on the Editorial Helm

1. Thurston Twigg-Smith, interview with Douglas Young, June 13, 1989.
2. Ibid.
3. *Newsweek*, June 22, 1959.
4. *Star-Bulletin*, June 30, 1959.
5. *Advertiser*, July 1, 1959.
6. *Advertiser*, August 1, 1959.
7. *Advertiser*, December 8, 1960.
8. *Advertiser*, December 16, 1960.
9. *Advertiser*, January 16, 1961.
10. *Advertiser*, January 27, 1961.
11. *Advertiser*, January 29, 1961.
12. *Advertiser*, February 5, 1961.
13. *Advertiser*, March 13, 1961.
14. *Advertiser*, March 16, 1961.
15. *Advertiser*, March 14, 1961.
16. *Advertiser*, March 16, 1961.
17. *Advertiser*, February 25, 1966.
18. Bob Krauss on Harry Lyons, *Advertiser*, July 13, 1989.

33. The Saga of Sammy Amalu

1. *Advertiser*, March 22, 1979.
2. Ibid.
3. Bob Krauss, *Advertiser*, February 23, 1986.
4. *Advertiser*, May 11, 1961.
5. *Advertiser*, May 15, 1961.
6. *Newsweek*, May 28, 1962.
7. *Advertiser*, March 19, 1979.
8. Ibid.
9. Krauss, *Advertiser*, March 19, 1979.
10. *Denver Post*, November 29, 1956.
11. *Star-Bulletin*, December 1, 1956.
12. United Press, January 5, 1971.
13. *Los Angeles Times*, June 29, 1970.

34. An All-Out Try to Rescue the Paper

1. Recollection of author and of Thurston Twigg-Smith in his interview with Douglas Young, June 13, 1989.

2. Ibid.

3. Ibid.

4. Ibid.

Part V. 1961–1995

35. Twigg-Smith Takes Over as Publisher

1. Twigg-Smith, pre-antitrust trial deposition.

2. Twigg-Smith, Young interview, June 13, 1989.

3. *Advertiser* legal brief in antitrust case, 1982.

4. Lorrin P. Thurston, pre-antitrust trial deposition.

36. Staff Talents Cover a Wide Spectrum

1. Ferd Borsch, memo to author, July 7, 1991.

2. *Advertiser*, January 14, 1968.

3. *Advertiser*, March 20, 1976.

4. Quoted by Bob Krauss, *Advertiser*, June 28, 1972.

5. Ibid.

6. Ibid.

7. *Advertiser*, June 30, 1969.

8. Ibid.

9. Ibid.

10. Ibid.

11. Ibid.

12. Ibid.

37. A Policy Shift from Conservatism

1. *Advertiser*, November 3, 1962.

2. Ibid.

3. *Advertiser*, September 23, 1964.

4. Ibid.

38. A "Joint Op," a Strike, and a Would-be Buyer

1. *The Guild Reporter*, Washington, D.C., August 10, 1962.

2. "Voice of the ILWU," June 21, 1963.

3. *Time* magazine, July 19, 1963.

4. Ibid.

5. United Press, August 3, 1963.

6. *Star-Bulletin*, February 25, 1964.

7. *Advertiser*, January 15, 1964.

8. *Time* magazine, September 23, 1966.

39. Historic Stamps, Art, and Journalism

1. *Advertiser*, June 24, 1977.

40. Right-to-Print Hits Official Snag

1. *Advertiser*, May 15, 1975.
2. *Advertiser*, October 5, 1975.
3. *Advertiser*, September 19, 1976.
4. *Advertiser*, October 5, 1979.

41. Neighbor Islands Make News Too

1. Ed Tanji, memo to author, August 18, 1994.
2. Ibid.
3. *Advertiser*, November 3, 1974.

42. Technology Brings a Host of Changes

1. Mike Middlesworth, memo to author, January 16, 1995.
2. Thurston Twigg-Smith, letter to stockholders, November 15, 1973.

43. Mayor Fasi's Battle with the Press

1. Fasi, letter to *Advertiser*, November 5, 1968.
2. Fasi, Windward Rotary Club, March 16, 1978, quoted in the *Advertiser*.
3. Fasi, letter to *Advertiser*, March 15, 1983.
4. George Chaplin, letter to *Sun Press*, January 1–7, 1975.
5. Chaplin, letter to *Sun Press*, April 1, 1981.
6. Thurston Twigg-Smith, talk to Exchange Club, June 21, 1979.
7. *Advertiser*, April 14, 1982.
8. Fasi statement.

44. A New Publisher and a New Mood

1. *Advertiser*, October 27, 1980.
2. *Advertiser*, October 15, 1989.
3. *Advertiser*, October, 1982.
4. *Advertiser*, August 31, 1986.
5. *Advertiser*, September 21, 1986.
6. Thurston Twigg-Smith, remarks at Gialanella's memorial services, February 3, 1994.
7. Sanford Zalburg, memo to author, November 28, 1988.
8. *Advertiser*, January 1, 1989.
9. Ibid.
10. *Advertiser*, June 11, 1989.
11. *Advertiser*, February 5, 1989.

45. Nearly a Century Ends in a Sale

1. *Advertiser*, September 3, 1992.
2. *Advertiser*, March 10, 1993.
3. *Advertiser*, January 31, 1993.
4. *Advertiser*, September 4, 1992.

Selected Bibliography

Adler, Jacob. *Claus Spreckels: The Sugar King in Hawaii*. Honolulu: University of Hawai'i Press, 1966.

Adler, Jacob, and Gwynn Barrett, ed. *The Diaries of Walter Murray Gibson, 1886, 1887*. Honolulu: University Press of Hawaii, 1973.

Allen, Gwenfread. *Hawaii's War Years*. Honolulu: University of Hawai'i Press, 1950.

Allen, Helena G. *Sanford Ballard Dole: Hawaii's Only President, 1844–1926*. Glendale, Calif.: Arthur H. Clark, 1988.

Anthony, J. Garner. *Hawaii Under Army Rule*. Palo Alto, Calif.: Stanford University Press, 1955.

Barber, Joseph, Jr. *Hawaii: Restless Rampart*. New York: Bobbs-Merrill, 1941.

Beechert, Edward D. *Working in Hawaii: A Labor History*. Honolulu: University of Hawai'i Press, 1985.

Bell, Roger. *Last Among Equals: Hawaiian Statehood and American Politics*. Honolulu: University of Hawai'i Press, 1984.

Castle, Henry N. *Letters of Henry Northrup Castle 1882–1895*. London, 1902.

Chang, Thelma. *"I Can Never Forget": Men of the 100th/442nd*. Honolulu: Sigi Productions, 1991.

Clarke, Thurston. *Pearl Harbor Ghosts: A Journey to Hawaii, Then and Now*. New York: William Morrow, 1991.

Conroy, Hilary. *The Japanese Frontier in Hawaii, 1868-1898*. Berkeley: University of California Press, 1953.

Davis, Eleanor H. *Abraham Fornander, A Biography*. Honolulu: University of Hawai'i Press, 1979.

Daws, Gavan. *Hawaii 1959–1989: The First Thirty Years of the Aloha State*. Honolulu: Publishers Group Hawaii, 1989.

———. *Holy Man: Father Damien of Molokai*. New York: Harper and Row, 1973.

———. *Shoal of Time: A History of the Hawaiian Islands*. Honolulu: University of Hawai'i Press, 1968.

Day, A. Grove. *Hawaii And Its People*. New York: Duell, Sloan and Pearce, 1955.

Fuchs, Lawrence H. *Hawaii Pono: A Social History*. New York: Harcourt, Brace and World, 1961.

Hawaiian Journal of History. Honolulu, 1967 to 1994.

Hardy, Thornton S. *Wallace Rider Farrington*. Honolulu: Honolulu Star-Bulletin, 1935.

Hazama, Dorothy O., and Jane O. Komeiji. *Okage Sama De: The Japanese in Hawaii 1885–1985*. Honolulu: Bess Press, 1986.

Hendricks, King, and Irving Shepard, eds. *Letters from Jack London*. New York: Odyssey Press, 1965.

Hitch, Thomas K. *Islands in Transition: The Past, Present, and Future of Hawaii's Economy*. Honolulu: First Hawaiian Bank, 1992.

Hooper, Paul F. *Elusive Destiny: The Internationalist Movement in Modern Hawaii*. Honolulu: University of Hawai'i Press, 1980.

Hopkins, Jerry. *The Hula*. Hong Kong: Apa Productions, 1982.

Joesting, Edward. *Kauai, The Separate Kingdom*. Honolulu: University of Hawai'i Press, 1984.

Johnson, Donald D. *The City and County of Honolulu: A Governmental Chronicle*. Honolulu: University of Hawai'i Press, 1991.

Johnson, Donald D., and Michael F. Miller. *Hawaii's Own: A History of the Hawaii Government Employees Association*. Honolulu: Hawaii Government Employees Association, 1986.

Judd, Gerrit P. IV. *Hawaii: An Informal History*. New York: Collier Books, 1961.

Judd, Lawrence M., as told to Hugh W. Lytle. *Lawrence M. Judd & Hawaii: An Autobiography*. Rutland, Vt.: Charles E. Tuttle, 1971.

Kimura, Yukiko. *Issei: Japanese Immigrants in Hawaii*. Honolulu: University of Hawai'i Press, 1988.

Krauss, Bob, and William P. Alexander. *Grove Farm Plantation: The Biography of a Hawaiian Sugar Plantation*. Palo Alto, Calif.: Pacific Books, 1965.

Krauss, Bob. *Keneti: South Seas Adventures of Kenneth Emory*. Honolulu: University of Hawai'i Press, 1988.

Kuykendall, Ralph. S. *The Hawaiian Kingdom, Vol. II, 1854–1874, Twenty Critical Years*. Honolulu, University of Hawai'i Press, 1953.

———. *The Hawaiian Kingdom, Vol. III, 1874–1893, The Kalakaua Dynasty*. Honolulu: University of Hawai'i Press, 1967.

Lee, W. Storrs. *The Islands*. New York: Holt, Rinehart and Winston, 1966.

MacDonald, Alexander. *Revolt in Paradise: The Social Revolution in Hawaii after Pearl Harbor*. New York: Stephen Daye Press, 1944.

Melendy, H. Brett. *The Oriental Americans*. New York: Twayne, 1972.

Mellen, Kathleen D. *An Island Kingdom Passes: Hawaii Becomes American*. New York: Hastings House, 1958.

Murphy, Thomas D. *Ambassadors in Arms: The Story of Hawaii's 100th Battalion*. Honolulu: University of Hawai'i Press, 1954.

Nordyke, Eleanor C. *The Peopling of Hawaii*. Honolulu: University of Hawai'i Press, 1977.

Okihiro, Gary Y. *Cane Fires: The Anti-Japanese Movement in Hawaii, 1865–1945*. Philadelphia: Temple University Press, 1991.

Potter, Norris W., and Lawrence M. Kasdon. *Hawaii, Our Island State*. Columbus, Ohio: C. E. Merrill Books, 1964.

Puette, William J. *The Hilo Massacre: Hawaii's Bloody Monday, August 1st, 1938*. Honolulu: University of Hawaii College of Continuing Education and Community Service, Center for Labor Education and Research, 1988.

Rayson, Ann. *Modern Hawaiian History*. Honolulu: Bess Press, 1984.

Richstad, Jim A. "The Press and the Courts Under Martial Law in Hawaii During World War II: From Pearl Harbor to Duncan v. Kahanamoku." Ph.D. diss., University of Minnesota, 1967.

———. *The Press Under Martial Law: The Hawaiian Experience*. Journalism Monograph no. 17. Lexington, Ky.: Association for Education in Journalism, 1970.

Russ, William A., Jr. *The Hawaiian Revolution (1893–94)*. Cranbury, N.J.: Associated University Presses, 1992.

———. *The Hawaiian Republic (1894–98)*. Cranbury, N.J.: Associated University Presses, 1992.

Scott, Edward B. *The Saga of the Sandwich Islands*. Lake Tahoe, Nev.: Sierra-Tahoe Publishing Co., 1968.

Sheehan, Ed, and Robert McCall. *One Sunday Morning*. Norfolk Island, Australia: Island Heritage, 1971.

Simpich, Frederick, Jr. *Anatomy of Hawaii*. New York: Coward, McCann and Geoghegan, 1971.

———. *Dynasty in the Pacific*. New York: McGraw-Hill, 1974.

Sung, B. L. *The Story of the Chinese in America*. New York, 1967.

Tabrah, Ruth M. *Hawaii, A Bicentennial History*. New York: Norton, 1980.

Tate, Merze. *The United States and the Hawaiian Kingdom: A Political History*. New Haven: Yale University Press, 1965.

———. *Hawaii: Reciprocity or Annexation*. East Lansing: Michigan State University Press, 1968.

Thomas, D. L. *The Story of American Statehood*. New York, 1961.

Thurston, Lorrin A. *Writings of Lorrin A. Thurston*. Edited by Andrew Farrell. Honolulu: Advertiser Publishing Co., 1936.

———. *Memoirs of the Hawaiian Revolution*. Edited by Andrew Farrell. Honolulu: Advertiser Publishing Co., 1936.

Van Slingerland, Peter. *Something Terrible Has Happened*. New York: Harper and Row, 1966.

Varigny, Charles de. *Fourteen Years in the Sandwich Islands, 1855–1868*. Honolulu: University of Hawai'i Press, 1981.

Webb, Nancy, and Jean F. Webb. *The Hawaiian Islands: From Monarchy to Democracy*. New York: Viking Press, 1956.

Wright, Theon. *Rape in Paradise*. New York: Hawthorne Books, 1966.

———. *The Disenchanted Isles*. New York: Dial Press, 1972.

Zalburg, S. *A Spark Is Struck! Jack Hall and the ILWU in Hawaii*. Honolulu: University Press of Hawai'i, 1979.

Index

Bold numerals indicate illustrations.

George Chaplin:
Journalist and Community Leader

By Daniel W. Tuttle, Jr.

A SOUTH Carolinian, the son of East European immigrants, George Chaplin edited the student newspaper at Clemson College and, in 1935, became a reporter and city editor in nearby Greenville. In 1940, he was chosen as one of the early Nieman Fellows at Harvard, where he focused on race relations.

Soon after the attack on Pearl Harbor, he joined the Army and ultimately was based in Hawaii, where he was the founding editor and officer-in-charge of the armed forces newspaper, the *Stars and Stripes*, mid-Pacific edition. Later, he became managing editor of newspapers in New Jersey and California and served for almost ten years as editor of the New Orleans *Item*.

In New Orleans, and even earlier, he wrote many editorials urging statehood for Hawaii. When the *Item* was sold, he was offered the editorship of *The Honolulu Advertiser* and returned to the Islands in December 1958, two and a half months before statehood.

He provided leadership in a quiet, steady style, transferring his own excitement over the vast potential of a new state to a general public that responded with enthusiasm to new ideas and to his notion that the "sky was the limit" to what Hawaii's people could achieve. He was tireless in the process, and before he retired in 1986, the *Advertiser*, once anemic and near death, had become Hawaii's preeminent newspaper.

Chaplin, as one observer noted in 1972, "turned the *Advertiser* from a reactionary pro-haole (pro-Caucasian) moth-eaten sheet into a lively, progressive, and important paper which visitors, expecting little but provincialism in the mid-Pacific press, are startled and delighted to discover."

George Chaplin was ever the activist, and his community service in Hawaii includes: Chairman of the Governor's Conference on the Year 2000 (1970) and co-editor of the book *Hawaii 2000* (University Press of Hawai'i, 1973); chairman, Commission on the Year 2000; co-chairman of the Committee on Alternative Economic Futures for Hawaii; charter member of the Goals for Hawaii and co-chairman of its Racial Tension Committee; alternate U.S. delegate to the South Pacific Commission; chairman of the regents' search committee for a new president at the University of Hawaii; chairman of the Governor's Advisory Council on Foreign Languages and International Studies; a charter director of the University of Hawaii Research Corporation; a board member of the Institute for Religion and Social Change; a director of the Japan-American Society of Honolulu; a director of the Jewish Federation of Hawaii; a director of the Pacific and Asian Affairs Council; a member of the Hawaii delegation, Japan-Hawaii Economic Council; a director of the Honolulu Symphony Society; a director of Hawaii Imin (Japanese Immigrants) Centennial Corporation; a founder and vice-president of the Coalition for a Drug-Free Hawaii; chairman of the Board of Governors of the East-West Center; and chairman of the twenty-fifth anniversary year of Temple Emanu-El. He was also generous with his time as a speaker before a broad spectrum of community organizations.

In the professional arena, Chaplin is a past president of the American Society of Newspaper Editors, having served also as its secretary, treasurer, and vice-president; a former chairman of the American Media Subcommittee of the U.S.-Japan Conference on Cultural and Educational Interchange; a member of the U.S. delegation to the Shimoda Conference in Japan; a former director of the American Committee of the International Press Institute; a representative of the World Press Freedom Committee for missions to Sri Lanka, Hong Kong, and Singapore; a Pulitzer Prize juror for two years; a member of the Society of Nieman Fellows; a former member of the Society of Professional Journalists (Sigma Delta Chi); a former member of the National Conference of Editorial Writers; and a former member of the World Future Society.

The numerous national awards bestowed on Chaplin include the Scripps-Howard Foundation's charter award for "a distinguished contribution to a free press"; two John Hancock awards for economic reporting on U.S.-Japan trade relations; a Champion Media award for writings promoting economic understanding; a Headliners award for feature writing; and two Overseas Press Club citations for series on Japan, China, and Southeast Asia.

Chaplin has been decorated by the governments of Japan (Order of the Rising Sun); Italy (the Star of Solidarity); and Israel (the Prime Minister's Medal). In 1987, he received the Judah Magnes Gold Medal from Hebrew University of Jerusalem and was named by the Honolulu Press Club to its Hall of Fame. He also has been honored by Clemson University with its Distinguished Alumni Award and by the University of Hawaii with its Trustees' Award for Distinguished Leadership. He received honorary doctorates from Clemson (humanities) in 1989 and from Hawaii Loa College (humane letters) in 1990. He was given the Meritorious Citation of the Navy League of the U.S. for starting a nationwide campaign in 1962 to raise funds to build the USS Arizona Memorial.

In 1989, Duty Free Shoppers Group presented $100,000 to the East-West Center to establish the George Chaplin Scholar-in-Residence Program to bring a distinguished author or journalist to Hawaii each year. Also, in 1991 the American Judicature Society hailed Chaplin as a "crusader for justice" and presented him with the Herbert Harley Award during the Hawaii Judicial Foresight Congress in Waikiki.

George Chaplin's career with *The Honolulu Advertiser* was never wholly smooth but always trended uphill. He seemed to be everywhere at once, armed in earlier years with a cigar or a pipe. A staunch competitor, *Honolulu Star-Bulletin* editor Bill Ewing, once said, "Statehood, Henry J. Kaiser, jet airplanes, and George Chaplin hit Hawaii at about the same time. I'm not sure where to list them in order of importance." When Chaplin came to the *Advertiser*, its circulation was 47,000. That increased by 23,000 in about two years, and when he retired in 1986, it had reached 86,596. Under his successor, long-time friend Buck Buchwach, it continued to climb and pass the *Star-Bulletin*.

The *Advertiser* turned the corner financially with the joint operating agreement with the *Star-Bulletin*, achieved after Thurston Twigg-Smith had assumed control from his uncle, Lorrin P. Thurston. Herbert Cornuelle, long-time corporate executive, university regent, and trustee of the Campbell Estate, phrased it well when he said, "My feeling about George Chaplin is that he's a caring, public-spirited grandfather who made it possible for Twigg to operate a financially successful paper."

Twigg-Smith put it this way: "*The Advertiser* was dying when George joined us in 1958 and he breathed new life into the paper. His participation was a principal factor in our renewed acceptance in the community. Without George Chaplin, *The Advertiser* wouldn't be the independent paper it is today." An editorial colleague, John Griffin, gives further insight. Chaplin and Twigg-Smith "were a business and editorial team with then managing editor Buck Buchwach in keeping the dying paper afloat long enough to get into the joint operating agreement with the prospering afternoon *Star-Bulletin*. They were stars in a business drama that influenced Hawaii journalism, and so local history."

Griffin says, "Chaplin revitalized *The Advertiser* from a poorly-run conservative paper to a liberal voice that pursued the news with nerve and vigor. Chaplin was an active community figure, making friends, showing the *Advertiser*'s new personality, and sometimes voicing challenging ideas to the old establishment. . . . In those early years, Chaplin showed a balance of courage, gambling and political skill in dealing with touchy stockholders, advertisers, and activist staffers who wanted to speak out even more. He was, in short, a journalist politician who constantly had to run for reelection."

Such accolades do not stand without modification. Griffin also observes: "There are other examples of Chaplin projecting his personal interest and involvement in ways that served to make him more of a community figure but possibly made *The Advertiser* less of a probing paper. But it was an honest disagreement that reflected generational differences and changing standards when today's younger journalists are less community involved. Any politician or editor over time picks up favorite allies or enemies, or is sometimes blinded to his or her own faults and ego. Chaplin was human in this regard, after all. But that should not obscure the fact that he was a great figure at an important time. Nor that he was a caring person—for family and friends, those who worked with him, and for Hawaii. Chaplin presented this personal involvement as something that showed *The Advertiser* cared."

Long-time *Advertiser* City Editor Sanford Zalburg gives personal insight into Chaplin's personality and work habits. "[He] is the rare editor who can write well and who has kept that skill sharply honed by constantly using it. . . . He wrote with clarity and intelligence, although often too lengthily. He never lost that vital spark. . . . He can reshape a wayward or cumbersome sentence; tone it down, lift it up, smooth it out, give it thrust and purpose. He has rescued many a reporter's work and made it sing a little."

Zalburg continues, "He's an open sort: hearty, loquacious, humorous. He did not bury himself in a fortress of an office, remote from the public. It was open house. He got around to see things for himself. The man is a bundle of energy. He likes the give and take of lively conversation. He loves politics, and even sweaty politicians. (He would have made a good politician himself, except there is no room for duplicity in his makeup.)"

Zalburg's further description of Chaplin as a person provides a classic word-picture: "George is a humorist. He carries a stack of jokes some old, some new, which he delights in telling. He loves to talk and is persistent in telling a story. He latches onto you like the Ancient Mariner. He's shrewd. People consult him: ordinary folk, businessmen, governors . . . he's a diplomat. He'd have made a first class chargé d'affaires, or even an ambassador. He's a Southerner, and in a sense he never left the South. The accent clings to him. He can deliver smooth Southern repartee . . . they're a talkative people. But, he has a commensurate skill: the ability to encourage and even to inspire.

"He knows how to cajole; how to prod and propel people to heights they did not believe they could attain. He leans on them like a benevolent elephant. Yet in the hurly-burly of the City Room, his was a gentling presence, a model of decorum and good cheer. I never heard him reproach a reporter; never heard him say anything to them that could sting or lacerate. As the 16th Century teacher Robert Whittington said of Sir Thomas More, so indeed George Chaplin is also 'a man of marvelous mirth and pastime, and sometimes of as sad a gravity; a man for all seasons!'"

Finally Zalburg adds, "If you wanted a single word to describe him that word would be *industrious*" (italics added).

George Chaplin's father, who came as a teenager from Poland, later voiced this credo: "Love this country. Treat other people the way you'd like to be treated. Work hard. Try to amount to something."

George has not only lived his father's credo but added substantially to it. Much that shines about society in Hawaii today bears his imprint. In a succinct statement made almost a decade ago, he observed: "[Hawaii's] got to recapture the sense of purpose it had at statehood. Hawaii needs a fresh dream. This is a place with a very special people. It would be a tragedy for us to settle for anything less than the best."